Luann 4

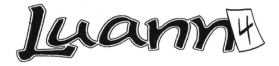

Get your daily dose
of LUANN at

Tiffany

LuannsRoom.com

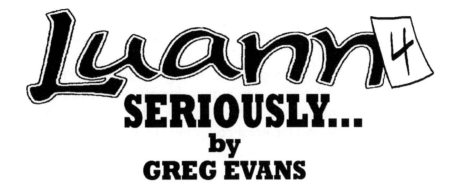

SERIOUSLY...
by
GREG EVANS

**Andrews McMeel
Publishing, LLC**

Kansas City

08 09 10 11 12 WKT 10 9 8 7 6 5 4 3 2 1

ISBN-13: 978-0-7407-7362-4
ISBN-10: 0-7407-7362-3

Library of Congress Control Number: 2008923404

www.LuannsRoom.com

www.andrewsmcmeel.com

──────── **ATTENTION: SCHOOLS AND BUSINESSES** ────────

Andrews McMeel books are available at quantity discounts with bulk purchase for educational, business, or sales promotional use. For information, please write to: Special Sales Department, Andrews McMeel Publishing, LLC, 1130 Walnut Street, Kansas City, Missouri 64106.

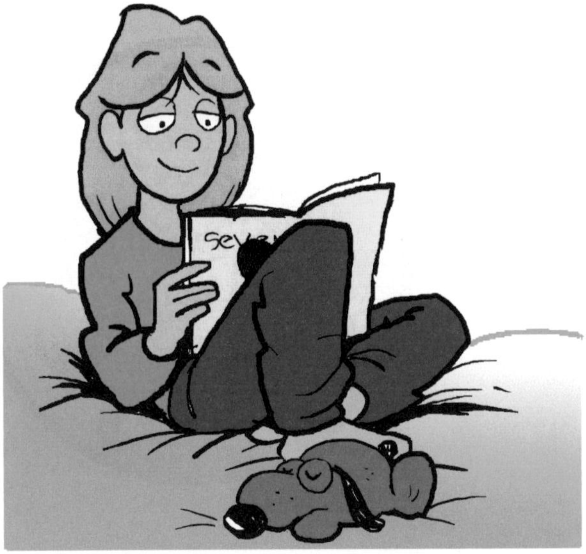

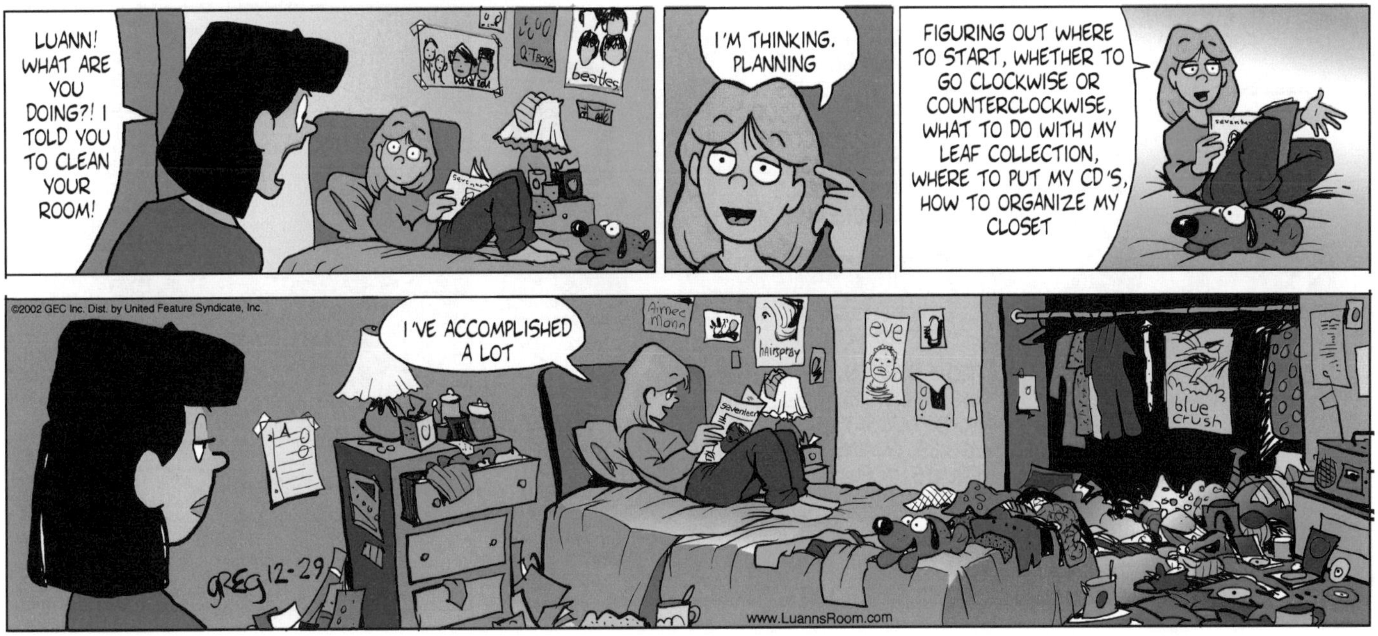

LUANN! WHAT ARE YOU DOING?! I TOLD YOU TO CLEAN YOUR ROOM!
I'M THINKING. PLANNING
FIGURING OUT WHERE TO START, WHETHER TO GO CLOCKWISE OR COUNTERCLOCKWISE, WHAT TO DO WITH MY LEAF COLLECTION, WHERE TO PUT MY CD'S, HOW TO ORGANIZE MY CLOSET
©2002 GEC Inc. Dist. by United Feature Syndicate, Inc.
I'VE ACCOMPLISHED A LOT
GREG 12-29
www.LuannsRoom.com

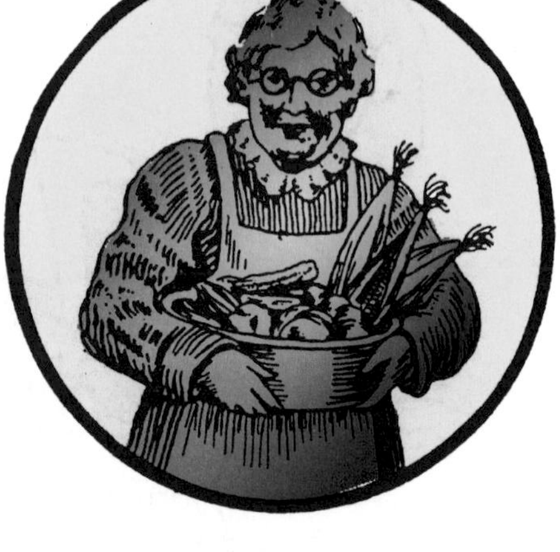

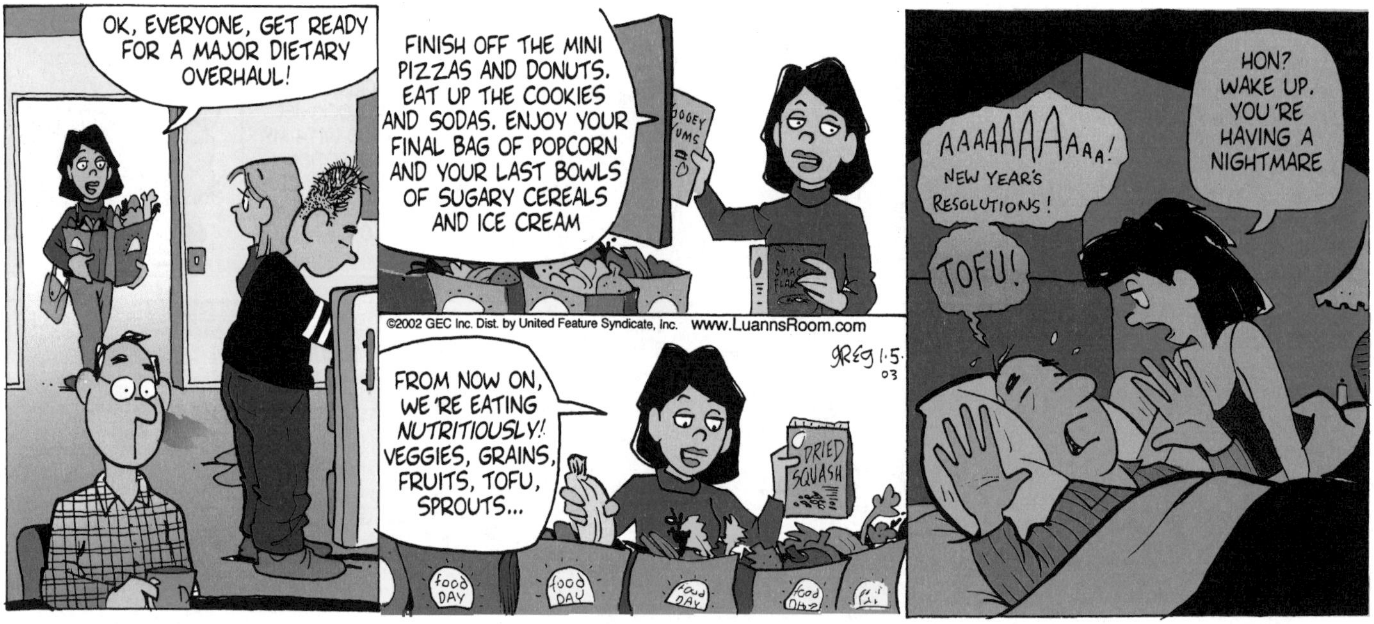

OK, EVERYONE, GET READY FOR A MAJOR DIETARY OVERHAUL!
FINISH OFF THE MINI PIZZAS AND DONUTS. EAT UP THE COOKIES AND SODAS. ENJOY YOUR FINAL BAG OF POPCORN AND YOUR LAST BOWLS OF SUGARY CEREALS AND ICE CREAM
©2002 GEC Inc. Dist. by United Feature Syndicate, Inc. www.LuannsRoom.com
GREG 1·5·03
FROM NOW ON, WE'RE EATING *NUTRITIOUSLY!* VEGGIES, GRAINS, FRUITS, TOFU, SPROUTS...
DRIED SQUASH
HON? WAKE UP. YOU'RE HAVING A NIGHTMARE
AAAAAAAAaa! NEW YEAR'S RESOLUTIONS!
TOFU!

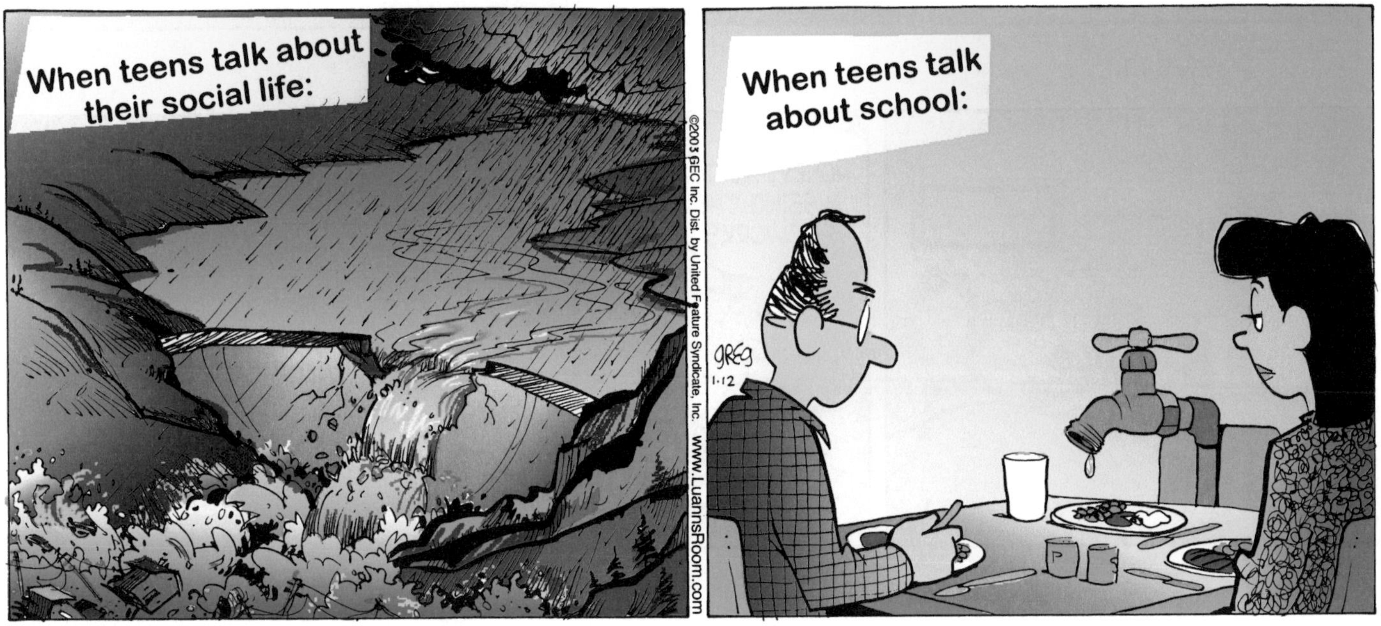
When teens talk about their social life:
©2003 GEC Inc. Dist. by United Feature Syndicate, Inc.
www.LuannsRoom.com
When teens talk about school:
GREG 1-12

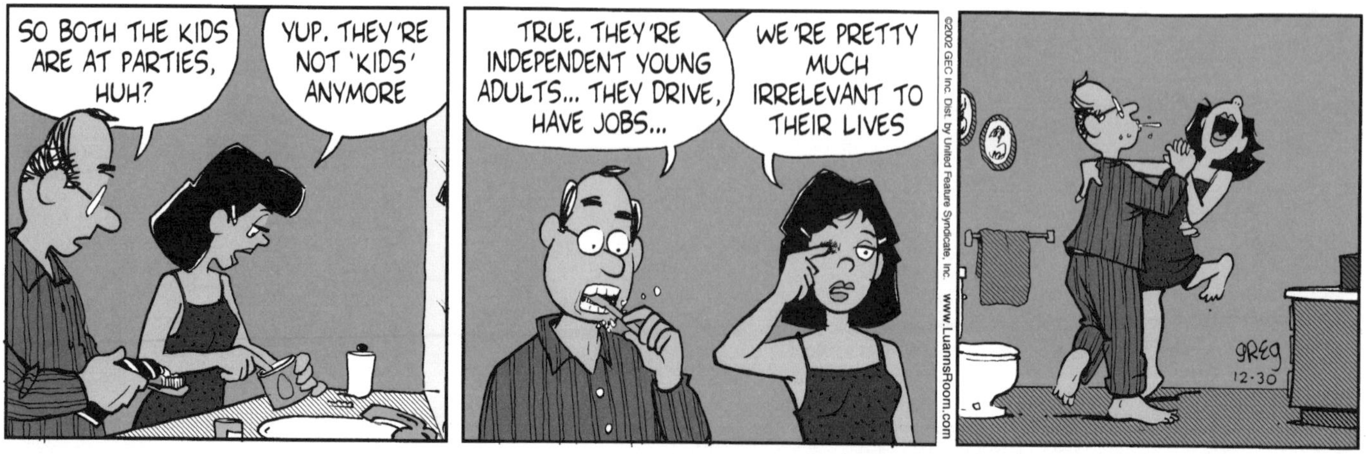
SO BOTH THE KIDS ARE AT PARTIES, HUH?
YUP. THEY'RE NOT 'KIDS' ANYMORE
TRUE. THEY'RE INDEPENDENT YOUNG ADULTS... THEY DRIVE, HAVE JOBS...
WE'RE PRETTY MUCH IRRELEVANT TO THEIR LIVES
©2002 GEC Inc. Dist. by United Feature Syndicate, Inc. www.LuannsRoom.com
GREG 12-30

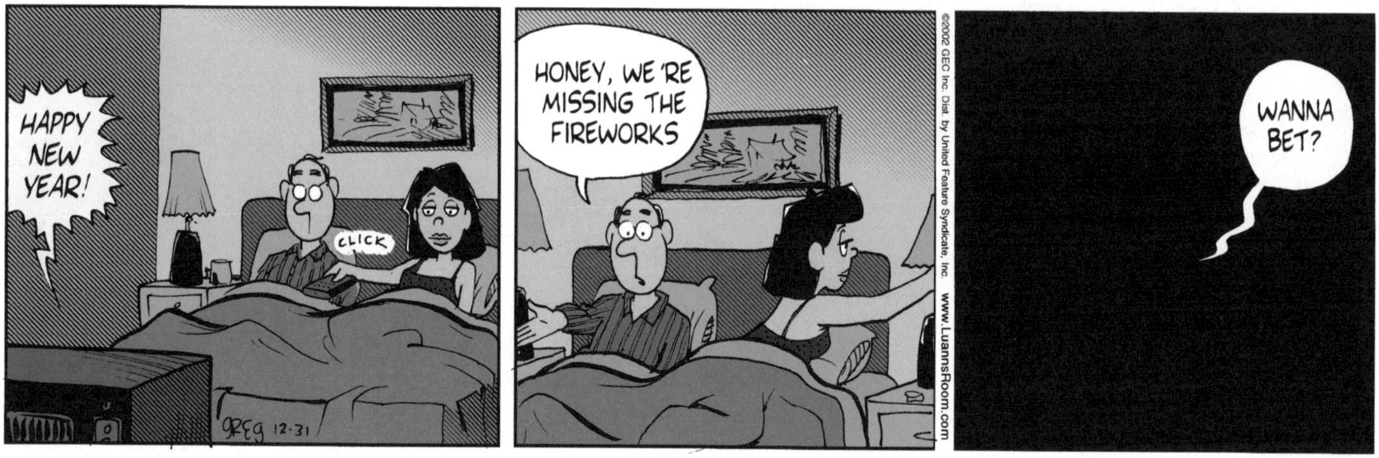
HAPPY NEW YEAR!
CLICK
GREG 12-31
HONEY, WE'RE MISSING THE FIREWORKS
©2002 GEC Inc. Dist. by United Feature Syndicate, Inc. www.LuannsRoom.com
WANNA BET?

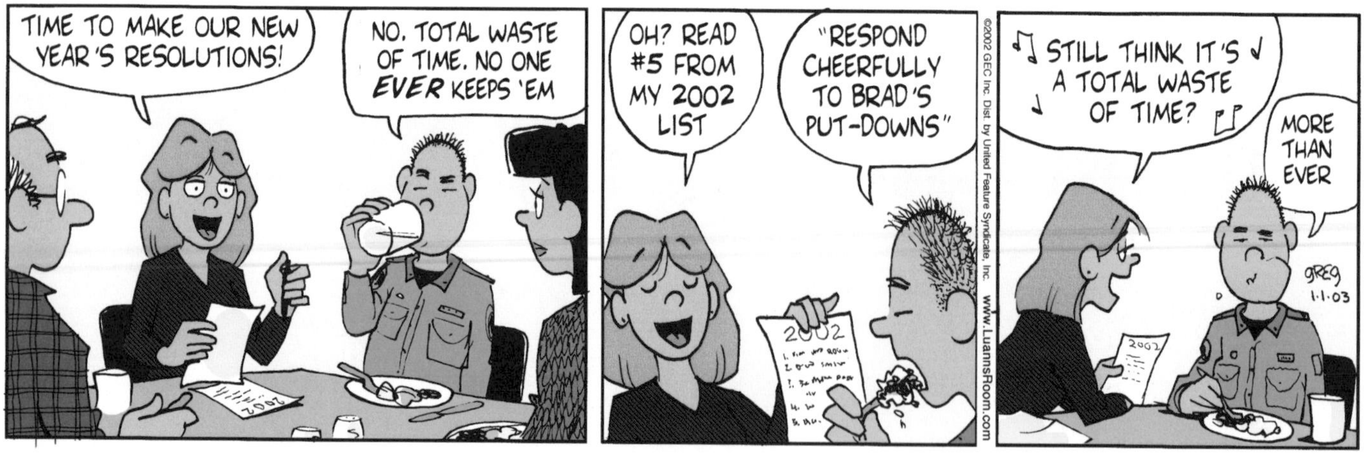
TIME TO MAKE OUR NEW YEAR'S RESOLUTIONS!
NO. TOTAL WASTE OF TIME. NO ONE EVER KEEPS 'EM
OH? READ #5 FROM MY 2002 LIST
"RESPOND CHEERFULLY TO BRAD'S PUT-DOWNS"
©2002 GEC Inc. Dist. by United Feature Syndicate, Inc. www.LuannsRoom.com
STILL THINK IT'S A TOTAL WASTE OF TIME?
MORE THAN EVER
GREG 1·1·03

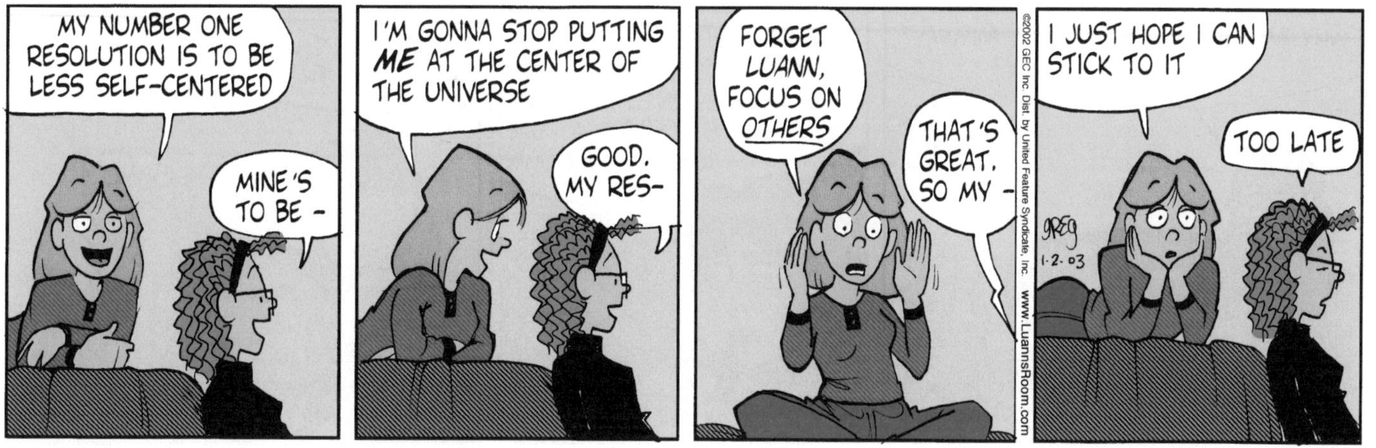
MY NUMBER ONE RESOLUTION IS TO BE LESS SELF-CENTERED
MINE'S TO BE -
I'M GONNA STOP PUTTING ME AT THE CENTER OF THE UNIVERSE
GOOD. MY RES-
FORGET LUANN, FOCUS ON OTHERS
THAT'S GREAT. SO MY -
©2002 GEC Inc. Dist. by United Feature Syndicate, Inc. www.LuannsRoom.com
I JUST HOPE I CAN STICK TO IT
TOO LATE
GREG 1-2-03

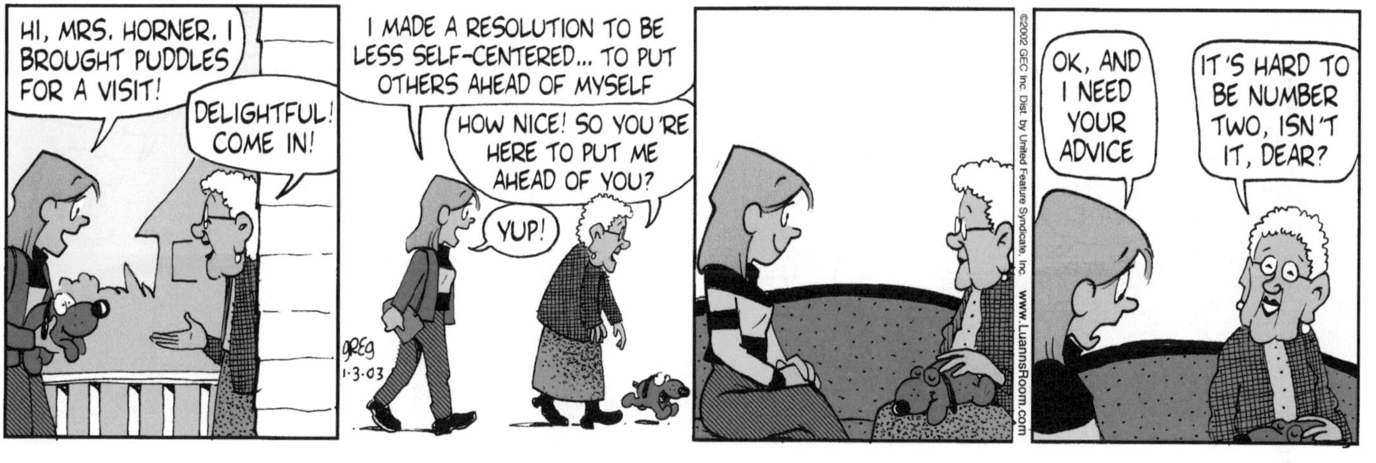
HI, MRS. HORNER. I BROUGHT PUDDLES FOR A VISIT!
DELIGHTFUL! COME IN!
I MADE A RESOLUTION TO BE LESS SELF-CENTERED... TO PUT OTHERS AHEAD OF MYSELF
HOW NICE! SO YOU'RE HERE TO PUT ME AHEAD OF YOU?
YUP!
GREG 1-3-03
©2002 GEC Inc. Dist. by United Feature Syndicate, Inc. www.LuannsRoom.com
OK, AND I NEED YOUR ADVICE
IT'S HARD TO BE NUMBER TWO, ISN'T IT, DEAR?

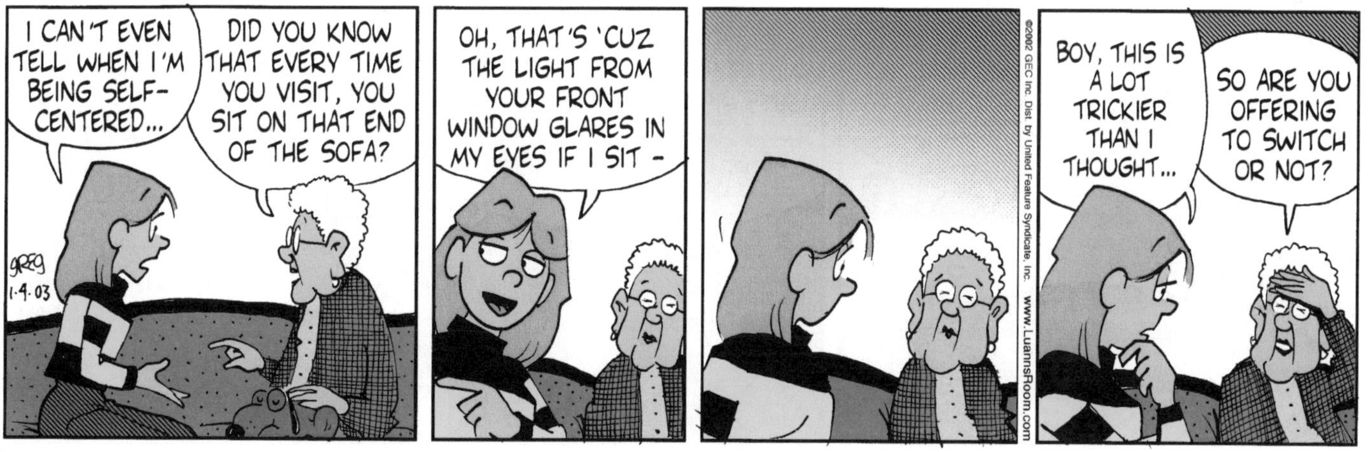
I CAN'T EVEN TELL WHEN I'M BEING SELF-CENTERED...
DID YOU KNOW THAT EVERY TIME YOU VISIT, YOU SIT ON THAT END OF THE SOFA?
GREG 1-4-03
OH, THAT'S 'CUZ THE LIGHT FROM YOUR FRONT WINDOW GLARES IN MY EYES IF I SIT -
©2002 GEC Inc. Dist. by United Feature Syndicate, Inc. www.LuannsRoom.com
BOY, THIS IS A LOT TRICKIER THAN I THOUGHT...
SO ARE YOU OFFERING TO SWITCH OR NOT?

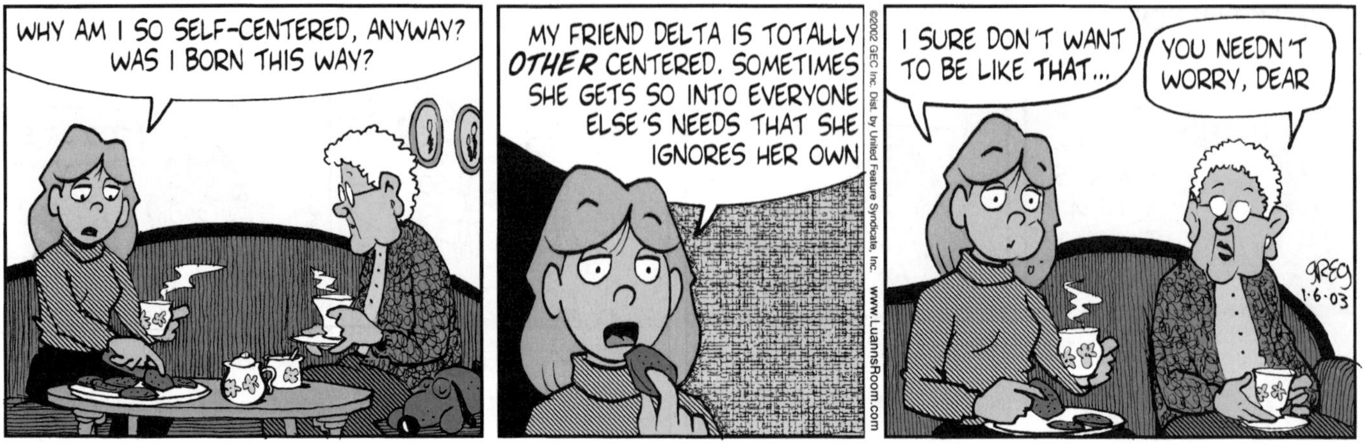
WHY AM I SO SELF-CENTERED, ANYWAY? WAS I BORN THIS WAY?
MY FRIEND DELTA IS TOTALLY *OTHER* CENTERED. SOMETIMES SHE GETS SO INTO EVERYONE ELSE'S NEEDS THAT SHE IGNORES HER OWN
©2002 GEC Inc. Dist. by United Feature Syndicate, Inc. www.LuannsRoom.com
I SURE DON'T WANT TO BE LIKE THAT...
YOU NEEDN'T WORRY, DEAR
GREG 1·6·03

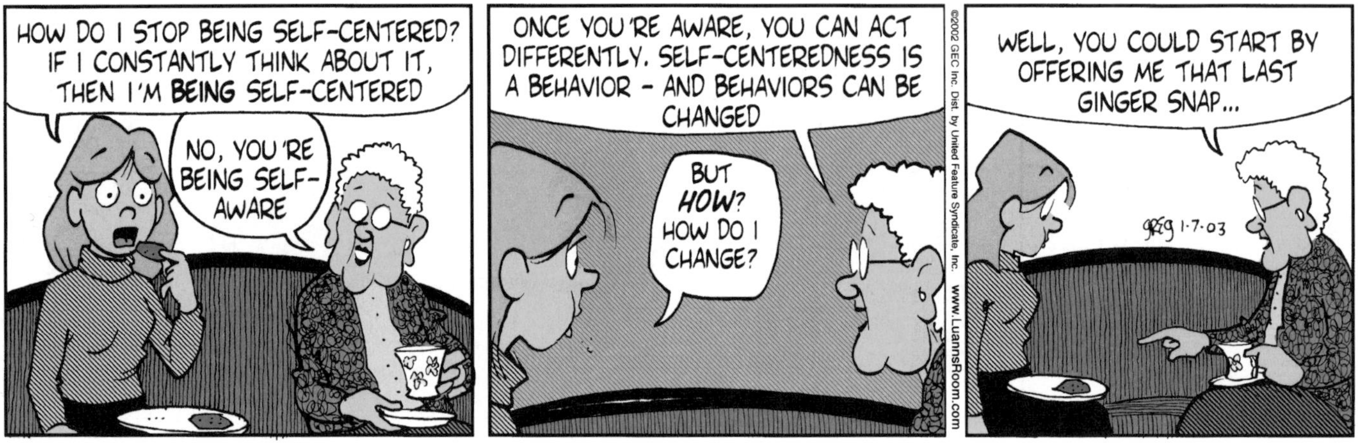
HOW DO I STOP BEING SELF-CENTERED? IF I CONSTANTLY THINK ABOUT IT, THEN I'M **BEING** SELF-CENTERED
NO, YOU'RE BEING SELF-AWARE
ONCE YOU'RE AWARE, YOU CAN ACT DIFFERENTLY. SELF-CENTEREDNESS IS A BEHAVIOR – AND BEHAVIORS CAN BE CHANGED
BUT *HOW*? HOW DO I CHANGE?
©2002 GEC Inc. Dist. by United Feature Syndicate, Inc. www.LuannsRoom.com
WELL, YOU COULD START BY OFFERING ME THAT LAST GINGER SNAP...
GREG 1·7·03

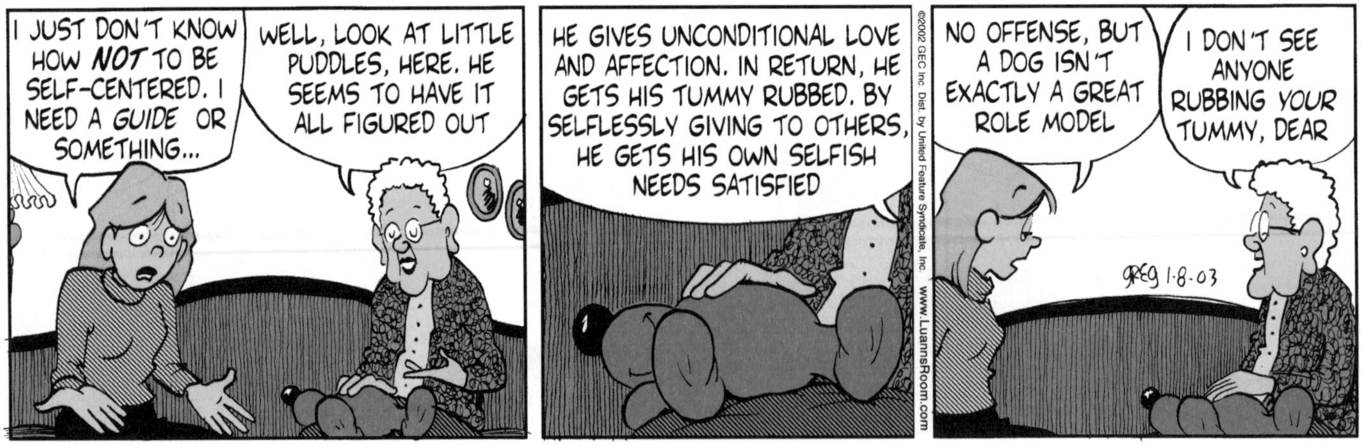
I JUST DON'T KNOW HOW *NOT* TO BE SELF-CENTERED. I NEED A *GUIDE* OR SOMETHING...
WELL, LOOK AT LITTLE PUDDLES, HERE. HE SEEMS TO HAVE IT ALL FIGURED OUT
HE GIVES UNCONDITIONAL LOVE AND AFFECTION. IN RETURN, HE GETS HIS TUMMY RUBBED. BY SELFLESSLY GIVING TO OTHERS, HE GETS HIS OWN SELFISH NEEDS SATISFIED
©2002 GEC Inc. Dist. by United Feature Syndicate, Inc. www.LuannsRoom.com
NO OFFENSE, BUT A DOG ISN'T EXACTLY A GREAT ROLE MODEL
I DON'T SEE ANYONE RUBBING *YOUR* TUMMY, DEAR
GREG 1·8·03

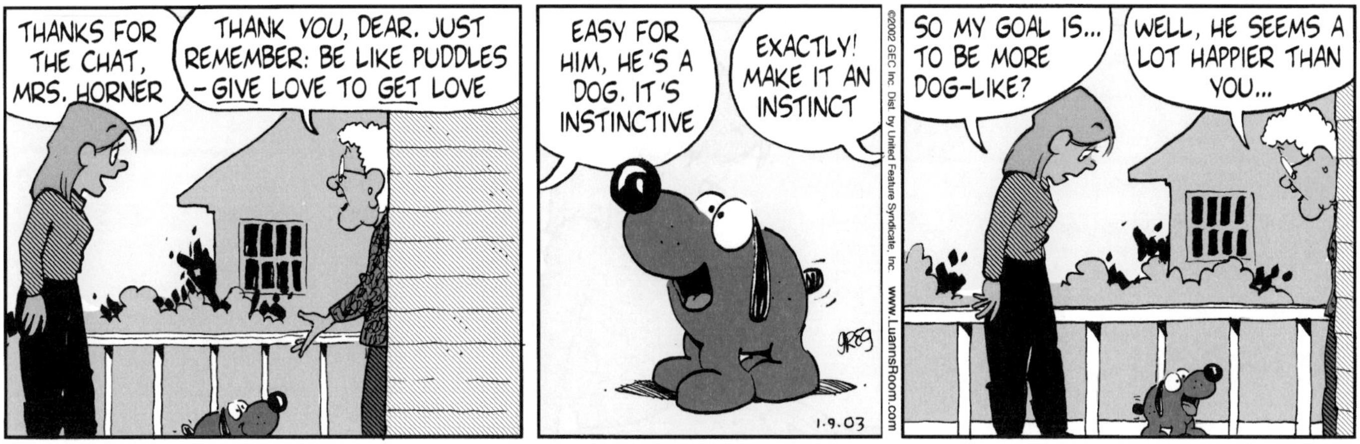
THANKS FOR THE CHAT, MRS. HORNER
THANK YOU, DEAR. JUST REMEMBER: BE LIKE PUDDLES – GIVE LOVE TO GET LOVE
EASY FOR HIM, HE'S A DOG. IT'S INSTINCTIVE
EXACTLY! MAKE IT AN INSTINCT
1·9·03
©2002 GEC Inc. Dist. by United Feature Syndicate, Inc. www.LuannsRoom.com
SO MY GOAL IS... TO BE MORE DOG-LIKE?
WELL, HE SEEMS A LOT HAPPIER THAN YOU...

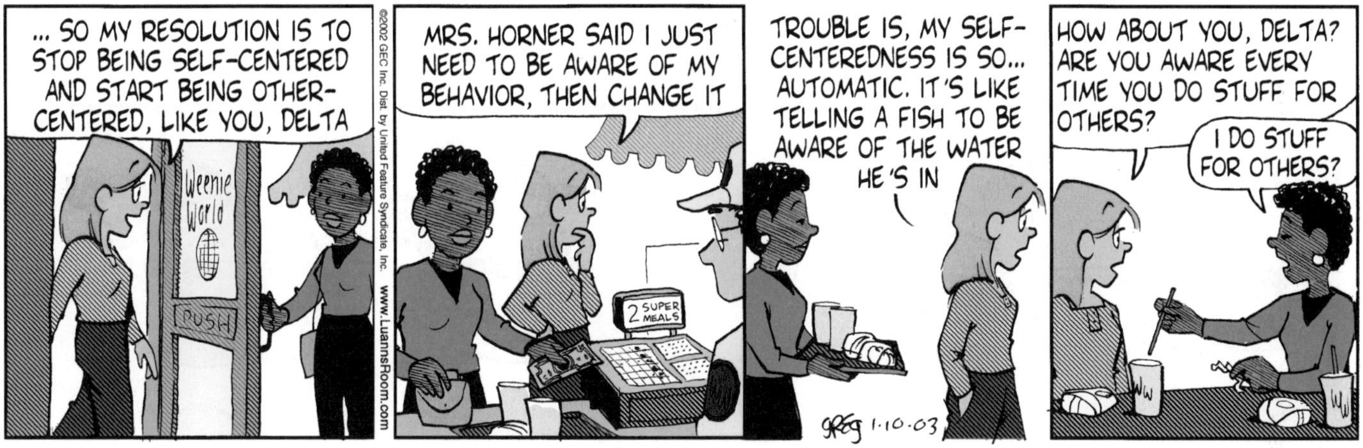
... SO MY RESOLUTION IS TO STOP BEING SELF-CENTERED AND START BEING OTHER-CENTERED, LIKE YOU, DELTA
Weenie World
PUSH
©2002 GEC Inc. Dist. by United Feature Syndicate, Inc. www.LuannsRoom.com
MRS. HORNER SAID I JUST NEED TO BE AWARE OF MY BEHAVIOR, THEN CHANGE IT
2 SUPER MEALS
TROUBLE IS, MY SELF-CENTEREDNESS IS SO... AUTOMATIC. IT'S LIKE TELLING A FISH TO BE AWARE OF THE WATER HE'S IN
1·10·03
HOW ABOUT YOU, DELTA? ARE YOU AWARE EVERY TIME YOU DO STUFF FOR OTHERS?
I DO STUFF FOR OTHERS?

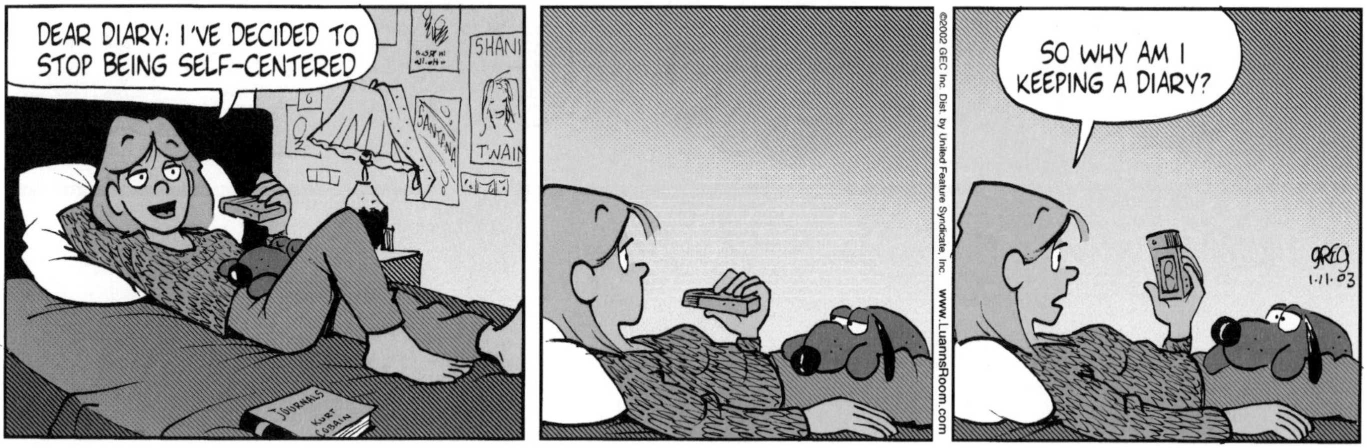
DEAR DIARY: I'VE DECIDED TO STOP BEING SELF-CENTERED
SANTANA
TWAIN
JOURNALS KURT COBAIN
©2002 GEC Inc. Dist. by United Feature Syndicate, Inc. www.LuannsRoom.com
SO WHY AM I KEEPING A DIARY?
1·11·03

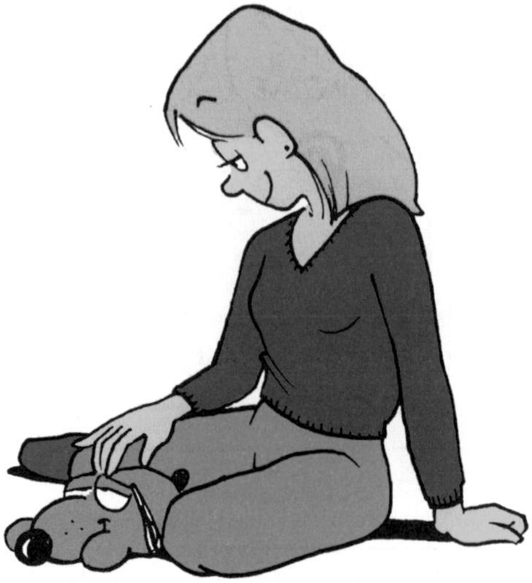

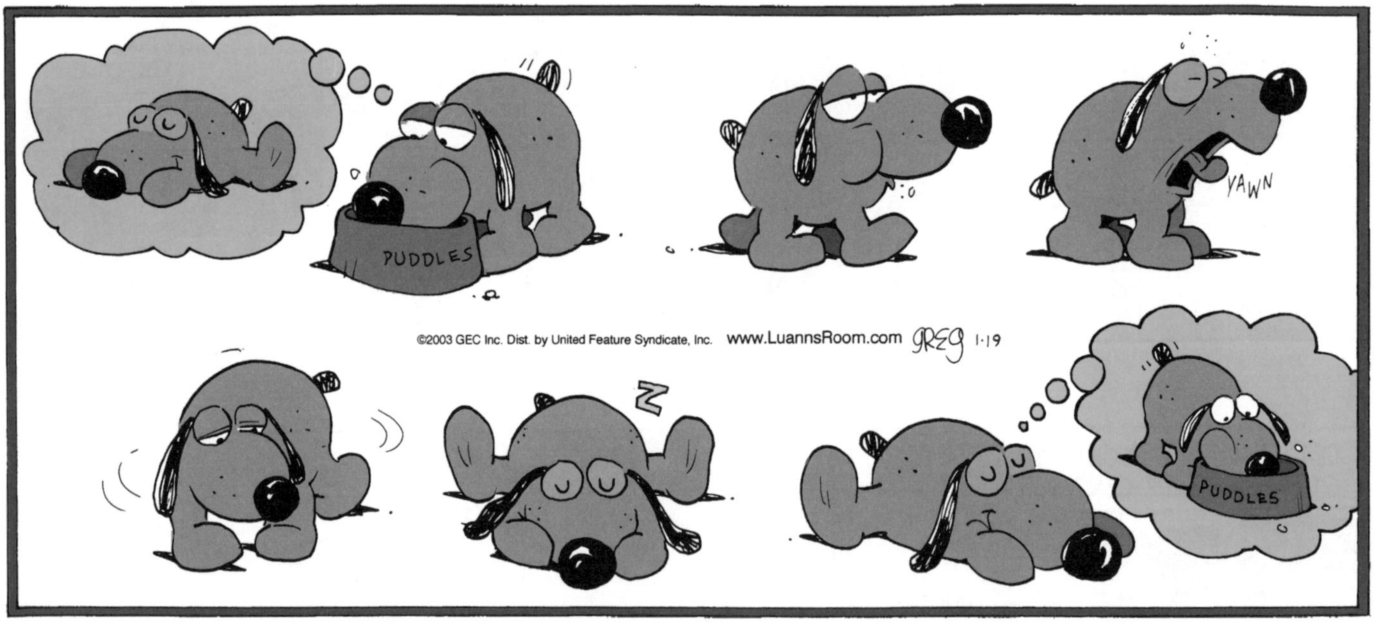
PUDDLES
YAWN
Z
PUDDLES
©2003 GEC Inc. Dist. by United Feature Syndicate, Inc. www.LuannsRoom.com GREG 1·19

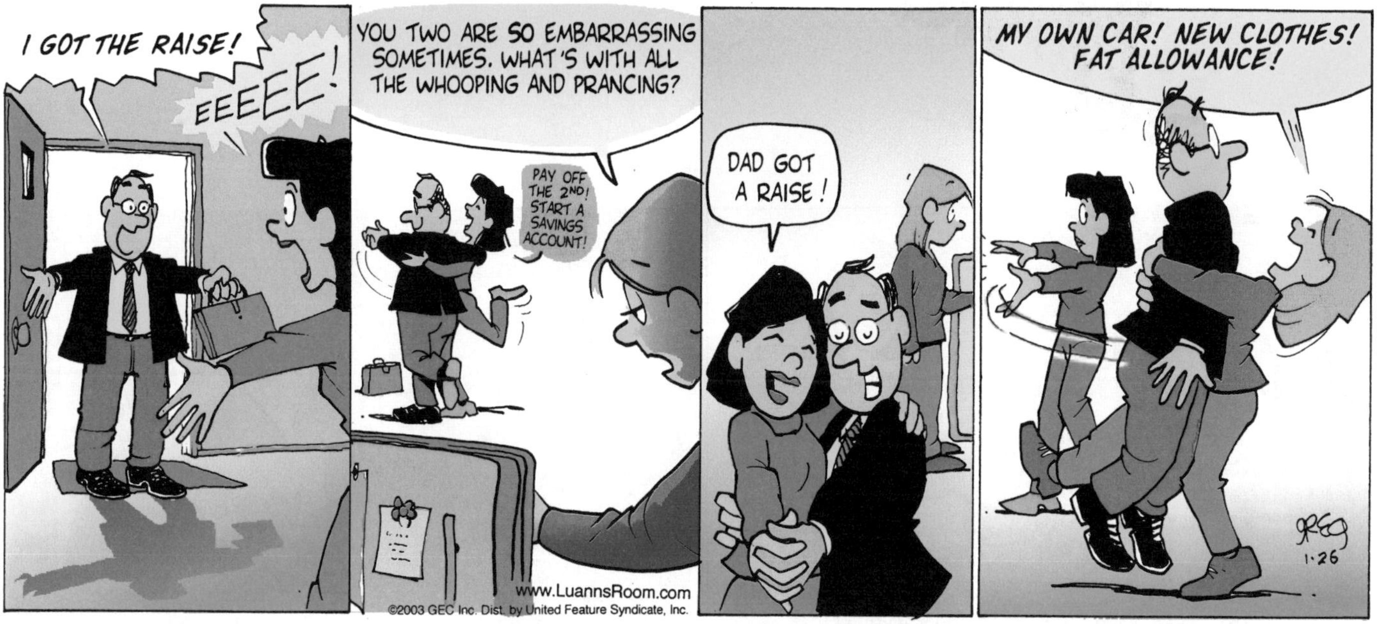
I GOT THE RAISE!
EEEEEE!
YOU TWO ARE SO EMBARRASSING SOMETIMES. WHAT'S WITH ALL THE WHOOPING AND PRANCING?
PAY OFF THE 2ND! START A SAVINGS ACCOUNT!
www.LuannsRoom.com
©2003 GEC Inc. Dist. by United Feature Syndicate, Inc.
DAD GOT A RAISE!
MY OWN CAR! NEW CLOTHES! FAT ALLOWANCE!
GREG
1·26

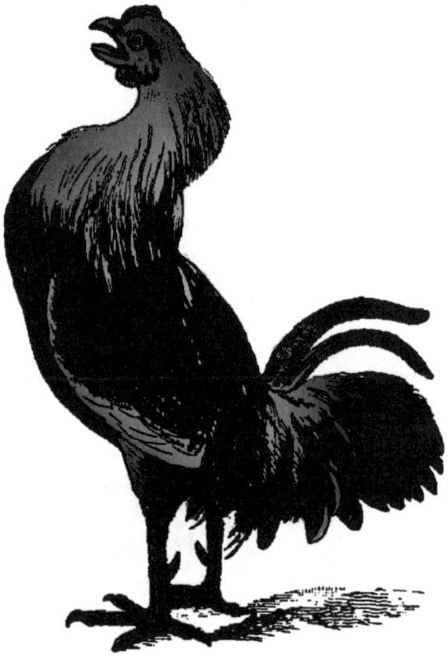

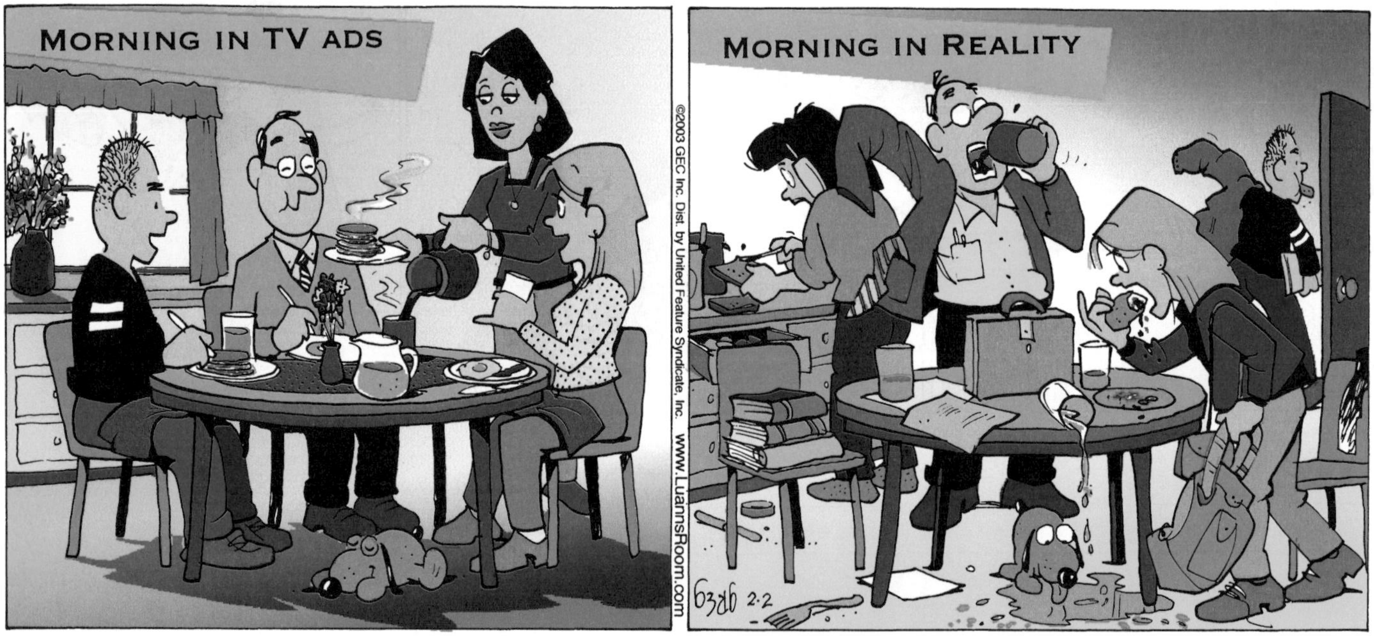
MORNING IN TV ADS
©2003 GEC Inc. Dist. by United Feature Syndicate, Inc.
www.LuannsRoom.com
MORNING IN REALITY

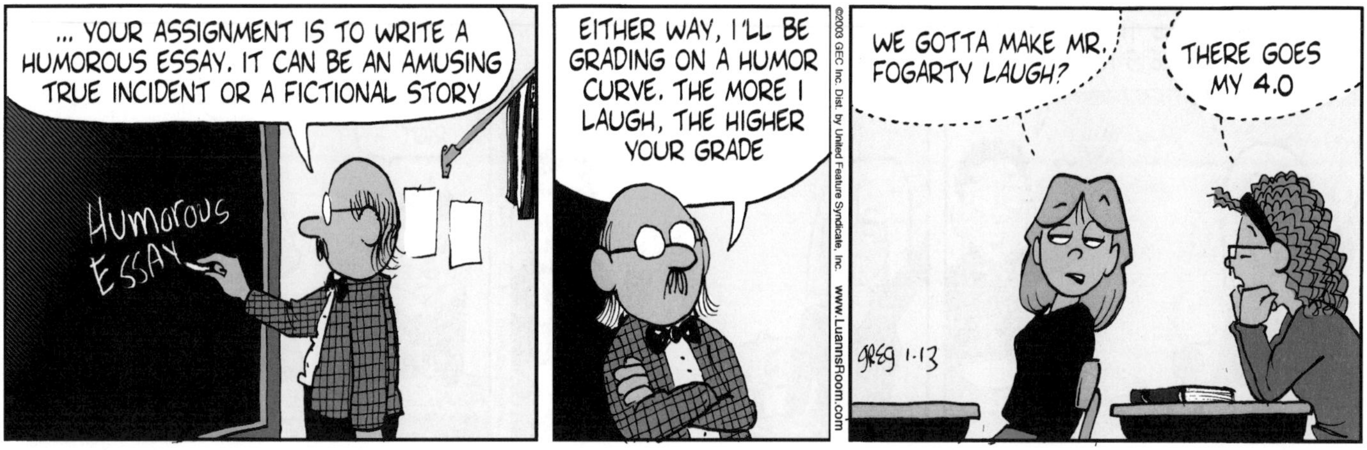
... YOUR ASSIGNMENT IS TO WRITE A HUMOROUS ESSAY. IT CAN BE AN AMUSING TRUE INCIDENT OR A FICTIONAL STORY
Humorous ESSAY
EITHER WAY, I'LL BE GRADING ON A HUMOR CURVE. THE MORE I LAUGH, THE HIGHER YOUR GRADE
©2003 GEC Inc. Dist. by United Feature Syndicate, Inc. www.LuannsRoom.com
WE GOTTA MAKE MR. FOGARTY LAUGH?
THERE GOES MY 4.0
GREG 1·13

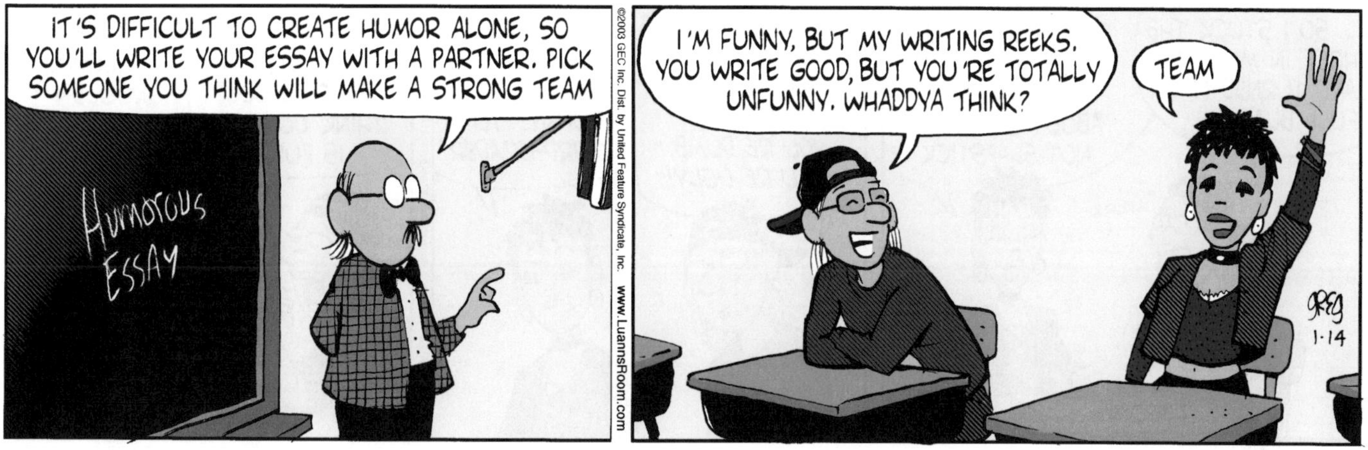
IT'S DIFFICULT TO CREATE HUMOR ALONE, SO YOU'LL WRITE YOUR ESSAY WITH A PARTNER. PICK SOMEONE YOU THINK WILL MAKE A STRONG TEAM
Humorous ESSAY
©2003 GEC Inc. Dist. by United Feature Syndicate, Inc. www.LuannsRoom.com
I'M FUNNY, BUT MY WRITING REEKS. YOU WRITE GOOD, BUT YOU'RE TOTALLY UNFUNNY. WHADDYA THINK?
TEAM
GREG 1·14

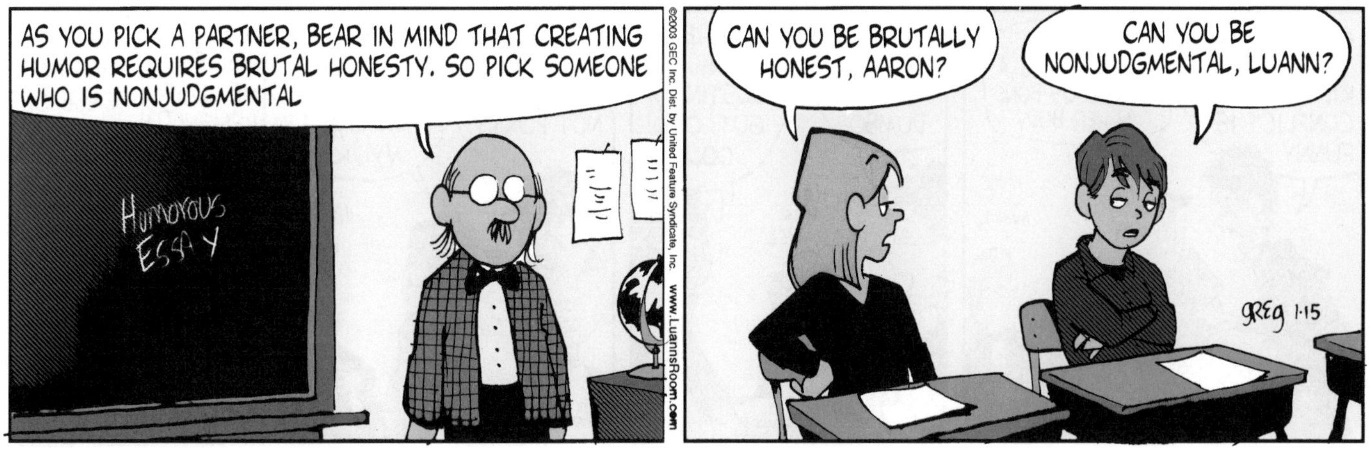
AS YOU PICK A PARTNER, BEAR IN MIND THAT CREATING HUMOR REQUIRES BRUTAL HONESTY. SO PICK SOMEONE WHO IS NONJUDGMENTAL
Humorous ESSAY
©2003 GEC Inc. Dist. by United Feature Syndicate, Inc. www.LuannsRoom.com
CAN YOU BE BRUTALLY HONEST, AARON?
CAN YOU BE NONJUDGMENTAL, LUANN?
GREG 1·15

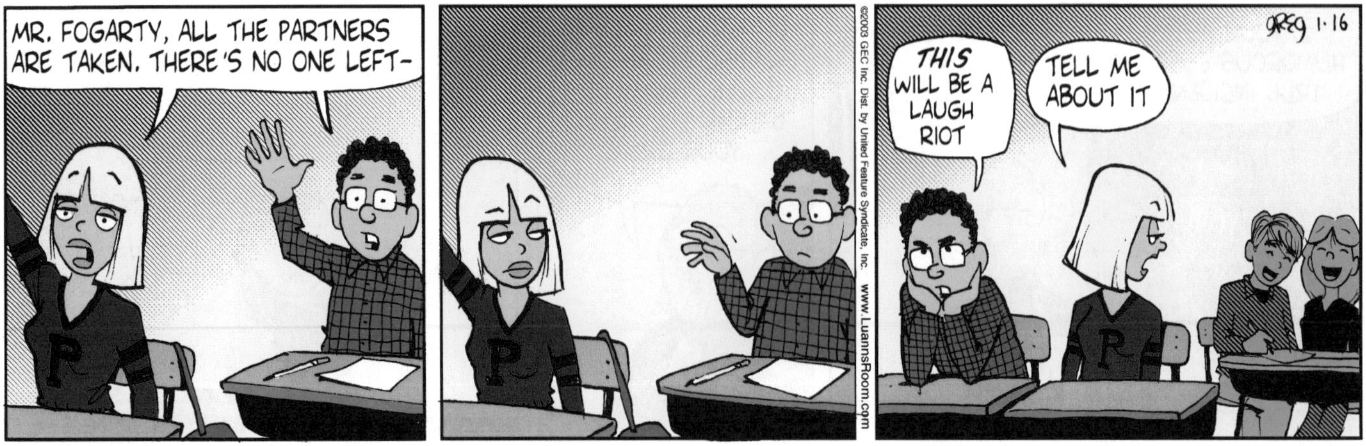
MR. FOGARTY, ALL THE PARTNERS ARE TAKEN. THERE'S NO ONE LEFT-
©2003 GEC Inc. Dist. by United Feature Syndicate, Inc. www.LuannsRoom.com
GREG 1·16
THIS WILL BE A LAUGH RIOT
TELL ME ABOUT IT

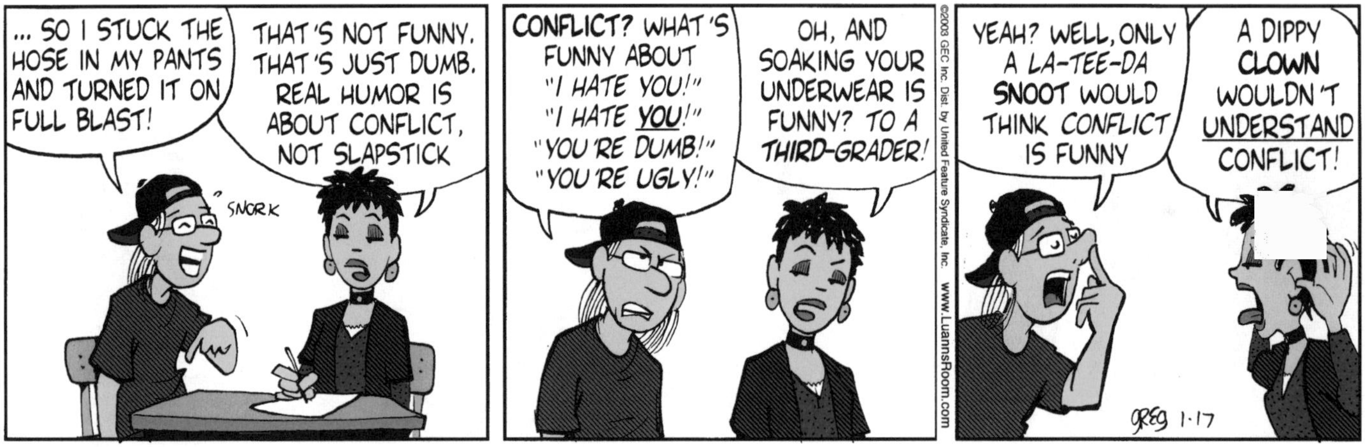
... SO I STUCK THE HOSE IN MY PANTS AND TURNED IT ON FULL BLAST!
SNORK
THAT'S NOT FUNNY. THAT'S JUST DUMB. REAL HUMOR IS ABOUT CONFLICT, NOT SLAPSTICK
CONFLICT? WHAT'S FUNNY ABOUT "I HATE YOU!" "I HATE YOU!" "YOU'RE DUMB!" "YOU'RE UGLY!"
OH, AND SOAKING YOUR UNDERWEAR IS FUNNY? TO A THIRD-GRADER!
©2003 GEC Inc. Dist. by United Feature Syndicate, Inc. www.LuannsRoom.com
YEAH? WELL, ONLY A LA-TEE-DA SNOOT WOULD THINK CONFLICT IS FUNNY
A DIPPY CLOWN WOULDN'T UNDERSTAND CONFLICT!
GREG 1·17

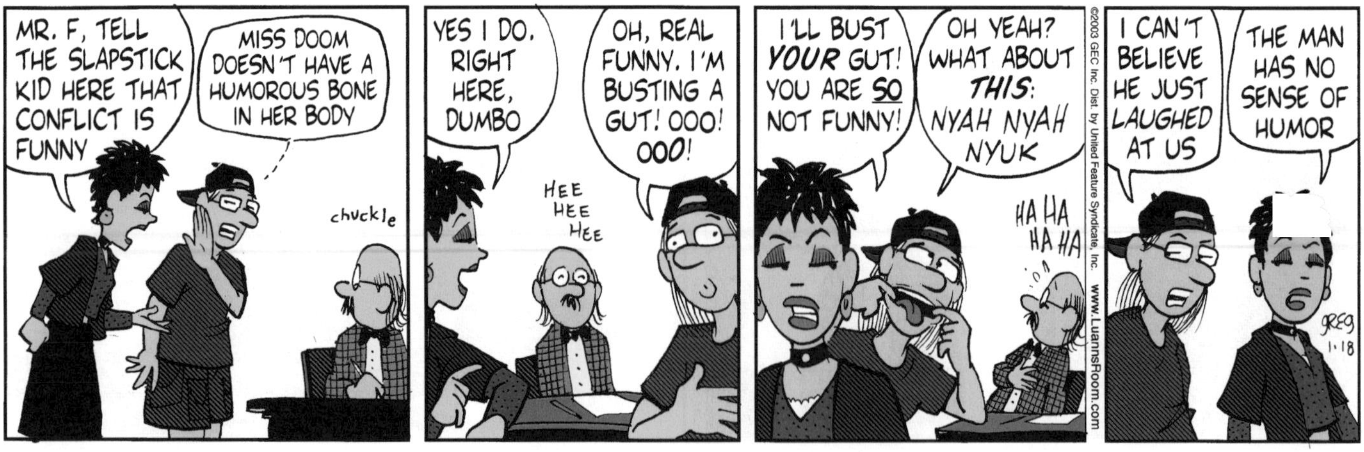
MR. F, TELL THE SLAPSTICK KID HERE THAT CONFLICT IS FUNNY
MISS DOOM DOESN'T HAVE A HUMOROUS BONE IN HER BODY
chuckle
YES I DO. RIGHT HERE, DUMBO
HEE HEE HEE
OH, REAL FUNNY. I'M BUSTING A GUT! OOO! OOO!
I'LL BUST YOUR GUT! YOU ARE SO NOT FUNNY!
OH YEAH? WHAT ABOUT THIS: NYAH NYAH NYUK
HA HA HA HA
©2003 GEC Inc. Dist. by United Feature Syndicate, Inc. www.LuannsRoom.com
I CAN'T BELIEVE HE JUST LAUGHED AT US
THE MAN HAS NO SENSE OF HUMOR
GREG 1·18

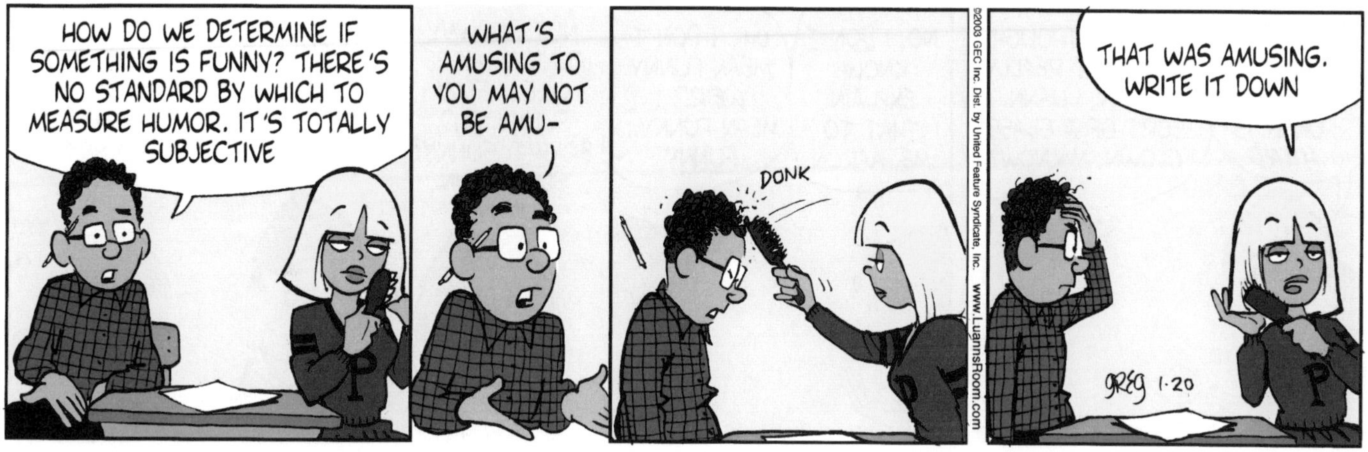
HOW DO WE DETERMINE IF SOMETHING IS FUNNY? THERE'S NO STANDARD BY WHICH TO MEASURE HUMOR. IT'S TOTALLY SUBJECTIVE
WHAT'S AMUSING TO YOU MAY NOT BE AMU-
DONK
THAT WAS AMUSING. WRITE IT DOWN
©2003 GEC Inc. Dist. by United Feature Syndicate, Inc.
www.LuannsRoom.com
GREG 1·20

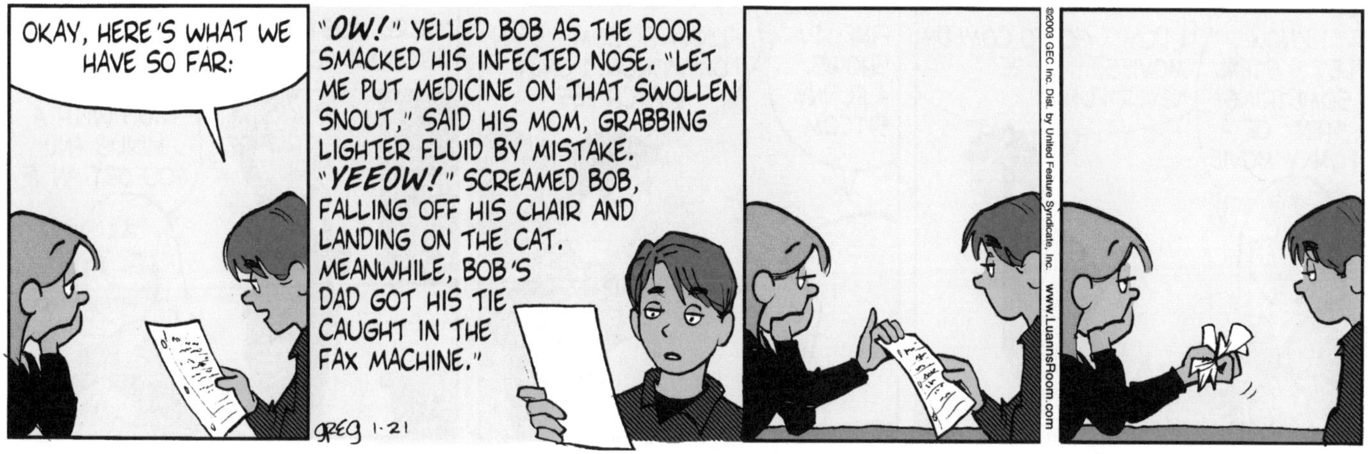
OKAY, HERE'S WHAT WE HAVE SO FAR:
"OW!" YELLED BOB AS THE DOOR SMACKED HIS INFECTED NOSE. "LET ME PUT MEDICINE ON THAT SWOLLEN SNOUT," SAID HIS MOM, GRABBING LIGHTER FLUID BY MISTAKE. "YEEOW!" SCREAMED BOB, FALLING OFF HIS CHAIR AND LANDING ON THE CAT. MEANWHILE, BOB'S DAD GOT HIS TIE CAUGHT IN THE FAX MACHINE."
GREG 1·21
©2003 GEC Inc. Dist. by United Feature Syndicate, Inc.
www.LuannsRoom.com

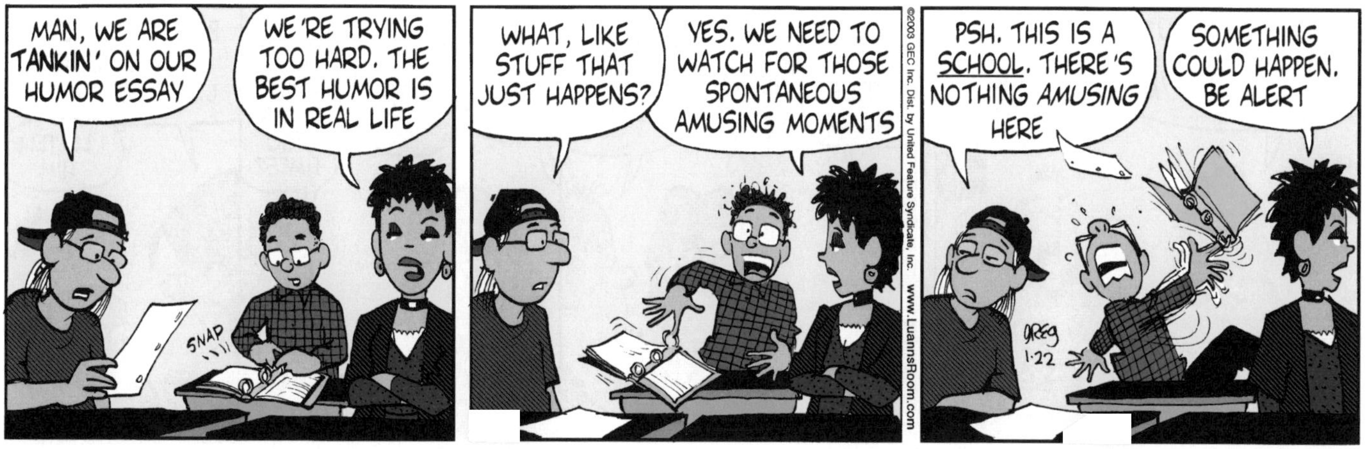
MAN, WE ARE TANKIN' ON OUR HUMOR ESSAY
WE'RE TRYING TOO HARD. THE BEST HUMOR IS IN REAL LIFE
SNAP
WHAT, LIKE STUFF THAT JUST HAPPENS?
YES. WE NEED TO WATCH FOR THOSE SPONTANEOUS AMUSING MOMENTS
©2003 GEC Inc. Dist. by United Feature Syndicate, Inc.
www.LuannsRoom.com
PSH. THIS IS A SCHOOL. THERE'S NOTHING AMUSING HERE
SOMETHING COULD HAPPEN. BE ALERT
GREG 1·22

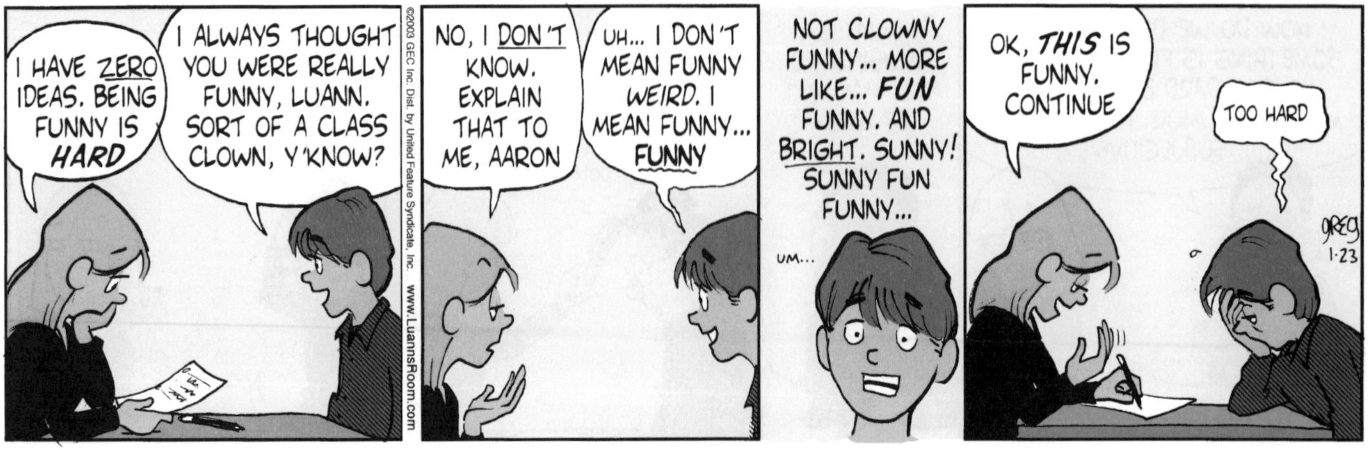
I HAVE ZERO IDEAS. BEING FUNNY IS HARD
I ALWAYS THOUGHT YOU WERE REALLY FUNNY, LUANN. SORT OF A CLASS CLOWN, Y'KNOW?
©2003 GEC Inc. Dist. by United Feature Syndicate, Inc. www.LuannsRoom.com
NO, I DON'T KNOW. EXPLAIN THAT TO ME, AARON
UH... I DON'T MEAN FUNNY WEIRD. I MEAN FUNNY... FUNNY
NOT CLOWNY FUNNY... MORE LIKE... FUN FUNNY. AND BRIGHT. SUNNY! SUNNY FUN FUNNY...
UM...
OK, THIS IS FUNNY. CONTINUE
TOO HARD
GREG 1·23

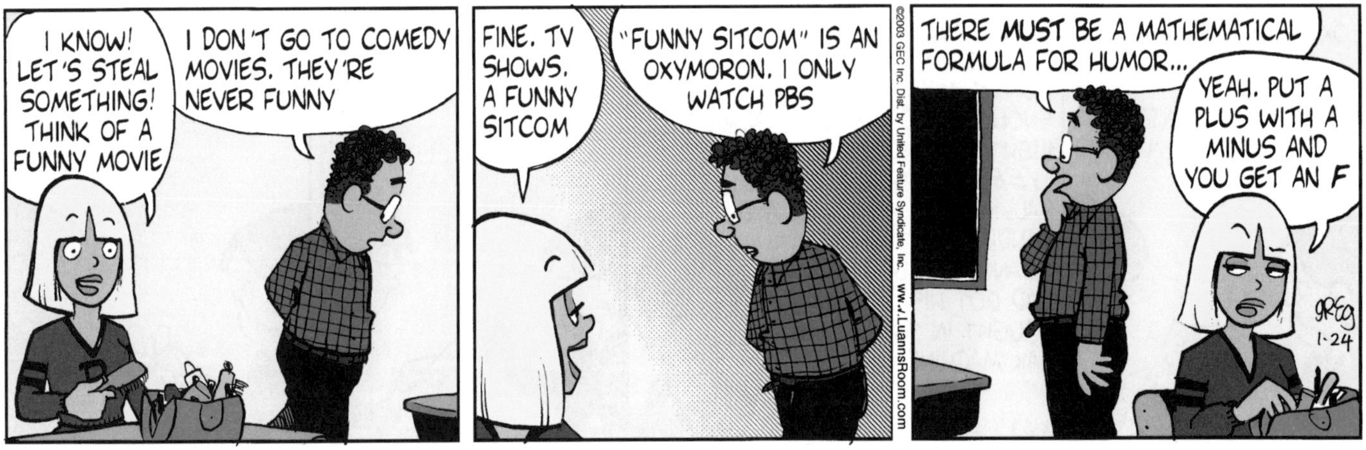
I KNOW! LET'S STEAL SOMETHING! THINK OF A FUNNY MOVIE
I DON'T GO TO COMEDY MOVIES. THEY'RE NEVER FUNNY
FINE. TV SHOWS. A FUNNY SITCOM
"FUNNY SITCOM" IS AN OXYMORON. I ONLY WATCH PBS
©2003 GEC Inc. Dist. by United Feature Syndicate, Inc. www.LuannsRoom.com
THERE MUST BE A MATHEMATICAL FORMULA FOR HUMOR...
YEAH. PUT A PLUS WITH A MINUS AND YOU GET AN F
GREG 1·24

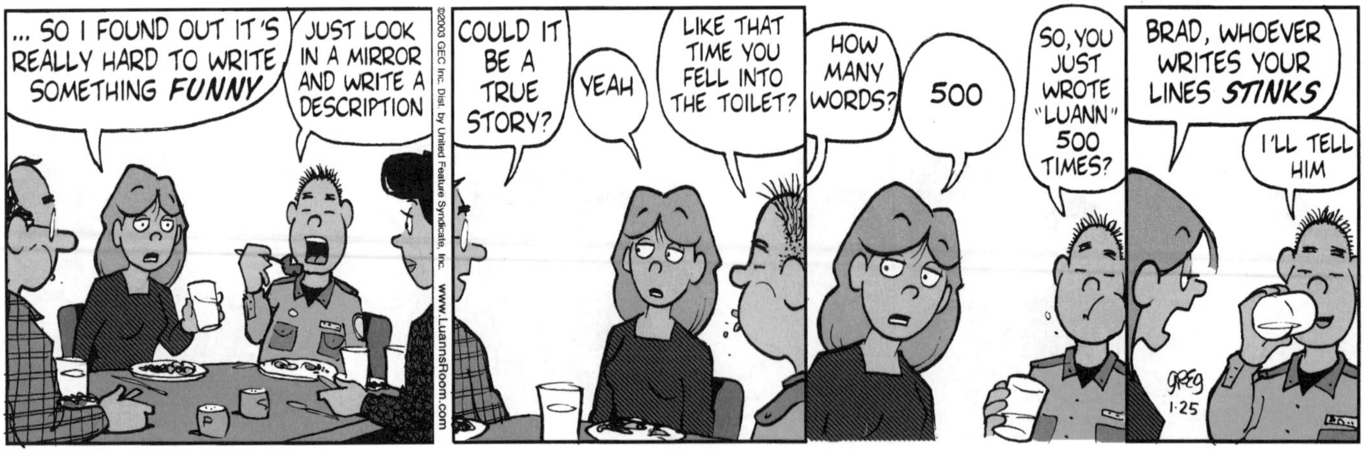
... SO I FOUND OUT IT'S REALLY HARD TO WRITE SOMETHING FUNNY
JUST LOOK IN A MIRROR AND WRITE A DESCRIPTION
©2003 GEC Inc. Dist. by United Feature Syndicate, Inc. www.LuannsRoom.com
COULD IT BE A TRUE STORY?
YEAH
LIKE THAT TIME YOU FELL INTO THE TOILET?
HOW MANY WORDS?
500
SO, YOU JUST WROTE "LUANN" 500 TIMES?
BRAD, WHOEVER WRITES YOUR LINES STINKS
I'LL TELL HIM
GREG 1·25

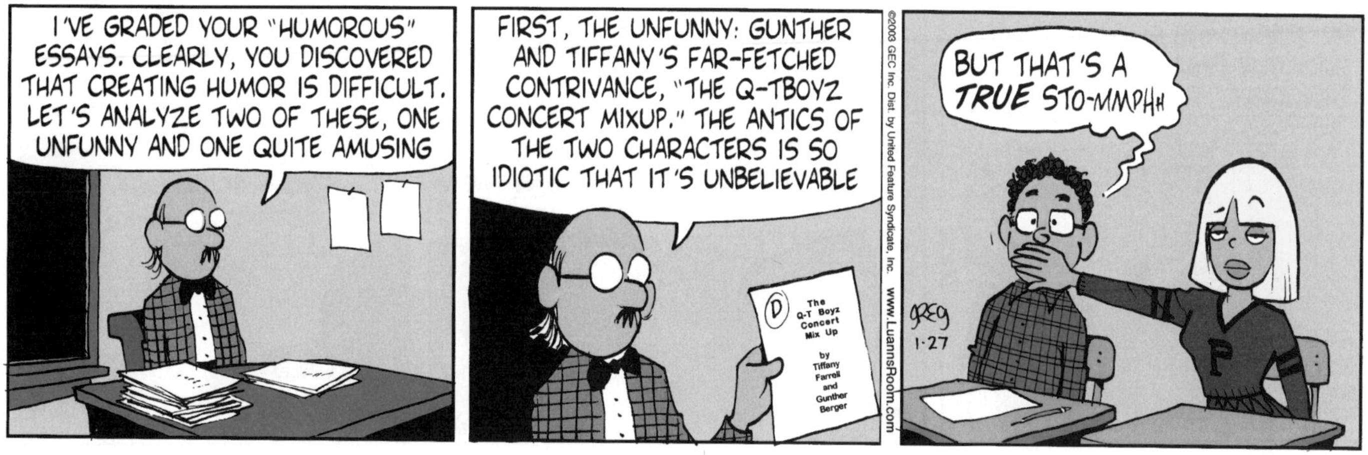
I'VE GRADED YOUR "HUMOROUS" ESSAYS. CLEARLY, YOU DISCOVERED THAT CREATING HUMOR IS DIFFICULT. LET'S ANALYZE TWO OF THESE, ONE UNFUNNY AND ONE QUITE AMUSING
FIRST, THE UNFUNNY: GUNTHER AND TIFFANY'S FAR-FETCHED CONTRIVANCE, "THE Q-TBOYZ CONCERT MIXUP." THE ANTICS OF THE TWO CHARACTERS IS SO IDIOTIC THAT IT'S UNBELIEVABLE
D
The Q-T Boyz Concert Mix Up
by Tiffany Farrell and Gunther Berger
©2003 GEC Inc. Dist. by United Feature Syndicate, Inc.
www.LuannsRoom.com
BUT THAT'S A *TRUE* STO-MMPHH
GREG
1·27

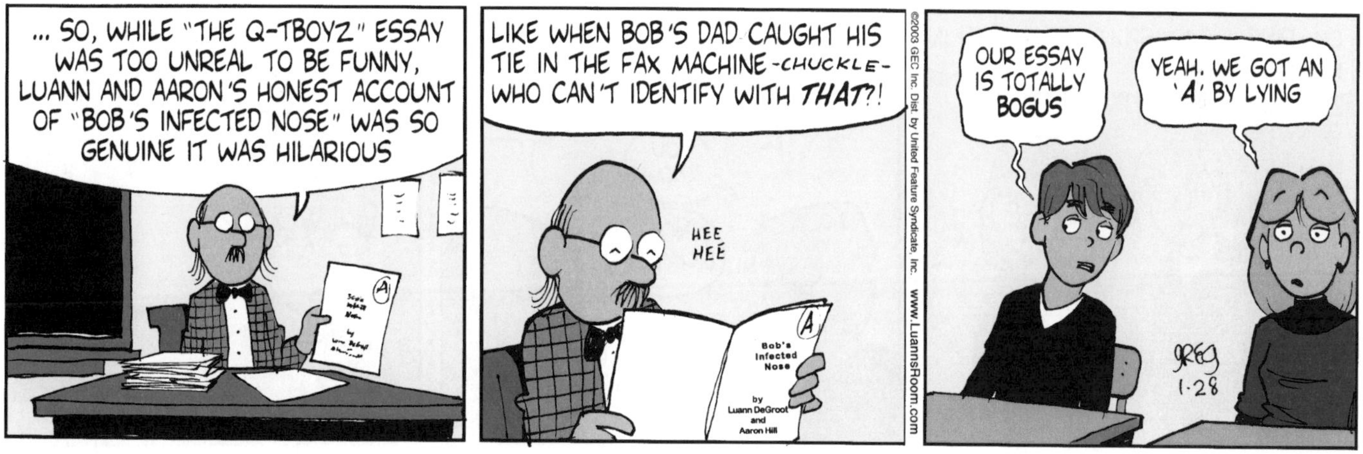
... SO, WHILE "THE Q-TBOYZ" ESSAY WAS TOO UNREAL TO BE FUNNY, LUANN AND AARON'S HONEST ACCOUNT OF "BOB'S INFECTED NOSE" WAS SO GENUINE IT WAS HILARIOUS
LIKE WHEN BOB'S DAD CAUGHT HIS TIE IN THE FAX MACHINE -CHUCKLE- WHO CAN'T IDENTIFY WITH *THAT*?!
HEE HEE
A
Bob's Infected Nose
by Luann DeGroot and Aaron Hill
©2003 GEC Inc. Dist. by United Feature Syndicate, Inc.
www.LuannsRoom.com
OUR ESSAY IS TOTALLY BOGUS
YEAH. WE GOT AN '*A*' BY LYING
GREG
1·28

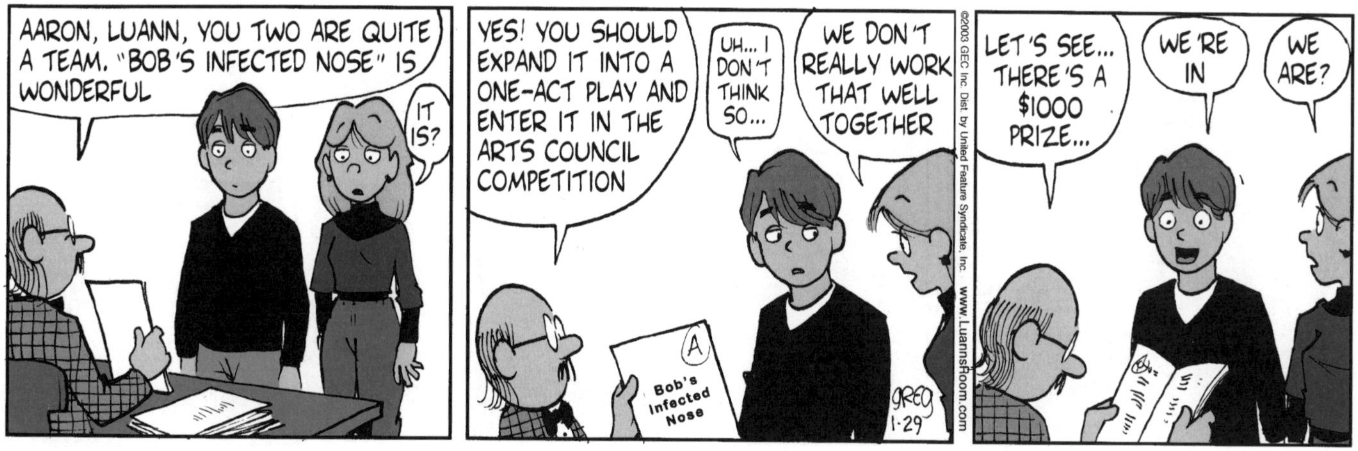
AARON, LUANN, YOU TWO ARE QUITE A TEAM. "BOB'S INFECTED NOSE" IS WONDERFUL
IT IS?
YES! YOU SHOULD EXPAND IT INTO A ONE-ACT PLAY AND ENTER IT IN THE ARTS COUNCIL COMPETITION
UH... I DON'T THINK SO...
WE DON'T REALLY WORK THAT WELL TOGETHER
A
Bob's Infected Nose
GREG
1·29
©2003 GEC Inc. Dist. by United Feature Syndicate, Inc.
www.LuannsRoom.com
LET'S SEE... THERE'S A $1000 PRIZE...
WE'RE IN
WE ARE?

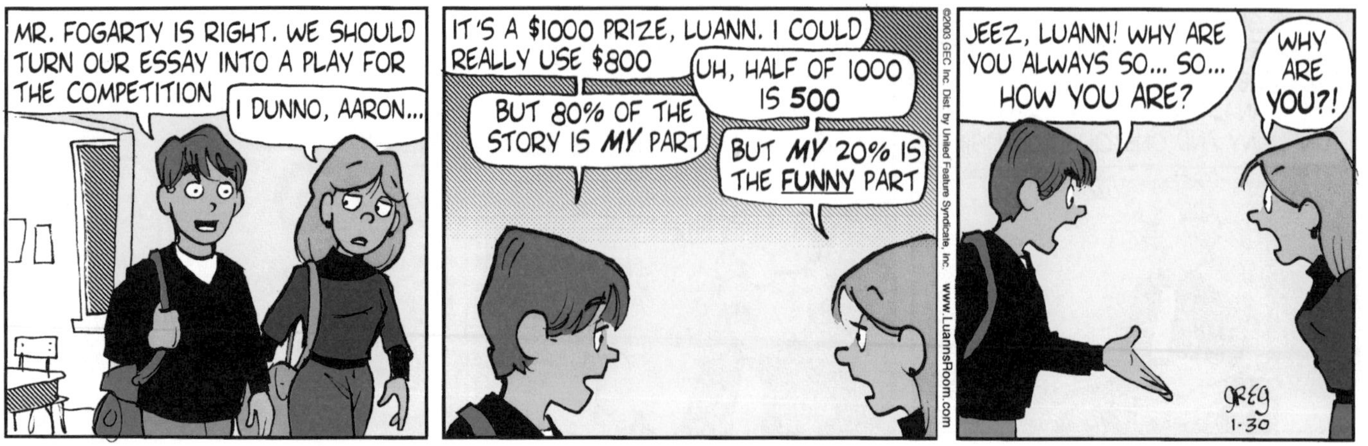
MR. FOGARTY IS RIGHT. WE SHOULD TURN OUR ESSAY INTO A PLAY FOR THE COMPETITION
I DUNNO, AARON...
IT'S A $1000 PRIZE, LUANN. I COULD REALLY USE $800
BUT 80% OF THE STORY IS MY PART
UH, HALF OF 1000 IS 500
BUT MY 20% IS THE FUNNY PART
©2003 GEC Inc. Dist. by United Feature Syndicate, Inc. www.LuannsRoom.com
JEEZ, LUANN! WHY ARE YOU ALWAYS SO... SO... HOW YOU ARE?
WHY ARE YOU?!
GREG 1·30

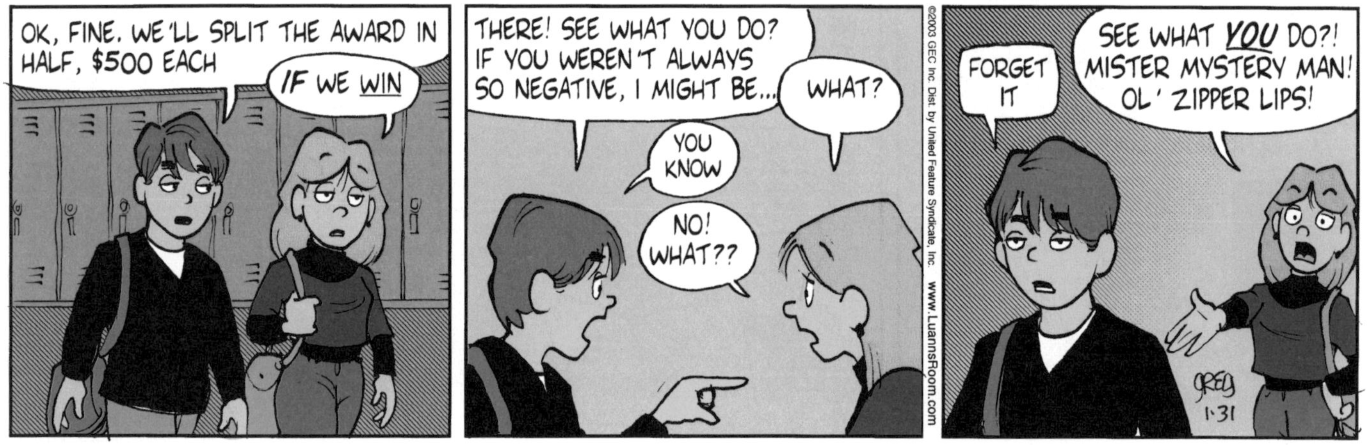
OK, FINE. WE'LL SPLIT THE AWARD IN HALF, $500 EACH
IF WE WIN
THERE! SEE WHAT YOU DO? IF YOU WEREN'T ALWAYS SO NEGATIVE, I MIGHT BE...
WHAT?
YOU KNOW
NO! WHAT??
©2003 GEC Inc. Dist. by United Feature Syndicate, Inc. www.LuannsRoom.com
FORGET IT
SEE WHAT YOU DO?! MISTER MYSTERY MAN! OL' ZIPPER LIPS!
GREG 1·31

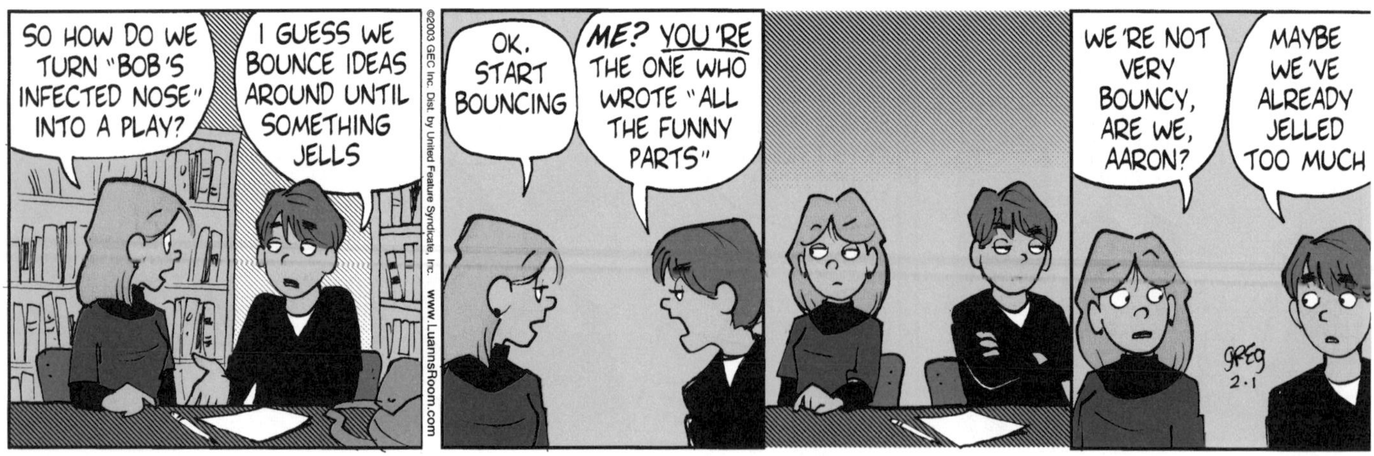
SO HOW DO WE TURN "BOB'S INFECTED NOSE" INTO A PLAY?
I GUESS WE BOUNCE IDEAS AROUND UNTIL SOMETHING JELLS
©2003 GEC Inc. Dist. by United Feature Syndicate, Inc. www.LuannsRoom.com
OK. START BOUNCING
ME? YOU'RE THE ONE WHO WROTE "ALL THE FUNNY PARTS"
WE'RE NOT VERY BOUNCY, ARE WE, AARON?
MAYBE WE'VE ALREADY JELLED TOO MUCH
GREG 2·1

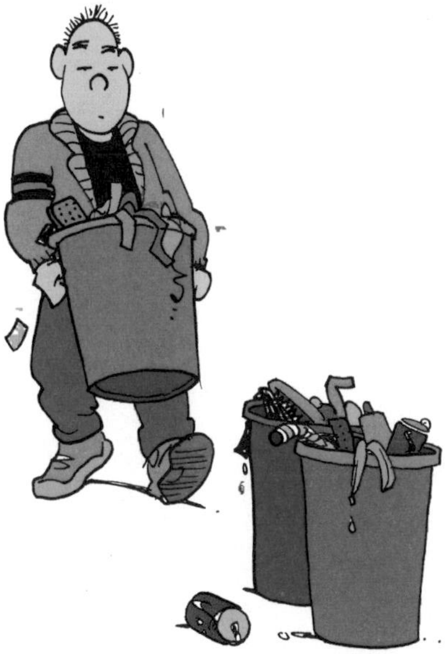

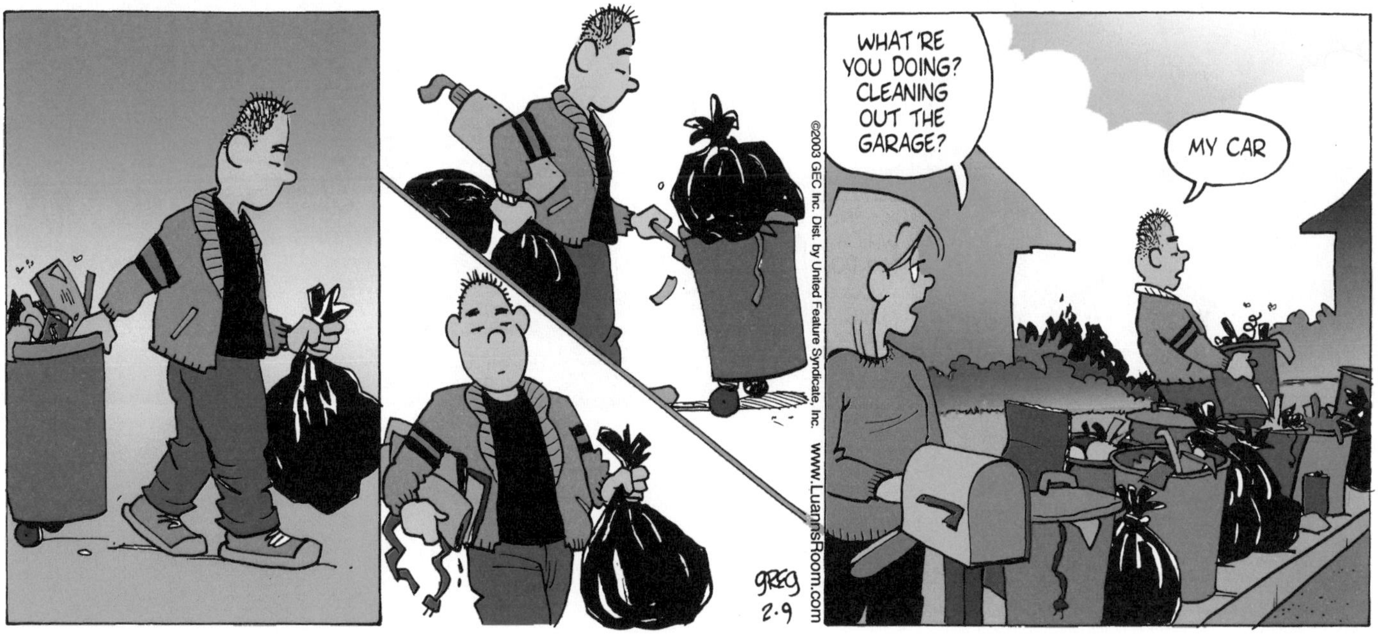
WHAT'RE YOU DOING? CLEANING OUT THE GARAGE?
MY CAR
©2003 GEC Inc. Dist. by United Feature Syndicate, Inc.
www.LuannsRoom.com
GREG 2.9

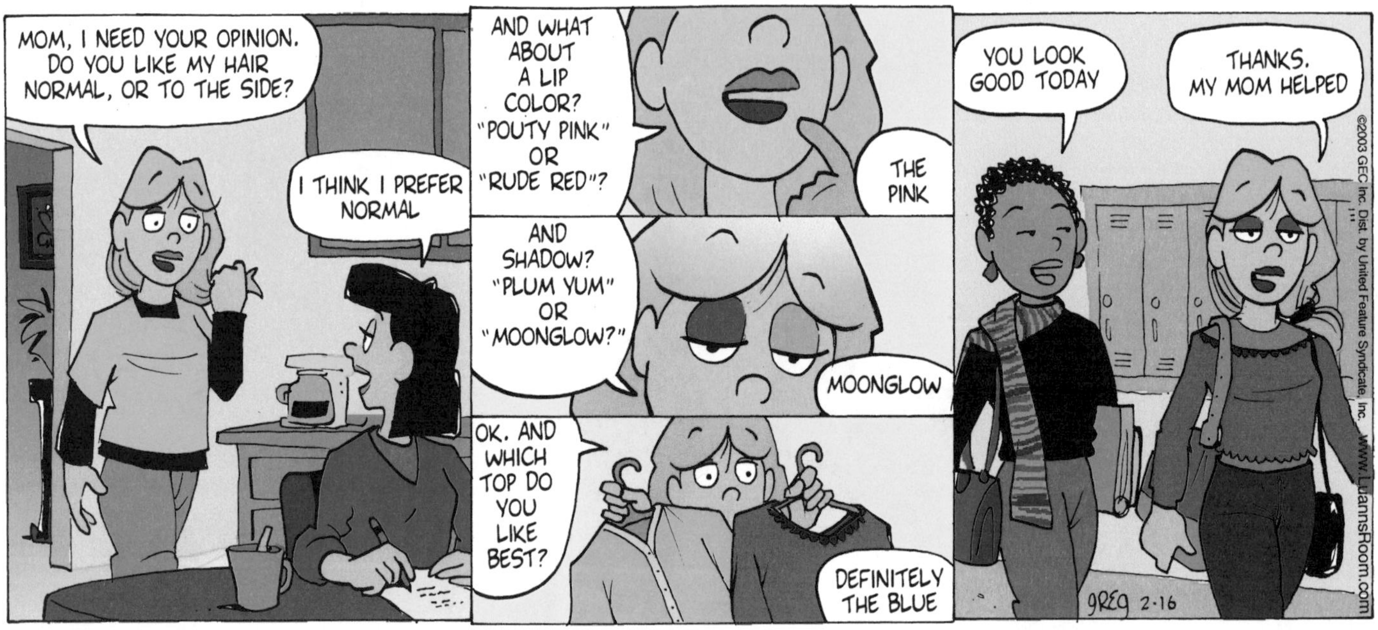
MOM, I NEED YOUR OPINION. DO YOU LIKE MY HAIR NORMAL, OR TO THE SIDE?
I THINK I PREFER NORMAL
AND WHAT ABOUT A LIP COLOR? "POUTY PINK" OR "RUDE RED"?
THE PINK
AND SHADOW? "PLUM YUM" OR "MOONGLOW?"
MOONGLOW
OK. AND WHICH TOP DO YOU LIKE BEST?
DEFINITELY THE BLUE
YOU LOOK GOOD TODAY
THANKS. MY MOM HELPED
©2003 GEC Inc. Dist. by United Feature Syndicate, Inc. www.LuannsRoom.com
GREG 2·16

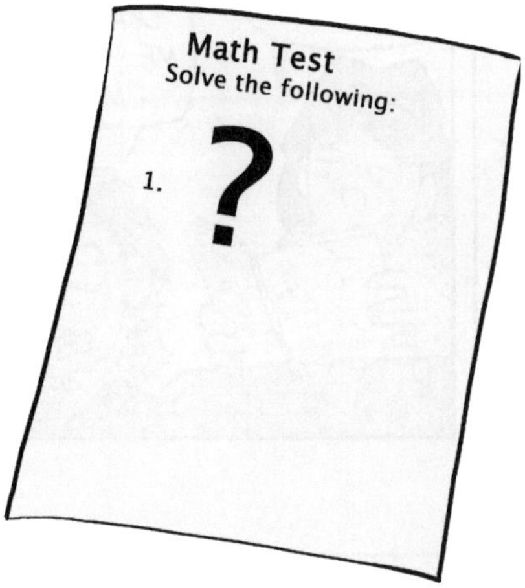
Math Test
Solve the following:
1. ?

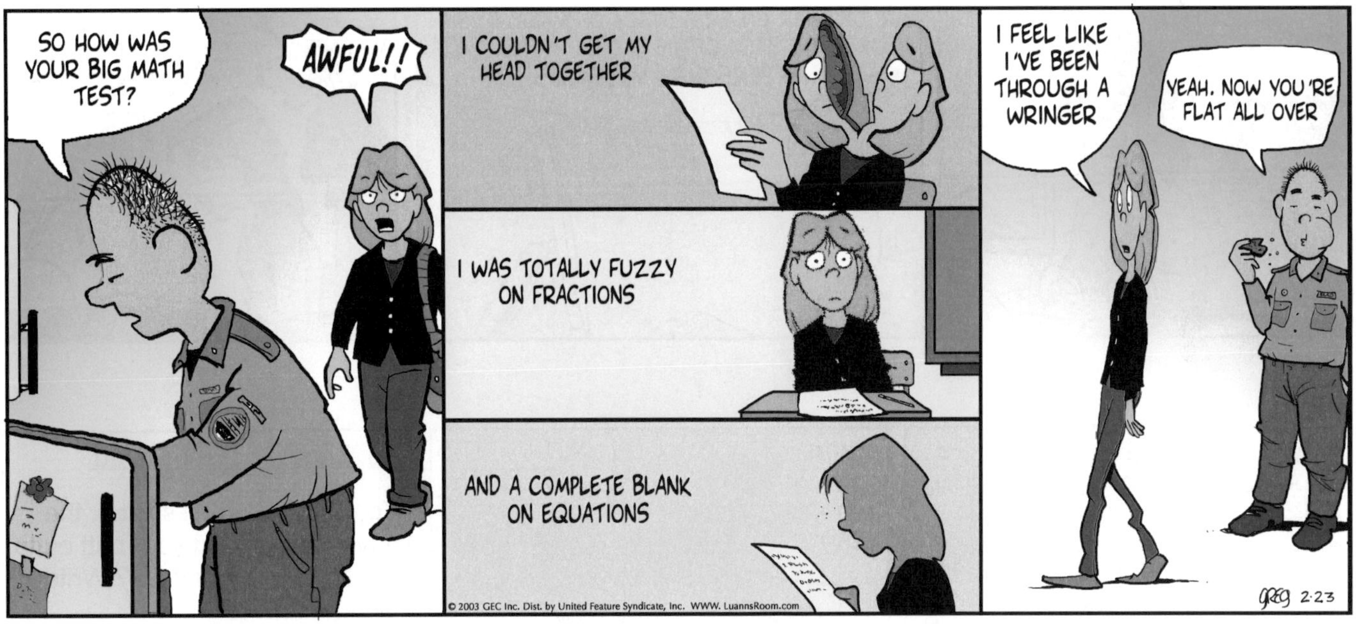
SO HOW WAS YOUR BIG MATH TEST?
AWFUL!!
I COULDN'T GET MY HEAD TOGETHER
I WAS TOTALLY FUZZY ON FRACTIONS
AND A COMPLETE BLANK ON EQUATIONS
© 2003 GEC Inc. Dist. by United Feature Syndicate, Inc. WWW. LuannsRoom.com
I FEEL LIKE I'VE BEEN THROUGH A WRINGER
YEAH. NOW YOU'RE FLAT ALL OVER
GREG 2·23

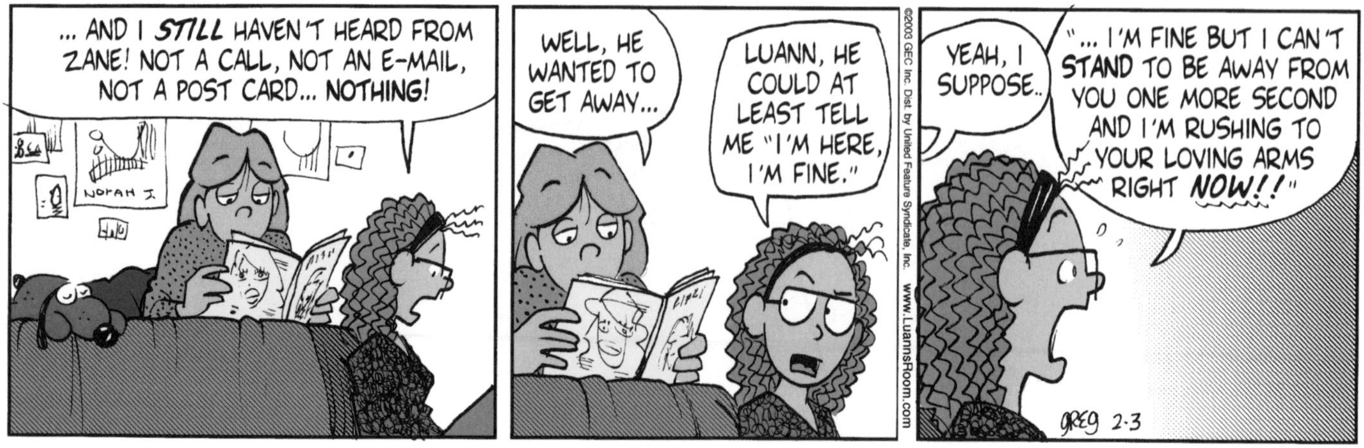
... AND I STILL HAVEN'T HEARD FROM ZANE! NOT A CALL, NOT AN E-MAIL, NOT A POST CARD... NOTHING!
WELL, HE WANTED TO GET AWAY...
LUANN, HE COULD AT LEAST TELL ME "I'M HERE, I'M FINE."
©2003 GEC Inc. Dist. by United Feature Syndicate, Inc. www.LuannsRoom.com
YEAH, I SUPPOSE..
"... I'M FINE BUT I CAN'T STAND TO BE AWAY FROM YOU ONE MORE SECOND AND I'M RUSHING TO YOUR LOVING ARMS RIGHT NOW!!"
GREG 2·3

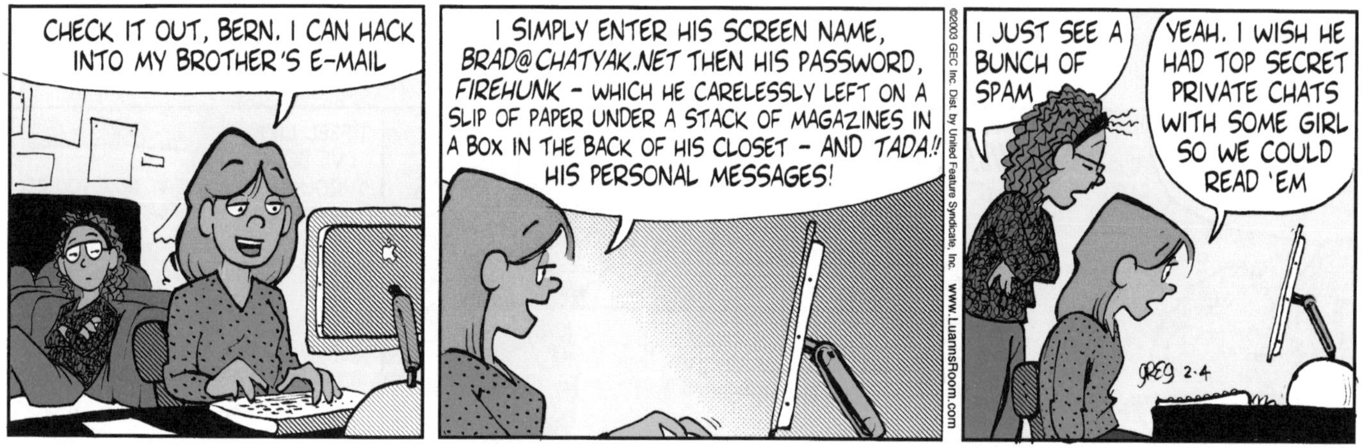
CHECK IT OUT, BERN. I CAN HACK INTO MY BROTHER'S E-MAIL
I SIMPLY ENTER HIS SCREEN NAME, BRAD@CHATYAK.NET THEN HIS PASSWORD, FIREHUNK - WHICH HE CARELESSLY LEFT ON A SLIP OF PAPER UNDER A STACK OF MAGAZINES IN A BOX IN THE BACK OF HIS CLOSET - AND TADA!! HIS PERSONAL MESSAGES!
©2003 GEC Inc. Dist. by United Feature Syndicate, Inc. www.LuannsRoom.com
I JUST SEE A BUNCH OF SPAM
YEAH. I WISH HE HAD TOP SECRET PRIVATE CHATS WITH SOME GIRL SO WE COULD READ 'EM
GREG 2·4

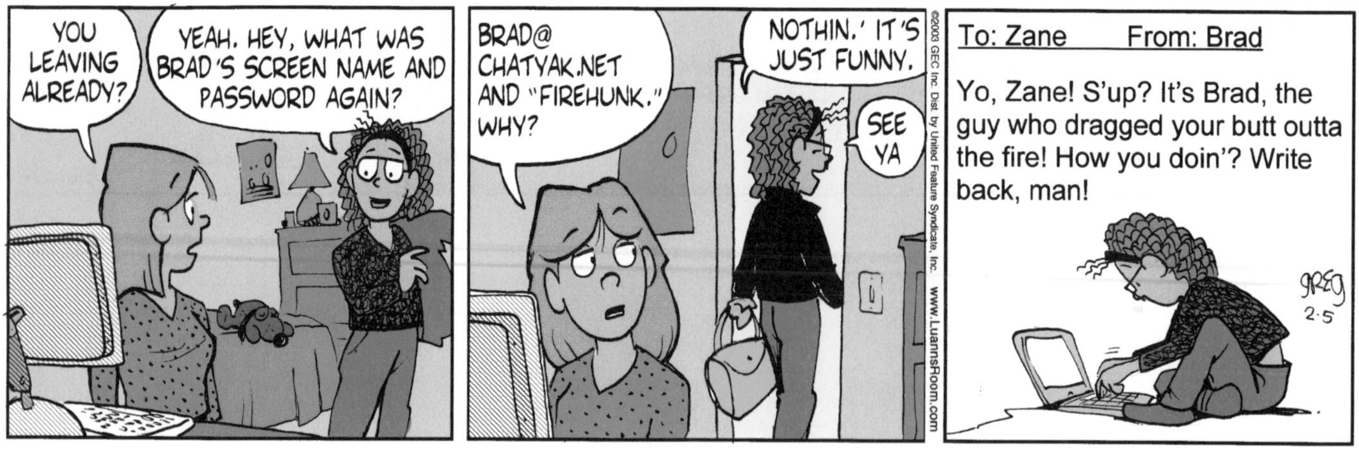
YOU LEAVING ALREADY?
YEAH. HEY, WHAT WAS BRAD'S SCREEN NAME AND PASSWORD AGAIN?
BRAD@ CHATYAK.NET AND "FIREHUNK." WHY?
NOTHIN.' IT'S JUST FUNNY.
SEE YA
©2003 GEC Inc. Dist. by United Feature Syndicate, Inc. www.LuannsRoom.com
To: Zane From: Brad
Yo, Zane! S'up? It's Brad, the guy who dragged your butt outta the fire! How you doin'? Write back, man!
GREG 2·5

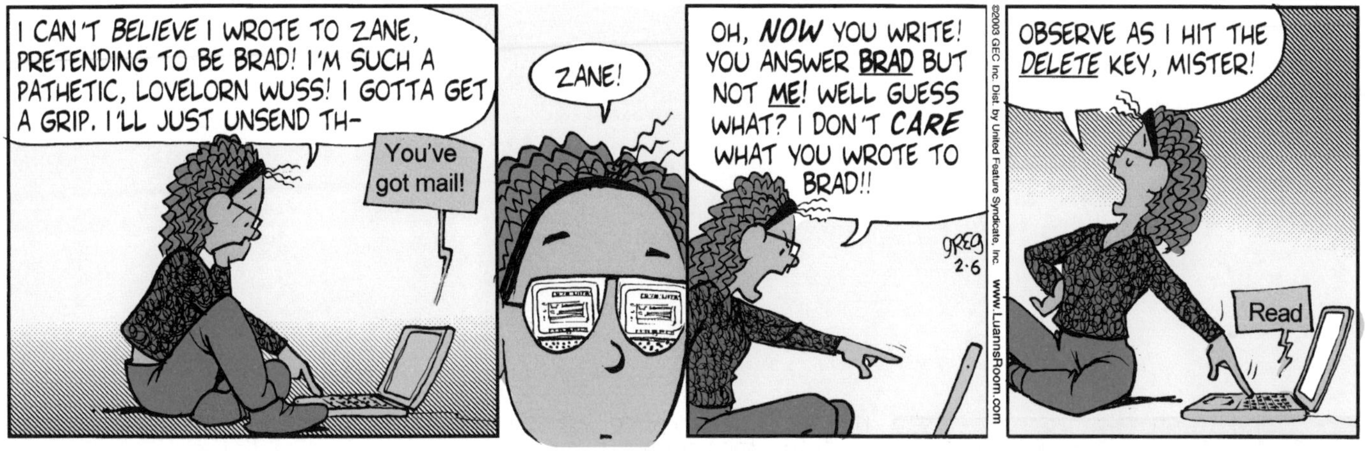
I CAN'T BELIEVE I WROTE TO ZANE, PRETENDING TO BE BRAD! I'M SUCH A PATHETIC, LOVELORN WUSS! I GOTTA GET A GRIP. I'LL JUST UNSEND TH-
You've got mail!
ZANE!
OH, NOW YOU WRITE! YOU ANSWER BRAD BUT NOT ME! WELL GUESS WHAT? I DON'T CARE WHAT YOU WROTE TO BRAD!!
GREG 2·6
©2003 GEC Inc. Dist. by United Feature Syndicate, Inc. www.LuannsRoom.com
OBSERVE AS I HIT THE DELETE KEY, MISTER!
Read

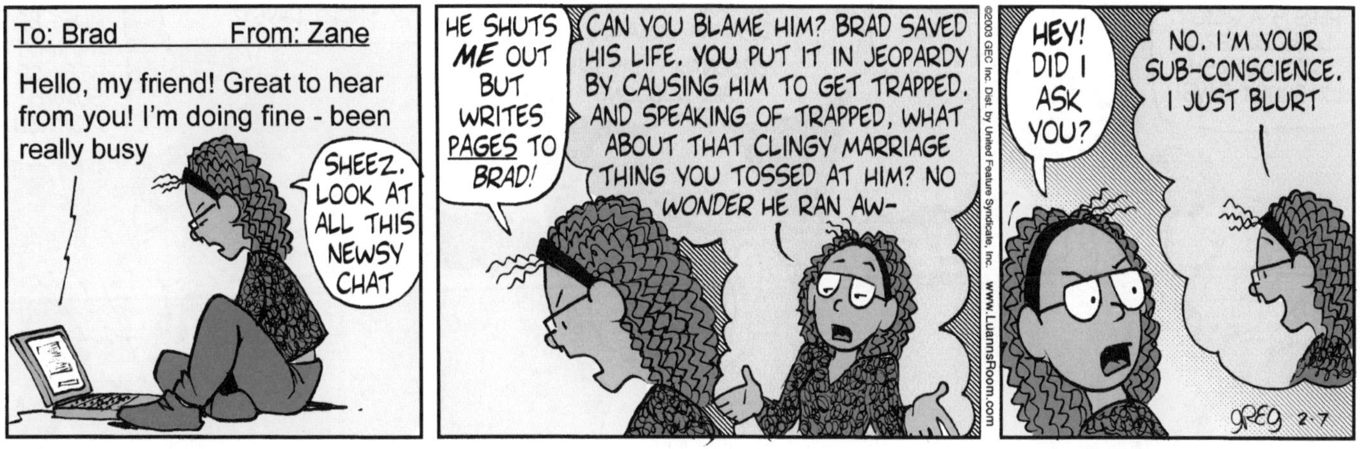
To: Brad From: Zane
Hello, my friend! Great to hear from you! I'm doing fine - been really busy
SHEEZ. LOOK AT ALL THIS NEWSY CHAT
HE SHUTS ME OUT BUT WRITES PAGES TO BRAD!
CAN YOU BLAME HIM? BRAD SAVED HIS LIFE. YOU PUT IT IN JEOPARDY BY CAUSING HIM TO GET TRAPPED. AND SPEAKING OF TRAPPED, WHAT ABOUT THAT CLINGY MARRIAGE THING YOU TOSSED AT HIM? NO WONDER HE RAN AW-
©2003 GEC Inc. Dist. by United Feature Syndicate, Inc. www.LuannsRoom.com
HEY! DID I ASK YOU?
NO. I'M YOUR SUB-CONSCIENCE. I JUST BLURT
GREG 2·7

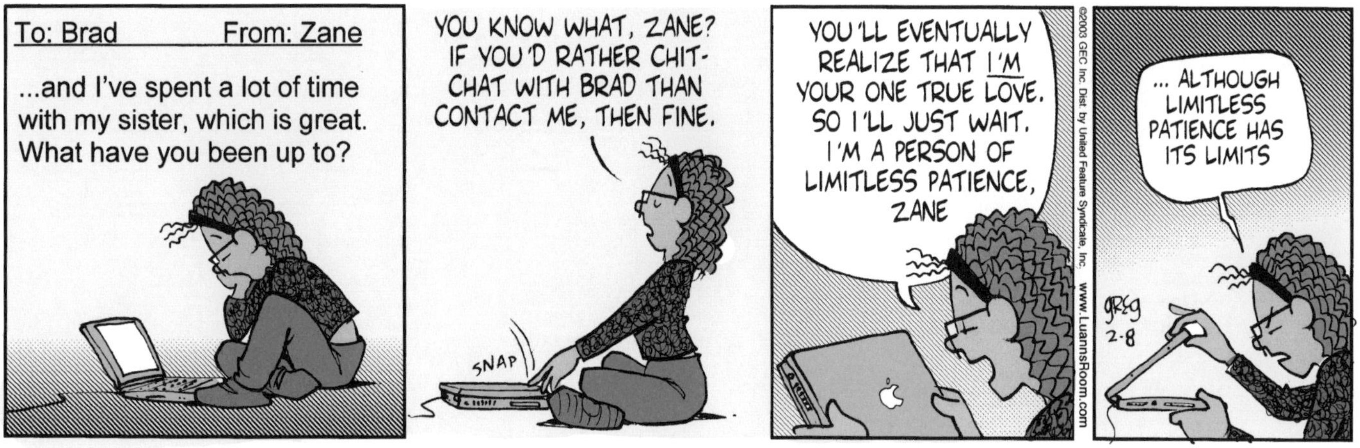
To: Brad From: Zane
...and I've spent a lot of time with my sister, which is great. What have you been up to?
YOU KNOW WHAT, ZANE? IF YOU'D RATHER CHIT-CHAT WITH BRAD THAN CONTACT ME, THEN FINE.
SNAP
YOU'LL EVENTUALLY REALIZE THAT I'M YOUR ONE TRUE LOVE. SO I'LL JUST WAIT. I'M A PERSON OF LIMITLESS PATIENCE, ZANE
©2003 GEC Inc. Dist. by United Feature Syndicate, Inc. www.LuannsRoom.com
... ALTHOUGH LIMITLESS PATIENCE HAS ITS LIMITS
GREG 2·8

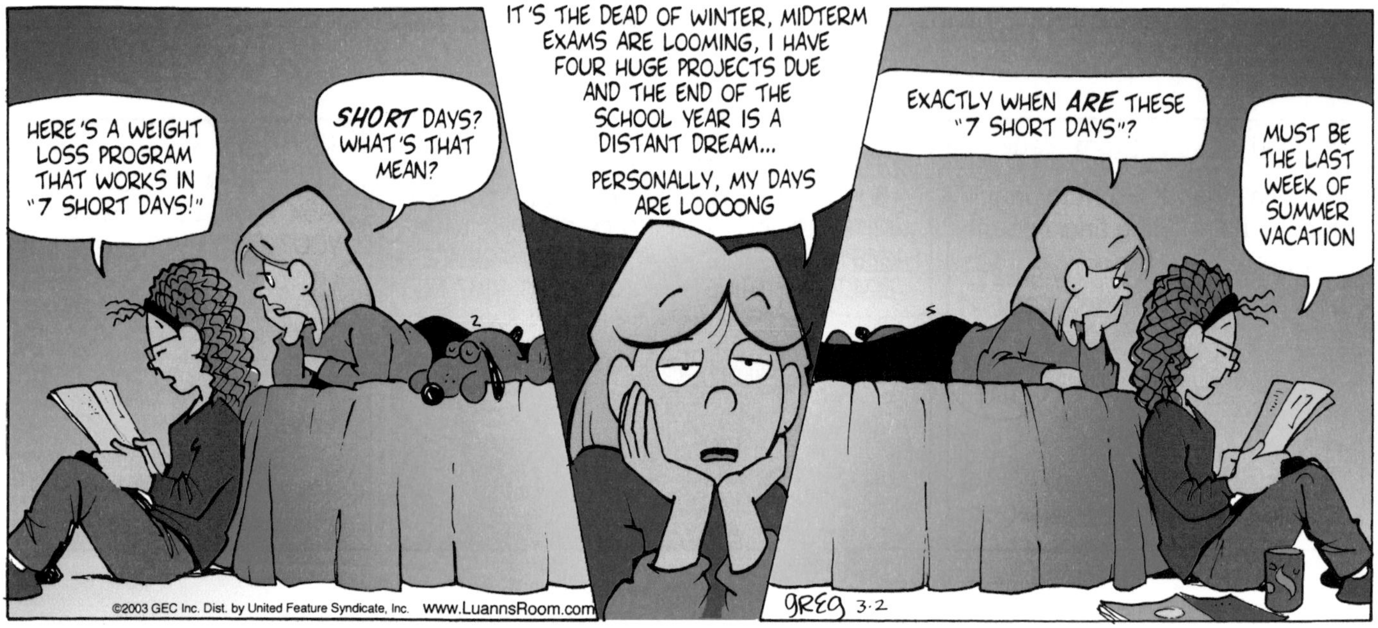
HERE'S A WEIGHT LOSS PROGRAM THAT WORKS IN "7 SHORT DAYS!"
SHORT DAYS? WHAT'S THAT MEAN?
Z
IT'S THE DEAD OF WINTER, MIDTERM EXAMS ARE LOOMING, I HAVE FOUR HUGE PROJECTS DUE AND THE END OF THE SCHOOL YEAR IS A DISTANT DREAM...
PERSONALLY, MY DAYS ARE LOOOONG
EXACTLY WHEN ARE THESE "7 SHORT DAYS"?
MUST BE THE LAST WEEK OF SUMMER VACATION
©2003 GEC Inc. Dist. by United Feature Syndicate, Inc.
www.LuannsRoom.com
GREG 3-2

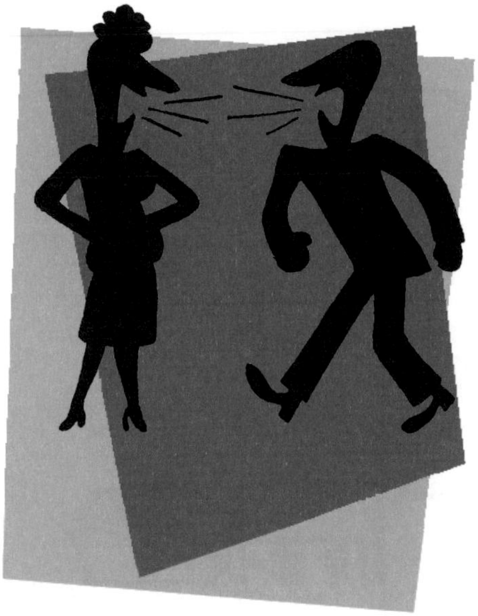

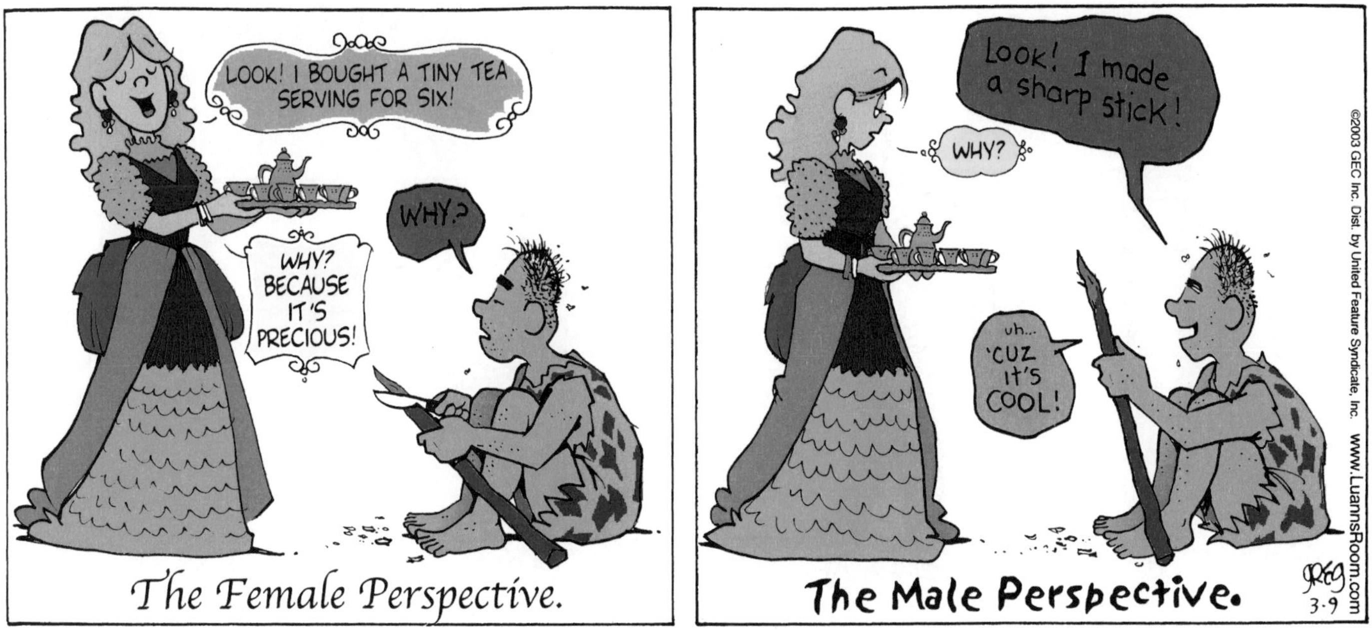
LOOK! I BOUGHT A TINY TEA SERVING FOR SIX!
WHY?
WHY? BECAUSE IT'S PRECIOUS!
The Female Perspective.
Look! I made a sharp stick!
WHY?
uh... 'CUZ IT'S COOL!
The Male Perspective.
GREG 3·9
©2003 GEC Inc. Dist. by United Feature Syndicate, Inc.
www.LuannsRoom.com

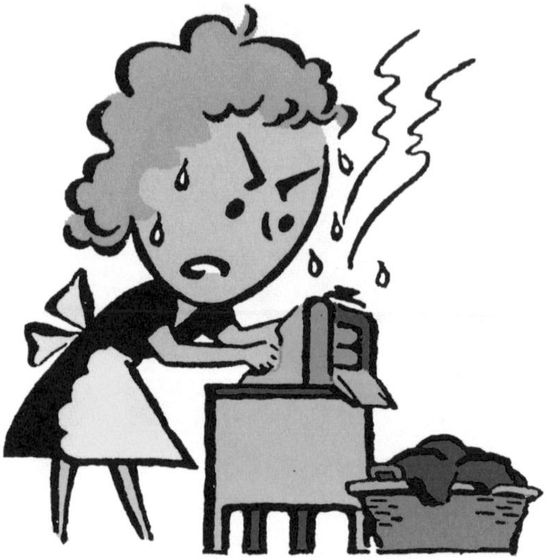

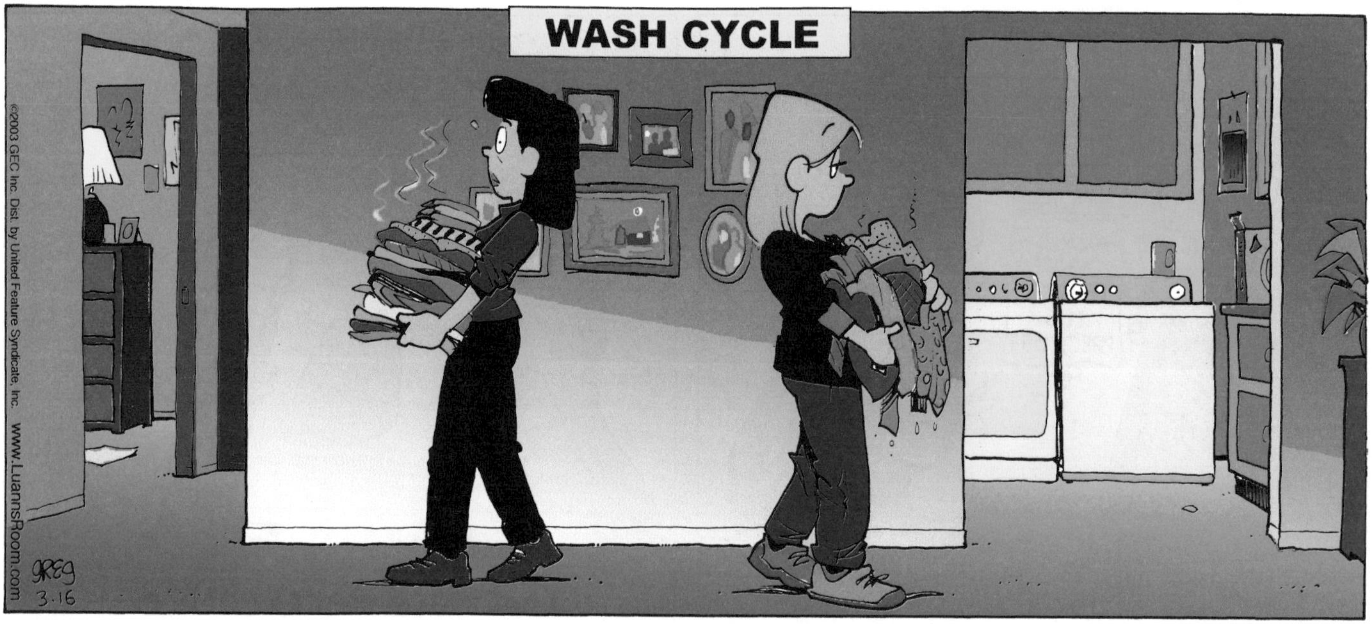
WASH CYCLE
©2003 GEC Inc. Dist. by United Feature Syndicate, Inc.
www.LuannsRoom.com
GREG
3.16

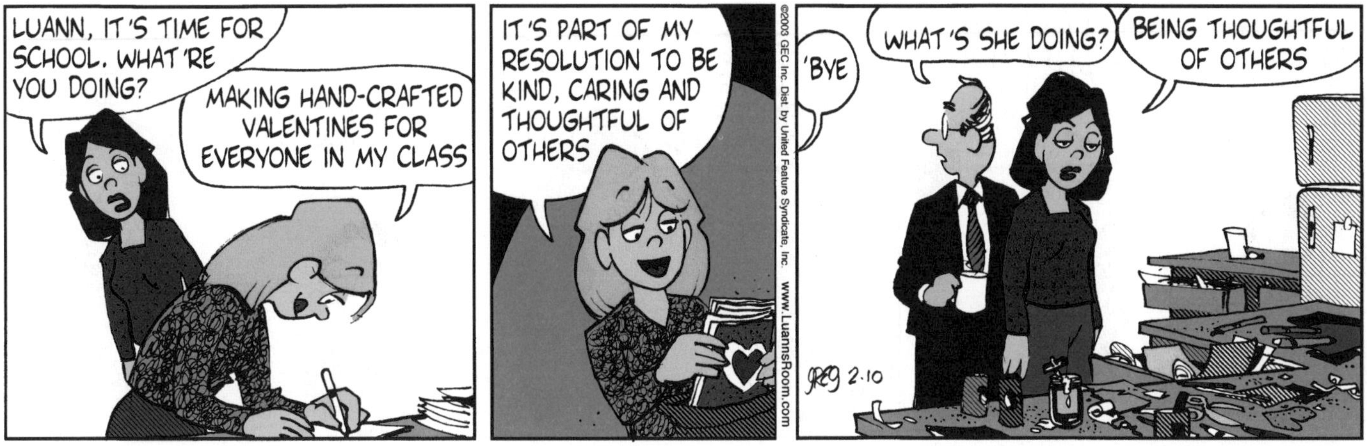
LUANN, IT'S TIME FOR SCHOOL. WHAT'RE YOU DOING?
MAKING HAND-CRAFTED VALENTINES FOR EVERYONE IN MY CLASS
IT'S PART OF MY RESOLUTION TO BE KIND, CARING AND THOUGHTFUL OF OTHERS
©2003 GEC Inc. Dist. by United Feature Syndicate, Inc. www.LuannsRoom.com
'BYE
WHAT'S SHE DOING?
BEING THOUGHTFUL OF OTHERS
GREG 2.10

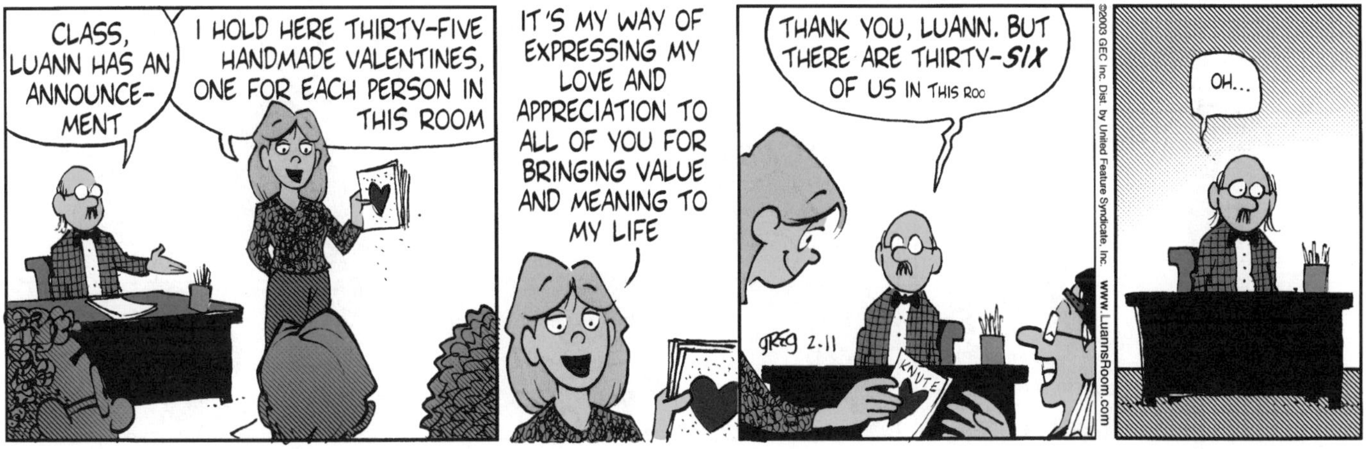
CLASS, LUANN HAS AN ANNOUNCEMENT
I HOLD HERE THIRTY-FIVE HANDMADE VALENTINES, ONE FOR EACH PERSON IN THIS ROOM
IT'S MY WAY OF EXPRESSING MY LOVE AND APPRECIATION TO ALL OF YOU FOR BRINGING VALUE AND MEANING TO MY LIFE
THANK YOU, LUANN. BUT THERE ARE THIRTY-SIX OF US IN THIS ROO
KNUTE
GREG 2.11
©2003 GEC Inc. Dist. by United Feature Syndicate, Inc. www.LuannsRoom.com
OH...

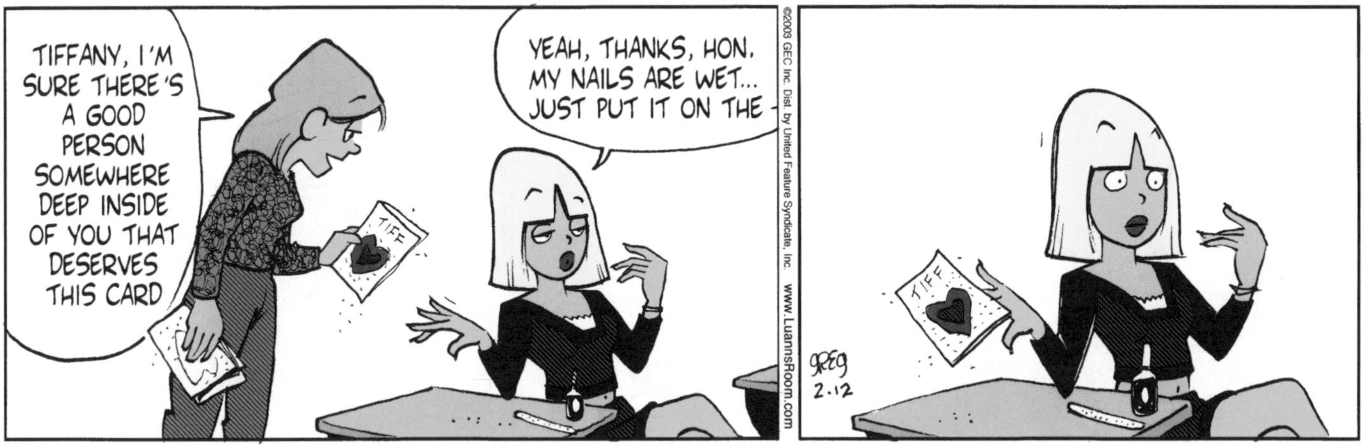
TIFFANY, I'M SURE THERE'S A GOOD PERSON SOMEWHERE DEEP INSIDE OF YOU THAT DESERVES THIS CARD
TIFF
YEAH, THANKS, HON. MY NAILS ARE WET... JUST PUT IT ON THE
©2003 GEC Inc. Dist. by United Feature Syndicate, Inc. www.LuannsRoom.com
GREG 2.12
TIFF

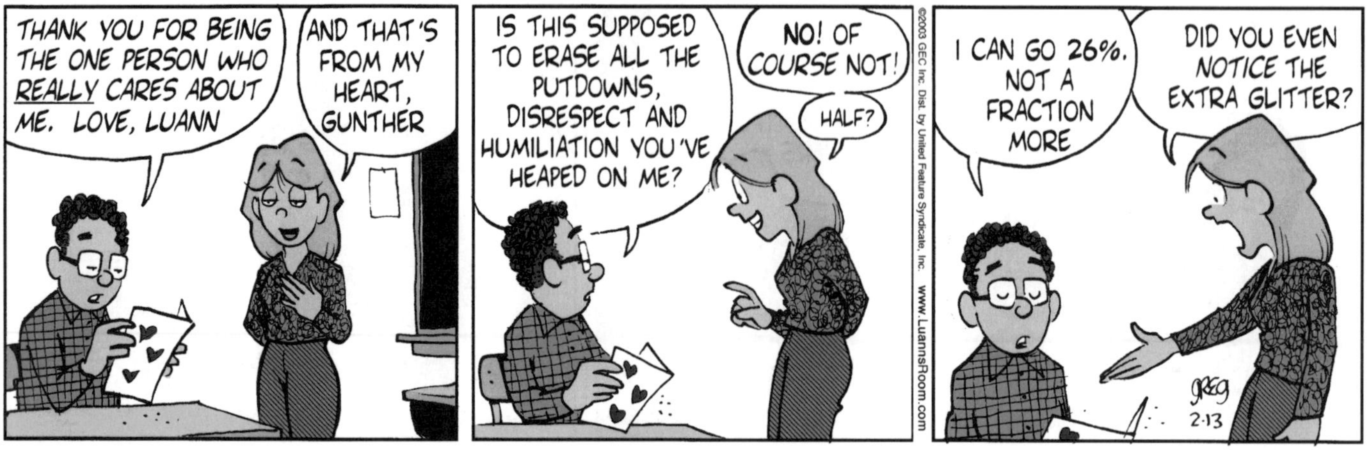
THANK YOU FOR BEING THE ONE PERSON WHO REALLY CARES ABOUT ME. LOVE, LUANN
AND THAT'S FROM MY HEART, GUNTHER
IS THIS SUPPOSED TO ERASE ALL THE PUTDOWNS, DISRESPECT AND HUMILIATION YOU'VE HEAPED ON ME?
NO! OF COURSE NOT!
HALF?
I CAN GO 26%. NOT A FRACTION MORE
DID YOU EVEN NOTICE THE EXTRA GLITTER?
©2003 GEC Inc. Dist. by United Feature Syndicate, Inc. www.LuannsRoom.com
GREG 2-13

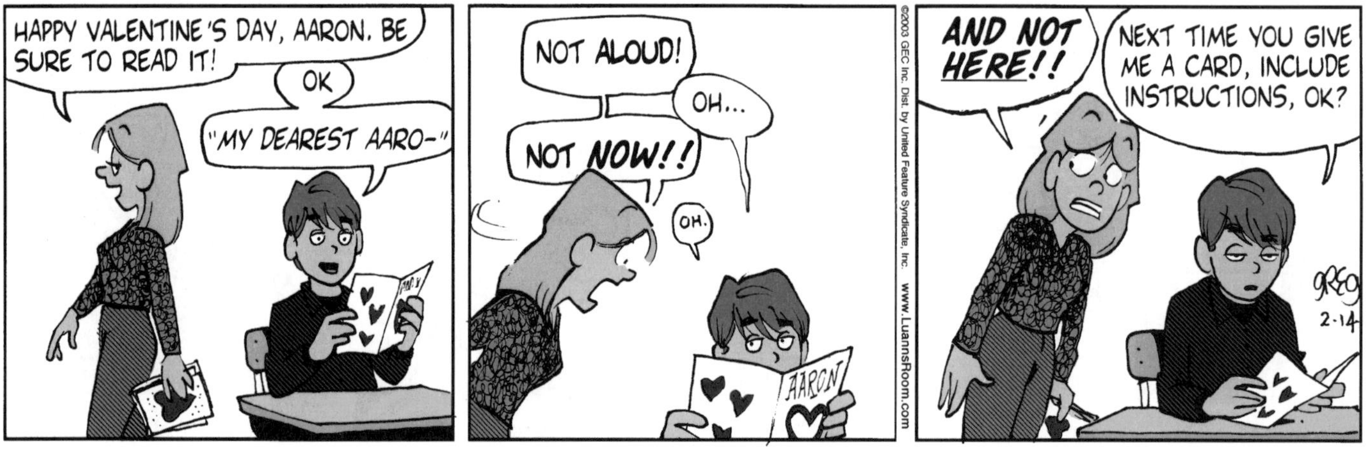
HAPPY VALENTINE'S DAY, AARON. BE SURE TO READ IT!
OK
"MY DEAREST AARO-"
NOT ALOUD!
OH...
NOT NOW!!
OH.
AND NOT HERE!!
NEXT TIME YOU GIVE ME A CARD, INCLUDE INSTRUCTIONS, OK?
AARON
©2003 GEC Inc. Dist. by United Feature Syndicate, Inc. www.LuannsRoom.com
GREG 2-14

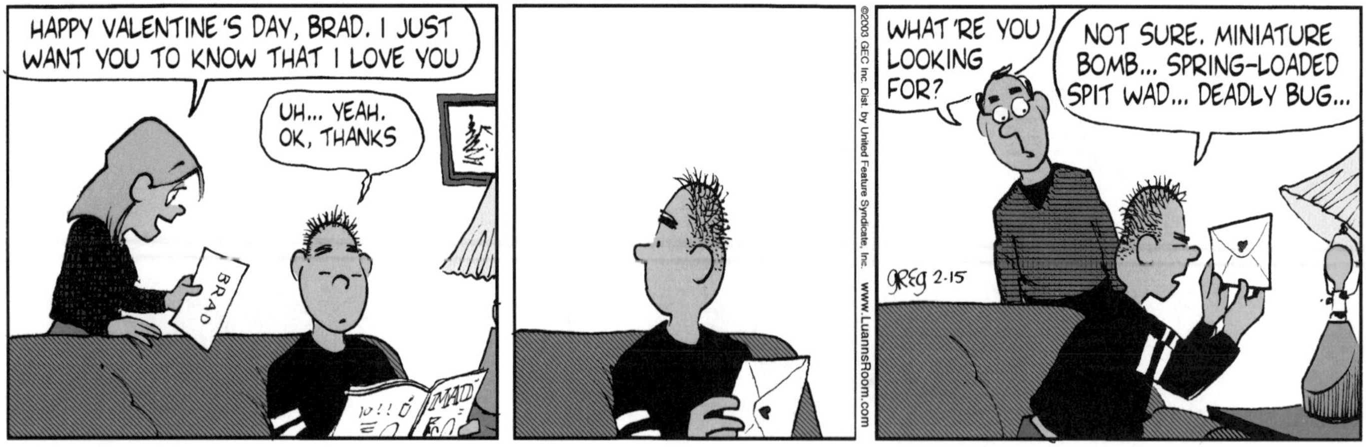
HAPPY VALENTINE'S DAY, BRAD. I JUST WANT YOU TO KNOW THAT I LOVE YOU
UH... YEAH. OK, THANKS
BRAD
WHAT'RE YOU LOOKING FOR?
NOT SURE. MINIATURE BOMB... SPRING-LOADED SPIT WAD... DEADLY BUG...
©2003 GEC Inc. Dist. by United Feature Syndicate, Inc. www.LuannsRoom.com
GREG 2-15

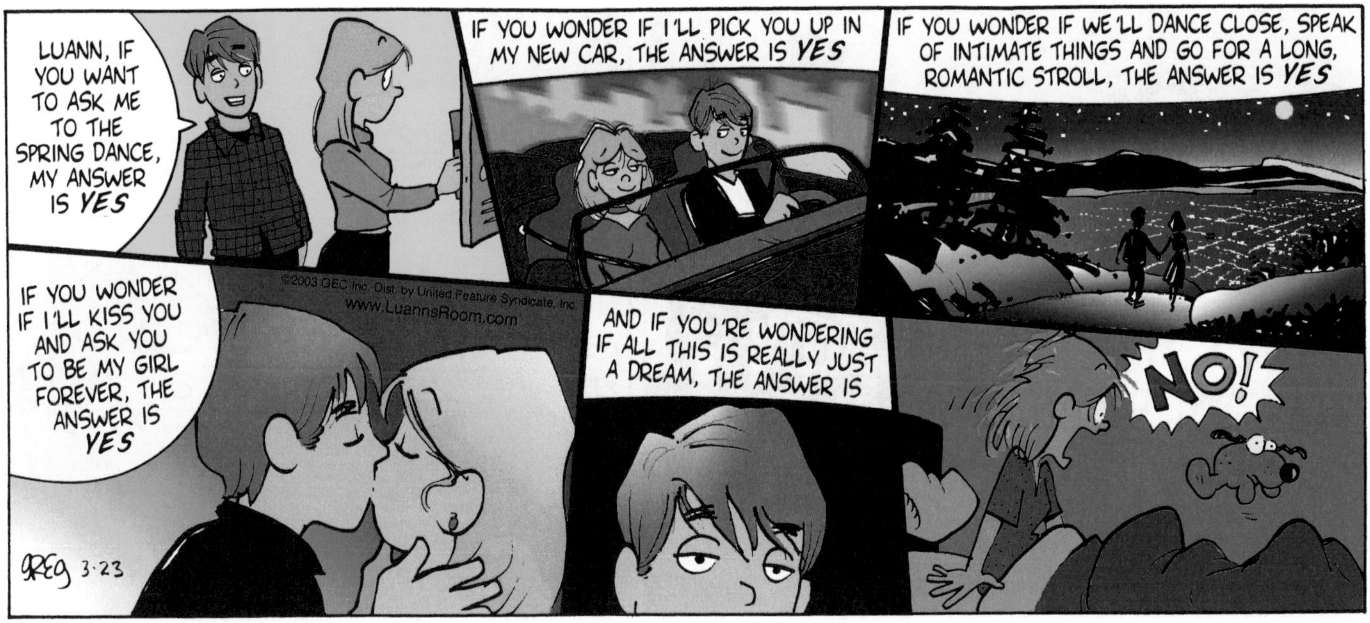
LUANN, IF YOU WANT TO ASK ME TO THE SPRING DANCE, MY ANSWER IS YES
IF YOU WONDER IF I'LL PICK YOU UP IN MY NEW CAR, THE ANSWER IS YES
IF YOU WONDER IF WE'LL DANCE CLOSE, SPEAK OF INTIMATE THINGS AND GO FOR A LONG, ROMANTIC STROLL, THE ANSWER IS YES
IF YOU WONDER IF I'LL KISS YOU AND ASK YOU TO BE MY GIRL FOREVER, THE ANSWER IS YES
©2003 GEC Inc. Dist. by United Feature Syndicate, Inc.
www.LuannsRoom.com
GREG 3·23
AND IF YOU'RE WONDERING IF ALL THIS IS REALLY JUST A DREAM, THE ANSWER IS
NO!

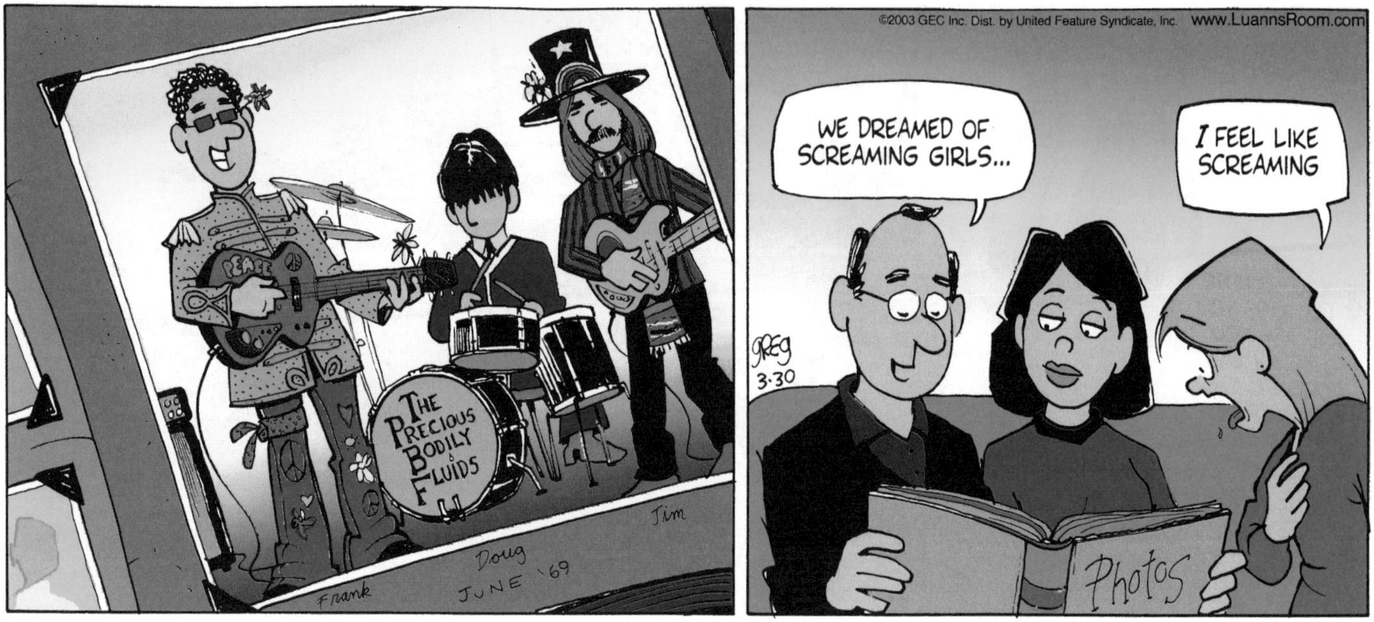
THE PRECIOUS BODILY FLUIDS
PEACE
Frank
Doug
JUNE '69
Jim
©2003 GEC Inc. Dist. by United Feature Syndicate, Inc. www.LuannsRoom.com
WE DREAMED OF SCREAMING GIRLS...
I FEEL LIKE SCREAMING
GREG 3·30
Photos

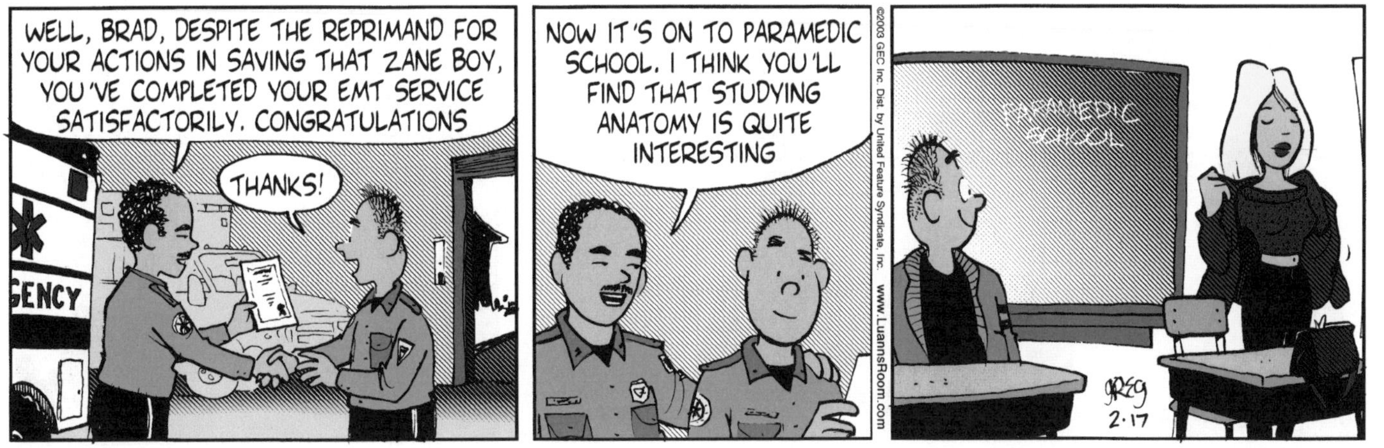
WELL, BRAD, DESPITE THE REPRIMAND FOR YOUR ACTIONS IN SAVING THAT ZANE BOY, YOU'VE COMPLETED YOUR EMT SERVICE SATISFACTORILY. CONGRATULATIONS
THANKS!
GENCY
NOW IT'S ON TO PARAMEDIC SCHOOL. I THINK YOU'LL FIND THAT STUDYING ANATOMY IS QUITE INTERESTING
©2003 GEC Inc. Dist. by United Feature Syndicate, Inc. www.LuannsRoom.com
PARAMEDIC SCHOOL
GREG 2·17

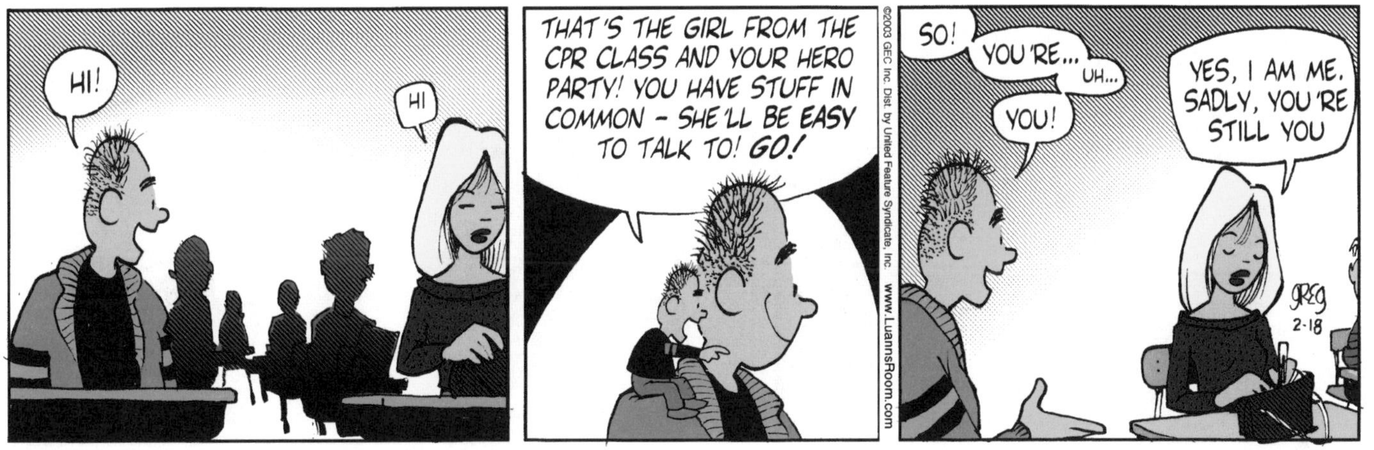
HI!
HI
THAT'S THE GIRL FROM THE CPR CLASS AND YOUR HERO PARTY! YOU HAVE STUFF IN COMMON – SHE'LL BE EASY TO TALK TO! GO!
©2003 GEC Inc. Dist. by United Feature Syndicate, Inc. www.LuannsRoom.com
SO!
YOU'RE...
UH...
YOU!
YES, I AM ME. SADLY, YOU'RE STILL YOU
GREG 2-18

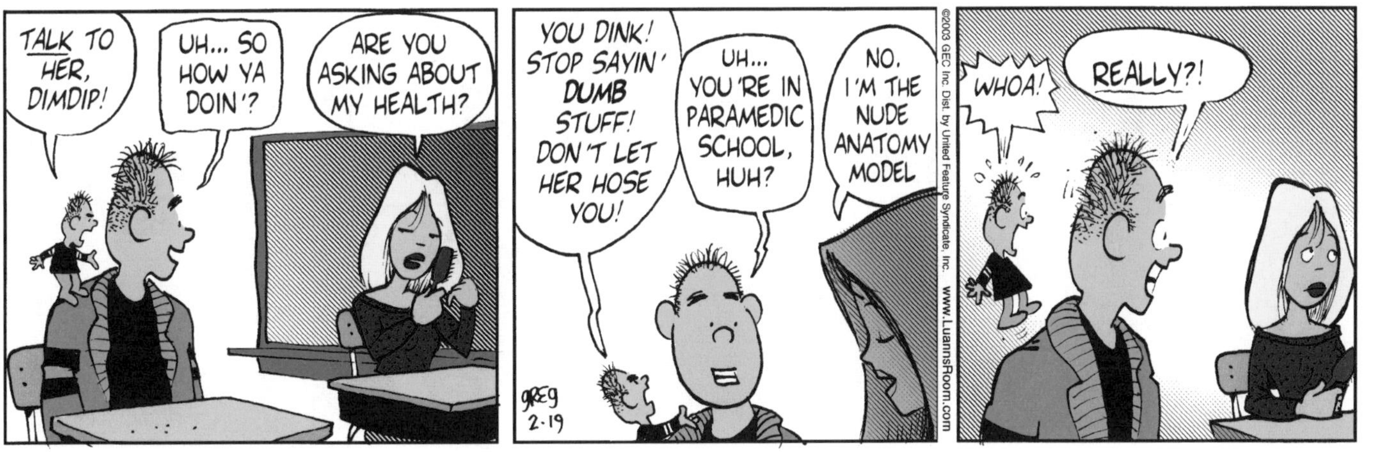
TALK TO HER, DIMDIP!
UH... SO HOW YA DOIN'?
ARE YOU ASKING ABOUT MY HEALTH?
YOU DINK! STOP SAYIN' DUMB STUFF! DON'T LET HER HOSE YOU!
UH... YOU'RE IN PARAMEDIC SCHOOL, HUH?
NO. I'M THE NUDE ANATOMY MODEL
GREG 2·19
©2003 GEC Inc. Dist. by United Feature Syndicate, Inc. www.LuannsRoom.com
WHOA!
REALLY?!

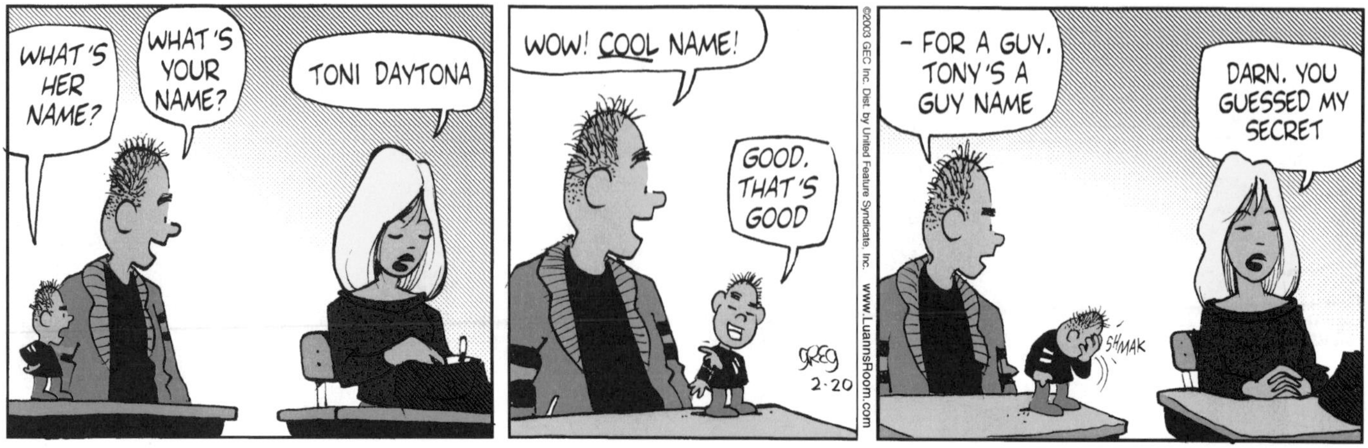
WHAT'S HER NAME?
WHAT'S YOUR NAME?
TONI DAYTONA
WOW! COOL NAME!
GOOD. THAT'S GOOD
GREG 2·20
- FOR A GUY. TONY'S A GUY NAME
DARN. YOU GUESSED MY SECRET
SHMAK

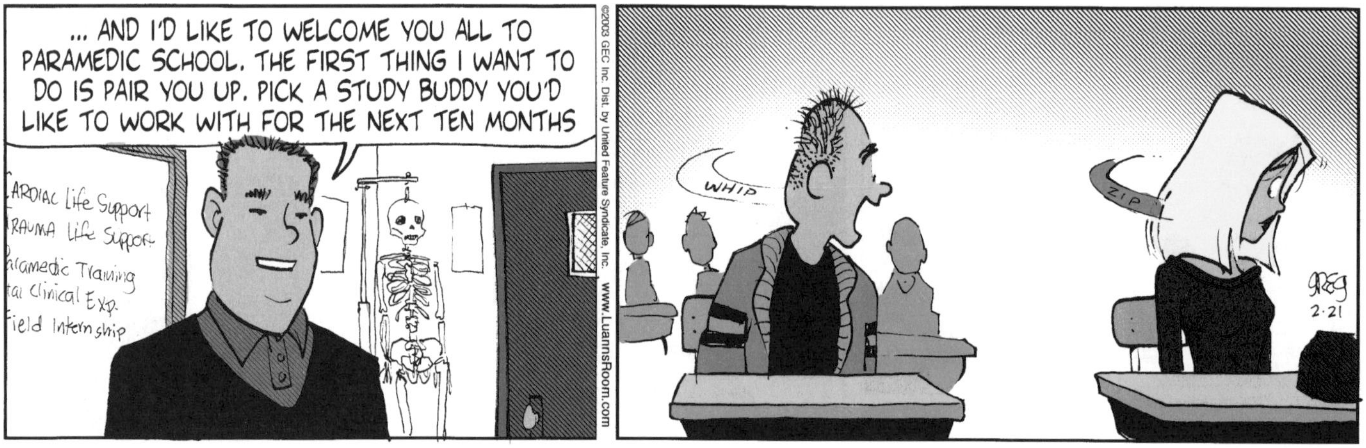
... AND I'D LIKE TO WELCOME YOU ALL TO PARAMEDIC SCHOOL. THE FIRST THING I WANT TO DO IS PAIR YOU UP. PICK A STUDY BUDDY YOU'D LIKE TO WORK WITH FOR THE NEXT TEN MONTHS
Field Internship
WHIP
ZIP
GREG 2·21

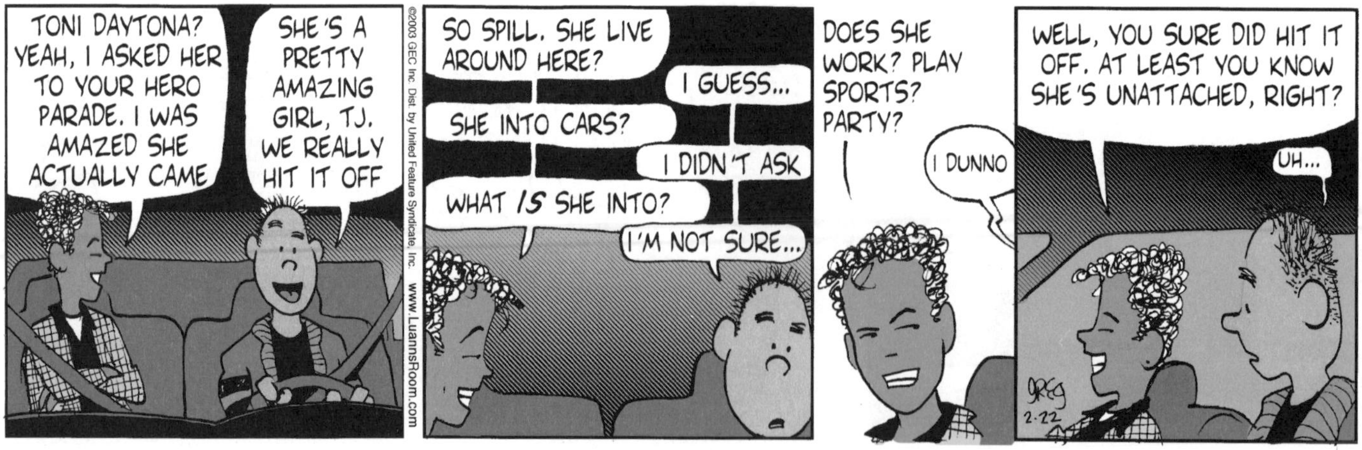
TONI DAYTONA? YEAH, I ASKED HER TO YOUR HERO PARADE. I WAS AMAZED SHE ACTUALLY CAME
SHE'S A PRETTY AMAZING GIRL, TJ. WE REALLY HIT IT OFF
SO SPILL. SHE LIVE AROUND HERE?
I GUESS...
SHE INTO CARS?
I DIDN'T ASK
WHAT IS SHE INTO?
I'M NOT SURE...
DOES SHE WORK? PLAY SPORTS? PARTY?
I DUNNO
WELL, YOU SURE DID HIT IT OFF. AT LEAST YOU KNOW SHE'S UNATTACHED, RIGHT?
UH...
GREG 2·22

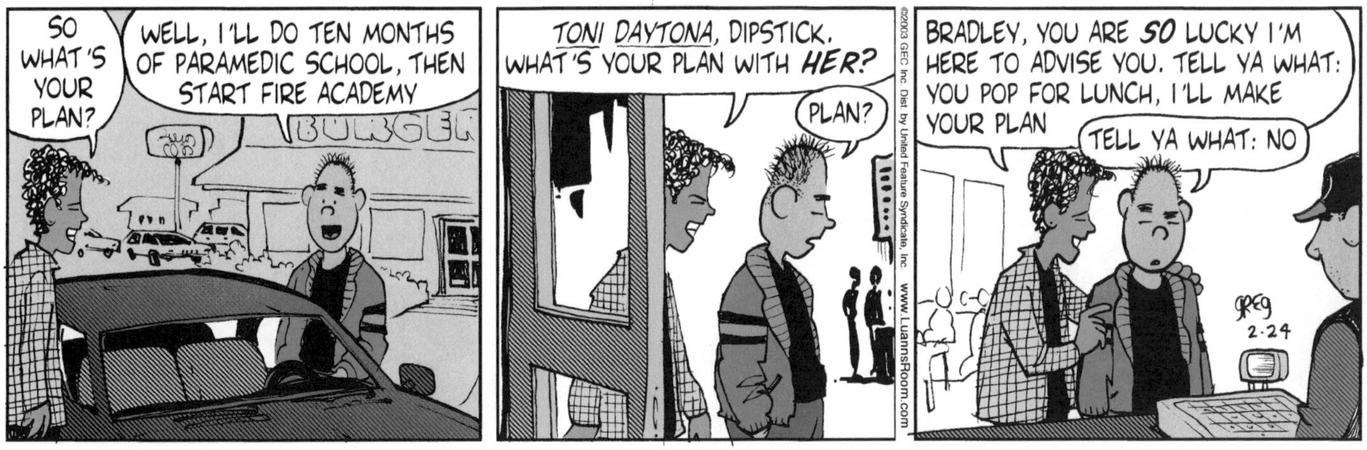
SO WHAT'S YOUR PLAN?
WELL, I'LL DO TEN MONTHS OF PARAMEDIC SCHOOL, THEN START FIRE ACADEMY
BURGER
TONI DAYTONA, DIPSTICK. WHAT'S YOUR PLAN WITH HER?
PLAN?
©2003 GEC Inc. Dist. by United Feature Syndicate, Inc.
www.LuannsRoom.com
BRADLEY, YOU ARE SO LUCKY I'M HERE TO ADVISE YOU. TELL YA WHAT: YOU POP FOR LUNCH, I'LL MAKE YOUR PLAN
TELL YA WHAT: NO
GREG 2.24

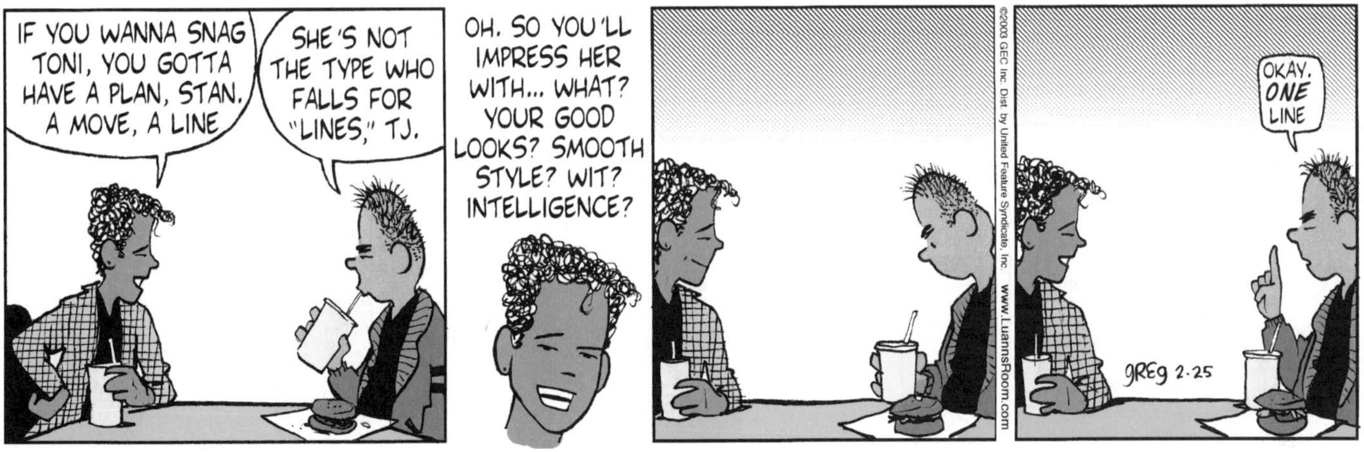
IF YOU WANNA SNAG TONI, YOU GOTTA HAVE A PLAN, STAN. A MOVE, A LINE
SHE'S NOT THE TYPE WHO FALLS FOR "LINES," TJ.
OH. SO YOU'LL IMPRESS HER WITH... WHAT? YOUR GOOD LOOKS? SMOOTH STYLE? WIT? INTELLIGENCE?
©2003 GEC Inc. Dist. by United Feature Syndicate, Inc.
www.LuannsRoom.com
OKAY. ONE LINE
GREG 2.25

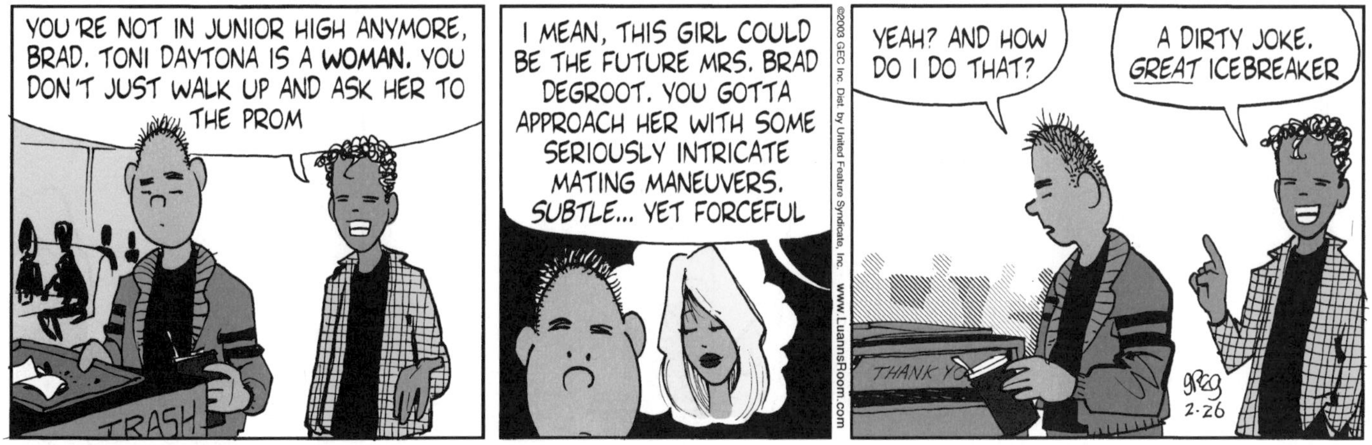
YOU'RE NOT IN JUNIOR HIGH ANYMORE, BRAD. TONI DAYTONA IS A WOMAN. YOU DON'T JUST WALK UP AND ASK HER TO THE PROM
TRASH
I MEAN, THIS GIRL COULD BE THE FUTURE MRS. BRAD DEGROOT. YOU GOTTA APPROACH HER WITH SOME SERIOUSLY INTRICATE MATING MANEUVERS. SUBTLE... YET FORCEFUL
©2003 GEC Inc. Dist. by United Feature Syndicate, Inc.
www.LuannsRoom.com
YEAH? AND HOW DO I DO THAT?
A DIRTY JOKE. GREAT ICEBREAKER
THANK YO
GREG 2.26

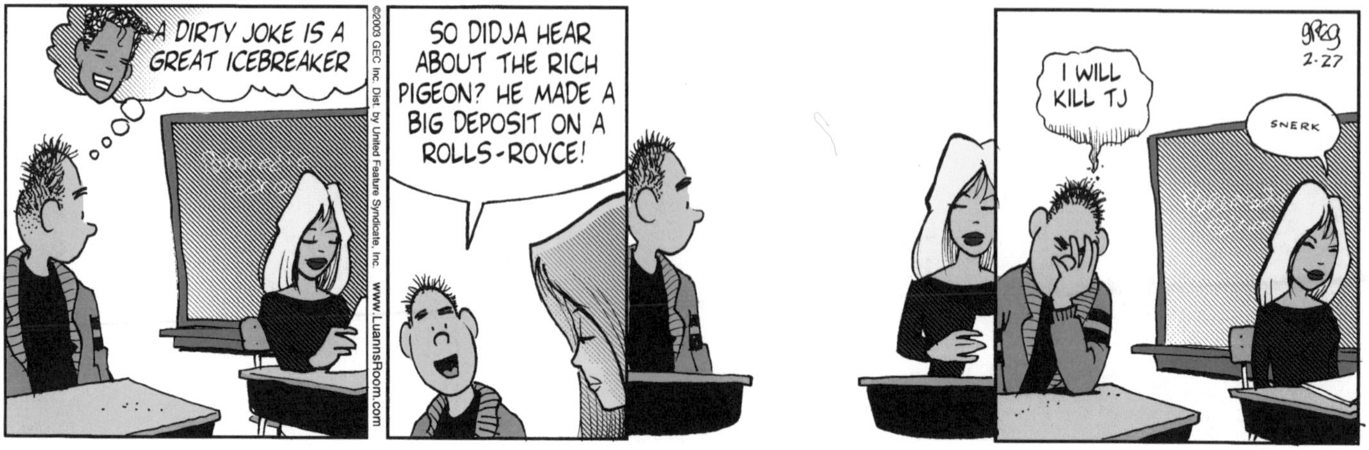
A DIRTY JOKE IS A GREAT ICEBREAKER
©2003 GEC Inc. Dist. by United Feature Syndicate, Inc. www.LuannsRoom.com
SO DIDJA HEAR ABOUT THE RICH PIGEON? HE MADE A BIG DEPOSIT ON A ROLLS-ROYCE!
I WILL KILL TJ
SNERK
GREG 2·27

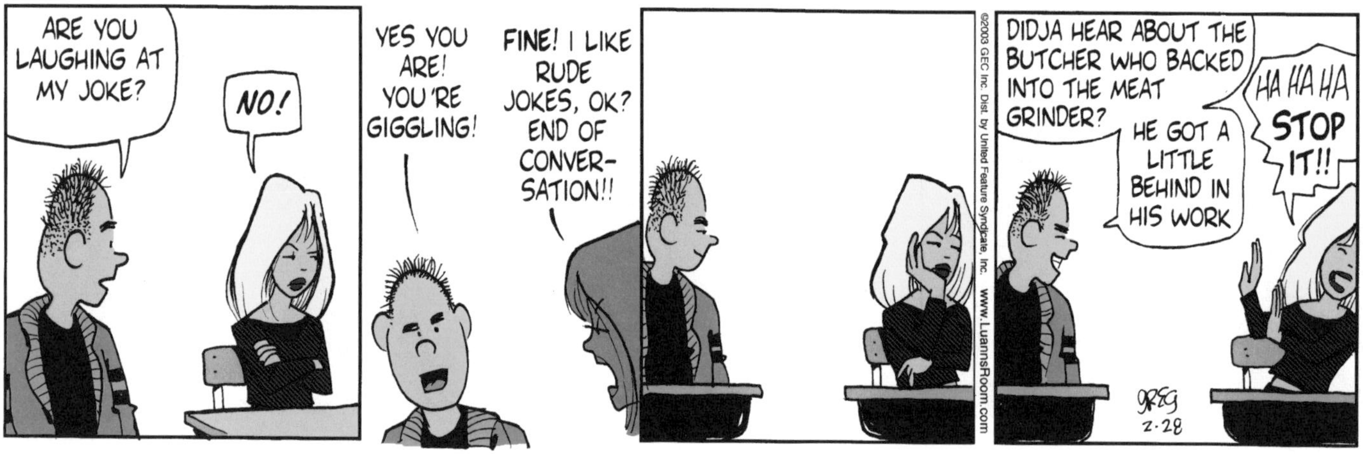
ARE YOU LAUGHING AT MY JOKE?
NO!
YES YOU ARE! YOU'RE GIGGLING!
FINE! I LIKE RUDE JOKES, OK? END OF CONVERSATION!!
©2003 GEC Inc. Dist. by United Feature Syndicate, Inc. www.LuannsRoom.com
DIDJA HEAR ABOUT THE BUTCHER WHO BACKED INTO THE MEAT GRINDER?
HE GOT A LITTLE BEHIND IN HIS WORK
HA HA HA STOP IT!!
GREG 2·28

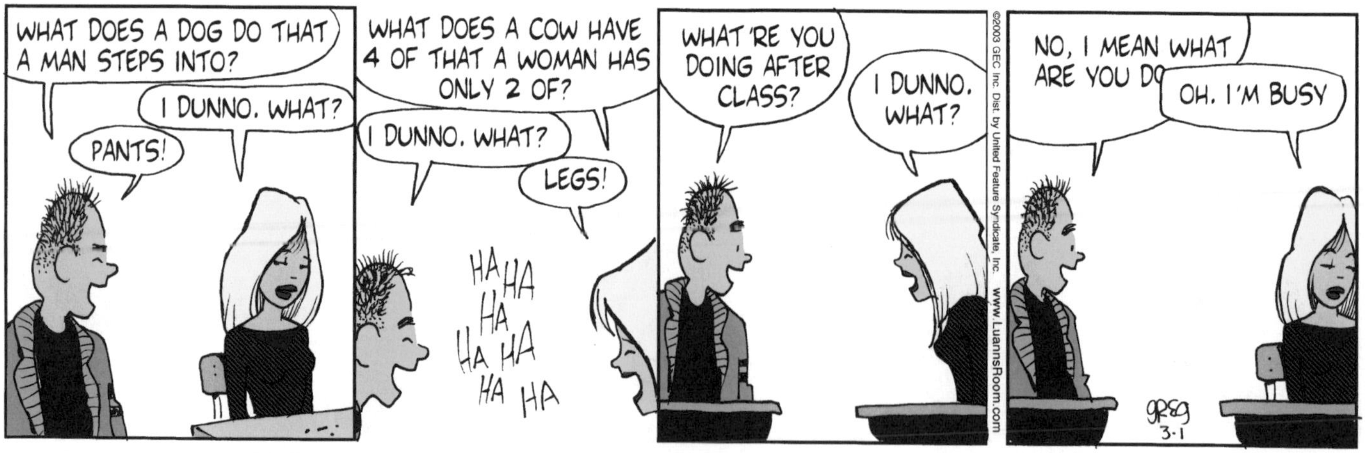
WHAT DOES A DOG DO THAT A MAN STEPS INTO?
I DUNNO. WHAT?
PANTS!
WHAT DOES A COW HAVE 4 OF THAT A WOMAN HAS ONLY 2 OF?
I DUNNO. WHAT?
LEGS!
HA HA HA HA HA HA HA
WHAT'RE YOU DOING AFTER CLASS?
I DUNNO. WHAT?
©2003 GEC Inc. Dist. by United Feature Syndicate, Inc. www.LuannsRoom.com
NO, I MEAN WHAT ARE YOU DO
OH. I'M BUSY
GREG 3·1

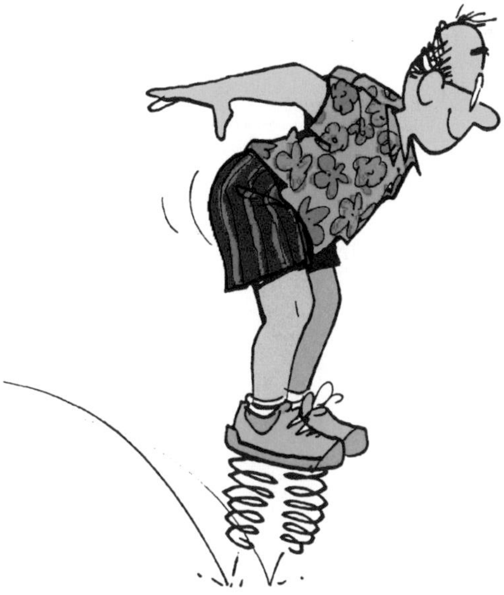

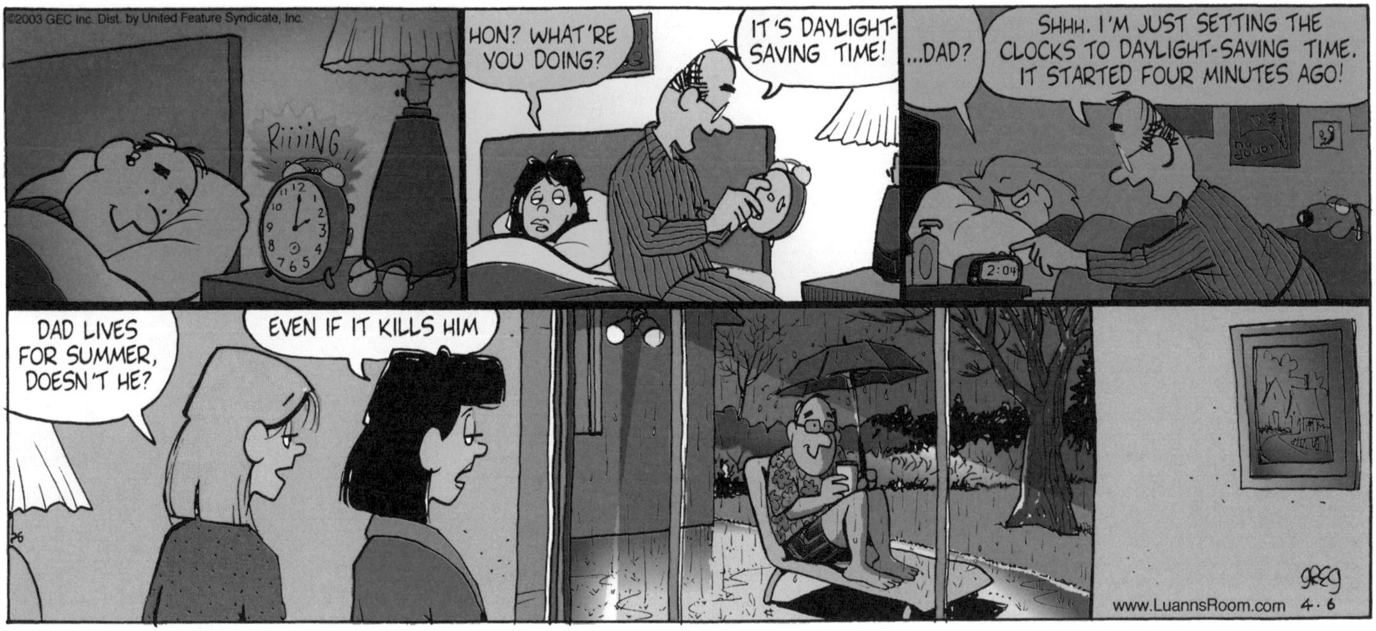

©2003 GEC Inc. Dist. by United Feature Syndicate, Inc.
RiiiiNG
HON? WHAT'RE YOU DOING?
IT'S DAYLIGHT-SAVING TIME!
...DAD?
SHHH. I'M JUST SETTING THE CLOCKS TO DAYLIGHT-SAVING TIME. IT STARTED FOUR MINUTES AGO!
2:04
DAD LIVES FOR SUMMER, DOESN'T HE?
EVEN IF IT KILLS HIM
GREG
www.LuannsRoom.com 4·6

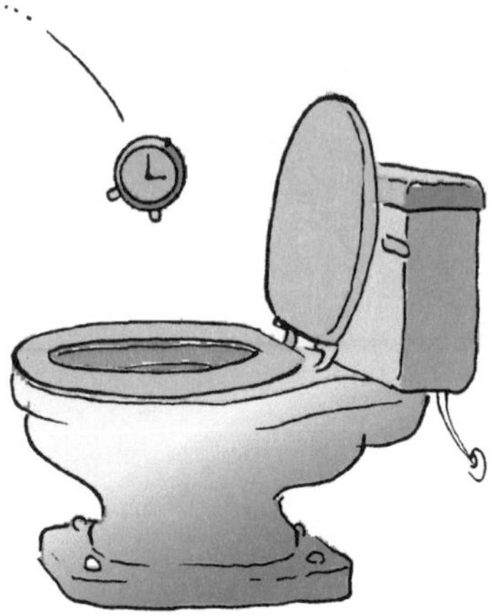

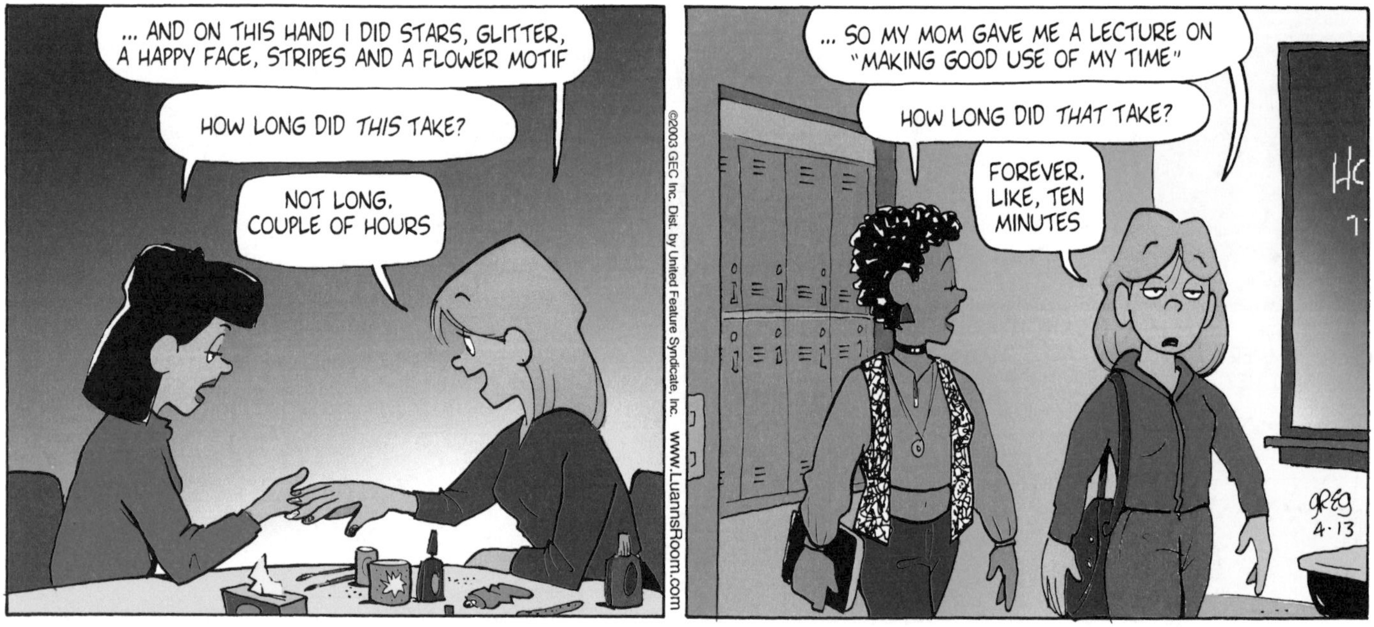

... AND ON THIS HAND I DID STARS, GLITTER, A HAPPY FACE, STRIPES AND A FLOWER MOTIF
HOW LONG DID *THIS* TAKE?
NOT LONG. COUPLE OF HOURS
©2003 GEC Inc. Dist. by United Feature Syndicate, Inc. www.LuannsRoom.com
... SO MY MOM GAVE ME A LECTURE ON "MAKING GOOD USE OF MY TIME"
HOW LONG DID *THAT* TAKE?
FOREVER. LIKE, TEN MINUTES
GREG 4·13

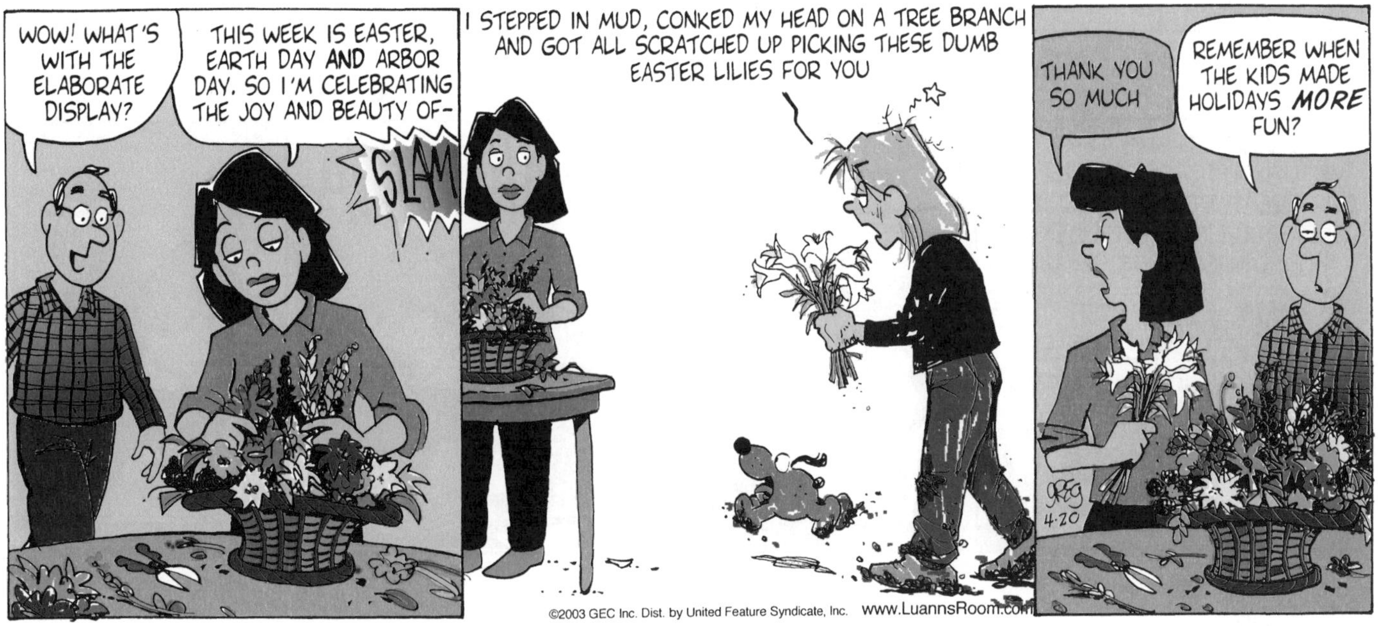
WOW! WHAT'S WITH THE ELABORATE DISPLAY?
THIS WEEK IS EASTER, EARTH DAY AND ARBOR DAY. SO I'M CELEBRATING THE JOY AND BEAUTY OF-
SLAM
I STEPPED IN MUD, CONKED MY HEAD ON A TREE BRANCH AND GOT ALL SCRATCHED UP PICKING THESE DUMB EASTER LILIES FOR YOU
THANK YOU SO MUCH
REMEMBER WHEN THE KIDS MADE HOLIDAYS MORE FUN?
GREG 4·20
©2003 GEC Inc. Dist. by United Feature Syndicate, Inc. www.LuannsRoom.com

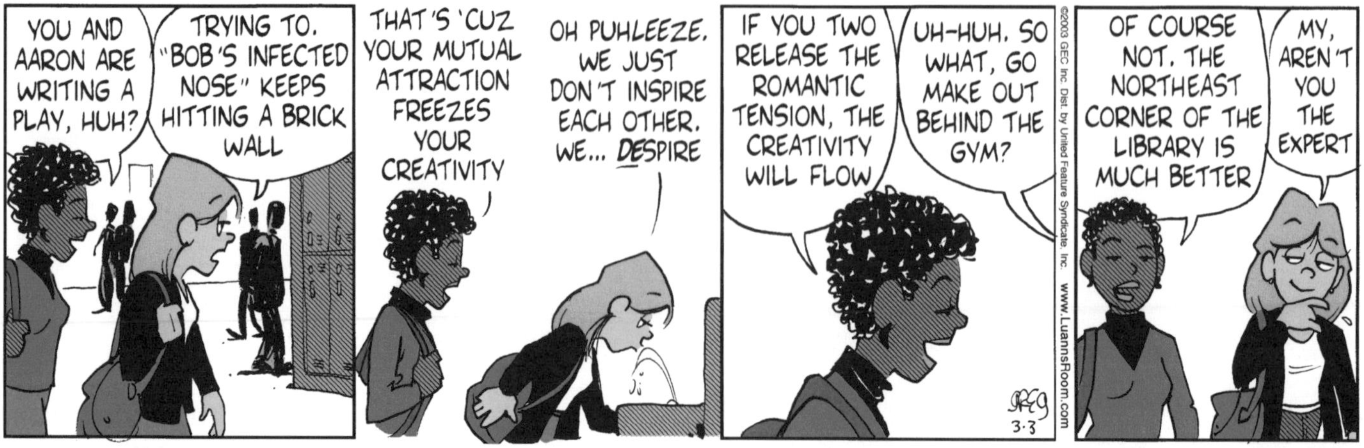
YOU AND AARON ARE WRITING A PLAY, HUH?
TRYING TO. "BOB'S INFECTED NOSE" KEEPS HITTING A BRICK WALL
THAT'S 'CUZ YOUR MUTUAL ATTRACTION FREEZES YOUR CREATIVITY
OH PUHLEEZE. WE JUST DON'T INSPIRE EACH OTHER. WE... DESPIRE
IF YOU TWO RELEASE THE ROMANTIC TENSION, THE CREATIVITY WILL FLOW
UH-HUH. SO WHAT, GO MAKE OUT BEHIND THE GYM?
©2003 GEC Inc. Dist. by United Feature Syndicate, Inc.
www.LuannsRoom.com
GREG 3·3
OF COURSE NOT. THE NORTHEAST CORNER OF THE LIBRARY IS MUCH BETTER
MY, AREN'T YOU THE EXPERT

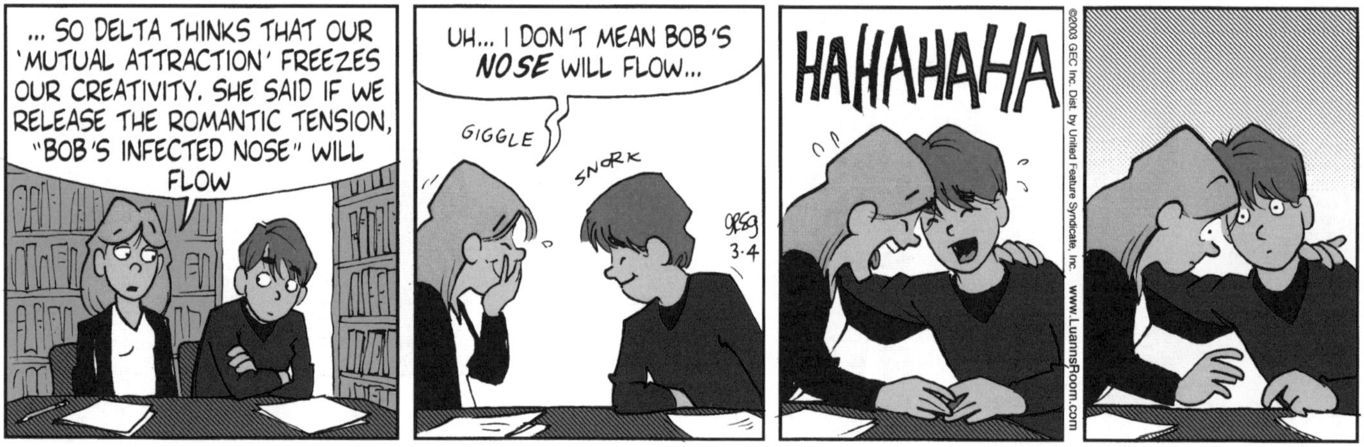
... SO DELTA THINKS THAT OUR 'MUTUAL ATTRACTION' FREEZES OUR CREATIVITY. SHE SAID IF WE RELEASE THE ROMANTIC TENSION, "BOB'S INFECTED NOSE" WILL FLOW
UH... I DON'T MEAN BOB'S NOSE WILL FLOW...
GIGGLE
SNORK
GREG 3·4
HAHAHAHA
©2003 GEC Inc. Dist. by United Feature Syndicate, Inc.
www.LuannsRoom.com

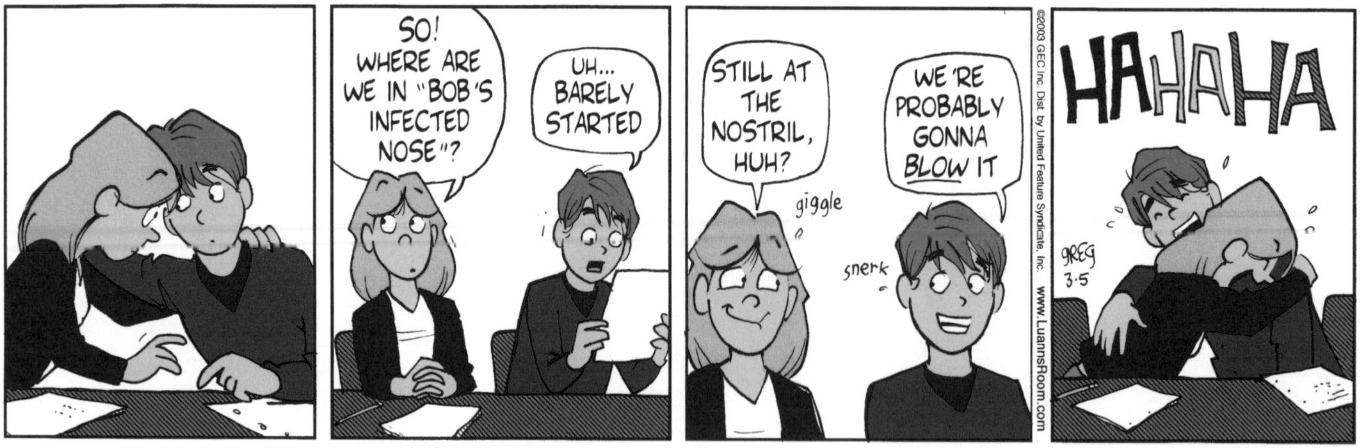
SO! WHERE ARE WE IN "BOB'S INFECTED NOSE"?
UH... BARELY STARTED
STILL AT THE NOSTRIL, HUH?
giggle
WE'RE PROBABLY GONNA BLOW IT
snerk
©2003 GEC Inc. Dist. by United Feature Syndicate, Inc.
www.LuannsRoom.com
HAHAHA
GREG 3·5

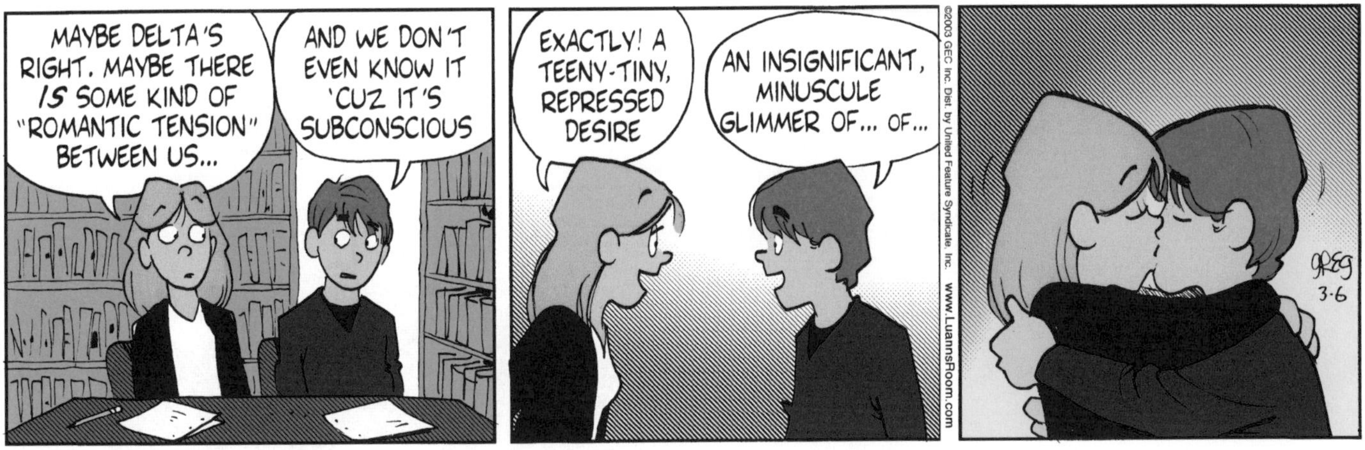

MAYBE DELTA'S RIGHT. MAYBE THERE *IS* SOME KIND OF "ROMANTIC TENSION" BETWEEN US...
AND WE DON'T EVEN KNOW IT 'CUZ IT'S SUBCONSCIOUS
EXACTLY! A TEENY-TINY, REPRESSED DESIRE
AN INSIGNIFICANT, MINUSCULE GLIMMER OF... OF...
©2003 GEC Inc. Dist. by United Feature Syndicate, Inc.
www.LuannsRoom.com
GREG 3·6

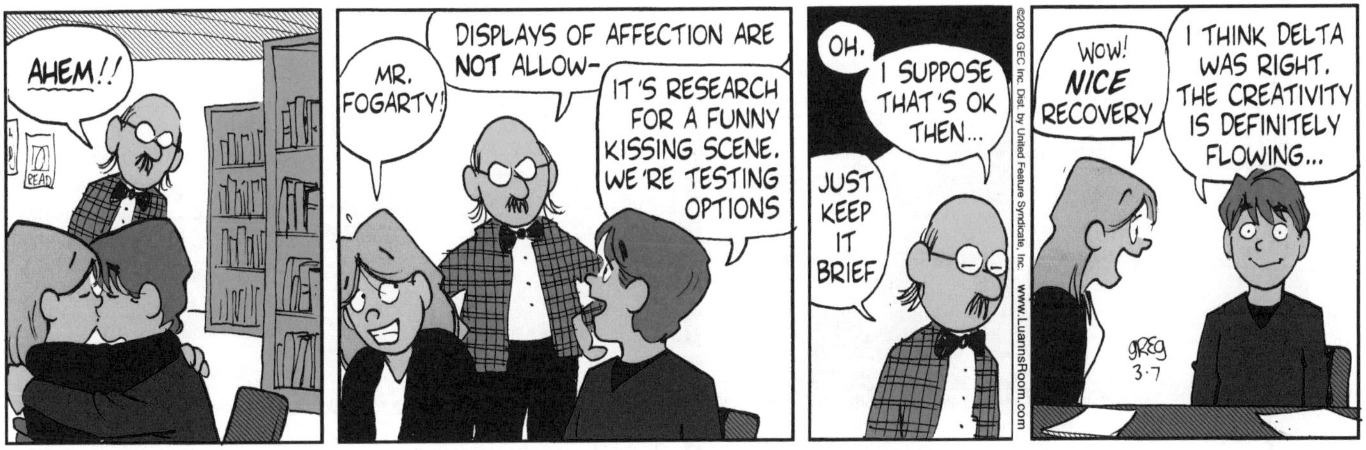

AHEM!!
READ
MR. FOGARTY!
DISPLAYS OF AFFECTION ARE NOT ALLOW–
IT'S RESEARCH FOR A FUNNY KISSING SCENE. WE'RE TESTING OPTIONS
OH.
I SUPPOSE THAT'S OK THEN...
JUST KEEP IT BRIEF
©2003 GEC Inc. Dist. by United Feature Syndicate, Inc.
www.LuannsRoom.com
WOW! *NICE* RECOVERY
I THINK DELTA WAS RIGHT. THE CREATIVITY IS DEFINITELY FLOWING...
GREG 3·7

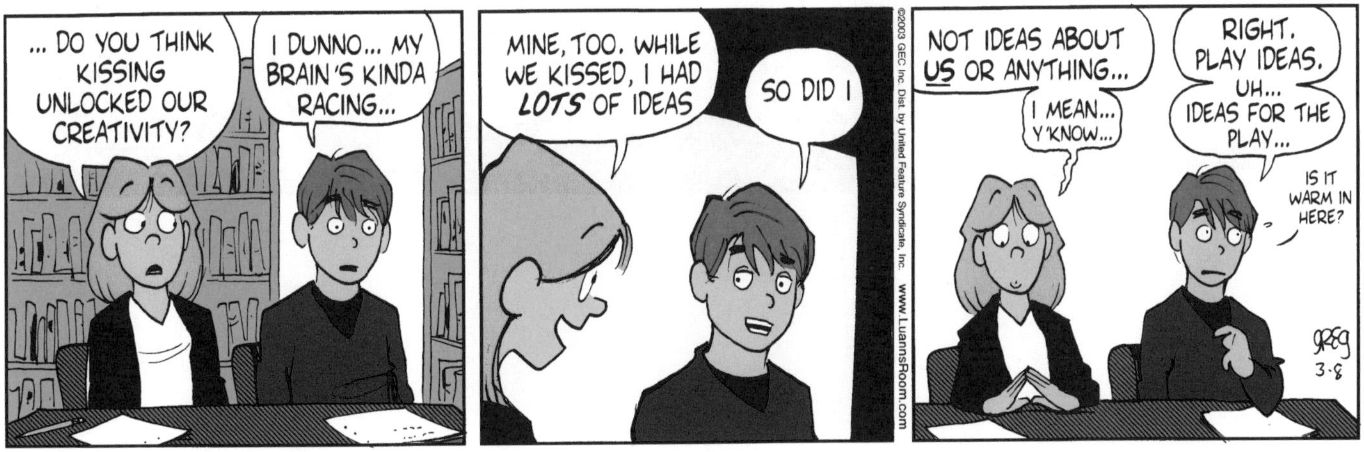

... DO YOU THINK KISSING UNLOCKED OUR CREATIVITY?
I DUNNO... MY BRAIN'S KINDA RACING...
MINE, TOO. WHILE WE KISSED, I HAD *LOTS* OF IDEAS
SO DID I
©2003 GEC Inc. Dist. by United Feature Syndicate, Inc.
www.LuannsRoom.com
NOT IDEAS ABOUT US OR ANYTHING...
I MEAN... Y'KNOW...
RIGHT. PLAY IDEAS. UH... IDEAS FOR THE PLAY...
IS IT WARM IN HERE?
GREG 3·8

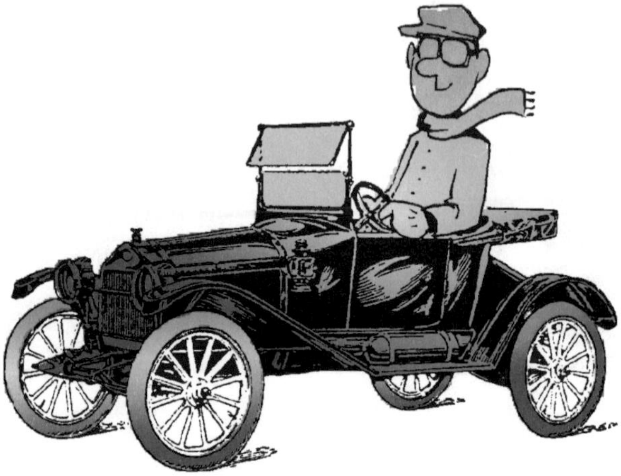

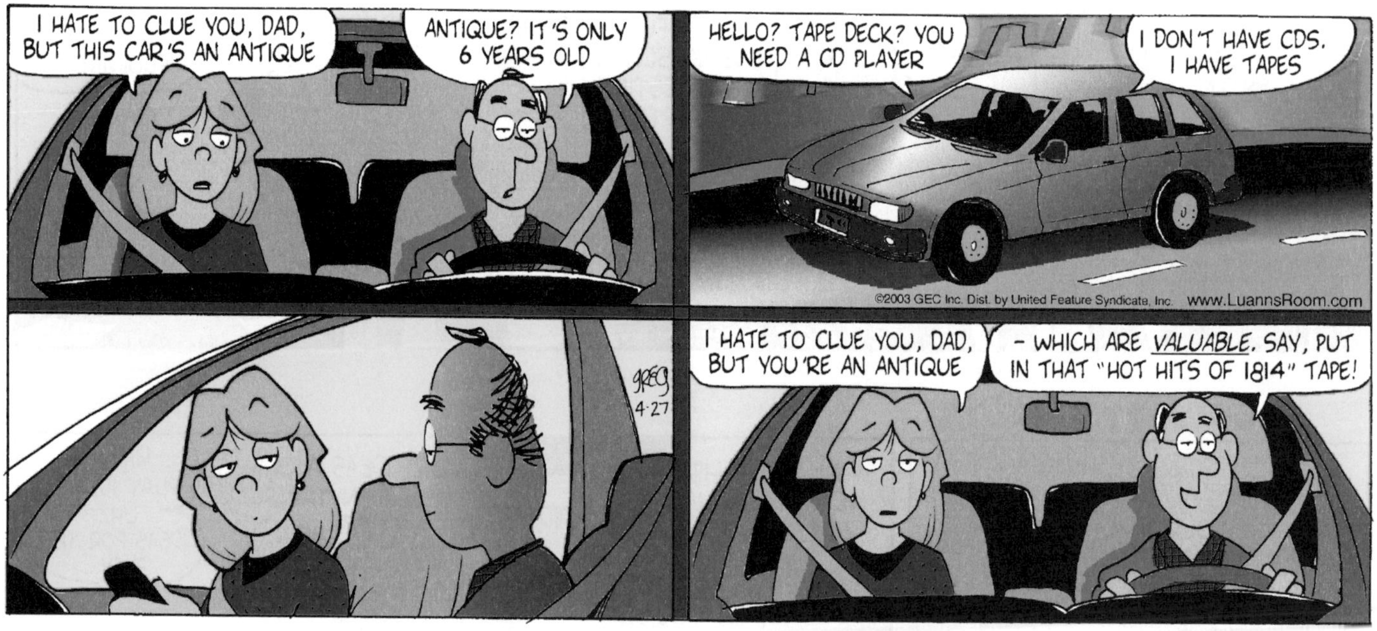
I HATE TO CLUE YOU, DAD, BUT THIS CAR'S AN ANTIQUE
ANTIQUE? IT'S ONLY 6 YEARS OLD
HELLO? TAPE DECK? YOU NEED A CD PLAYER
I DON'T HAVE CDS. I HAVE TAPES
©2003 GEC Inc. Dist. by United Feature Syndicate, Inc. www.LuannsRoom.com
GREG 4-27
I HATE TO CLUE YOU, DAD, BUT YOU'RE AN ANTIQUE
- WHICH ARE VALUABLE. SAY, PUT IN THAT "HOT HITS OF 1814" TAPE!

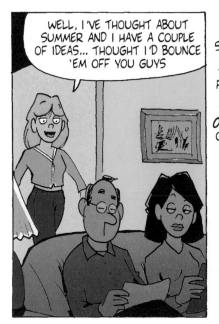

WELL, I'VE THOUGHT ABOUT SUMMER AND I HAVE A COUPLE OF IDEAS... THOUGHT I'D BOUNCE 'EM OFF YOU GUYS
I WAS THINKIN' I COULD HITCHHIKE TO SOUTH AMERICA, MAYBE ALL THE WAY TO RIO, THEN RIDE HOME ON A FISHING BOAT OR NAVY SHIP OR SOMETHING.
OR, I COULD JUST HANG OUT HERE AND RELAX... DO THE MALL, HAVE A FEW PARTIES, STUFF LIKE THAT
©2003 GEC Inc. Dist. by United Feature Syndicate, Inc
SO. ANY PREFERENCE?
www.LuannsRoom.com
WELL? DID IT WORK?
NO. THEY HAD THEIR OWN IDEA: GET A JOB
chicago
GREG
5.4

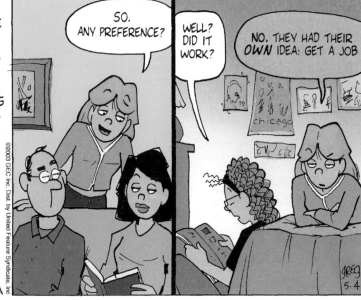

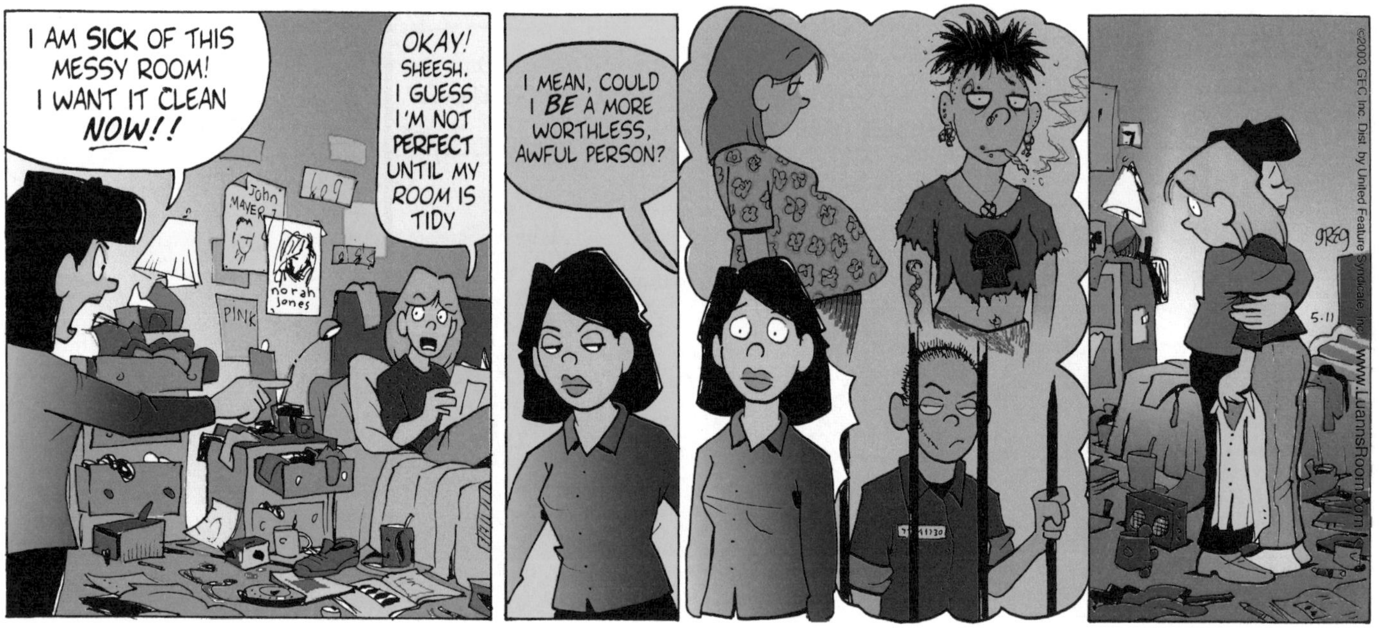
I AM SICK OF THIS MESSY ROOM! I WANT IT CLEAN NOW!!
OKAY! SHEESH. I GUESS I'M NOT PERFECT UNTIL MY ROOM IS TIDY
John MAYER
norah jones
PINK
I MEAN, COULD I BE A MORE WORTHLESS, AWFUL PERSON?
GREG
5-11
©2003 GEC Inc. Dist. by United Feature Syndicate, Inc.
www.LuannsRoom.com

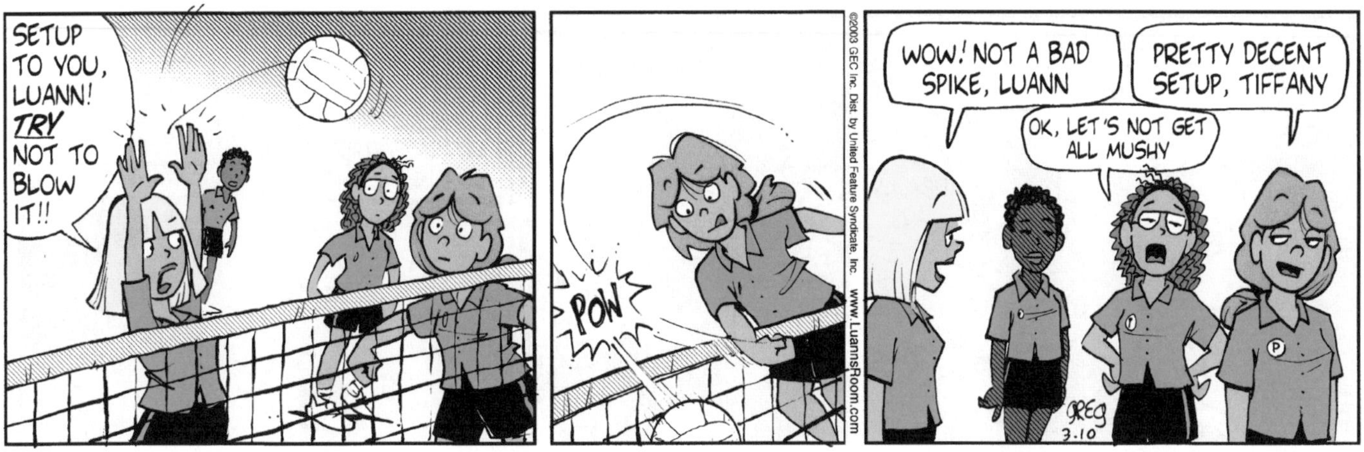
SETUP TO YOU, LUANN! TRY NOT TO BLOW IT!!
POW
©2003 GEC Inc. Dist. by United Feature Syndicate, Inc. www.LuannsRoom.com
WOW! NOT A BAD SPIKE, LUANN
PRETTY DECENT SETUP, TIFFANY
OK, LET'S NOT GET ALL MUSHY
GREG 3-10

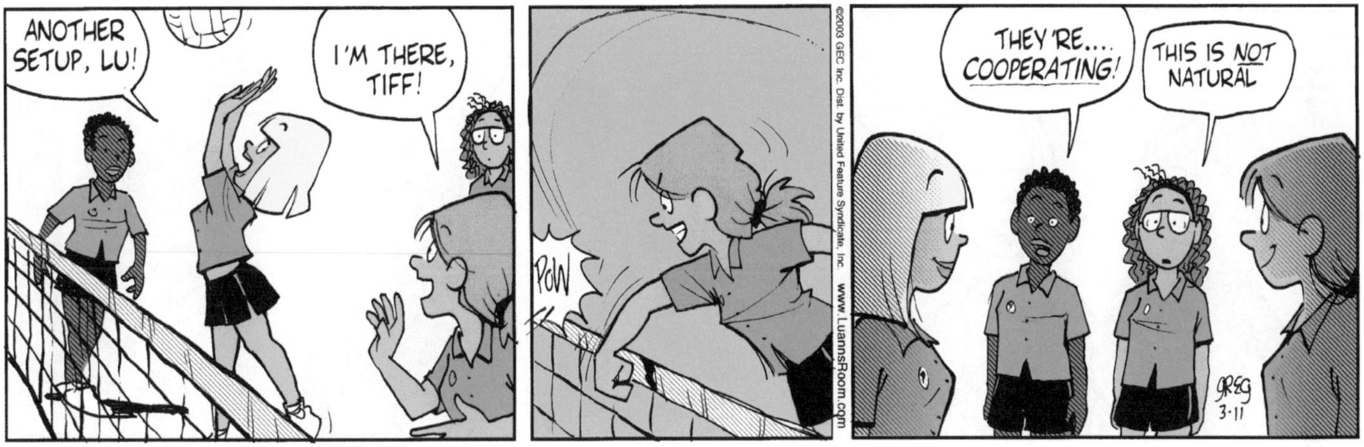
ANOTHER SETUP, LU!
I'M THERE, TIFF!
POW
©2003 GEC Inc. Dist. by United Feature Syndicate, Inc. www.LuannsRoom.com
THEY'RE.... COOPERATING!
THIS IS NOT NATURAL
GREG 3-11

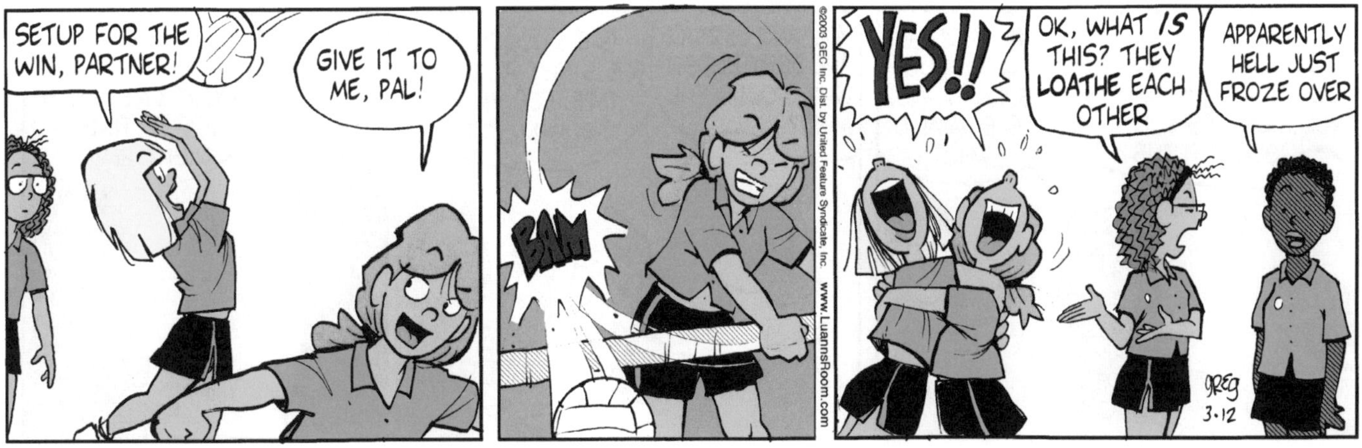
SETUP FOR THE WIN, PARTNER!
GIVE IT TO ME, PAL!
BAM
©2003 GEC Inc. Dist. by United Feature Syndicate, Inc. www.LuannsRoom.com
YES!!
OK, WHAT IS THIS? THEY LOATHE EACH OTHER
APPARENTLY HELL JUST FROZE OVER
GREG 3-12

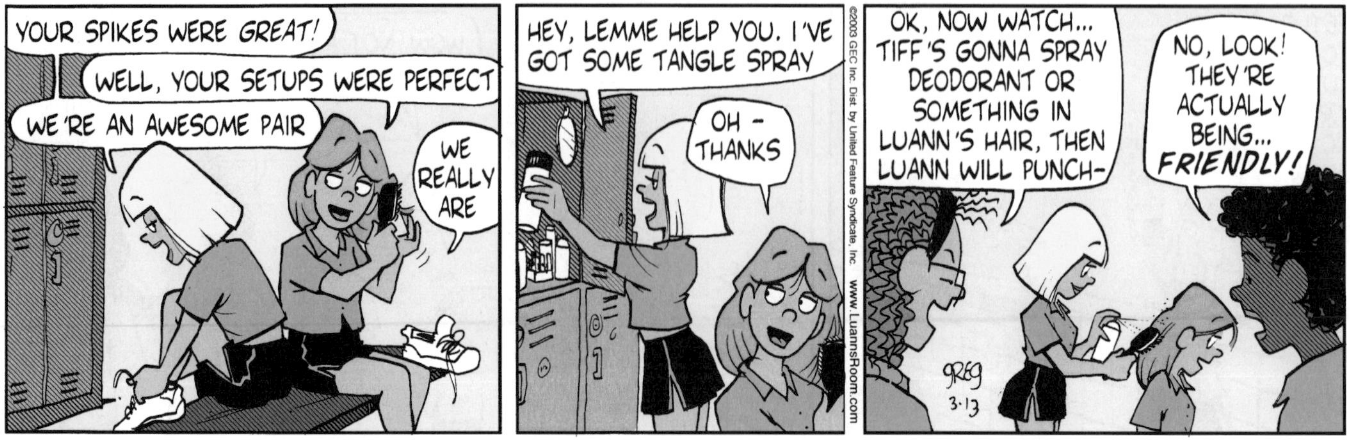
YOUR SPIKES WERE GREAT!
WELL, YOUR SETUPS WERE PERFECT
WE'RE AN AWESOME PAIR
WE REALLY ARE
HEY, LEMME HELP YOU. I'VE GOT SOME TANGLE SPRAY
OH - THANKS
©2003 GEC Inc. Dist. by United Feature Syndicate, Inc.
www.LuannsRoom.com
OK, NOW WATCH... TIFF'S GONNA SPRAY DEODORANT OR SOMETHING IN LUANN'S HAIR, THEN LUANN WILL PUNCH-
NO, LOOK! THEY'RE ACTUALLY BEING... ***FRIENDLY!***
GREG
3·13

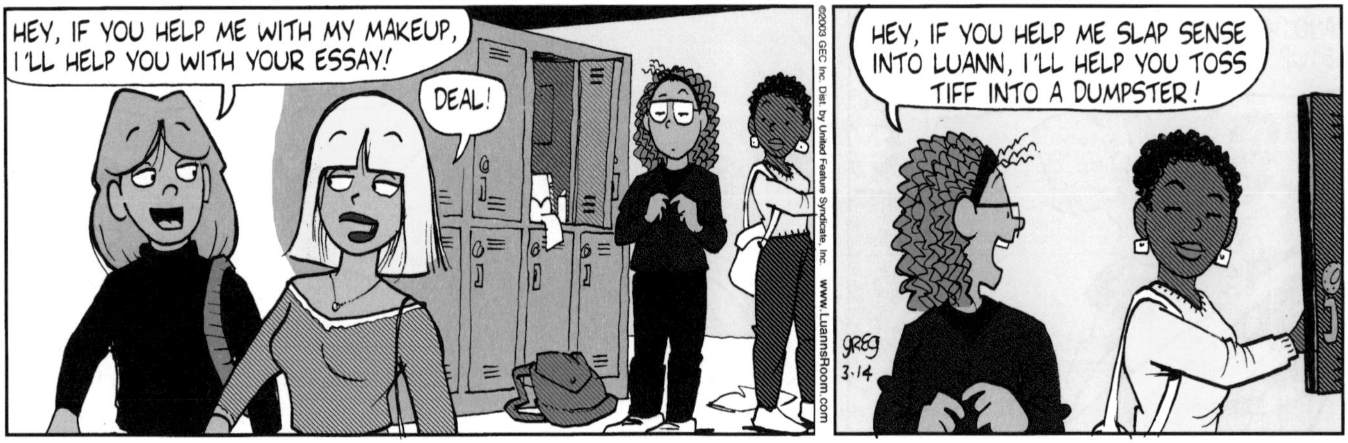
HEY, IF YOU HELP ME WITH MY MAKEUP, I'LL HELP YOU WITH YOUR ESSAY!
DEAL!
©2003 GEC Inc. Dist. by United Feature Syndicate, Inc.
www.LuannsRoom.com
HEY, IF YOU HELP ME SLAP SENSE INTO LUANN, I'LL HELP YOU TOSS TIFF INTO A DUMPSTER!
GREG
3·14

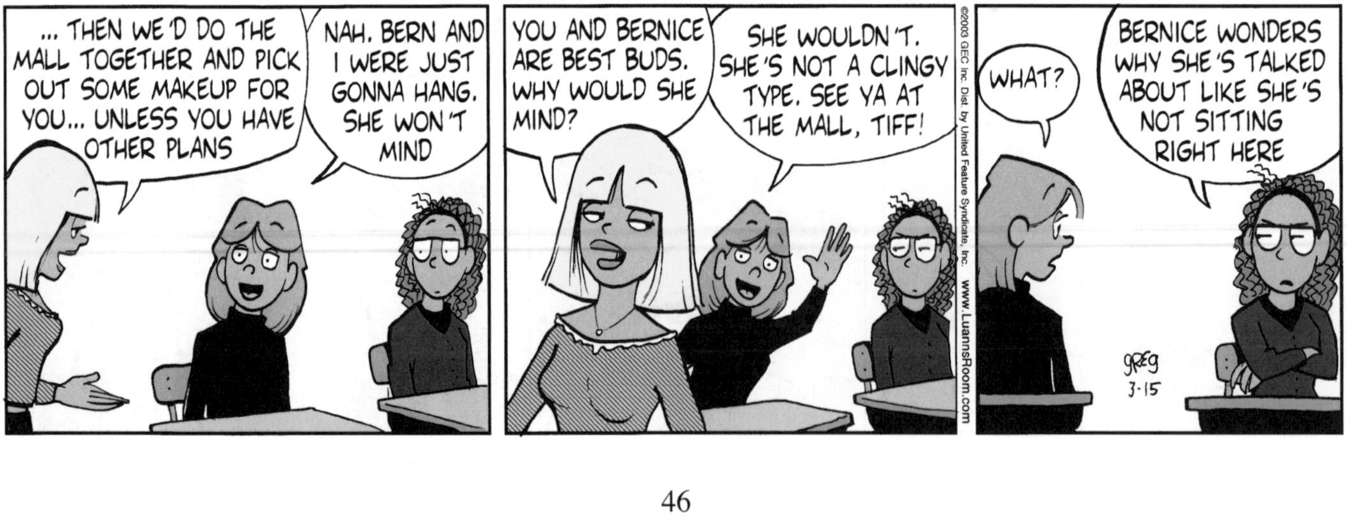
... THEN WE'D DO THE MALL TOGETHER AND PICK OUT SOME MAKEUP FOR YOU... UNLESS YOU HAVE OTHER PLANS
NAH. BERN AND I WERE JUST GONNA HANG. SHE WON'T MIND
YOU AND BERNICE ARE BEST BUDS. WHY WOULD SHE MIND?
SHE WOULDN'T. SHE'S NOT A CLINGY TYPE. SEE YA AT THE MALL, TIFF!
©2003 GEC Inc. Dist. by United Feature Syndicate, Inc.
www.LuannsRoom.com
WHAT?
BERNICE WONDERS WHY SHE'S TALKED ABOUT LIKE SHE'S NOT SITTING RIGHT HERE
GREG
3·15

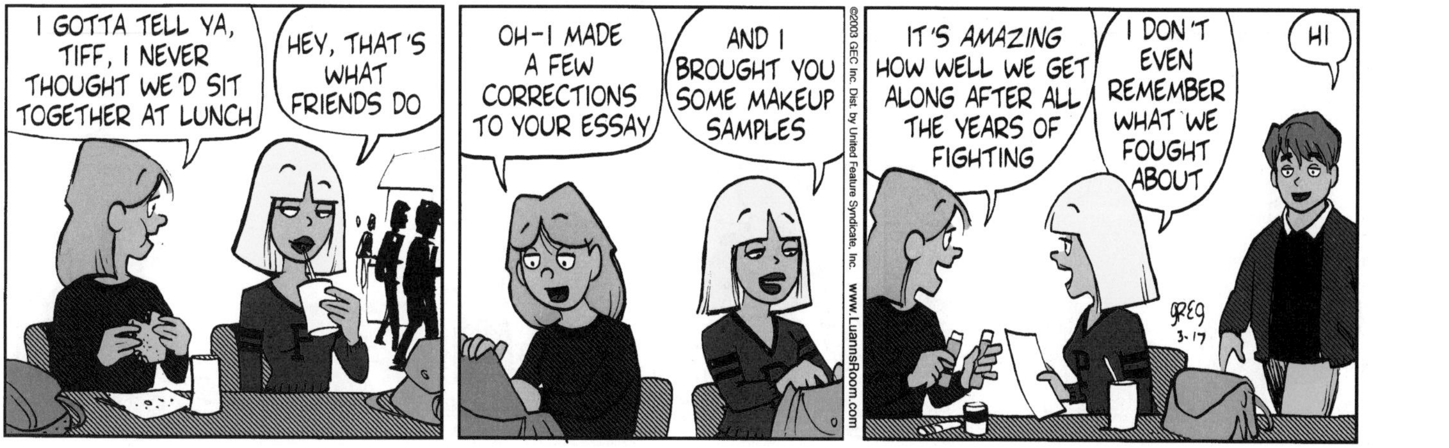
I GOTTA TELL YA, TIFF, I NEVER THOUGHT WE'D SIT TOGETHER AT LUNCH
HEY, THAT'S WHAT FRIENDS DO
OH-I MADE A FEW CORRECTIONS TO YOUR ESSAY
AND I BROUGHT YOU SOME MAKEUP SAMPLES
©2003 GEC Inc. Dist. by United Feature Syndicate, Inc. www.LuannsRoom.com
IT'S *AMAZING* HOW WELL WE GET ALONG AFTER ALL THE YEARS OF FIGHTING
I DON'T EVEN REMEMBER WHAT WE FOUGHT ABOUT
HI
GREG 3-17

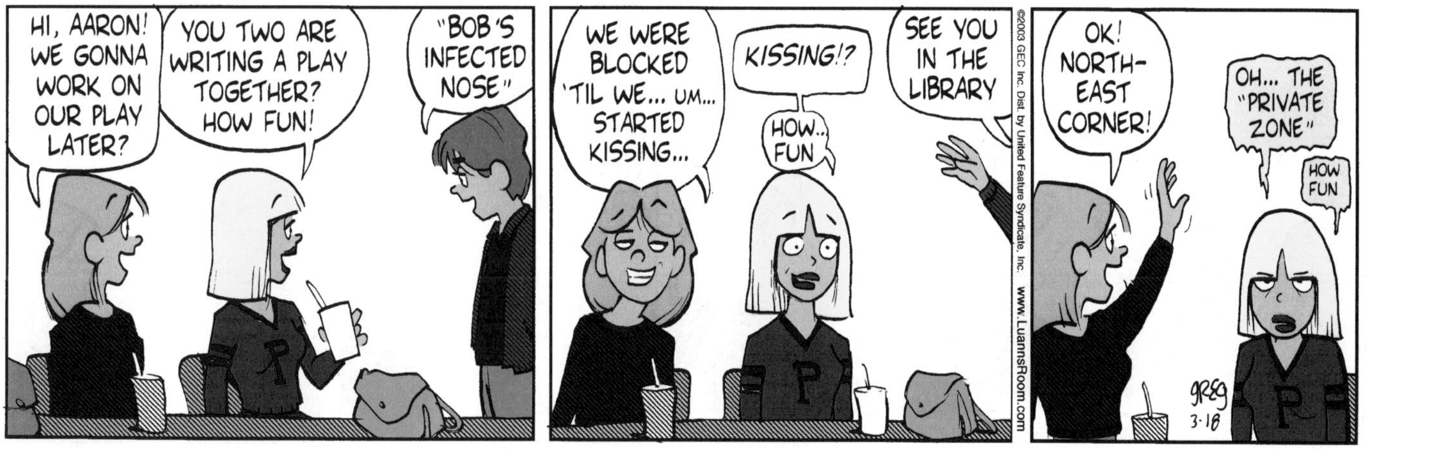
HI, AARON! WE GONNA WORK ON OUR PLAY LATER?
YOU TWO ARE WRITING A PLAY TOGETHER? HOW FUN!
"BOB'S INFECTED NOSE"
WE WERE BLOCKED 'TIL WE... UM... STARTED KISSING...
KISSING!?
HOW... FUN
SEE YOU IN THE LIBRARY
©2003 GEC Inc. Dist. by United Feature Syndicate, Inc. www.LuannsRoom.com
OK! NORTH-EAST CORNER!
OH... THE "PRIVATE ZONE"
HOW FUN
GREG 3-18

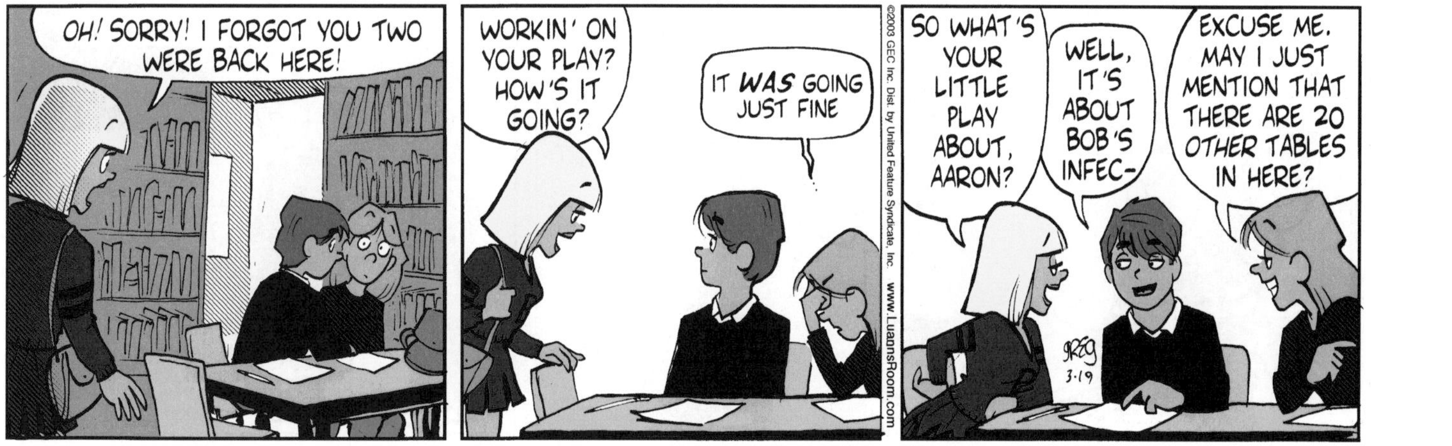
OH! SORRY! I FORGOT YOU TWO WERE BACK HERE!
WORKIN' ON YOUR PLAY? HOW'S IT GOING?
IT ***WAS*** GOING JUST FINE
©2003 GEC Inc. Dist. by United Feature Syndicate, Inc. www.LuannsRoom.com
SO WHAT'S YOUR LITTLE PLAY ABOUT, AARON?
WELL, IT'S ABOUT BOB'S INFEC-
EXCUSE ME. MAY I JUST MENTION THAT THERE ARE 20 *OTHER* TABLES IN HERE?
GREG 3-19

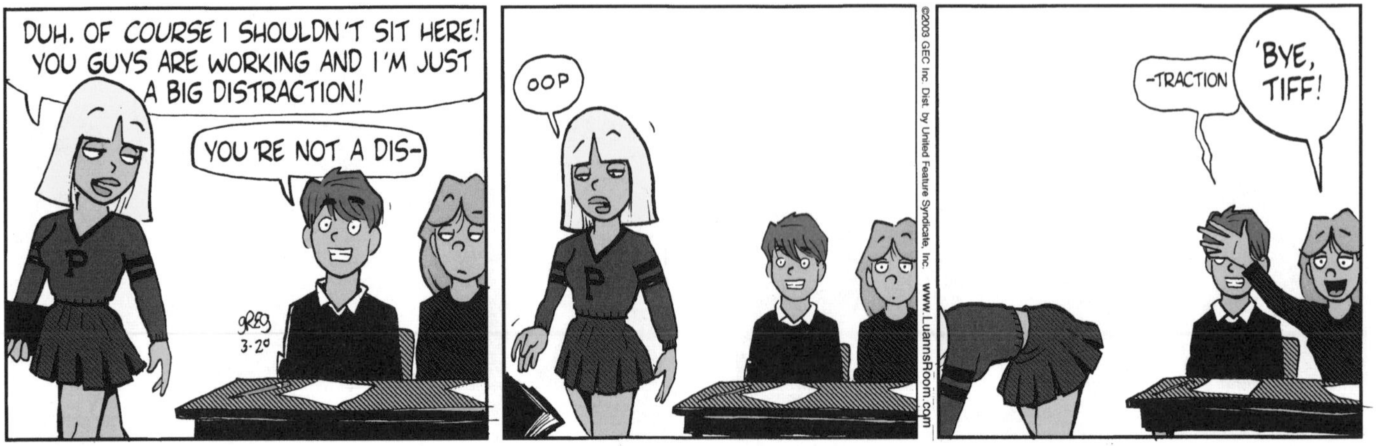
DUH. OF COURSE I SHOULDN'T SIT HERE! YOU GUYS ARE WORKING AND I'M JUST A BIG DISTRACTION!
YOU'RE NOT A DIS-
GREG 3·20
OOP
©2003 GEC Inc. Dist. by United Feature Syndicate, Inc. www.LuannsRoom.com
-TRACTION
'BYE, TIFF!

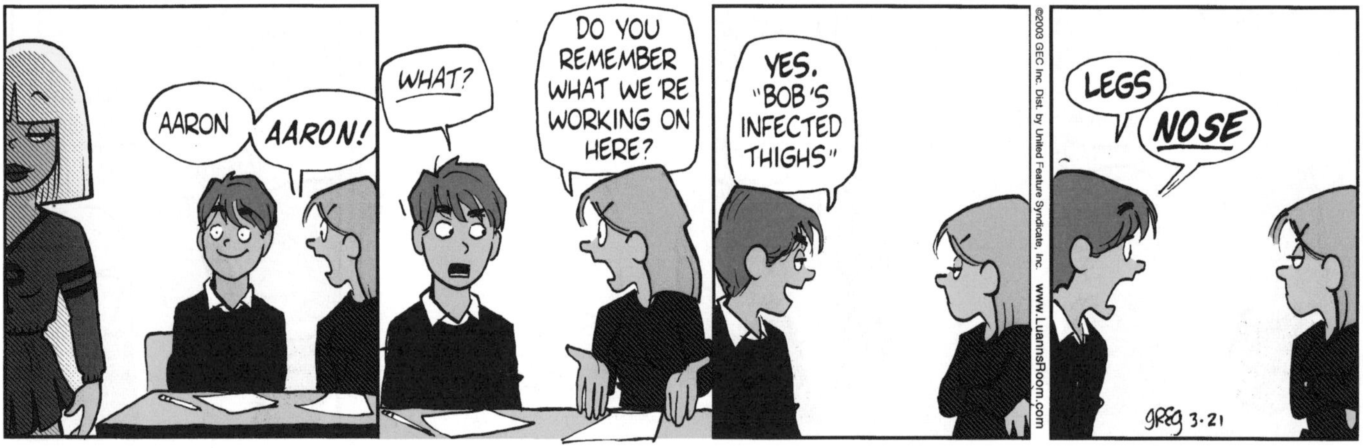
AARON
AARON!
WHAT?
DO YOU REMEMBER WHAT WE'RE WORKING ON HERE?
YES. "BOB'S INFECTED THIGHS"
©2003 GEC Inc. Dist. by United Feature Syndicate, Inc. www.LuannsRoom.com
LEGS
NOSE
GREG 3·21

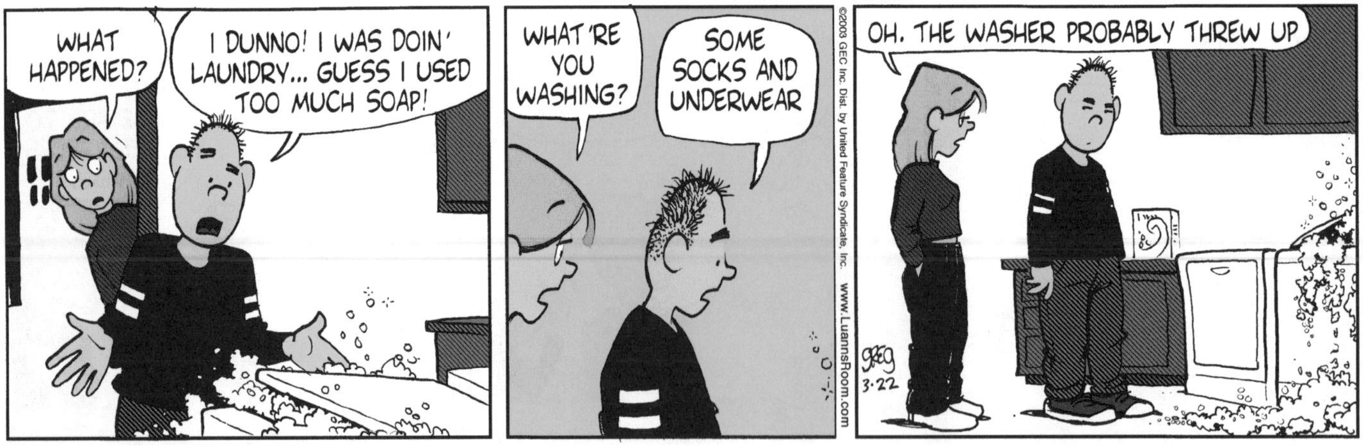
WHAT HAPPENED?
I DUNNO! I WAS DOIN' LAUNDRY... GUESS I USED TOO MUCH SOAP!
WHAT'RE YOU WASHING?
SOME SOCKS AND UNDERWEAR
©2003 GEC Inc. Dist. by United Feature Syndicate, Inc. www.LuannsRoom.com
GREG 3·22
OH. THE WASHER PROBABLY THREW UP

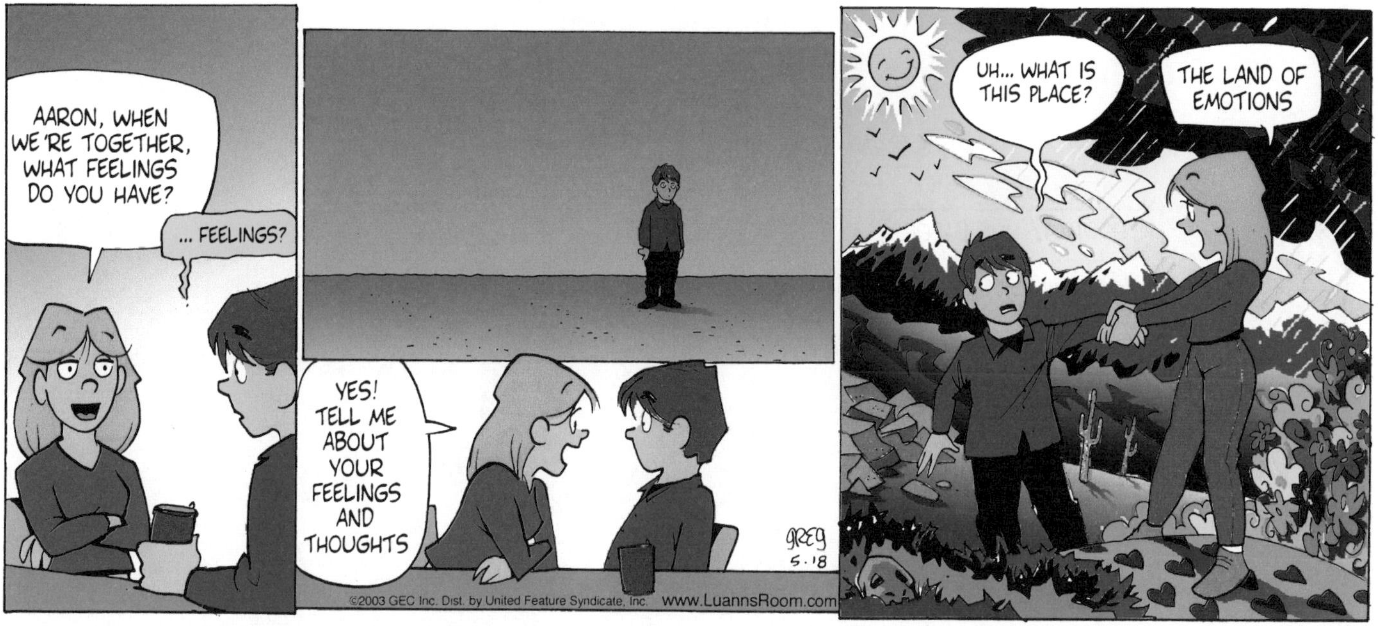
AARON, WHEN WE'RE TOGETHER, WHAT FEELINGS DO YOU HAVE?
... FEELINGS?
YES! TELL ME ABOUT YOUR FEELINGS AND THOUGHTS
GREG 5.18
©2003 GEC Inc. Dist. by United Feature Syndicate, Inc.
www.LuannsRoom.com
UH... WHAT IS THIS PLACE?
THE LAND OF EMOTIONS

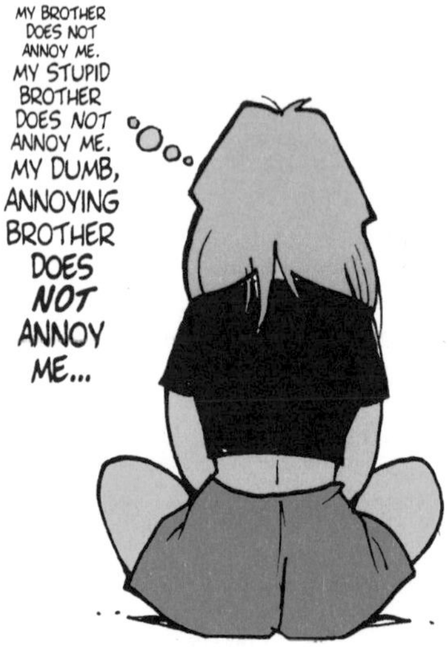
MY BROTHER DOES NOT ANNOY ME. MY STUPID BROTHER DOES NOT ANNOY ME. MY DUMB, ANNOYING BROTHER DOES NOT ANNOY ME...

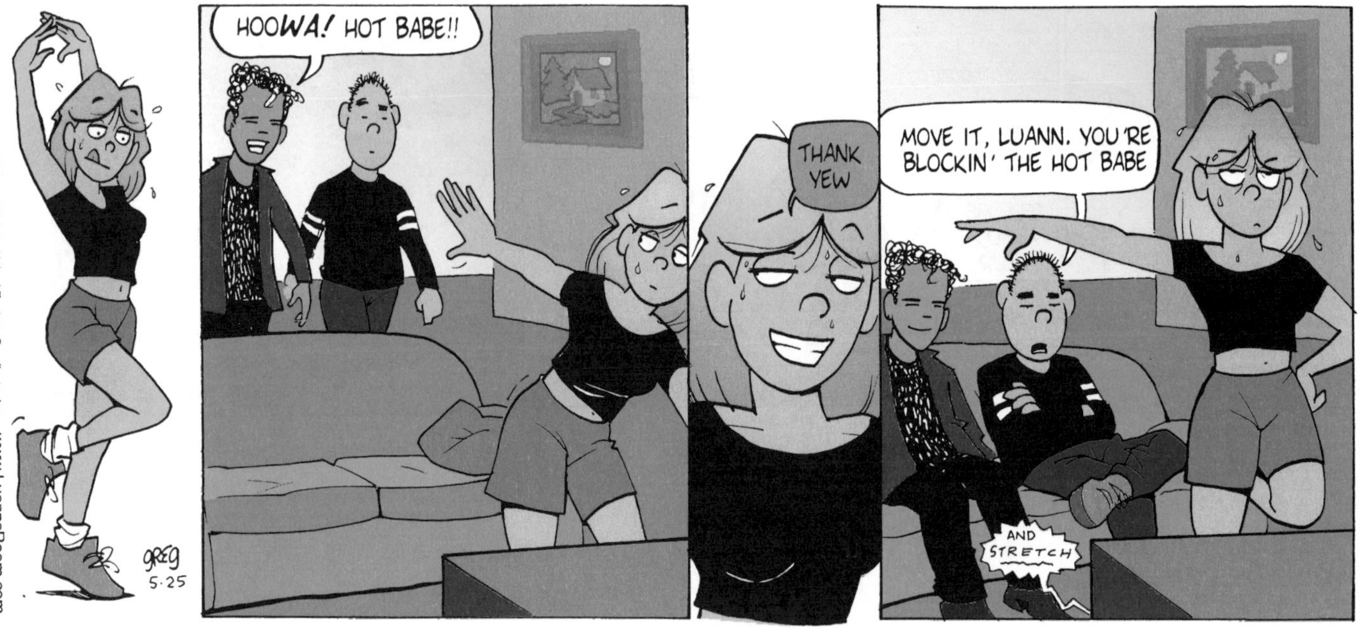
HOOWA! HOT BABE!!
THANK YEW
MOVE IT, LUANN. YOU'RE BLOCKIN' THE HOT BABE
AND STRETCH
GREG 5·25

IDEAL vs REAL
1. Hair full of body...
...body full of hair.
2. Long, thick lashes...
...lashes?
3. Small nose, big lips...
...oops, got it backward.
4. Moist, glowing skin...
...yeah, in the armpit.
5. Flat tummy, round rear...
...darn. Backward again.
6. Nicely shaped nails...
...well, 2 out of 10.
7. Soft skin, tough muscles...
...another one backward!
8. Ideal feet...
...define "ideal."
GREG
6.1

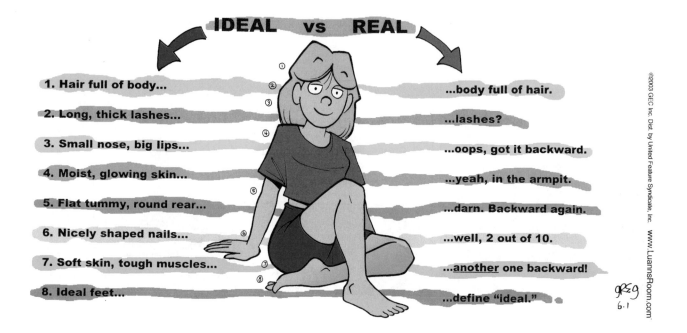

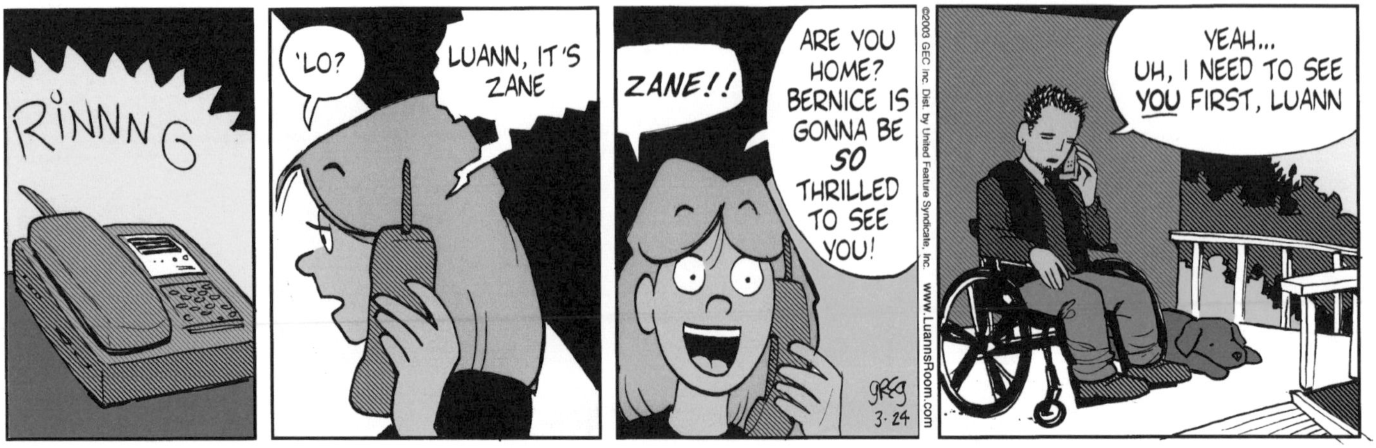
RINNNG
'LO?
LUANN, IT'S ZANE
ZANE!!
ARE YOU HOME? BERNICE IS GONNA BE SO THRILLED TO SEE YOU!
©2003 GEC Inc. Dist. by United Feature Syndicate, Inc. www.LuannsRoom.com
GREG 3·24
YEAH... UH, I NEED TO SEE YOU FIRST, LUANN

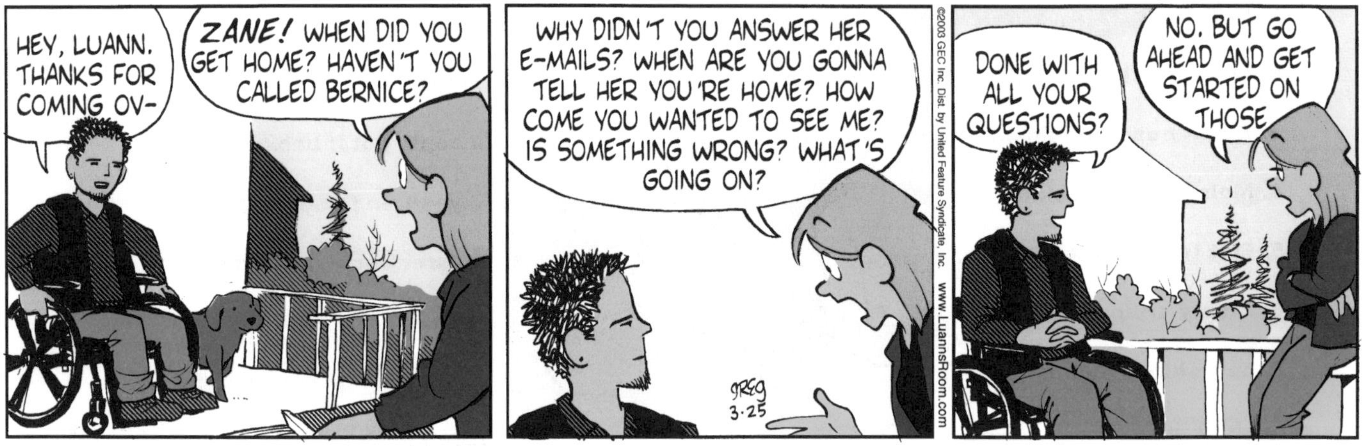
HEY, LUANN. THANKS FOR COMING OV-
ZANE! WHEN DID YOU GET HOME? HAVEN'T YOU CALLED BERNICE?
WHY DIDN'T YOU ANSWER HER E-MAILS? WHEN ARE YOU GONNA TELL HER YOU'RE HOME? HOW COME YOU WANTED TO SEE ME? IS SOMETHING WRONG? WHAT'S GOING ON?
GREG 3·25
©2003 GEC Inc. Dist. by United Feature Syndicate, Inc. www.LuannsRoom.com
DONE WITH ALL YOUR QUESTIONS?
NO. BUT GO AHEAD AND GET STARTED ON THOSE

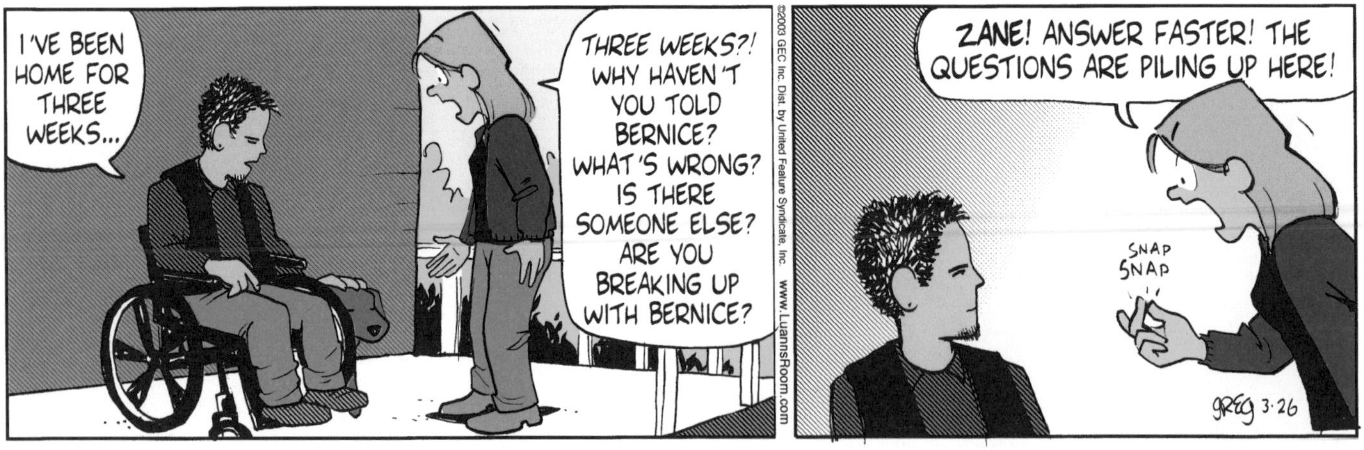
I'VE BEEN HOME FOR THREE WEEKS...
THREE WEEKS?! WHY HAVEN'T YOU TOLD BERNICE? WHAT'S WRONG? IS THERE SOMEONE ELSE? ARE YOU BREAKING UP WITH BERNICE?
©2003 GEC Inc. Dist. by United Feature Syndicate, Inc. www.LuannsRoom.com
ZANE! ANSWER FASTER! THE QUESTIONS ARE PILING UP HERE!
SNAP SNAP
GREG 3·26

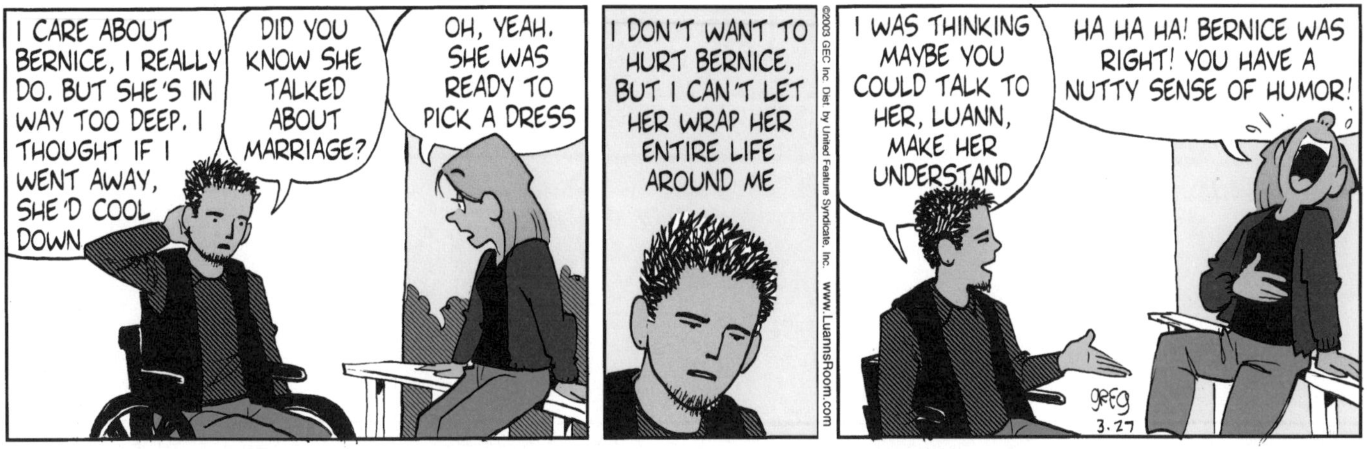
I CARE ABOUT BERNICE, I REALLY DO. BUT SHE'S IN WAY TOO DEEP. I THOUGHT IF I WENT AWAY, SHE'D COOL DOWN
DID YOU KNOW SHE TALKED ABOUT MARRIAGE?
OH, YEAH. SHE WAS READY TO PICK A DRESS
I DON'T WANT TO HURT BERNICE, BUT I CAN'T LET HER WRAP HER ENTIRE LIFE AROUND ME
©2003 GEC Inc. Dist. by United Feature Syndicate, Inc.
www.LuannsRoom.com
I WAS THINKING MAYBE YOU COULD TALK TO HER, LUANN, MAKE HER UNDERSTAND
HA HA HA! BERNICE WAS RIGHT! YOU HAVE A NUTTY SENSE OF HUMOR!
GREG 3.27

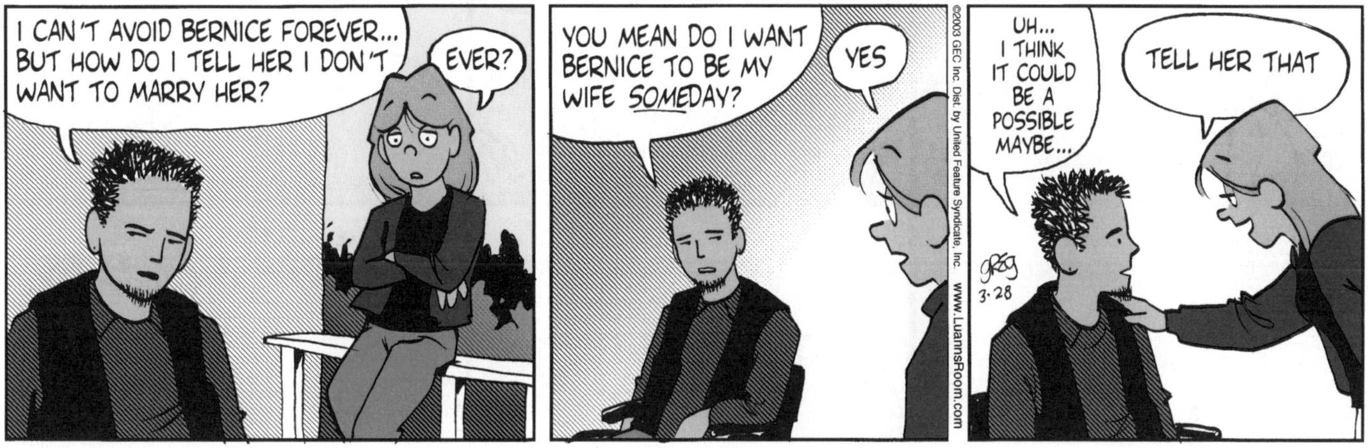
I CAN'T AVOID BERNICE FOREVER... BUT HOW DO I TELL HER I DON'T WANT TO MARRY HER?
EVER?
YOU MEAN DO I WANT BERNICE TO BE MY WIFE SOMEDAY?
YES
©2003 GEC Inc. Dist. by United Feature Syndicate, Inc.
www.LuannsRoom.com
UH... I THINK IT COULD BE A POSSIBLE MAYBE...
TELL HER THAT
GREG 3.28

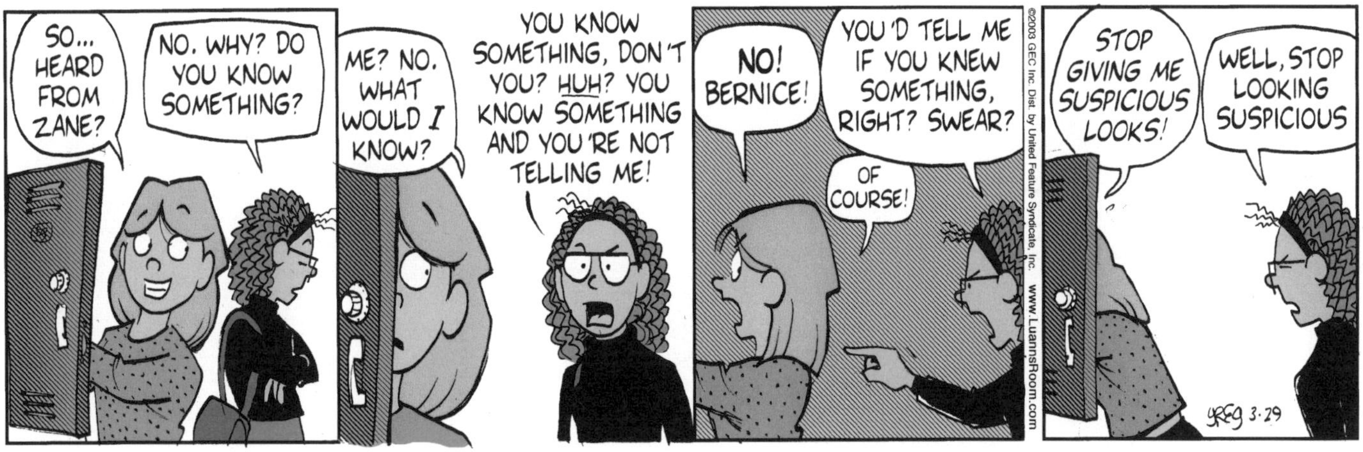
SO... HEARD FROM ZANE?
NO. WHY? DO YOU KNOW SOMETHING?
ME? NO. WHAT WOULD I KNOW?
YOU KNOW SOMETHING, DON'T YOU? HUH? YOU KNOW SOMETHING AND YOU'RE NOT TELLING ME!
NO! BERNICE!
YOU'D TELL ME IF YOU KNEW SOMETHING, RIGHT? SWEAR?
OF COURSE!
©2003 GEC Inc. Dist. by United Feature Syndicate, Inc.
www.LuannsRoom.com
STOP GIVING ME SUSPICIOUS LOOKS!
WELL, STOP LOOKING SUSPICIOUS
GREG 3.29

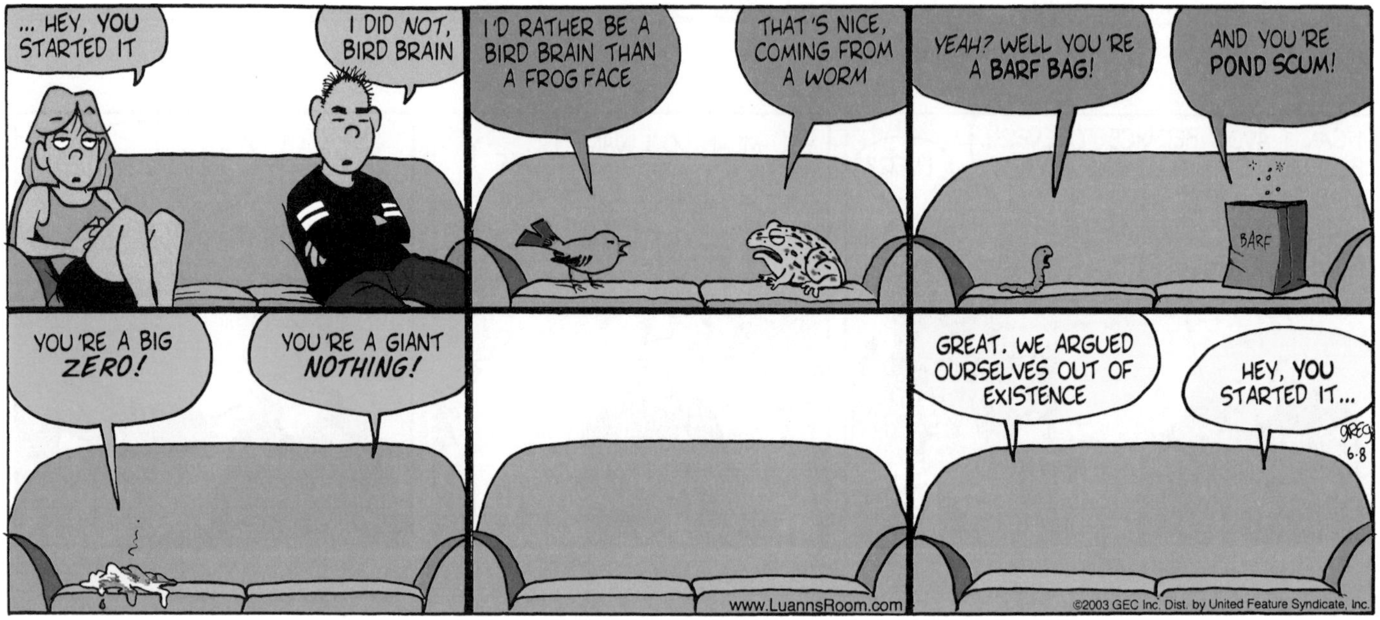
... HEY, YOU STARTED IT
I DID NOT, BIRD BRAIN
I'D RATHER BE A BIRD BRAIN THAN A FROG FACE
THAT'S NICE, COMING FROM A WORM
YEAH? WELL YOU'RE A BARF BAG!
AND YOU'RE POND SCUM!
BARF
YOU'RE A BIG ZERO!
YOU'RE A GIANT NOTHING!
GREAT. WE ARGUED OURSELVES OUT OF EXISTENCE
HEY, YOU STARTED IT...
GREG 6-8
www.LuannsRoom.com
©2003 GEC Inc. Dist. by United Feature Syndicate, Inc.

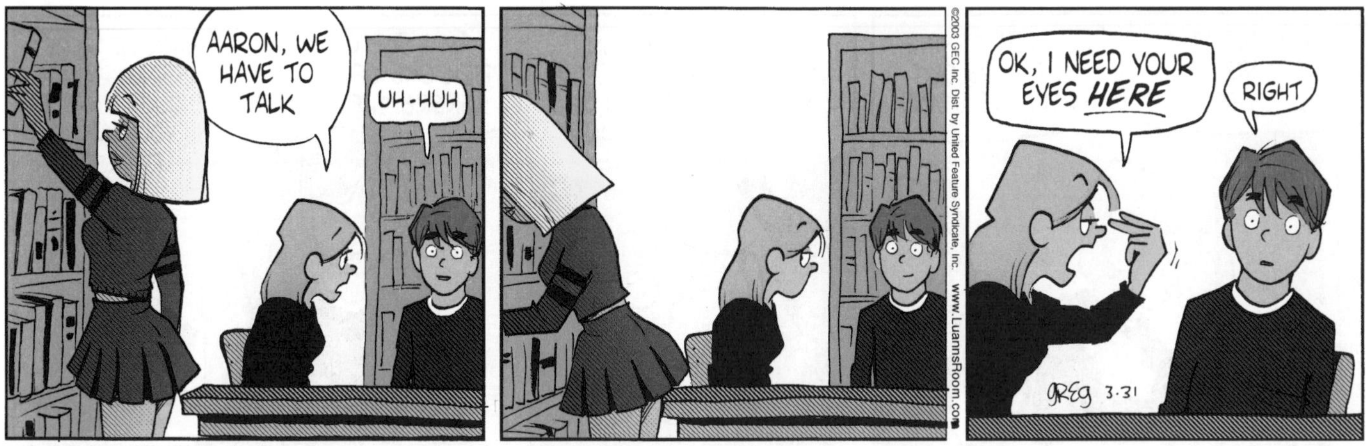
AARON, WE HAVE TO TALK
UH-HUH
©2003 GEC Inc. Dist. by United Feature Syndicate, Inc. www.LuannsRoom.com
OK, I NEED YOUR EYES HERE
RIGHT
GREG 3·31

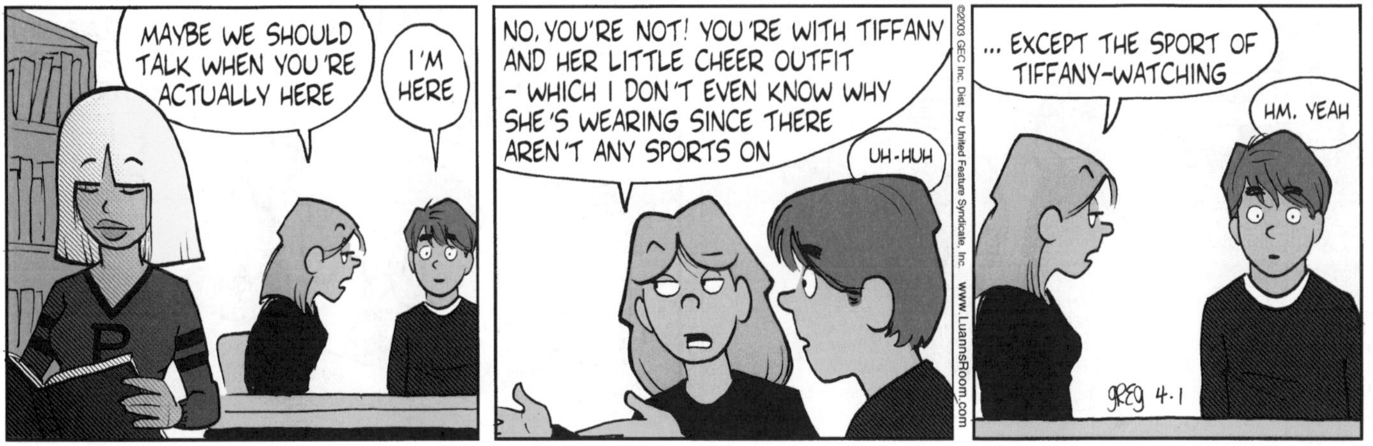
MAYBE WE SHOULD TALK WHEN YOU'RE ACTUALLY HERE
I'M HERE
NO, YOU'RE NOT! YOU'RE WITH TIFFANY AND HER LITTLE CHEER OUTFIT - WHICH I DON'T EVEN KNOW WHY SHE'S WEARING SINCE THERE AREN'T ANY SPORTS ON
UH-HUH
©2003 GEC Inc. Dist. by United Feature Syndicate, Inc. www.LuannsRoom.com
... EXCEPT THE SPORT OF TIFFANY-WATCHING
HM. YEAH
GREG 4·1

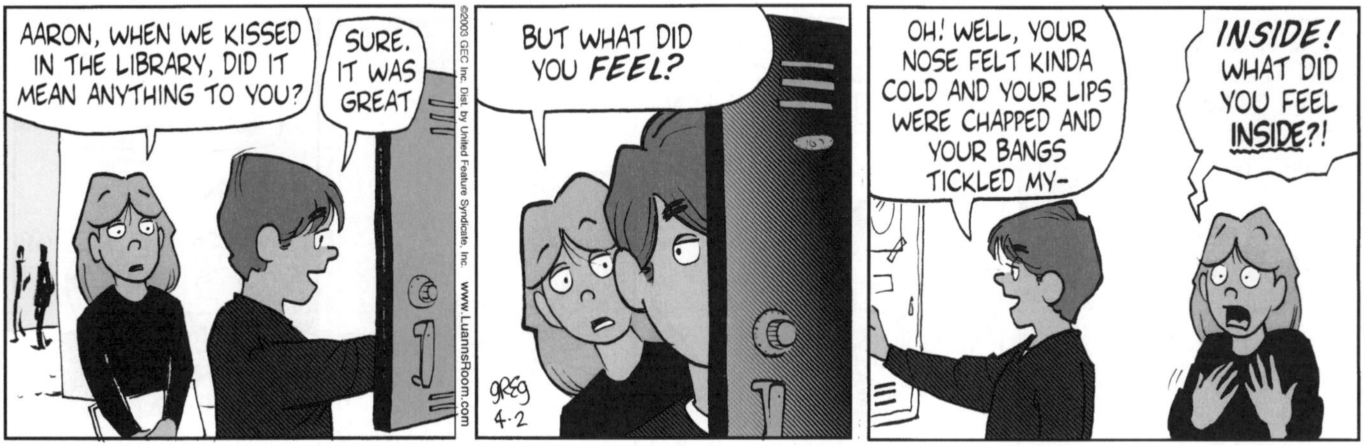
AARON, WHEN WE KISSED IN THE LIBRARY, DID IT MEAN ANYTHING TO YOU?
SURE. IT WAS GREAT
©2003 GEC Inc. Dist. by United Feature Syndicate, Inc. www.LuannsRoom.com
GREG 4·2
BUT WHAT DID YOU FEEL?
OH! WELL, YOUR NOSE FELT KINDA COLD AND YOUR LIPS WERE CHAPPED AND YOUR BANGS TICKLED MY-
INSIDE! WHAT DID YOU FEEL INSIDE?!

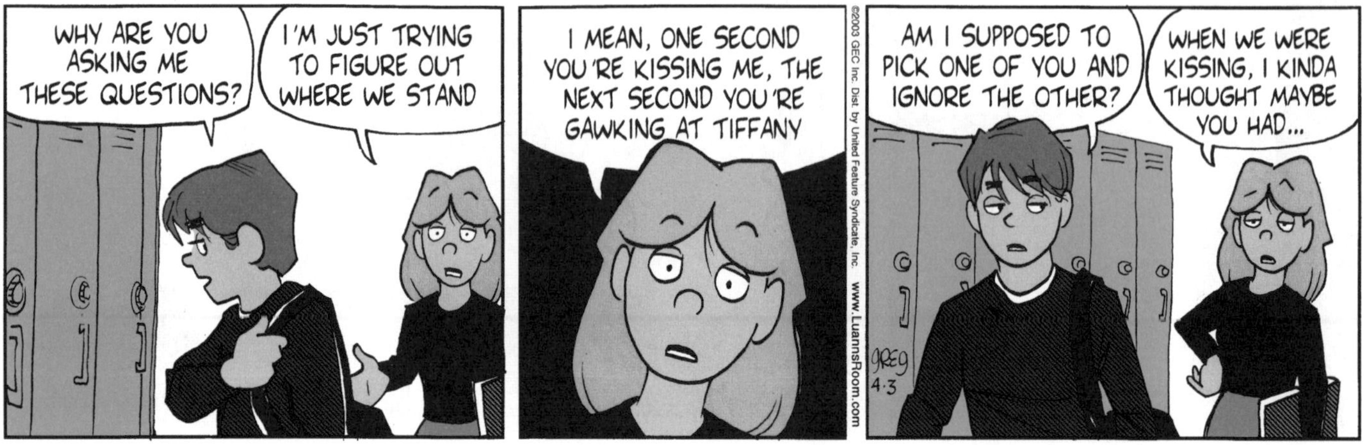
WHY ARE YOU ASKING ME THESE QUESTIONS?
I'M JUST TRYING TO FIGURE OUT WHERE WE STAND
I MEAN, ONE SECOND YOU'RE KISSING ME, THE NEXT SECOND YOU'RE GAWKING AT TIFFANY
©2003 GEC Inc. Dist. by United Feature Syndicate, Inc. www.LuannsRoom.com
AM I SUPPOSED TO PICK ONE OF YOU AND IGNORE THE OTHER?
WHEN WE WERE KISSING, I KINDA THOUGHT MAYBE YOU HAD...
GREG 4·3

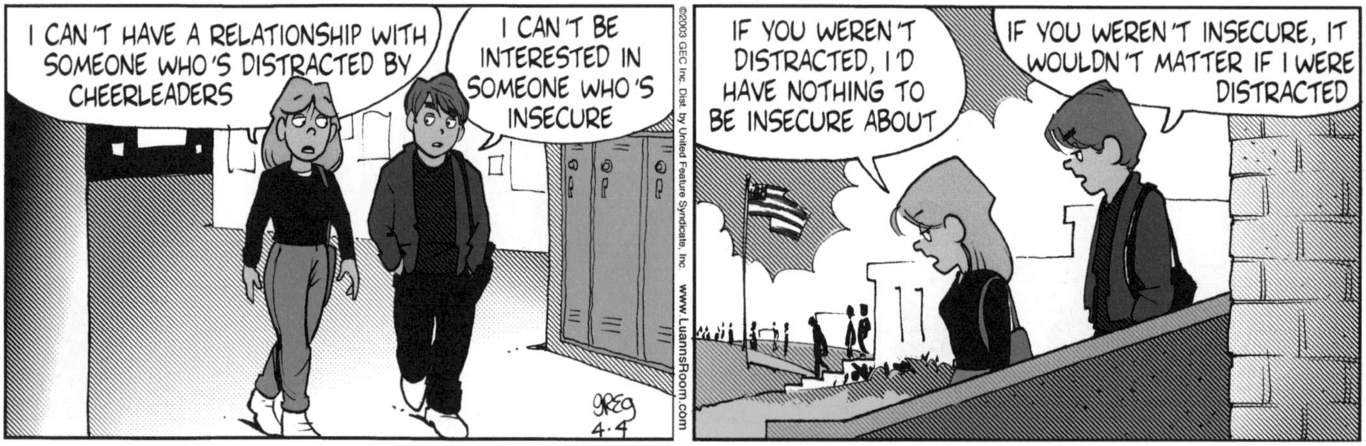
I CAN'T HAVE A RELATIONSHIP WITH SOMEONE WHO'S DISTRACTED BY CHEERLEADERS
I CAN'T BE INTERESTED IN SOMEONE WHO'S INSECURE
GREG 4·4
©2003 GEC Inc. Dist. by United Feature Syndicate, Inc. www.LuannsRoom.com
IF YOU WEREN'T DISTRACTED, I'D HAVE NOTHING TO BE INSECURE ABOUT
IF YOU WEREN'T INSECURE, IT WOULDN'T MATTER IF I WERE DISTRACTED

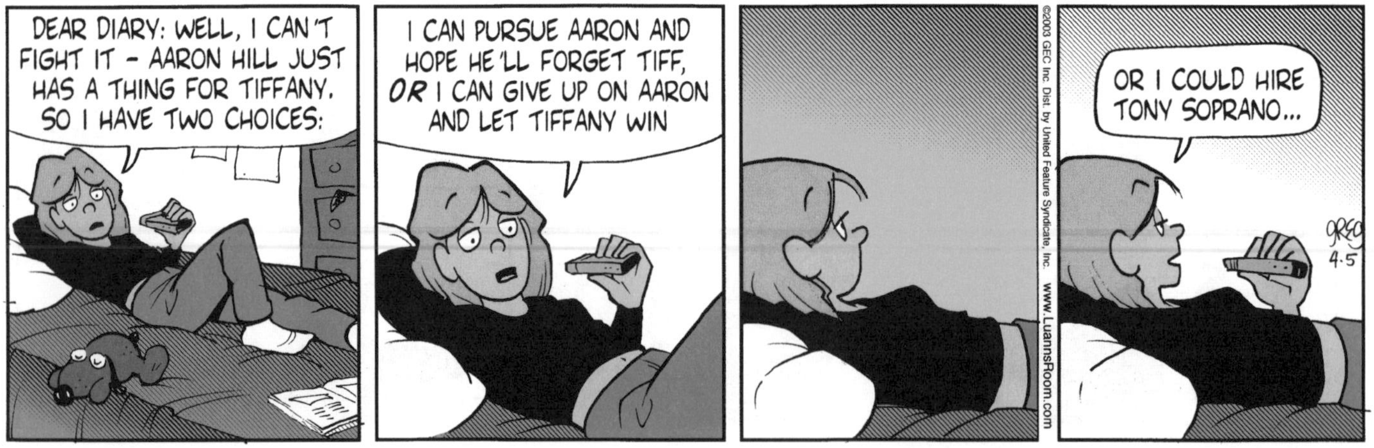
DEAR DIARY: WELL, I CAN'T FIGHT IT - AARON HILL JUST HAS A THING FOR TIFFANY. SO I HAVE TWO CHOICES:
I CAN PURSUE AARON AND HOPE HE'LL FORGET TIFF, *OR* I CAN GIVE UP ON AARON AND LET TIFFANY WIN
©2003 GEC Inc. Dist. by United Feature Syndicate, Inc. www.LuannsRoom.com
OR I COULD HIRE TONY SOPRANO...
GREG 4·5

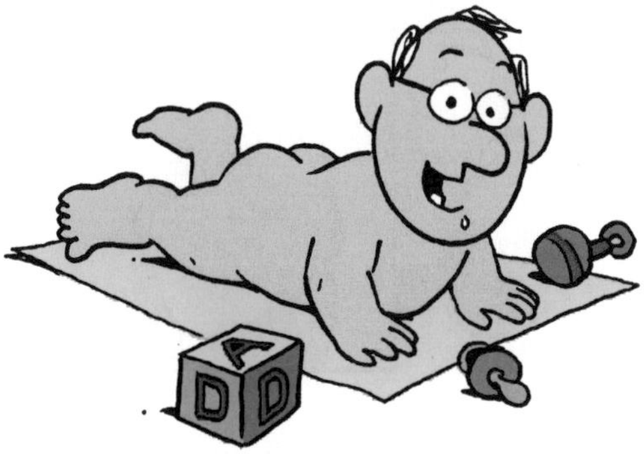
D
D
A

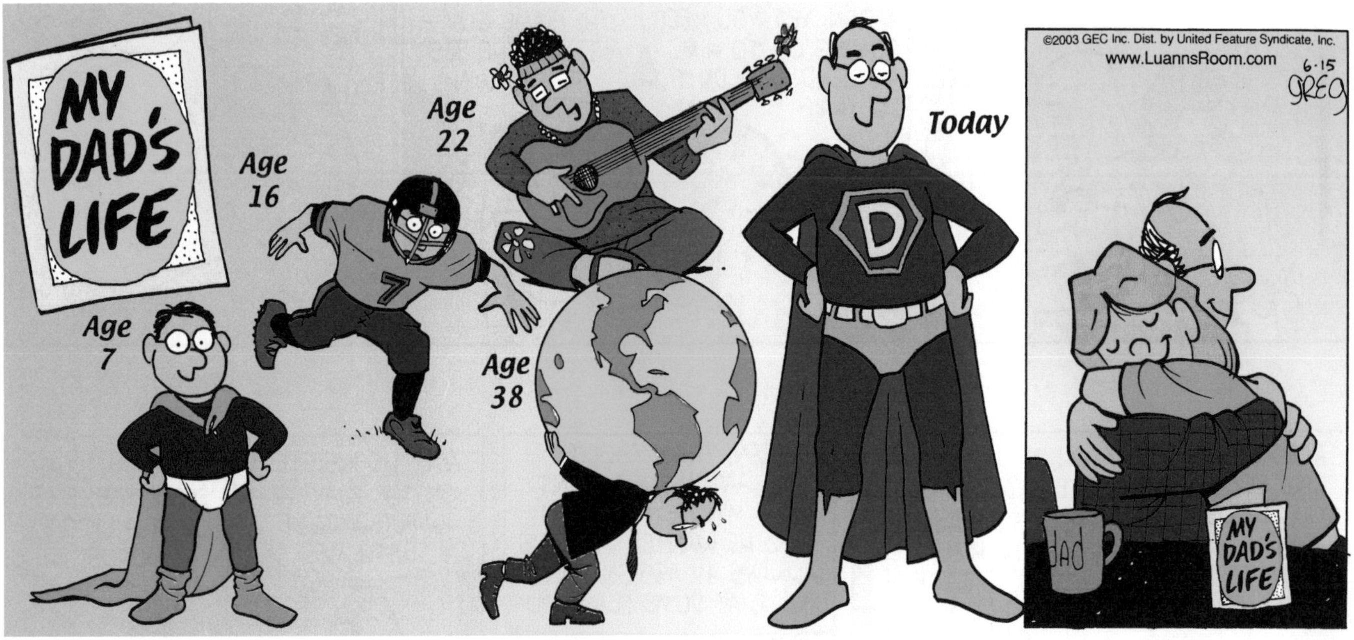
MY DAD'S LIFE
Age 7
Age 16
Age 22
Age 38
Today
©2003 GEC Inc. Dist. by United Feature Syndicate, Inc.
www.LuannsRoom.com
6·15
GREG
dad
MY DAD'S LIFE

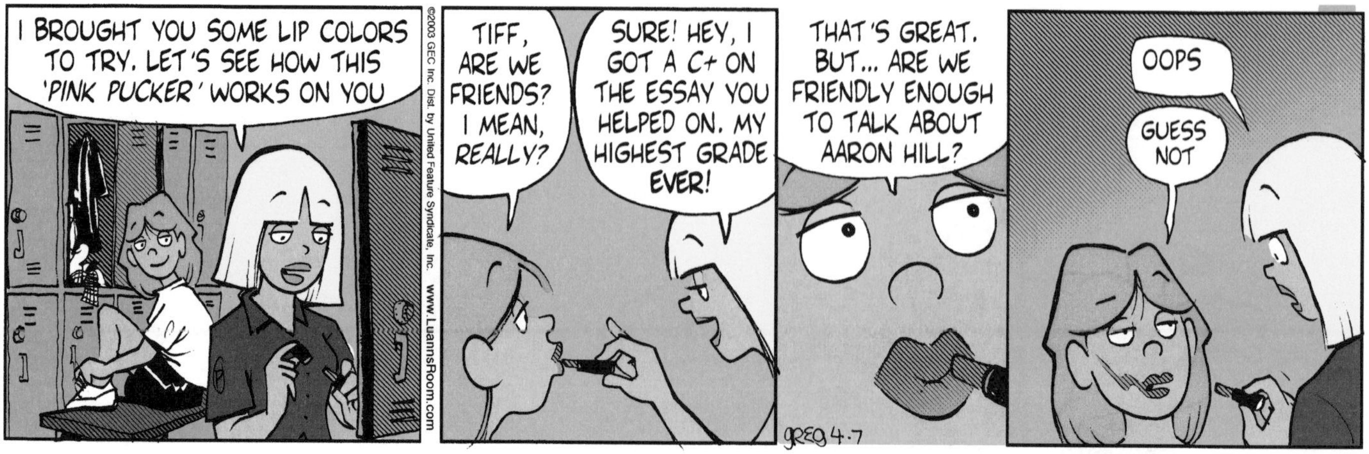
I BROUGHT YOU SOME LIP COLORS TO TRY. LET'S SEE HOW THIS 'PINK PUCKER' WORKS ON YOU
©2003 GEC Inc. Dist. by United Feature Syndicate, Inc. www.LuannsRoom.com
TIFF, ARE WE FRIENDS? I MEAN, REALLY?
SURE! HEY, I GOT A C+ ON THE ESSAY YOU HELPED ON. MY HIGHEST GRADE EVER!
THAT'S GREAT. BUT... ARE WE FRIENDLY ENOUGH TO TALK ABOUT AARON HILL?
GREG 4-7
OOPS
GUESS NOT

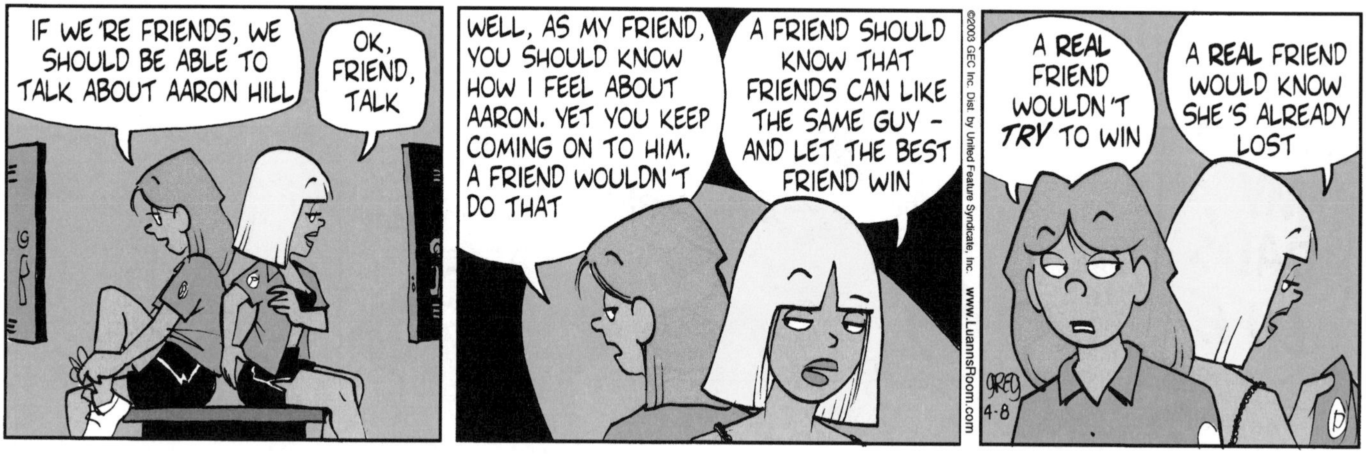
IF WE'RE FRIENDS, WE SHOULD BE ABLE TO TALK ABOUT AARON HILL
OK, FRIEND, TALK
WELL, AS MY FRIEND, YOU SHOULD KNOW HOW I FEEL ABOUT AARON. YET YOU KEEP COMING ON TO HIM. A FRIEND WOULDN'T DO THAT
A FRIEND SHOULD KNOW THAT FRIENDS CAN LIKE THE SAME GUY – AND LET THE BEST FRIEND WIN
©2003 GEC Inc. Dist. by United Feature Syndicate, Inc. www.LuannsRoom.com
A REAL FRIEND WOULDN'T TRY TO WIN
A REAL FRIEND WOULD KNOW SHE'S ALREADY LOST
GREG 4-8

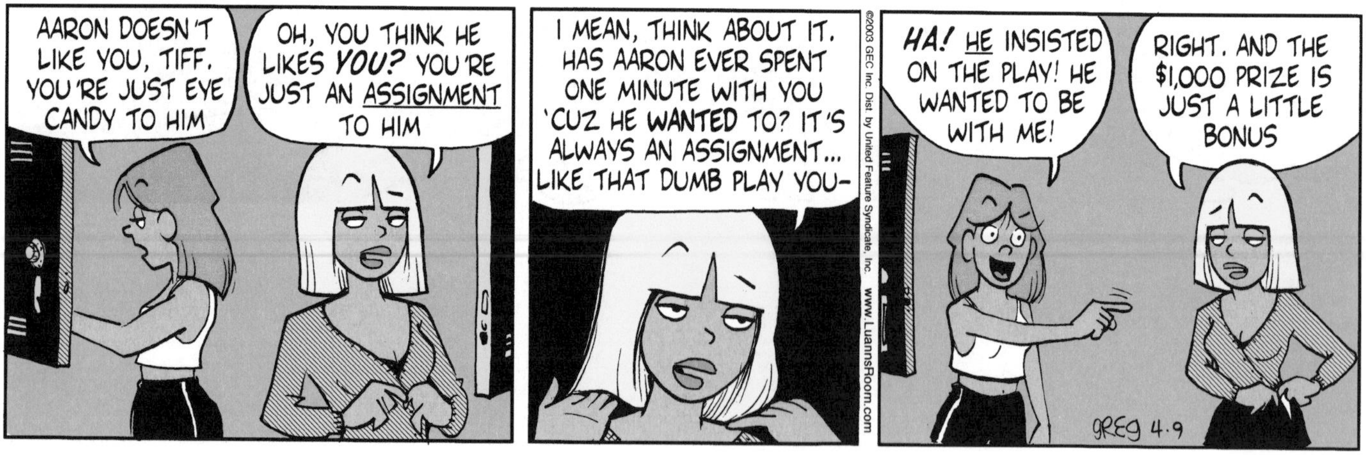
AARON DOESN'T LIKE YOU, TIFF. YOU'RE JUST EYE CANDY TO HIM
OH, YOU THINK HE LIKES YOU? YOU'RE JUST AN ASSIGNMENT TO HIM
I MEAN, THINK ABOUT IT. HAS AARON EVER SPENT ONE MINUTE WITH YOU 'CUZ HE WANTED TO? IT'S ALWAYS AN ASSIGNMENT... LIKE THAT DUMB PLAY YOU-
©2003 GEC Inc. Dist. by United Feature Syndicate, Inc. www.LuannsRoom.com
HA! HE INSISTED ON THE PLAY! HE WANTED TO BE WITH ME!
RIGHT. AND THE $1,000 PRIZE IS JUST A LITTLE BONUS
GREG 4-9

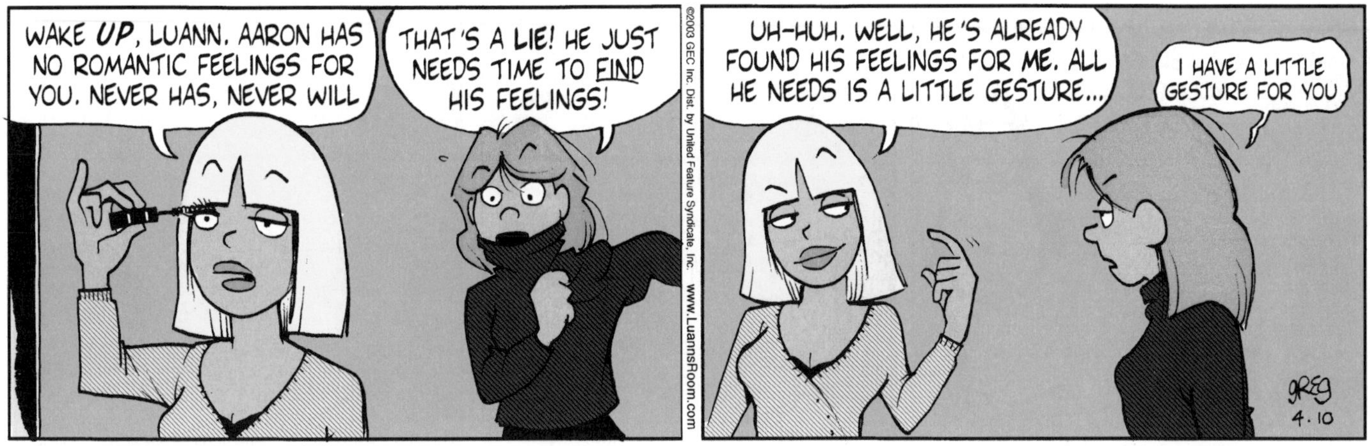
WAKE UP, LUANN. AARON HAS NO ROMANTIC FEELINGS FOR YOU. NEVER HAS, NEVER WILL
THAT'S A LIE! HE JUST NEEDS TIME TO FIND HIS FEELINGS!
©2003 GEC Inc. Dist. by United Feature Syndicate, Inc. www.LuannsRoom.com
UH-HUH. WELL, HE'S ALREADY FOUND HIS FEELINGS FOR ME. ALL HE NEEDS IS A LITTLE GESTURE...
I HAVE A LITTLE GESTURE FOR YOU
GREG 4.10

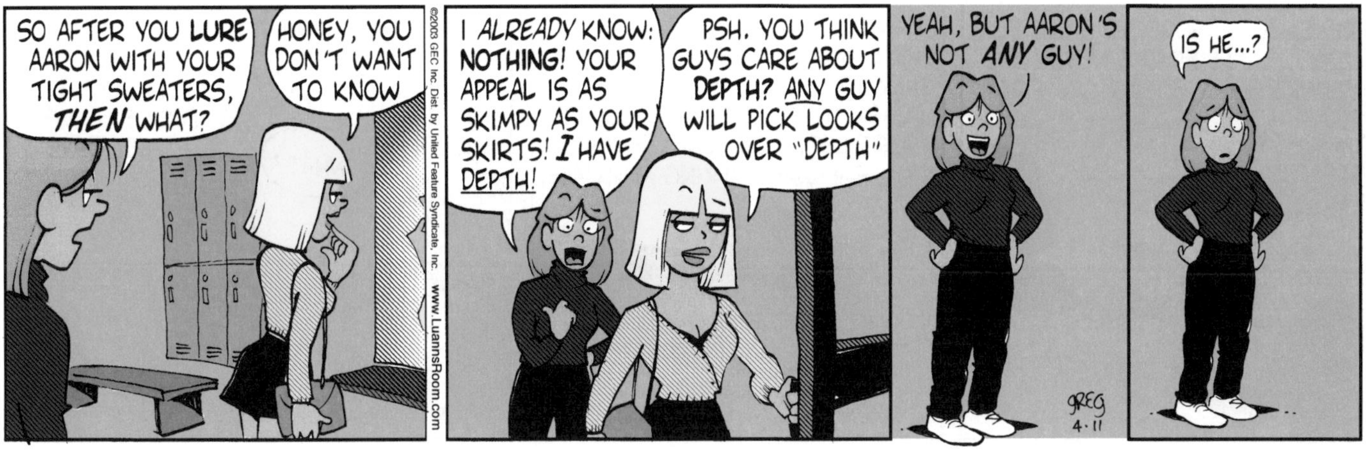
SO AFTER YOU LURE AARON WITH YOUR TIGHT SWEATERS, THEN WHAT?
HONEY, YOU DON'T WANT TO KNOW
©2003 GEC Inc. Dist. by United Feature Syndicate, Inc. www.LuannsRoom.com
I ALREADY KNOW: NOTHING! YOUR APPEAL IS AS SKIMPY AS YOUR SKIRTS! I HAVE DEPTH!
PSH. YOU THINK GUYS CARE ABOUT DEPTH? ANY GUY WILL PICK LOOKS OVER "DEPTH"
YEAH, BUT AARON'S NOT ANY GUY!
GREG 4.11
IS HE...?

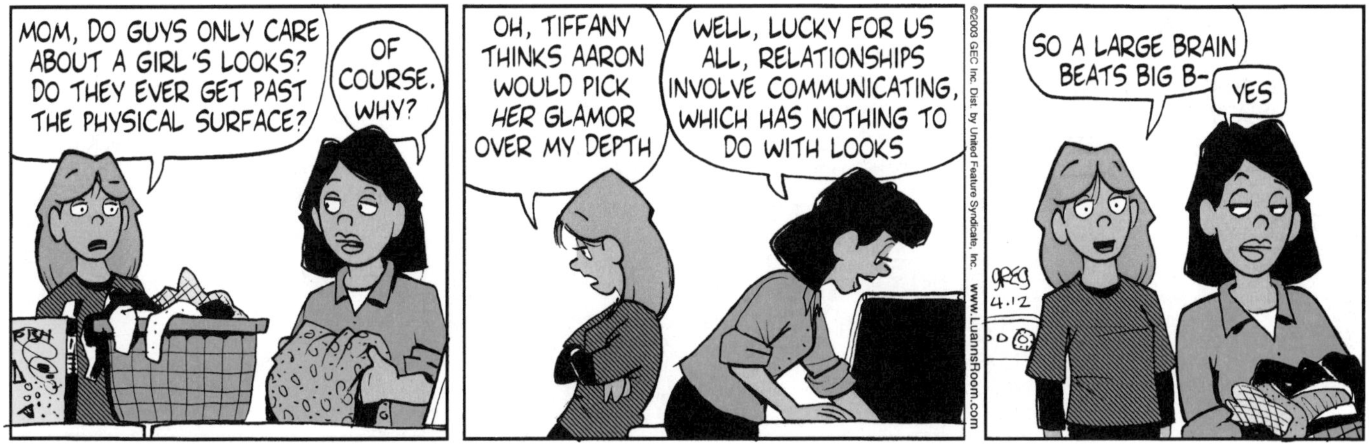
MOM, DO GUYS ONLY CARE ABOUT A GIRL'S LOOKS? DO THEY EVER GET PAST THE PHYSICAL SURFACE?
OF COURSE. WHY?
OH, TIFFANY THINKS AARON WOULD PICK HER GLAMOR OVER MY DEPTH
WELL, LUCKY FOR US ALL, RELATIONSHIPS INVOLVE COMMUNICATING, WHICH HAS NOTHING TO DO WITH LOOKS
©2003 GEC Inc. Dist. by United Feature Syndicate, Inc. www.LuannsRoom.com
GREG 4.12
SO A LARGE BRAIN BEATS BIG B-
YES

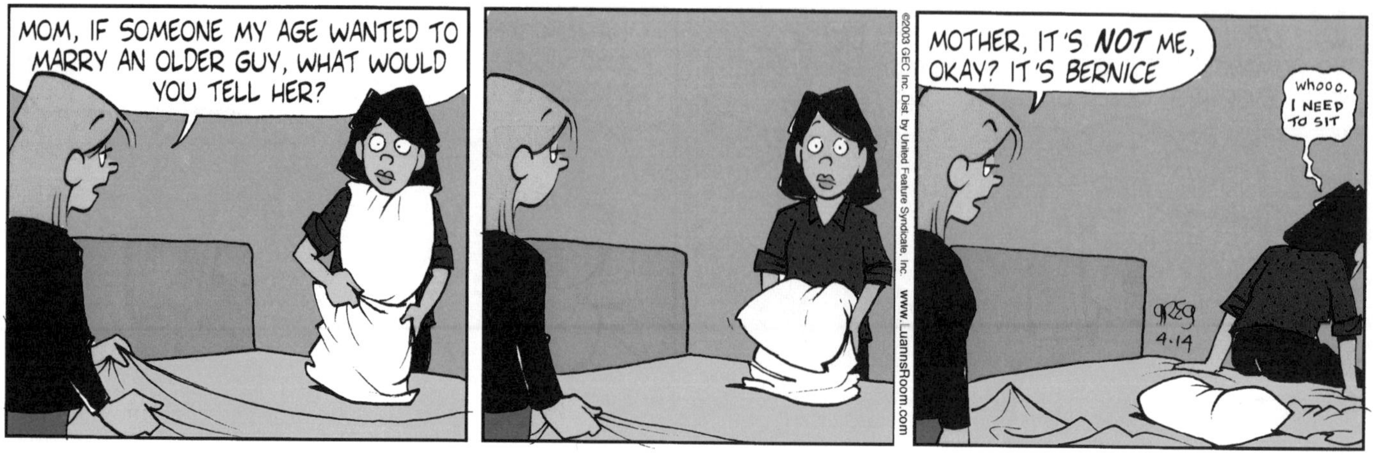
MOM, IF SOMEONE MY AGE WANTED TO MARRY AN OLDER GUY, WHAT WOULD YOU TELL HER?
©2003 GEC Inc. Dist. by United Feature Syndicate, Inc.
www.LuannsRoom.com
MOTHER, IT'S **NOT** ME, OKAY? IT'S BERNICE
Whooo. I NEED TO SIT
GREG 4.14

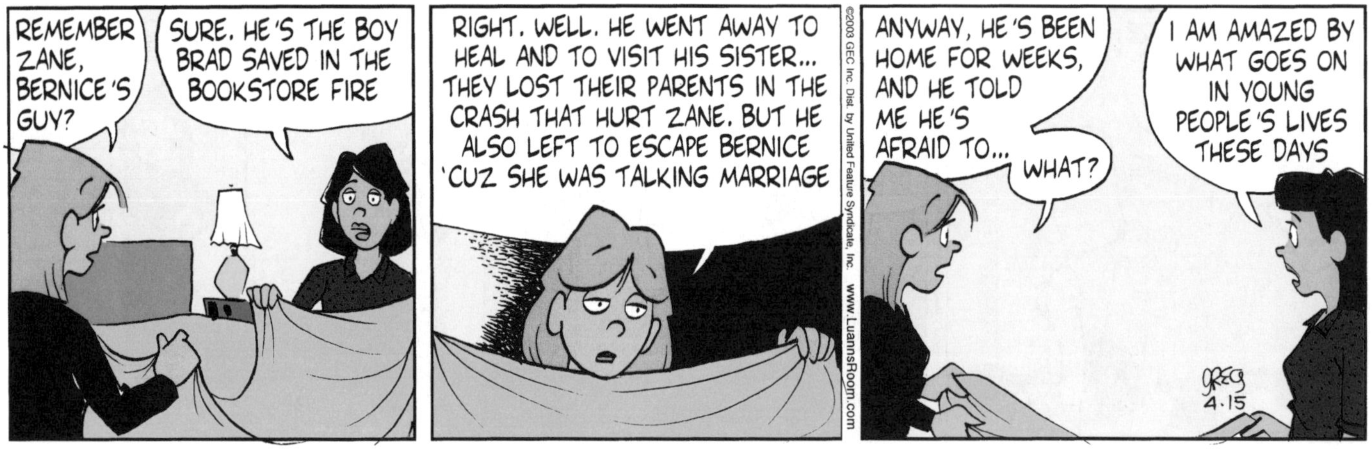
REMEMBER ZANE, BERNICE'S GUY?
SURE. HE'S THE BOY BRAD SAVED IN THE BOOKSTORE FIRE
RIGHT. WELL. HE WENT AWAY TO HEAL AND TO VISIT HIS SISTER... THEY LOST THEIR PARENTS IN THE CRASH THAT HURT ZANE. BUT HE ALSO LEFT TO ESCAPE BERNICE 'CUZ SHE WAS TALKING MARRIAGE
©2003 GEC Inc. Dist. by United Feature Syndicate, Inc.
www.LuannsRoom.com
ANYWAY, HE'S BEEN HOME FOR WEEKS, AND HE TOLD ME HE'S AFRAID TO...
WHAT?
I AM AMAZED BY WHAT GOES ON IN YOUNG PEOPLE'S LIVES THESE DAYS
GREG 4.15

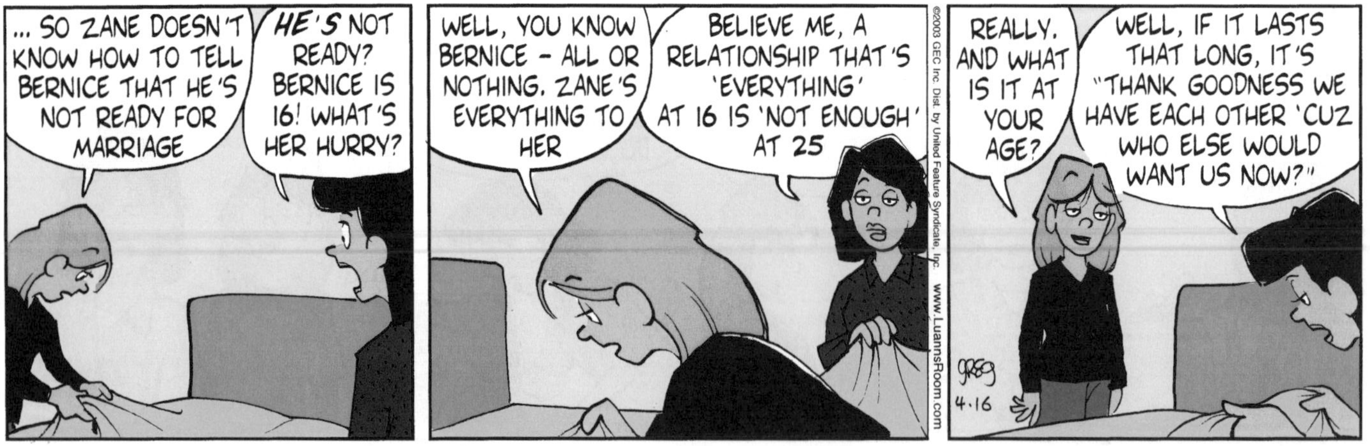
... SO ZANE DOESN'T KNOW HOW TO TELL BERNICE THAT HE'S NOT READY FOR MARRIAGE
HE'S NOT READY? BERNICE IS 16! WHAT'S HER HURRY?
WELL, YOU KNOW BERNICE - ALL OR NOTHING. ZANE'S EVERYTHING TO HER
BELIEVE ME, A RELATIONSHIP THAT'S 'EVERYTHING' AT 16 IS 'NOT ENOUGH' AT 25
©2003 GEC Inc. Dist. by United Feature Syndicate, Inc.
www.LuannsRoom.com
REALLY. AND WHAT IS IT AT YOUR AGE?
WELL, IF IT LASTS THAT LONG, IT'S "THANK GOODNESS WE HAVE EACH OTHER 'CUZ WHO ELSE WOULD WANT US NOW?"
GREG 4.16

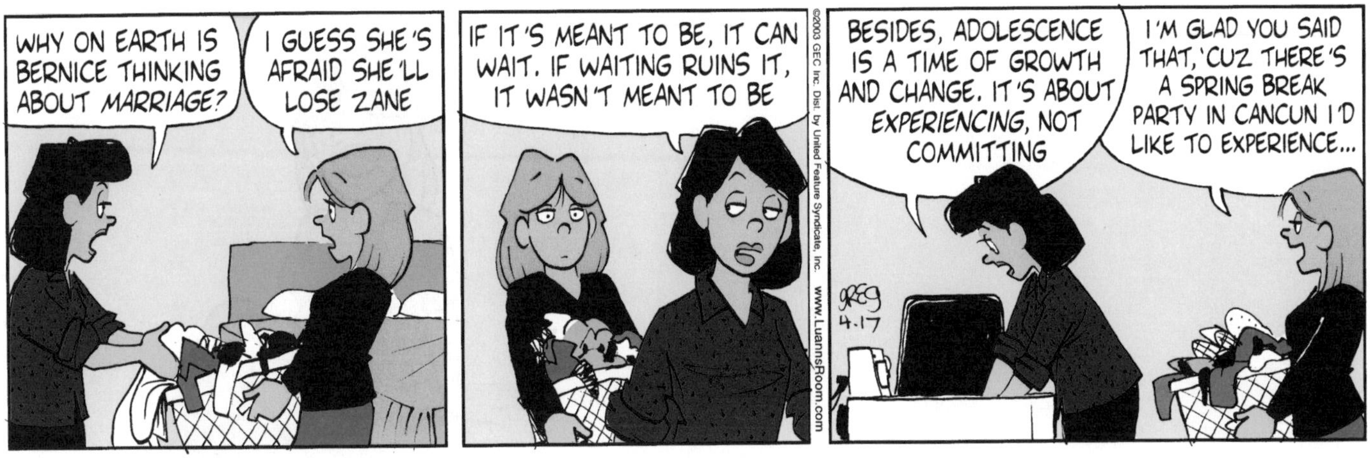
WHY ON EARTH IS BERNICE THINKING ABOUT *MARRIAGE?*
I GUESS SHE'S AFRAID SHE'LL LOSE ZANE
IF IT'S MEANT TO BE, IT CAN WAIT. IF WAITING RUINS IT, IT WASN'T MEANT TO BE
BESIDES, ADOLESCENCE IS A TIME OF GROWTH AND CHANGE. IT'S ABOUT *EXPERIENCING*, NOT COMMITTING
I'M GLAD YOU SAID THAT, 'CUZ THERE'S A SPRING BREAK PARTY IN CANCUN I'D LIKE TO EXPERIENCE...
©2003 GEC Inc. Dist. by United Feature Syndicate, Inc.
www.LuannsRoom.com
GREG 4-17

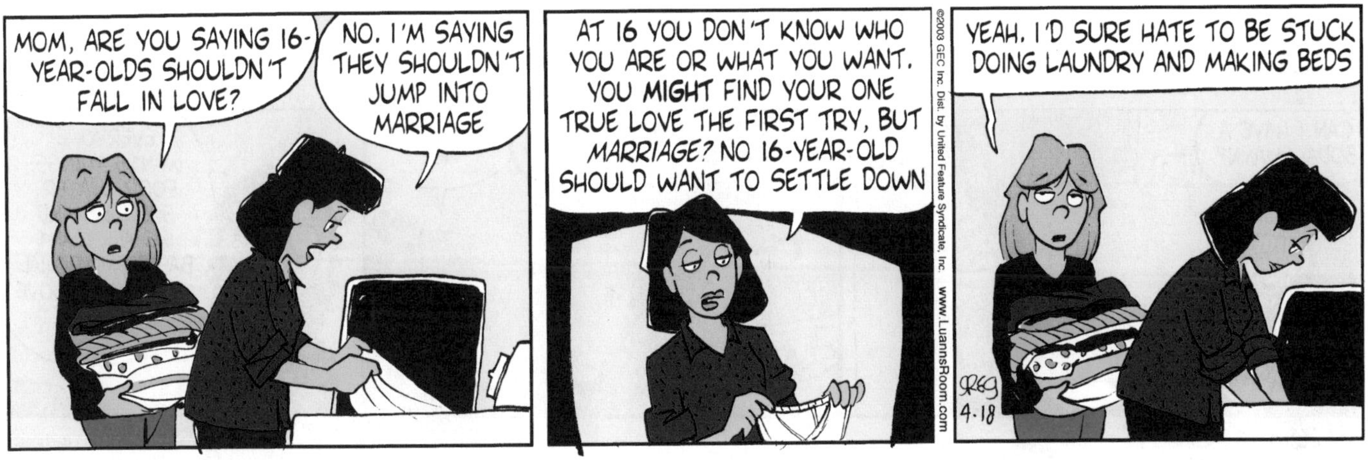
MOM, ARE YOU SAYING 16-YEAR-OLDS SHOULDN'T FALL IN LOVE?
NO. I'M SAYING THEY SHOULDN'T JUMP INTO MARRIAGE
AT 16 YOU DON'T KNOW WHO YOU ARE OR WHAT YOU WANT. YOU **MIGHT** FIND YOUR ONE TRUE LOVE THE FIRST TRY, BUT *MARRIAGE?* NO 16-YEAR-OLD SHOULD WANT TO SETTLE DOWN
YEAH. I'D SURE HATE TO BE STUCK DOING LAUNDRY AND MAKING BEDS
©2003 GEC Inc. Dist. by United Feature Syndicate, Inc.
www.LuannsRoom.com
GREG 4-18

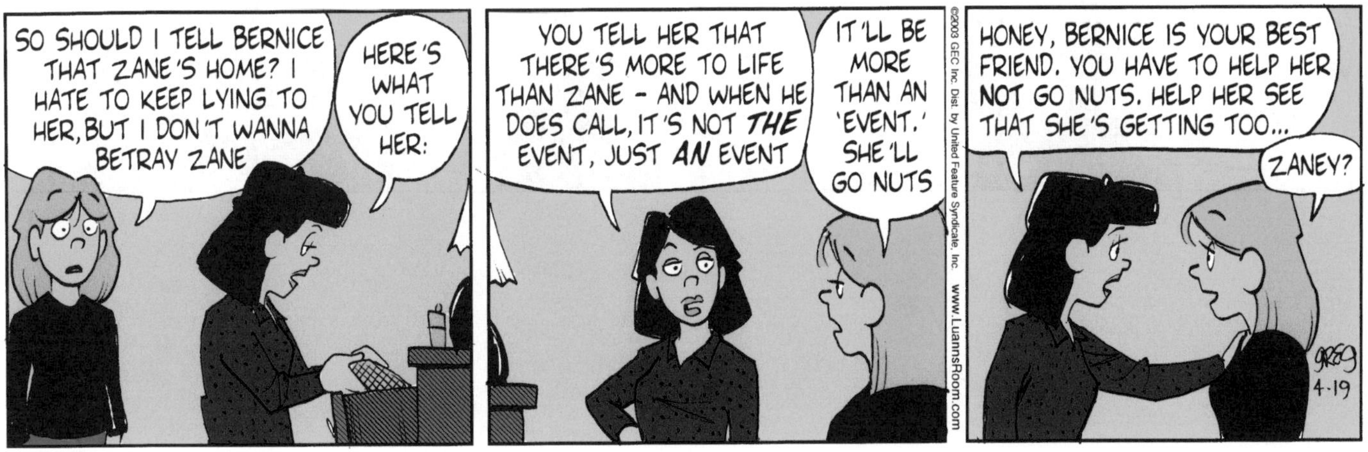
SO SHOULD I TELL BERNICE THAT ZANE'S HOME? I HATE TO KEEP LYING TO HER, BUT I DON'T WANNA BETRAY ZANE
HERE'S WHAT YOU TELL HER:
YOU TELL HER THAT THERE'S MORE TO LIFE THAN ZANE - AND WHEN HE DOES CALL, IT'S NOT ***THE*** EVENT, JUST ***AN*** EVENT
IT'LL BE MORE THAN AN 'EVENT.' SHE'LL GO NUTS
HONEY, BERNICE IS YOUR BEST FRIEND. YOU HAVE TO HELP HER **NOT** GO NUTS. HELP HER SEE THAT SHE'S GETTING TOO...
ZANEY?
©2003 GEC Inc. Dist. by United Feature Syndicate, Inc.
www.LuannsRoom.com
GREG 4-19

Panel 1:
CAN I HAVE A SODA, LUANN?

SURE

www.LuannsRoom.com

Panel 2:
BERNICE, DO YOU THINK IT'S WRONG TO WANT STUFF?

OF COURSE NOT

Panel 3:
EVERYONE WANTS THINGS: FOOD, WATER, SHELTER. AND WE ALL WANT BASIC EMOTIONAL THINGS LIKE LOVE AND RESPECT

Panel 4:
OF COURSE, SOME PEOPLE WANT TOO MANY MATERIAL THINGS – OR EVEN EMOTIONAL THINGS. AND SOME PEOPLE WANT EVERYTHING: WEALTH, POWER, ADORATION...

©2003 GEC Inc. Dist. by United Feature Syndicate, Inc.

Panel 5:
HUMANS CAN'T AVOID WANTING. IT'S PART OF OUR SURVIVAL INSTINCT. WHY?

GREG 6-22

Panel 6:
THERE'S ONLY ONE SODA LEFT, AND I WANT IT

62

www.LuannsRoom.com

GREG 6·29

... SO YOU FIGURE THE DIFFERENCE IS $5,000, AND YOU WANT IT IN A LUMP SUM?

PAYMENTS WOULD BE OKAY, TOO

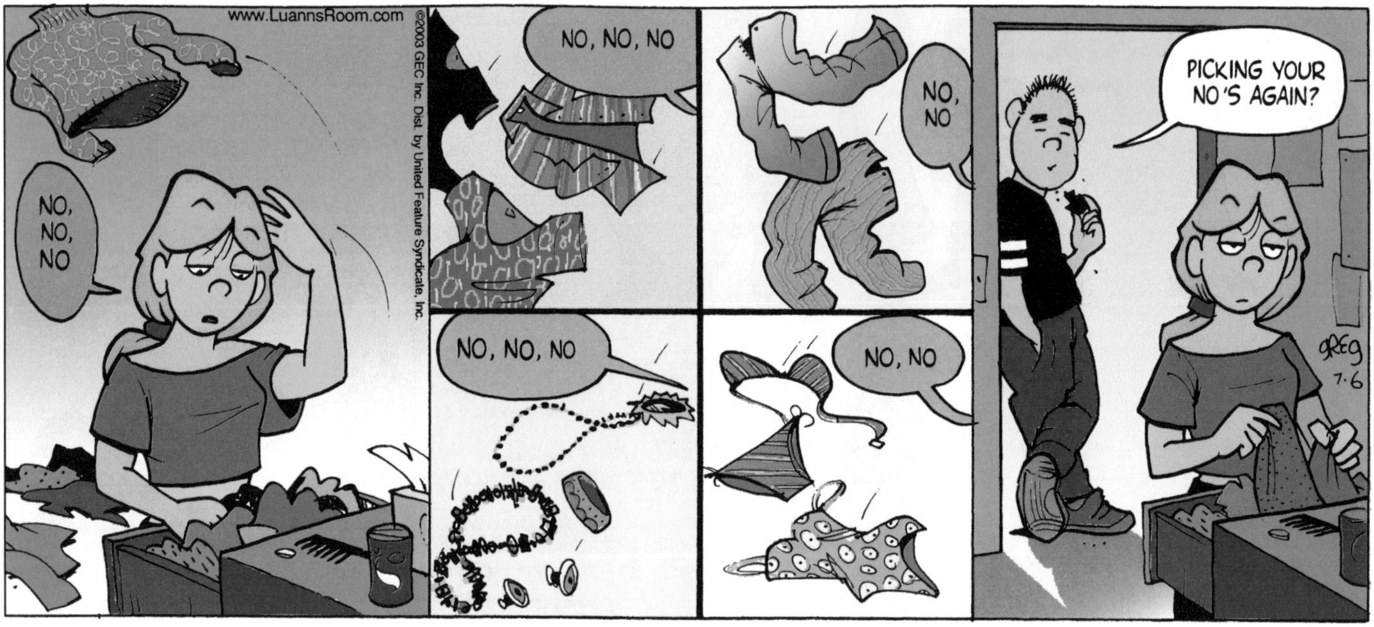
www.LuannsRoom.com
©2003 GEC Inc. Dist. by United Feature Syndicate, Inc.
NO, NO, NO
NO, NO, NO
NO, NO
NO, NO, NO
NO, NO
PICKING YOUR NO'S AGAIN?
GREG 7·6

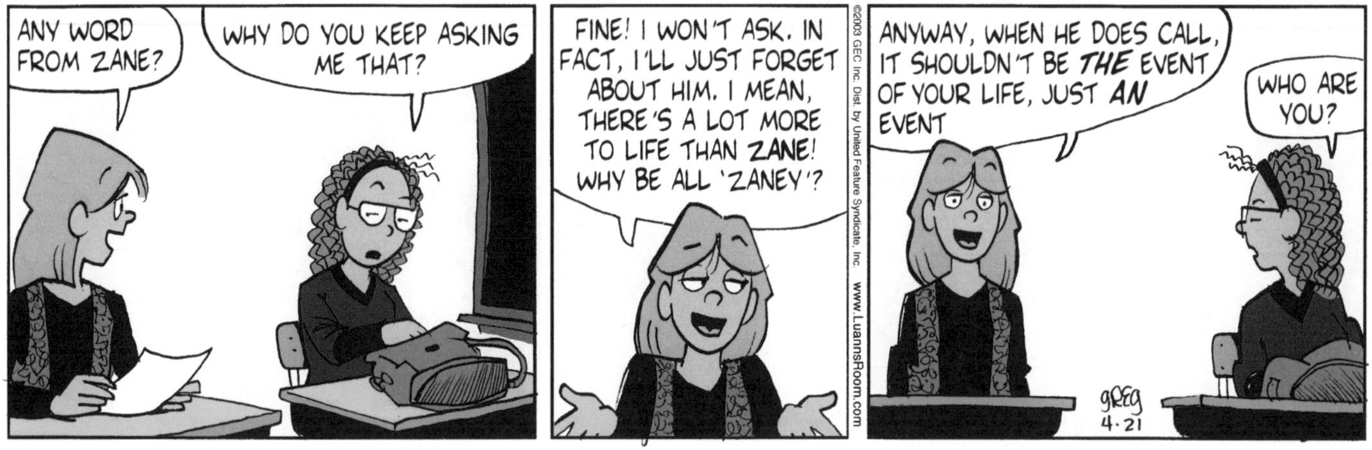
ANY WORD FROM ZANE?
WHY DO YOU KEEP ASKING ME THAT?
FINE! I WON'T ASK. IN FACT, I'LL JUST FORGET ABOUT HIM. I MEAN, THERE'S A LOT MORE TO LIFE THAN ZANE! WHY BE ALL 'ZANEY'?
ANYWAY, WHEN HE DOES CALL, IT SHOULDN'T BE *THE* EVENT OF YOUR LIFE, JUST *AN* EVENT
WHO ARE YOU?
©2003 GEC Inc. Dist. by United Feature Syndicate, Inc.
www.LuannsRoom.com
GREG 4·21

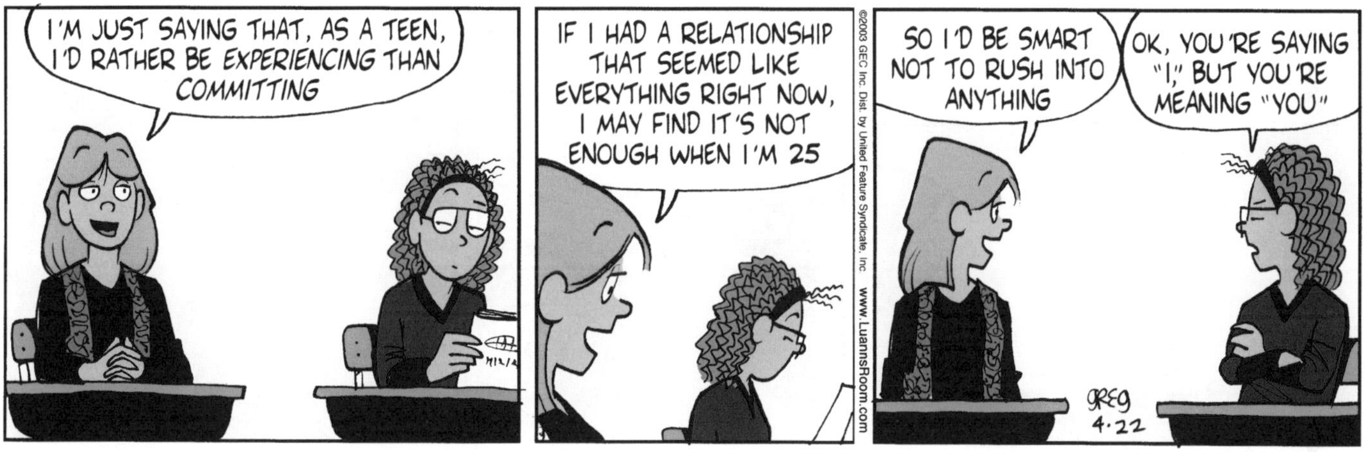
I'M JUST SAYING THAT, AS A TEEN, I'D RATHER BE *EXPERIENCING* THAN *COMMITTING*
IF I HAD A RELATIONSHIP THAT SEEMED LIKE EVERYTHING RIGHT NOW, I MAY FIND IT'S NOT ENOUGH WHEN I'M 25
SO I'D BE SMART NOT TO RUSH INTO ANYTHING
OK, YOU'RE SAYING "I," BUT YOU'RE MEANING "YOU"
©2003 GEC Inc. Dist. by United Feature Syndicate, Inc.
www.LuannsRoom.com
GREG 4·22

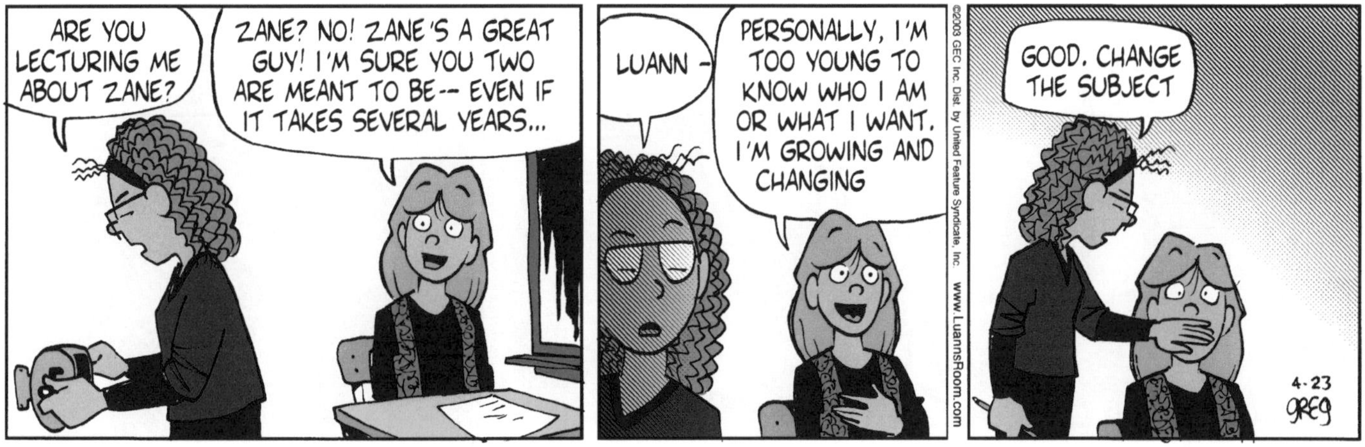
ARE YOU LECTURING ME ABOUT ZANE?
ZANE? NO! ZANE'S A GREAT GUY! I'M SURE YOU TWO ARE MEANT TO BE-- EVEN IF IT TAKES SEVERAL YEARS...
LUANN -
PERSONALLY, I'M TOO YOUNG TO KNOW WHO I AM OR WHAT I WANT. I'M GROWING AND CHANGING
GOOD. CHANGE THE SUBJECT
©2003 GEC Inc. Dist. by United Feature Syndicate, Inc.
www.LuannsRoom.com
4-23 GREG

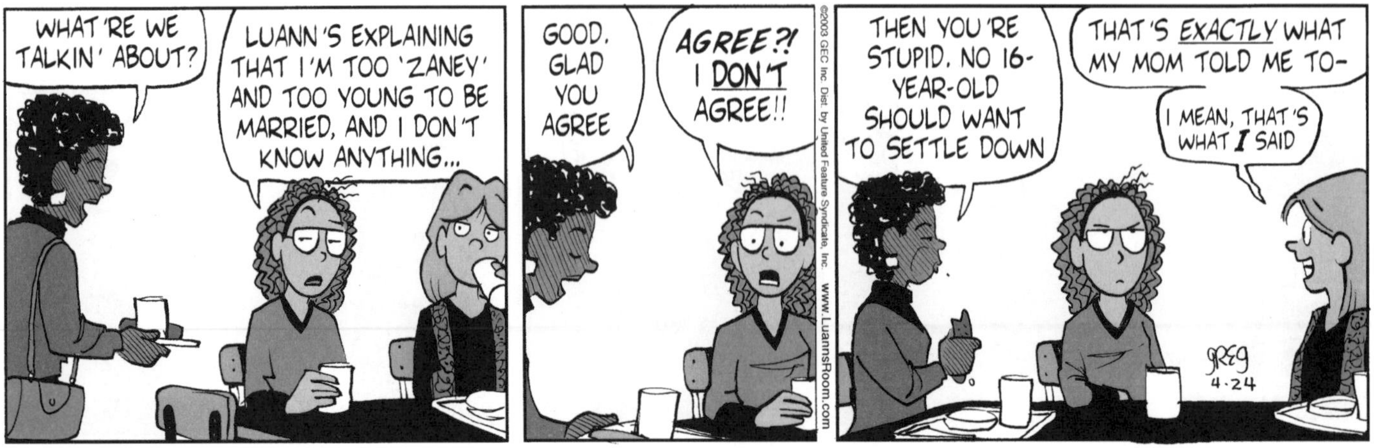
WHAT'RE WE TALKIN' ABOUT?
LUANN'S EXPLAINING THAT I'M TOO 'ZANEY' AND TOO YOUNG TO BE MARRIED, AND I DON'T KNOW ANYTHING...
GOOD. GLAD YOU AGREE
AGREE?! I DON'T AGREE!!
©2003 GEC Inc. Dist. by United Feature Syndicate, Inc. www.LuannsRoom.com
THEN YOU'RE STUPID. NO 16-YEAR-OLD SHOULD WANT TO SETTLE DOWN
THAT'S EXACTLY WHAT MY MOM TOLD ME TO-
I MEAN, THAT'S WHAT I SAID
GREG 4·24

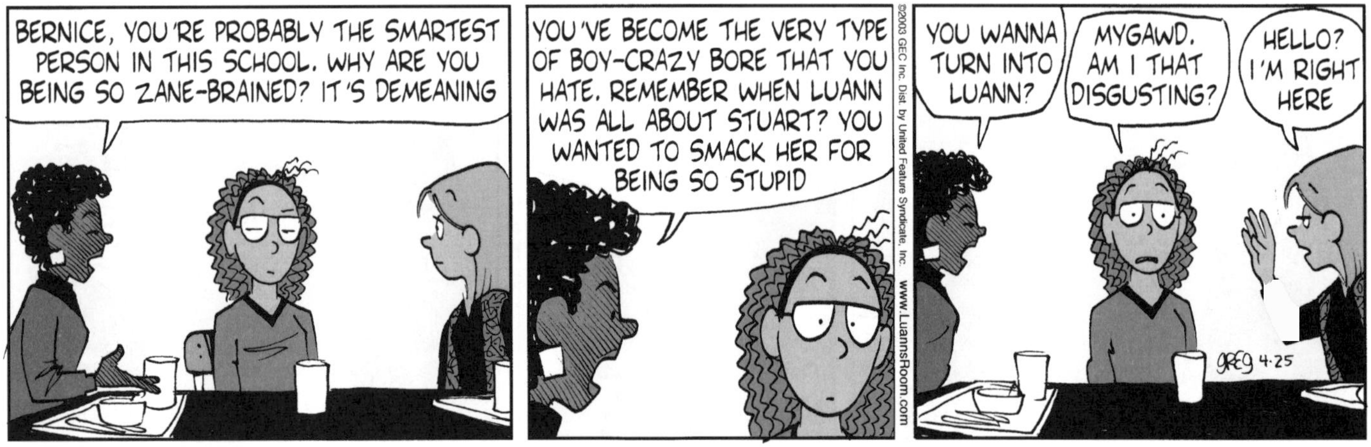
BERNICE, YOU'RE PROBABLY THE SMARTEST PERSON IN THIS SCHOOL. WHY ARE YOU BEING SO ZANE-BRAINED? IT'S DEMEANING
YOU'VE BECOME THE VERY TYPE OF BOY-CRAZY BORE THAT YOU HATE. REMEMBER WHEN LUANN WAS ALL ABOUT STUART? YOU WANTED TO SMACK HER FOR BEING SO STUPID
©2003 GEC Inc. Dist. by United Feature Syndicate, Inc. www.LuannsRoom.com
YOU WANNA TURN INTO LUANN?
MYGAWD. AM I THAT DISGUSTING?
HELLO? I'M RIGHT HERE
GREG 4·25

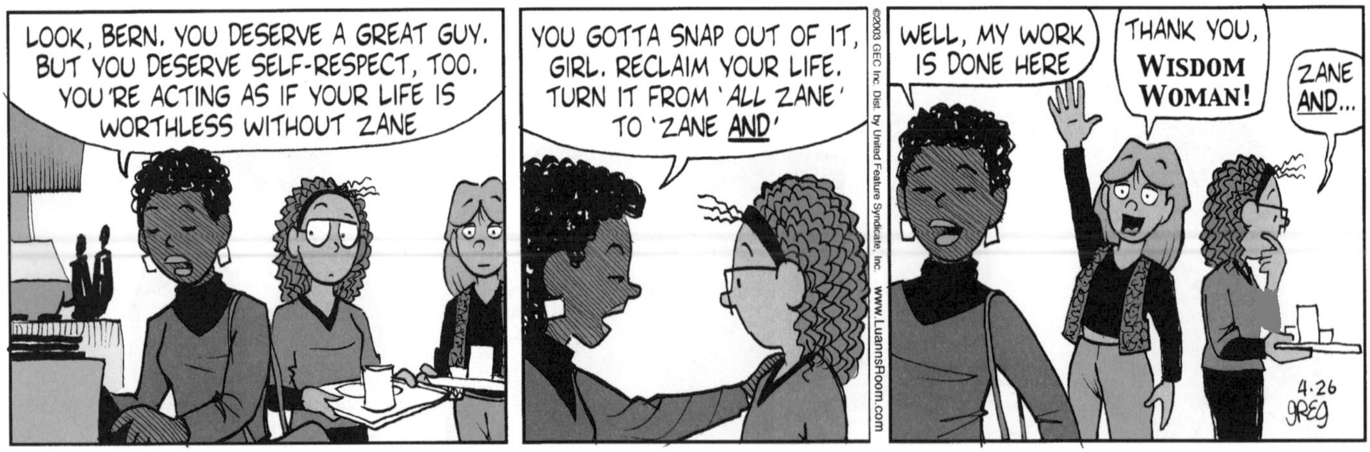
LOOK, BERN. YOU DESERVE A GREAT GUY. BUT YOU DESERVE SELF-RESPECT, TOO. YOU'RE ACTING AS IF YOUR LIFE IS WORTHLESS WITHOUT ZANE
YOU GOTTA SNAP OUT OF IT, GIRL. RECLAIM YOUR LIFE. TURN IT FROM 'ALL ZANE' TO 'ZANE AND'
©2003 GEC Inc. Dist. by United Feature Syndicate, Inc. www.LuannsRoom.com
WELL, MY WORK IS DONE HERE
THANK YOU, WISDOM WOMAN!
ZANE AND...
4·26 GREG

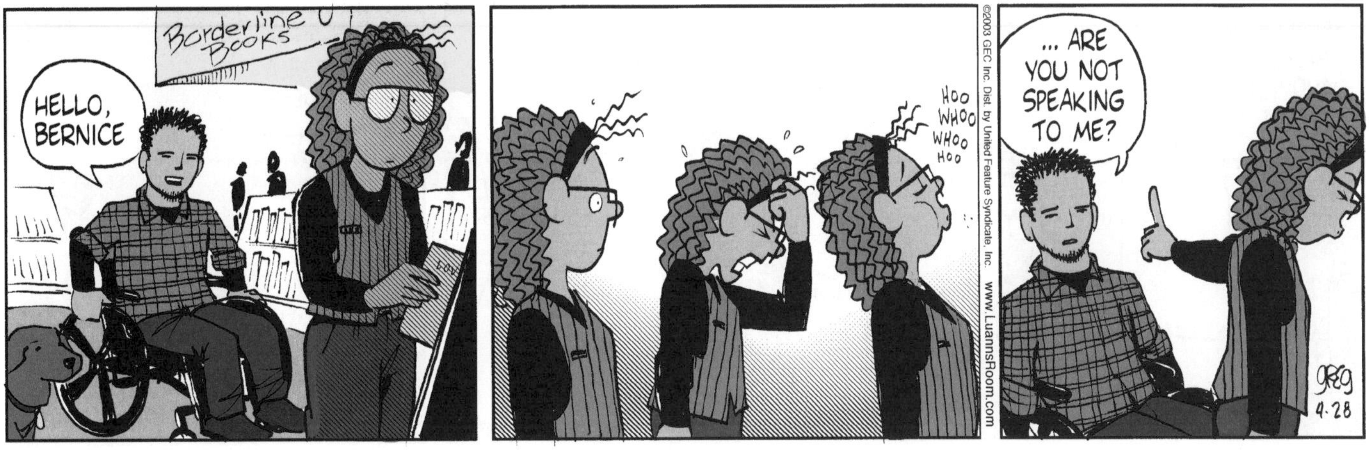
Borderline Books
HELLO, BERNICE
HOO WHOO WHOO HOO
©2003 GEC Inc. Dist. by United Feature Syndicate, Inc.
www.LuannsRoom.com
... ARE YOU NOT SPEAKING TO ME?
GREG 4.28

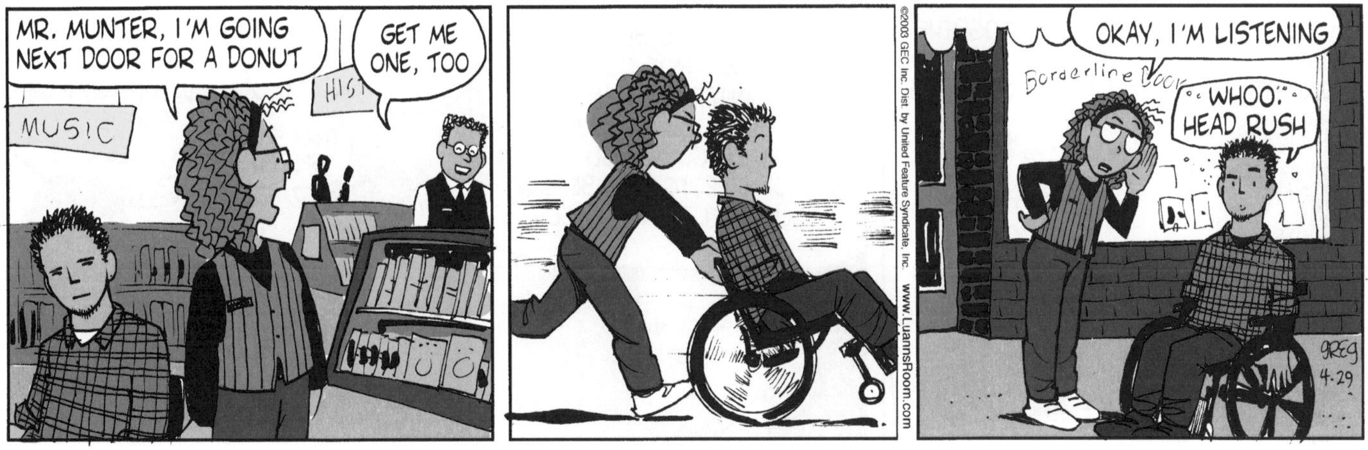
MR. MUNTER, I'M GOING NEXT DOOR FOR A DONUT
GET ME ONE, TOO
MUSIC
HIST
©2003 GEC Inc. Dist. by United Feature Syndicate, Inc.
www.LuannsRoom.com
OKAY, I'M LISTENING
WHOO. HEAD RUSH
GREG 4.29

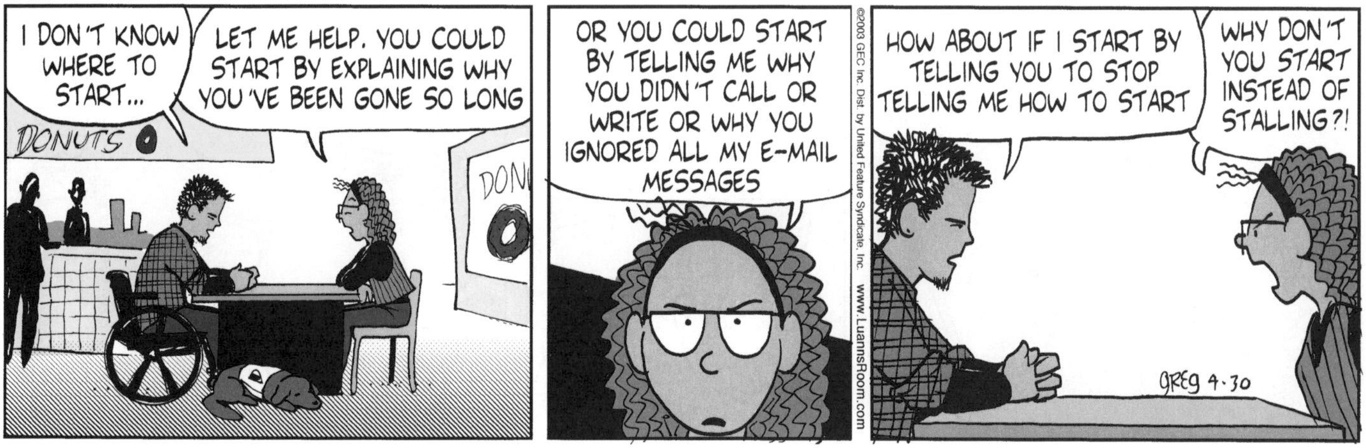
I DON'T KNOW WHERE TO START...
LET ME HELP. YOU COULD START BY EXPLAINING WHY YOU'VE BEEN GONE SO LONG
DONUTS
OR YOU COULD START BY TELLING ME WHY YOU DIDN'T CALL OR WRITE OR WHY YOU IGNORED ALL MY E-MAIL MESSAGES
©2003 GEC Inc. Dist. by United Feature Syndicate, Inc.
www.LuannsRoom.com
HOW ABOUT IF I START BY TELLING YOU TO STOP TELLING ME HOW TO START
WHY DON'T YOU START INSTEAD OF STALLING?!
GREG 4.30

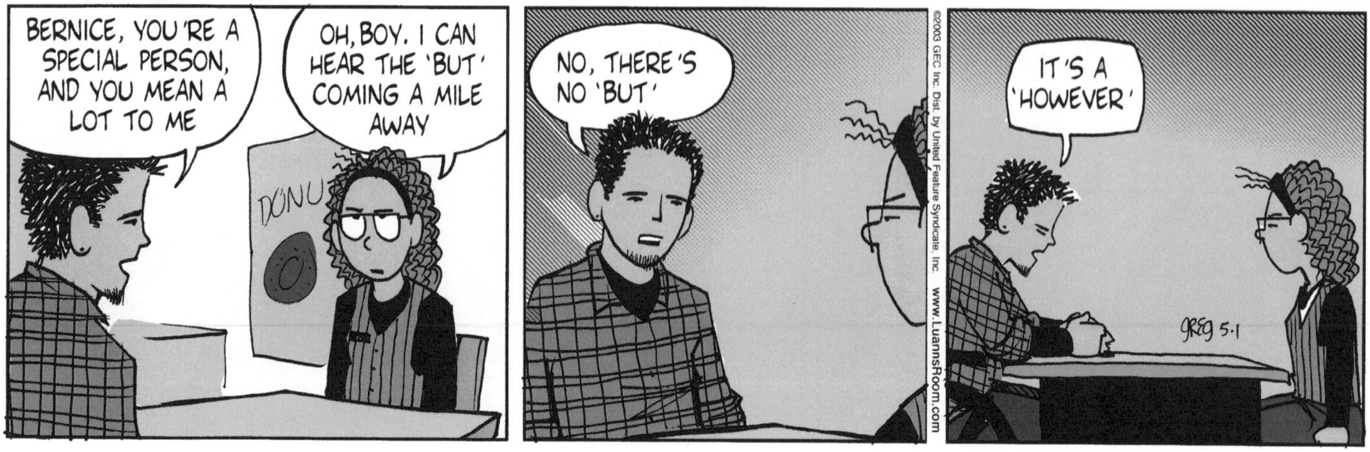
BERNICE, YOU'RE A SPECIAL PERSON, AND YOU MEAN A LOT TO ME
OH, BOY. I CAN HEAR THE 'BUT' COMING A MILE AWAY
DONU
NO, THERE'S NO 'BUT'
©2003 GEC Inc. Dist. by United Feature Syndicate, Inc.
www.LuannsRoom.com
IT'S A 'HOWEVER'
GREG 5·1

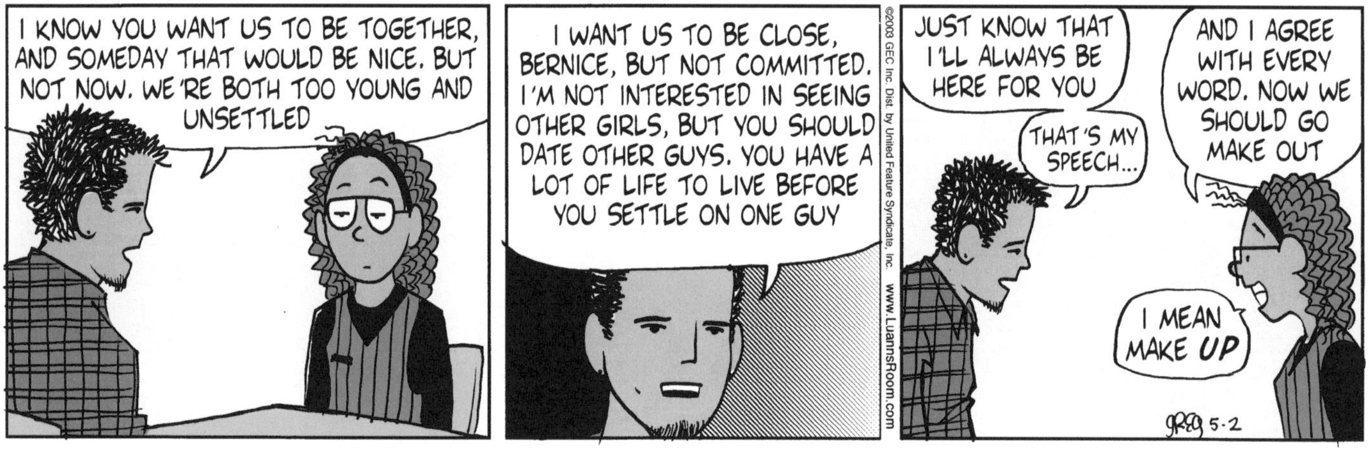
I KNOW YOU WANT US TO BE TOGETHER, AND SOMEDAY THAT WOULD BE NICE. BUT NOT NOW. WE'RE BOTH TOO YOUNG AND UNSETTLED
I WANT US TO BE CLOSE, BERNICE, BUT NOT COMMITTED. I'M NOT INTERESTED IN SEEING OTHER GIRLS, BUT YOU SHOULD DATE OTHER GUYS. YOU HAVE A LOT OF LIFE TO LIVE BEFORE YOU SETTLE ON ONE GUY
©2003 GEC Inc. Dist. by United Feature Syndicate, Inc.
www.LuannsRoom.com
JUST KNOW THAT I'LL ALWAYS BE HERE FOR YOU
THAT'S MY SPEECH...
AND I AGREE WITH EVERY WORD. NOW WE SHOULD GO MAKE OUT
I MEAN MAKE ***UP***
GREG 5·2

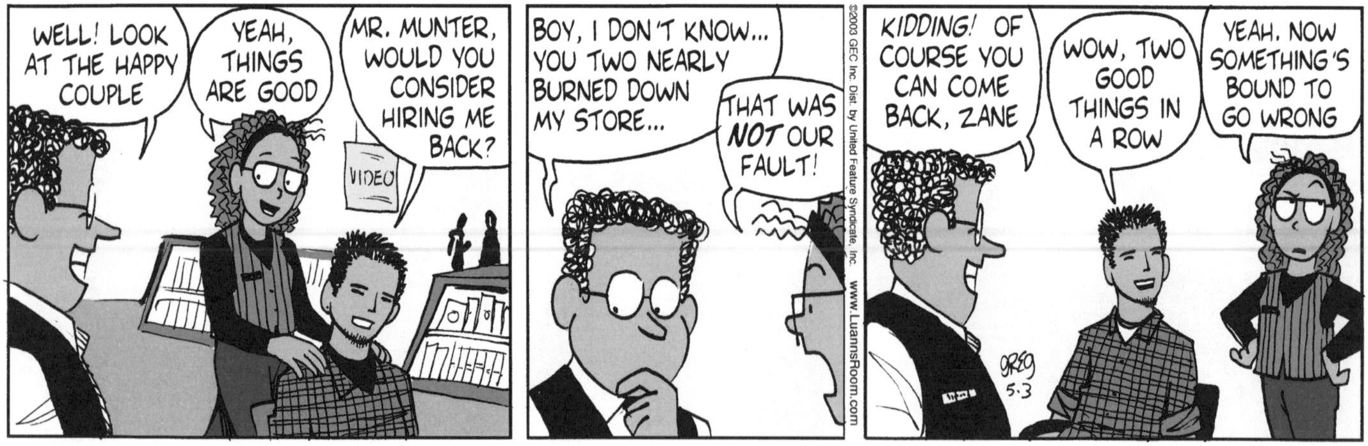
WELL! LOOK AT THE HAPPY COUPLE
YEAH, THINGS ARE GOOD
MR. MUNTER, WOULD YOU CONSIDER HIRING ME BACK?
VIDEO
BOY, I DON'T KNOW... YOU TWO NEARLY BURNED DOWN MY STORE...
THAT WAS ***NOT*** OUR FAULT!
©2003 GEC Inc. Dist. by United Feature Syndicate, Inc.
www.LuannsRoom.com
KIDDING! OF COURSE YOU CAN COME BACK, ZANE
WOW, TWO GOOD THINGS IN A ROW
YEAH. NOW SOMETHING'S BOUND TO GO WRONG
GREG 5·3

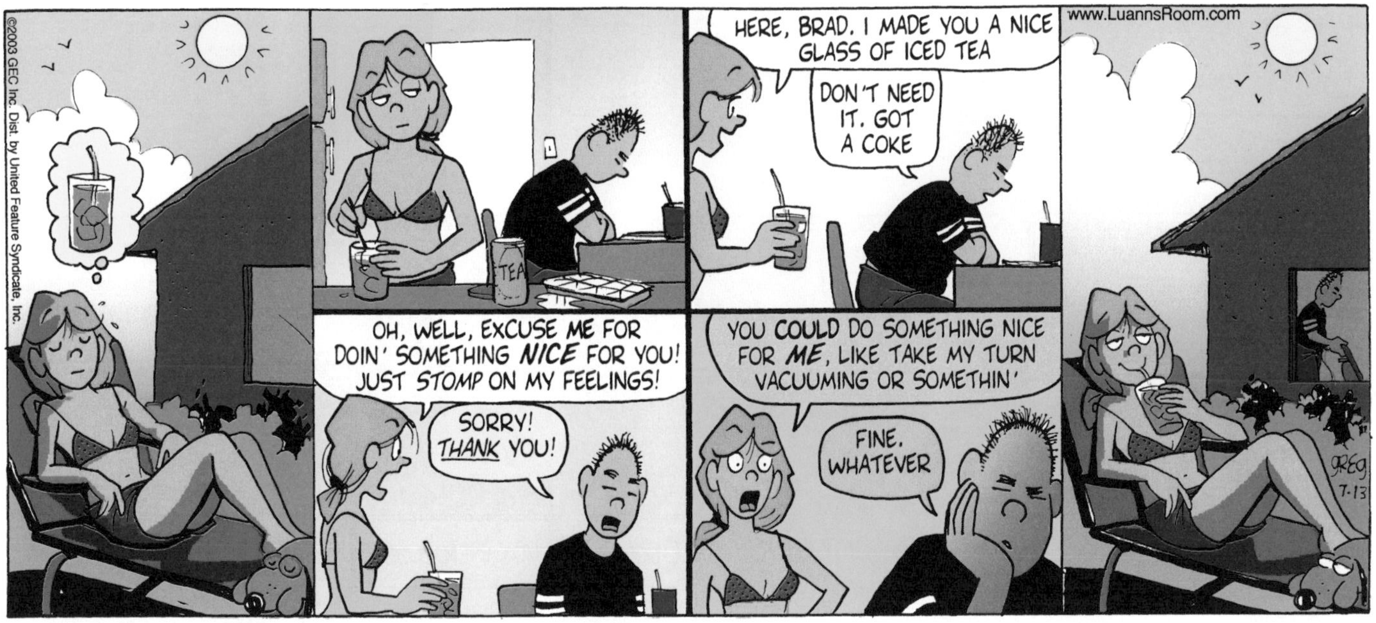
©2003 GEC Inc. Dist. by United Feature Syndicate, Inc.
TEA
HERE, BRAD. I MADE YOU A NICE GLASS OF ICED TEA
DON'T NEED IT. GOT A COKE
OH, WELL, EXCUSE ME FOR DOIN' SOMETHING NICE FOR YOU! JUST STOMP ON MY FEELINGS!
SORRY! THANK YOU!
YOU COULD DO SOMETHING NICE FOR ME, LIKE TAKE MY TURN VACUUMING OR SOMETHIN'
FINE. WHATEVER
www.LuannsRoom.com
GREG 7-13

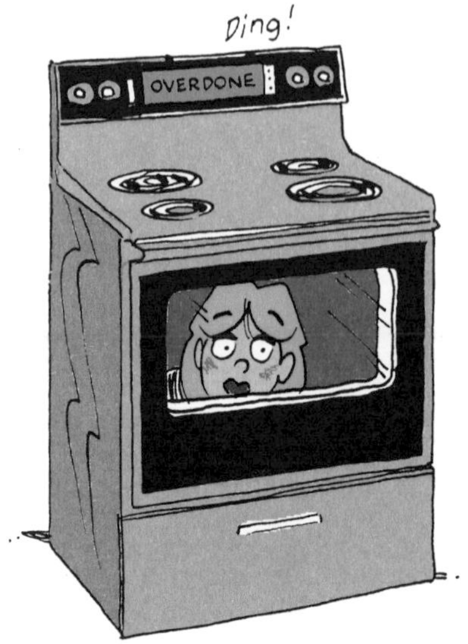
Ding!
OVERDONE

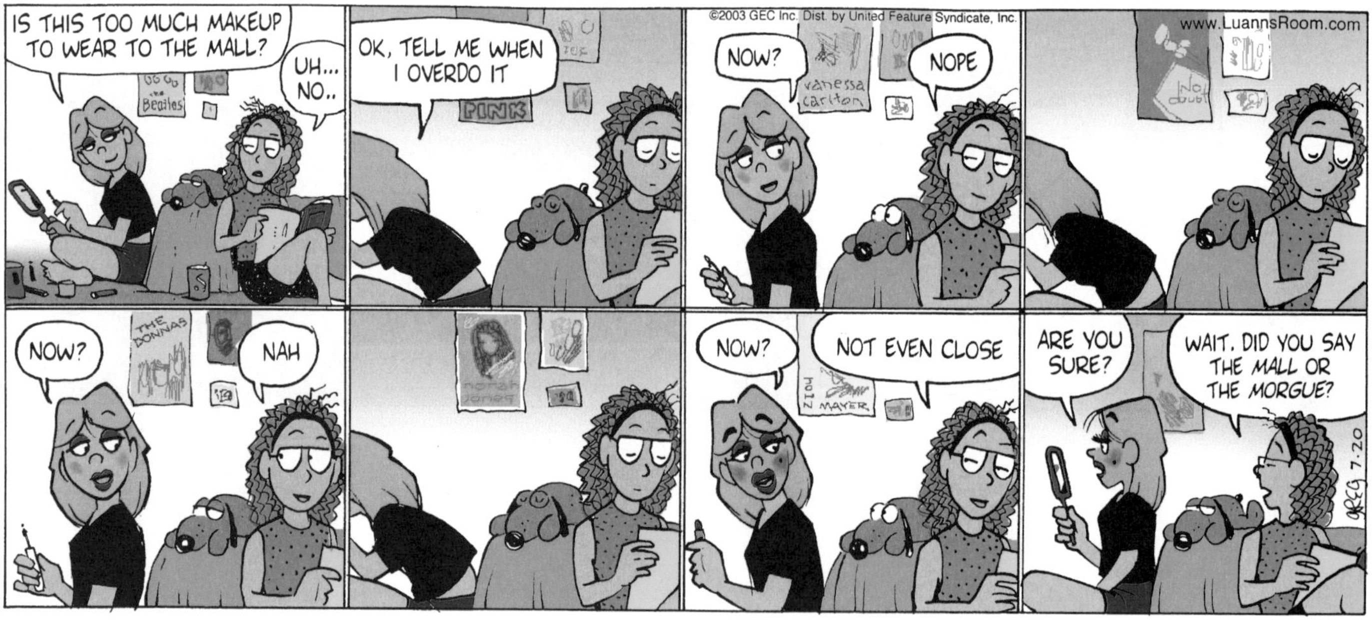
IS THIS TOO MUCH MAKEUP TO WEAR TO THE MALL?
UH... NO..
OK, TELL ME WHEN I OVERDO IT
©2003 GEC Inc. Dist. by United Feature Syndicate, Inc.
NOW?
NOPE
www.LuannsRoom.com
NOW?
NAH
NOW?
NOT EVEN CLOSE
ARE YOU SURE?
WAIT. DID YOU SAY THE MALL OR THE MORGUE?
GREG 7.20

MAN, I COULD NEVER BE A SWIMSUIT MODEL
WHY NOT?
ALL YOU GOTTA DO IS WALK LIKE THIS...
LOOK TOTALLY BORED...
MESS YOUR HAIR AND SPRAWL IN THE SAND...
©2003 GEC Inc. Dist. by United Feature Syndicate, Inc.
www.LuannsRoom.com
SEE? DON'T I LOOK LIKE A SWIMSUIT MODEL?
NO. YOU LOOK LIKE SOMETHING A WHALE THREW UP
GREG 7·27

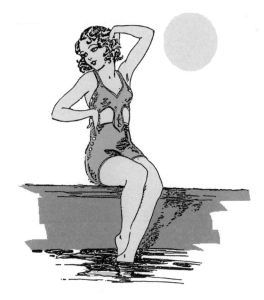

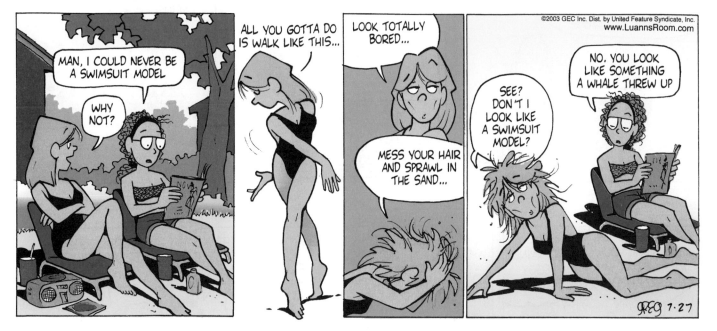

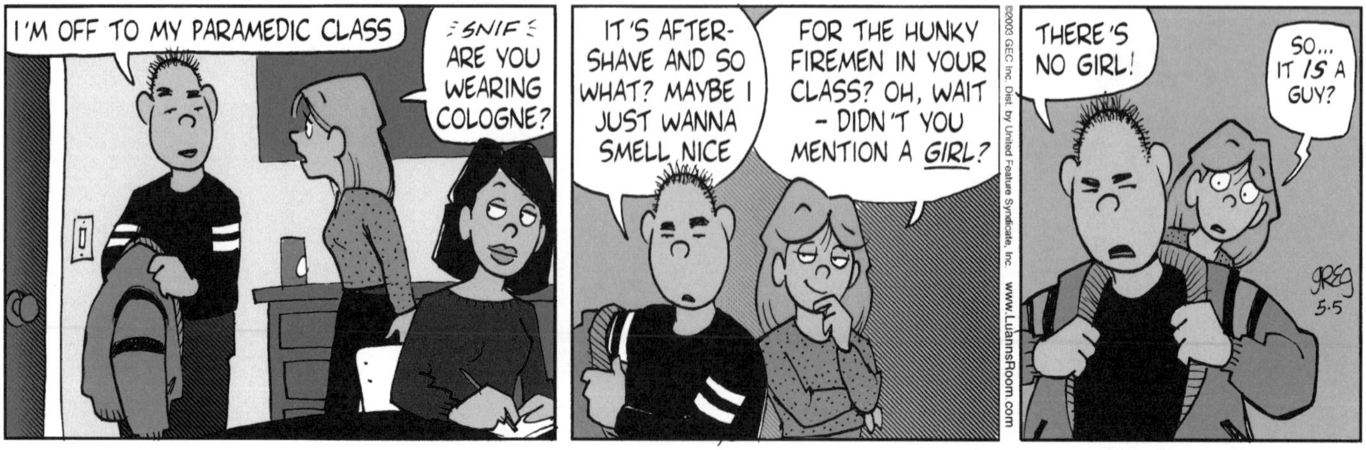
I'M OFF TO MY PARAMEDIC CLASS
SNIF ARE YOU WEARING COLOGNE?
IT'S AFTER-SHAVE AND SO WHAT? MAYBE I JUST WANNA SMELL NICE
FOR THE HUNKY FIREMEN IN YOUR CLASS? OH, WAIT - DIDN'T YOU MENTION A GIRL?
©2003 GEC Inc. Dist. by United Feature Syndicate, Inc. www.LuannsRoom.com
THERE'S NO GIRL!
SO... IT IS A GUY?
GREG 5·5

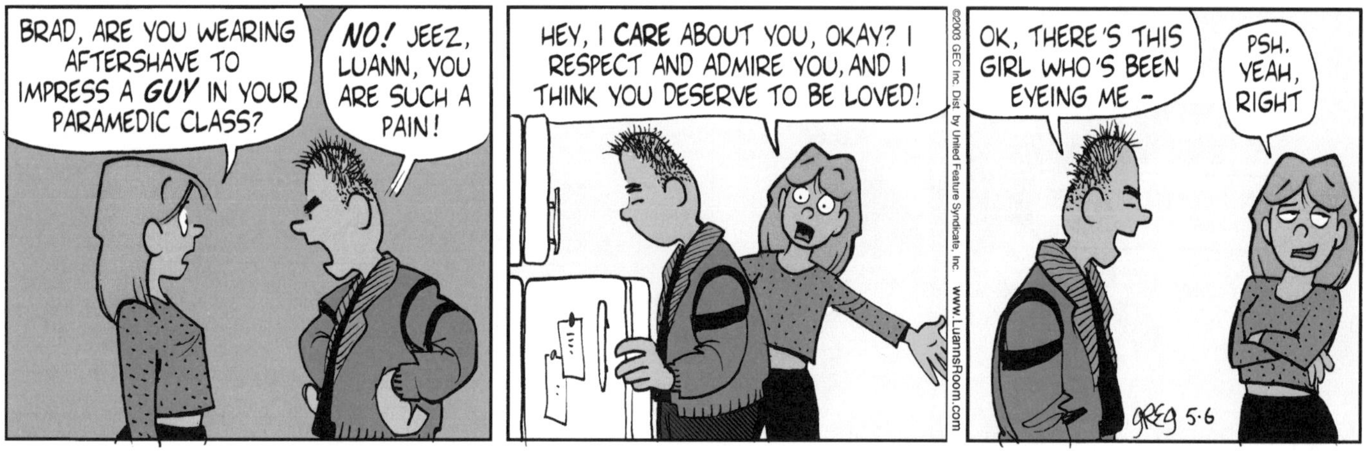
BRAD, ARE YOU WEARING AFTERSHAVE TO IMPRESS A GUY IN YOUR PARAMEDIC CLASS?
NO! JEEZ, LUANN, YOU ARE SUCH A PAIN!
HEY, I CARE ABOUT YOU, OKAY? I RESPECT AND ADMIRE YOU, AND I THINK YOU DESERVE TO BE LOVED!
©2003 GEC Inc. Dist. by United Feature Syndicate, Inc. www.LuannsRoom.com
OK, THERE'S THIS GIRL WHO'S BEEN EYEING ME -
PSH. YEAH, RIGHT
GREG 5·6

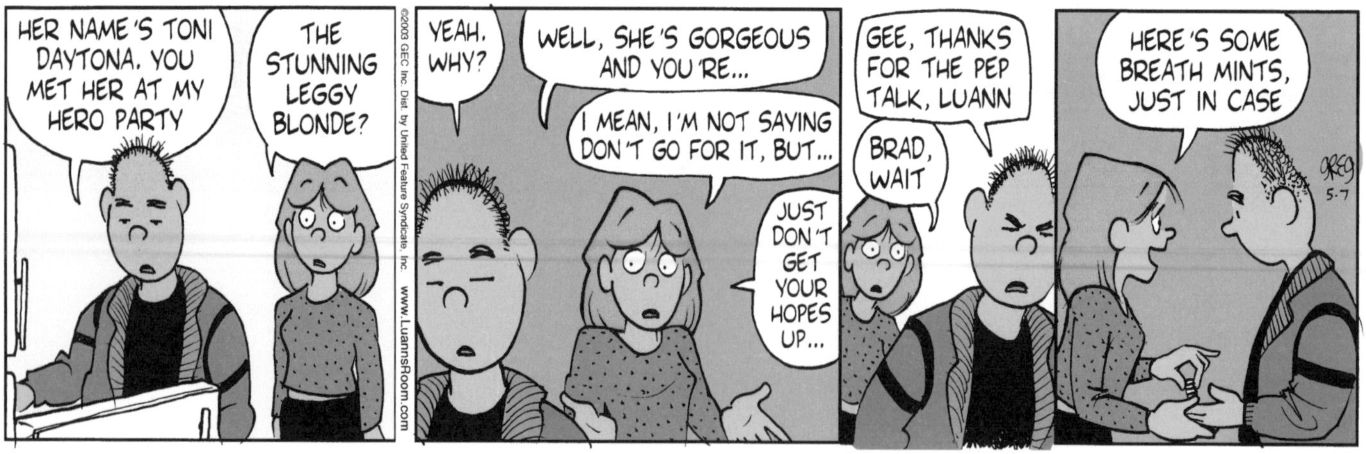
HER NAME'S TONI DAYTONA. YOU MET HER AT MY HERO PARTY
THE STUNNING LEGGY BLONDE?
©2003 GEC Inc. Dist. by United Feature Syndicate, Inc. www.LuannsRoom.com
YEAH. WHY?
WELL, SHE'S GORGEOUS AND YOU'RE...
I MEAN, I'M NOT SAYING DON'T GO FOR IT, BUT...
JUST DON'T GET YOUR HOPES UP...
GEE, THANKS FOR THE PEP TALK, LUANN
BRAD, WAIT
HERE'S SOME BREATH MINTS, JUST IN CASE
GREG 5·7

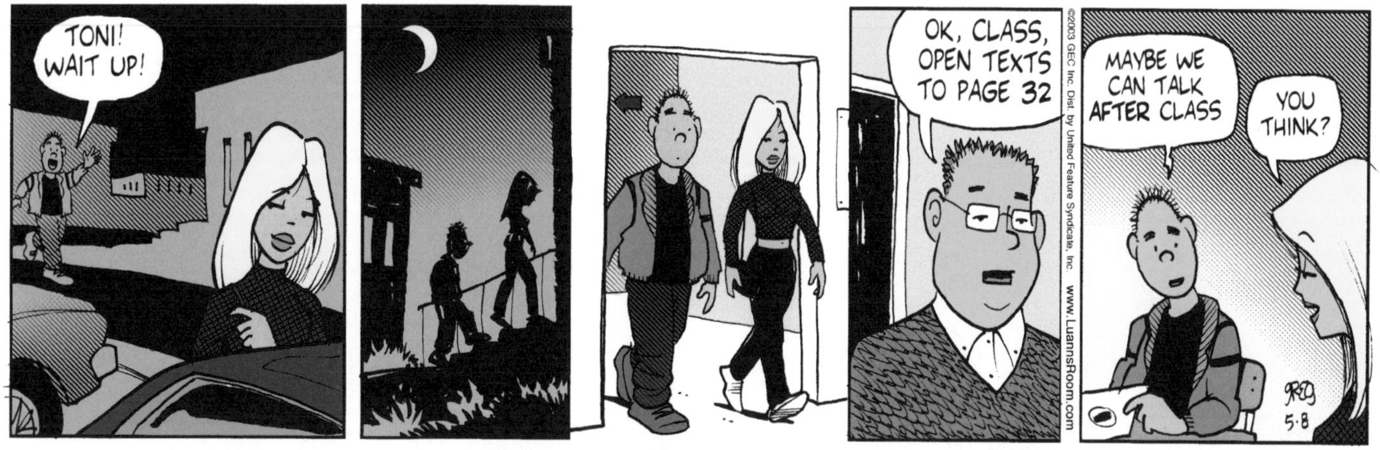
TONI! WAIT UP!
OK, CLASS, OPEN TEXTS TO PAGE 32
©2003 GEC Inc. Dist. by United Feature Syndicate, Inc.
www.LuannsRoom.com
MAYBE WE CAN TALK AFTER CLASS
YOU THINK?
GREG 5·8

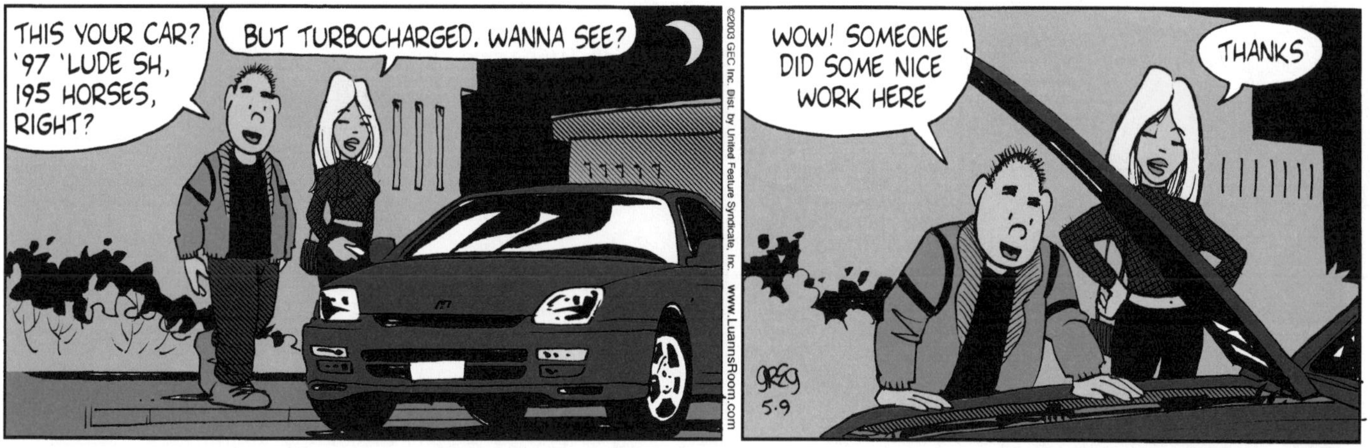
THIS YOUR CAR? '97 'LUDE SH, 195 HORSES, RIGHT?
BUT TURBOCHARGED. WANNA SEE?
©2003 GEC Inc. Dist. by United Feature Syndicate, Inc.
www.LuannsRoom.com
WOW! SOMEONE DID SOME NICE WORK HERE
THANKS
GREG 5·9

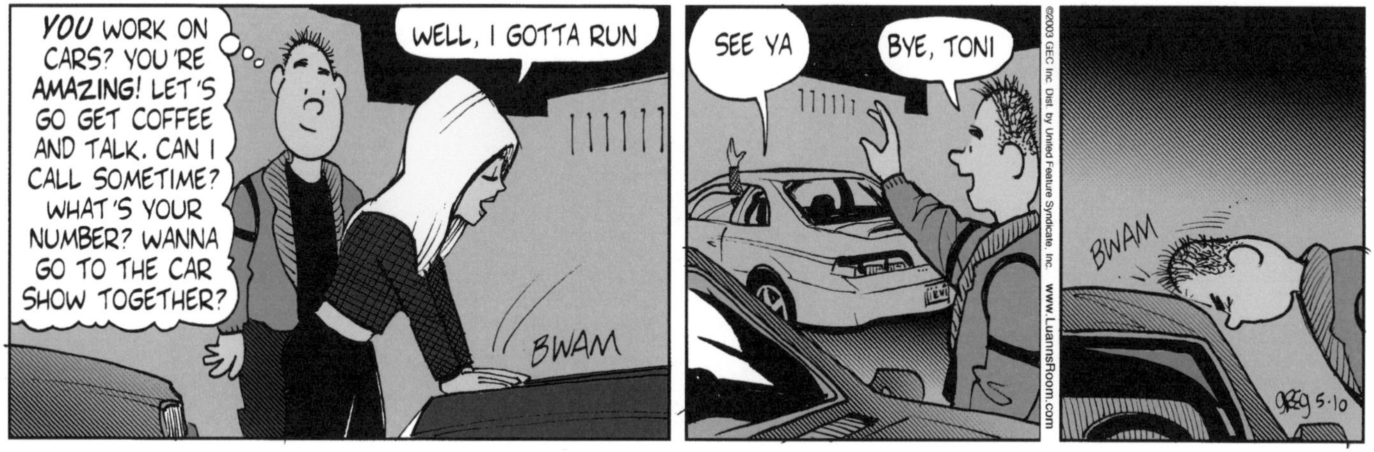
YOU WORK ON CARS? YOU'RE AMAZING! LET'S GO GET COFFEE AND TALK. CAN I CALL SOMETIME? WHAT'S YOUR NUMBER? WANNA GO TO THE CAR SHOW TOGETHER?
WELL, I GOTTA RUN
BWAM
SEE YA
BYE, TONI
©2003 GEC Inc. Dist. by United Feature Syndicate, Inc.
www.LuannsRoom.com
BWAM
GREG 5·10

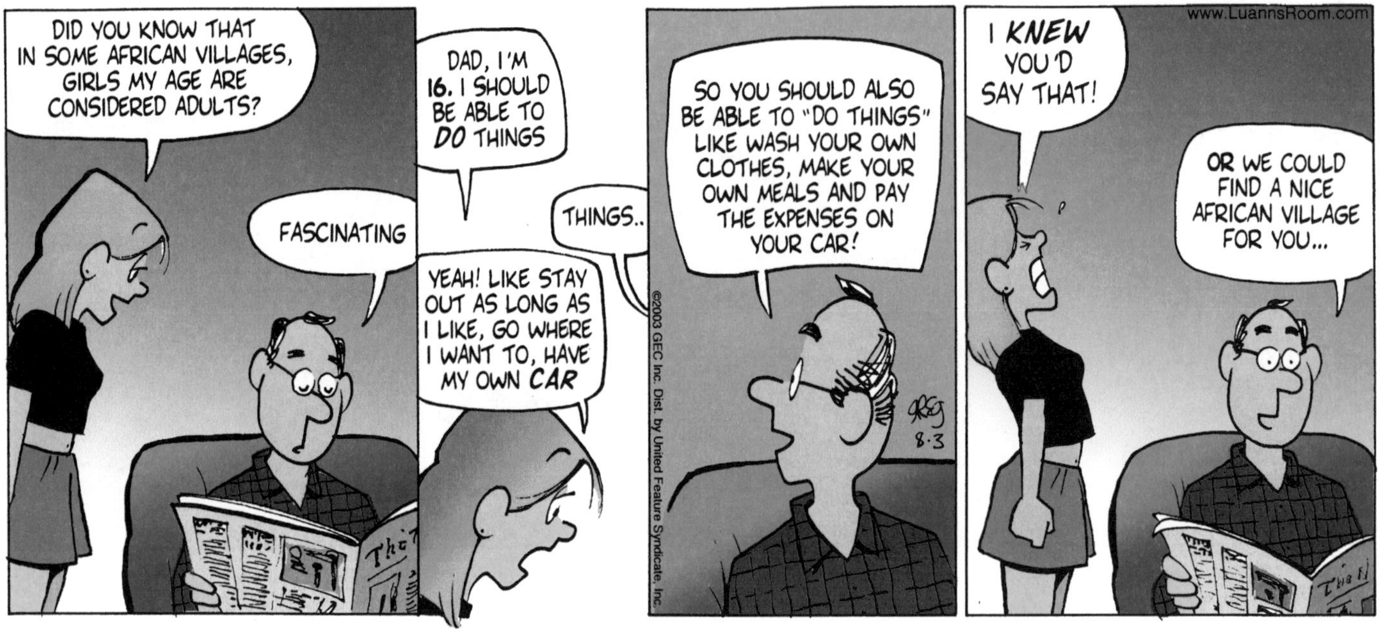
www.LuannsRoom.com
DID YOU KNOW THAT IN SOME AFRICAN VILLAGES, GIRLS MY AGE ARE CONSIDERED ADULTS?
FASCINATING
DAD, I'M 16. I SHOULD BE ABLE TO DO THINGS
THINGS..
YEAH! LIKE STAY OUT AS LONG AS I LIKE, GO WHERE I WANT TO, HAVE MY OWN CAR
SO YOU SHOULD ALSO BE ABLE TO "DO THINGS" LIKE WASH YOUR OWN CLOTHES, MAKE YOUR OWN MEALS AND PAY THE EXPENSES ON YOUR CAR!
©2003 GEC Inc. Dist. by United Feature Syndicate, Inc.
8·3
I KNEW YOU'D SAY THAT!
OR WE COULD FIND A NICE AFRICAN VILLAGE FOR YOU...

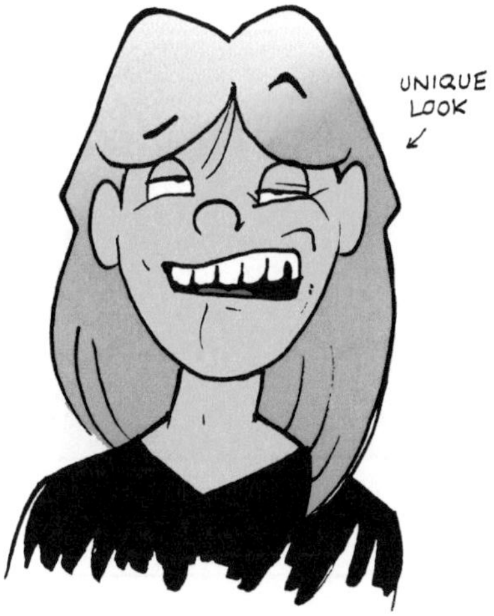
UNIQUE LOOK

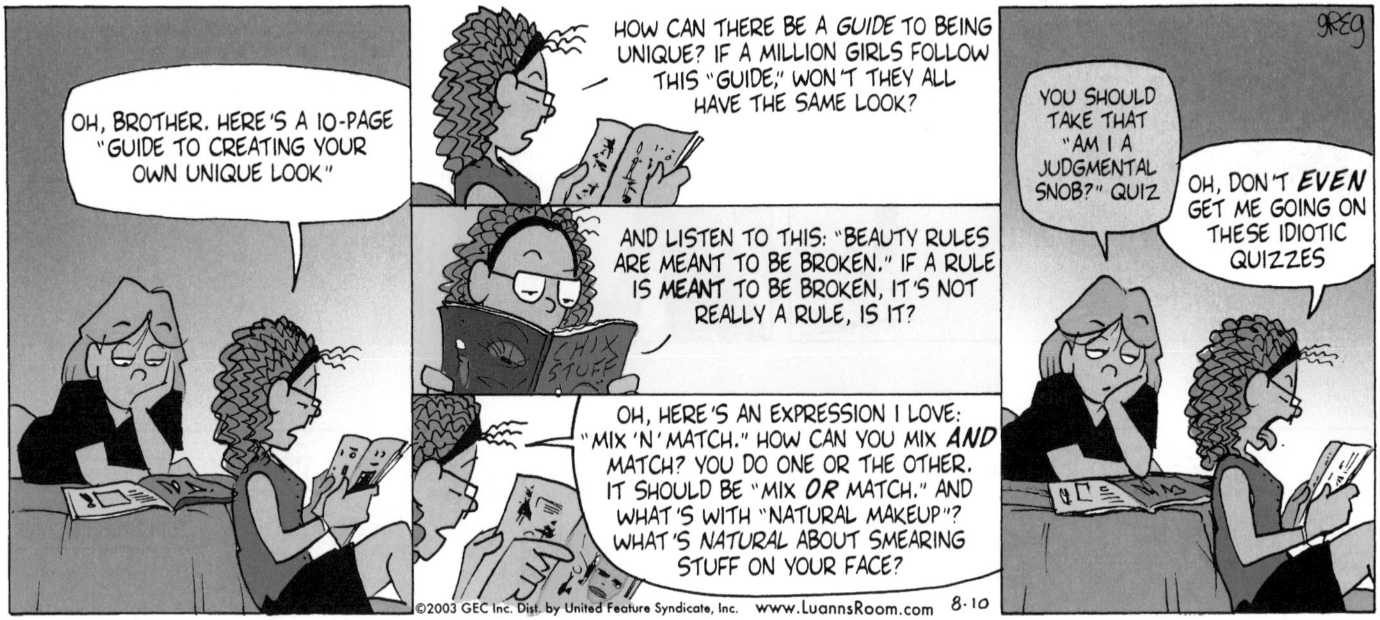
OH, BROTHER. HERE'S A 10-PAGE "GUIDE TO CREATING YOUR OWN UNIQUE LOOK"
HOW CAN THERE BE A *GUIDE* TO BEING UNIQUE? IF A MILLION GIRLS FOLLOW THIS "GUIDE," WON'T THEY ALL HAVE THE SAME LOOK?
AND LISTEN TO THIS: "BEAUTY RULES ARE MEANT TO BE BROKEN." IF A RULE IS **MEANT** TO BE BROKEN, IT'S NOT REALLY A RULE, IS IT?
CHIX STUFF
OH, HERE'S AN EXPRESSION I LOVE: "MIX 'N' MATCH." HOW CAN YOU MIX ***AND*** MATCH? YOU DO ONE OR THE OTHER. IT SHOULD BE "MIX ***OR*** MATCH." AND WHAT'S WITH "NATURAL MAKEUP"? WHAT'S *NATURAL* ABOUT SMEARING STUFF ON YOUR FACE?
YOU SHOULD TAKE THAT "AM I A JUDGMENTAL SNOB?" QUIZ
OH, DON'T ***EVEN*** GET ME GOING ON THESE IDIOTIC QUIZZES
GREG
©2003 GEC Inc. Dist. by United Feature Syndicate, Inc. www.LuannsRoom.com 8-10

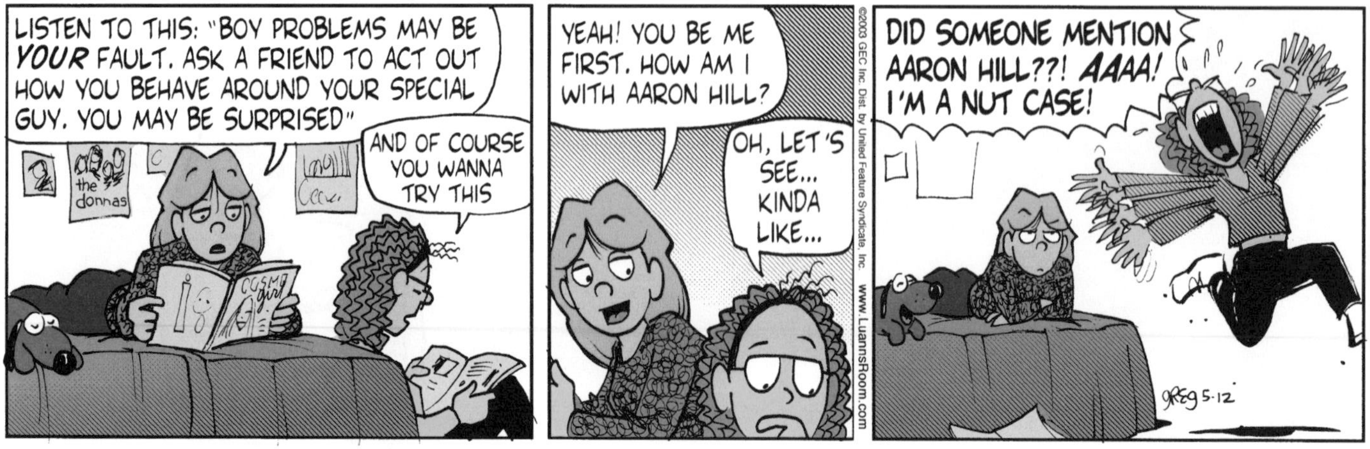
LISTEN TO THIS: "BOY PROBLEMS MAY BE ***YOUR*** FAULT. ASK A FRIEND TO ACT OUT HOW YOU BEHAVE AROUND YOUR SPECIAL GUY. YOU MAY BE SURPRISED"
AND OF COURSE YOU WANNA TRY THIS
the donnas
YEAH! YOU BE ME FIRST. HOW AM I WITH AARON HILL?
OH, LET'S SEE... KINDA LIKE...
©2003 GEC Inc. Dist. by United Feature Syndicate, Inc. www.LuannsRoom.com
DID SOMEONE MENTION AARON HILL??! ***AAAA!*** I'M A NUT CASE!
GREG 5-12

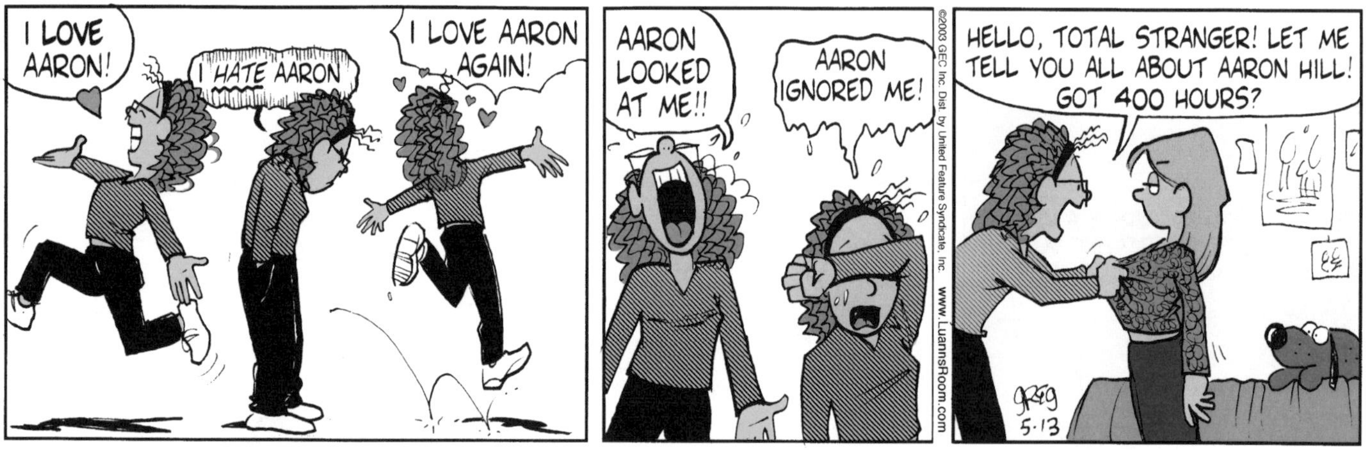
I **LOVE** AARON!
I *HATE* AARON
I LOVE AARON AGAIN!
AARON LOOKED AT ME!!
AARON IGNORED ME!
©2003 GEC Inc. Dist. by United Feature Syndicate, Inc. www.LuannsRoom.com
HELLO, TOTAL STRANGER! LET ME TELL YOU ALL ABOUT AARON HILL! GOT 400 HOURS?
GREG 5-13

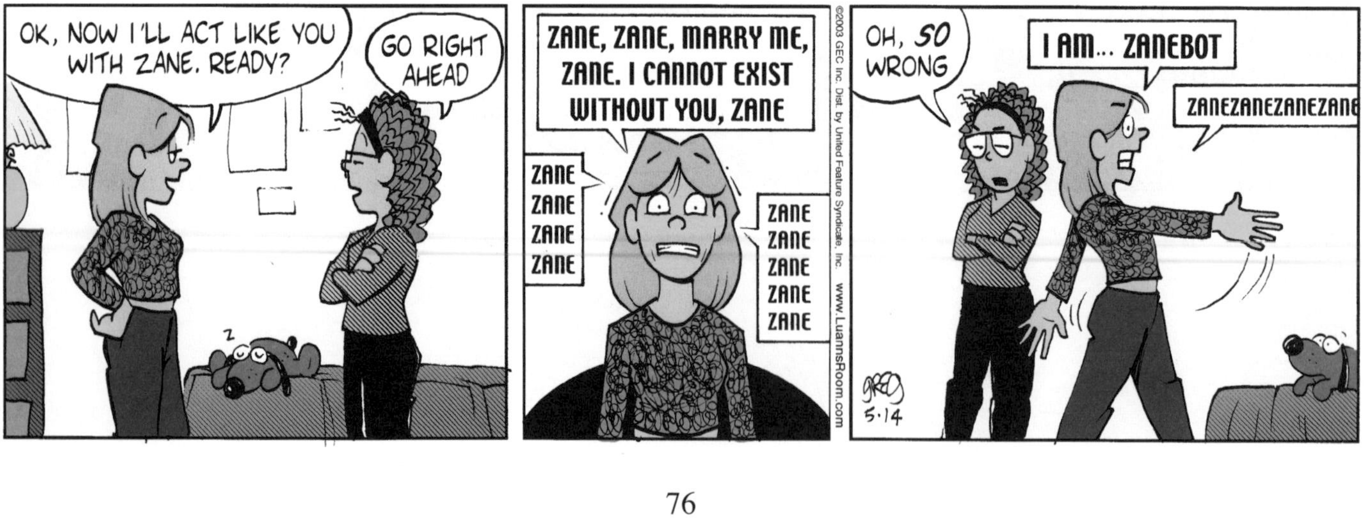
OK, NOW I'LL ACT LIKE YOU WITH ZANE. READY?
GO RIGHT AHEAD
ZANE, ZANE, MARRY ME, ZANE. I CANNOT EXIST WITHOUT YOU, ZANE
ZANE ZANE ZANE ZANE
ZANE ZANE ZANE ZANE ZANE
©2003 GEC Inc. Dist. by United Feature Syndicate, Inc. www.LuannsRoom.com
OH, *SO* WRONG
I AM... ZANEBOT
ZANEZANEZANEZANE
GREG 5-14

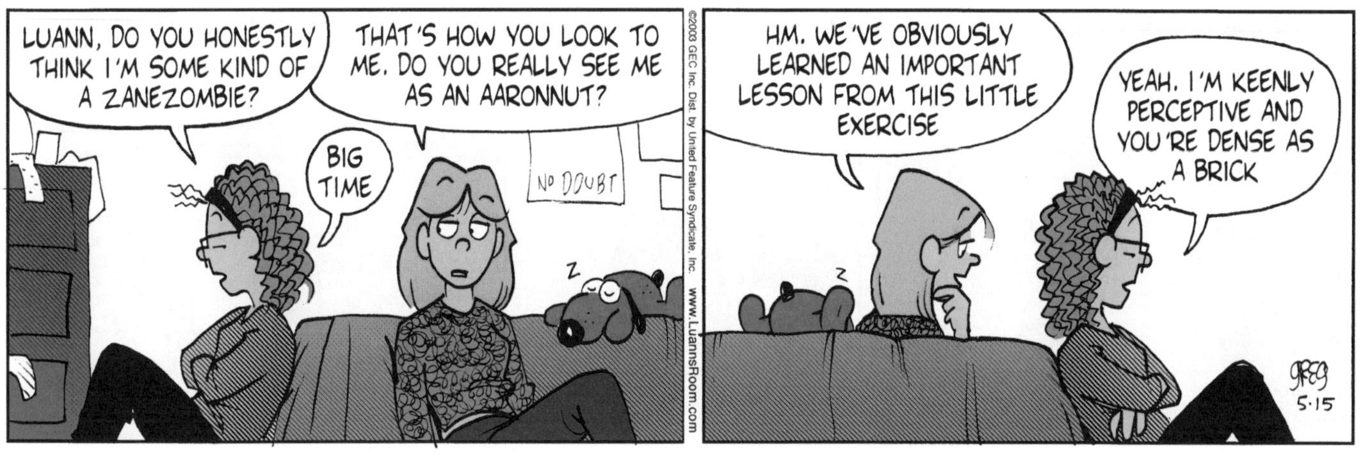
LUANN, DO YOU HONESTLY THINK I'M SOME KIND OF A ZANEZOMBIE?
BIG TIME
THAT'S HOW YOU LOOK TO ME. DO YOU REALLY SEE ME AS AN AARONNUT?
NO DOUBT
©2003 GEC Inc. Dist. by United Feature Syndicate, Inc. www.LuannsRoom.com
HM. WE'VE OBVIOUSLY LEARNED AN IMPORTANT LESSON FROM THIS LITTLE EXERCISE
YEAH. I'M KEENLY PERCEPTIVE AND YOU'RE DENSE AS A BRICK
GREG 5·15

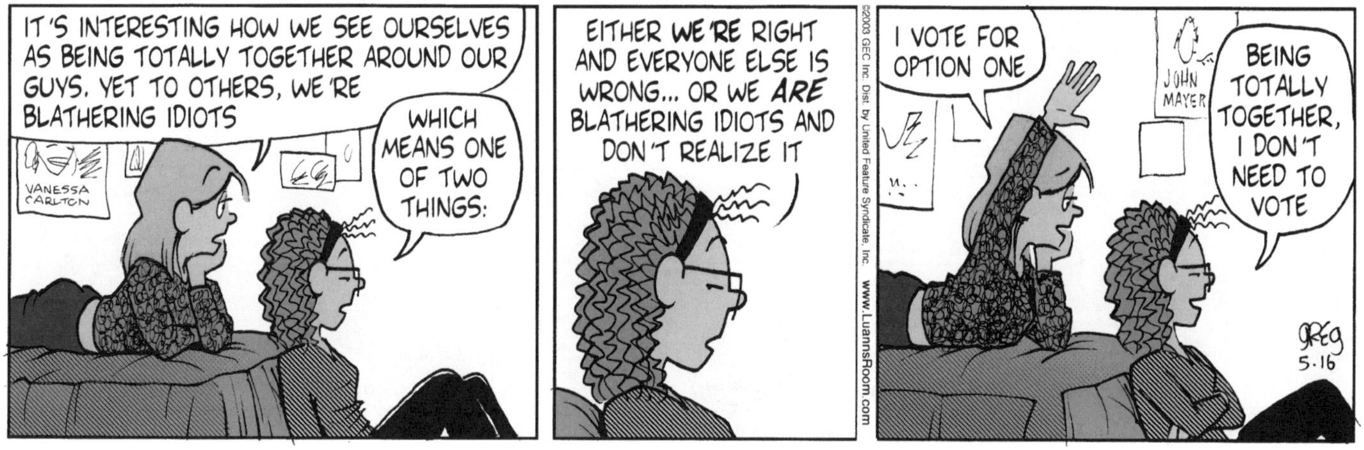
IT'S INTERESTING HOW WE SEE OURSELVES AS BEING TOTALLY TOGETHER AROUND OUR GUYS. YET TO OTHERS, WE'RE BLATHERING IDIOTS
VANESSA CARLTON
WHICH MEANS ONE OF TWO THINGS:
EITHER **WE'RE** RIGHT AND EVERYONE ELSE IS WRONG... OR WE ***ARE*** BLATHERING IDIOTS AND DON'T REALIZE IT
©2003 GEC Inc. Dist. by United Feature Syndicate, Inc. www.LuannsRoom.com
I VOTE FOR OPTION ONE
JOHN MAYER
BEING TOTALLY TOGETHER, I DON'T NEED TO VOTE
GREG 5·16

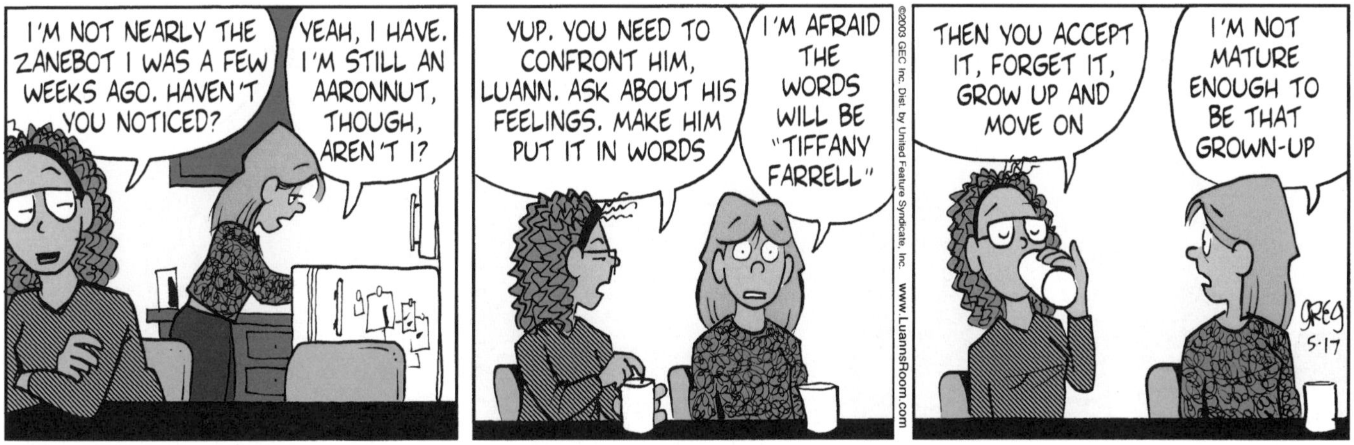
I'M NOT NEARLY THE ZANEBOT I WAS A FEW WEEKS AGO. HAVEN'T YOU NOTICED?
YEAH, I HAVE. I'M STILL AN AARONNUT, THOUGH, AREN'T I?
YUP. YOU NEED TO CONFRONT HIM, LUANN. ASK ABOUT HIS FEELINGS. MAKE HIM PUT IT IN WORDS
I'M AFRAID THE WORDS WILL BE "TIFFANY FARRELL"
©2003 GEC Inc. Dist. by United Feature Syndicate, Inc. www.LuannsRoom.com
THEN YOU ACCEPT IT, FORGET IT, GROW UP AND MOVE ON
I'M NOT MATURE ENOUGH TO BE THAT GROWN-UP
GREG 5·17

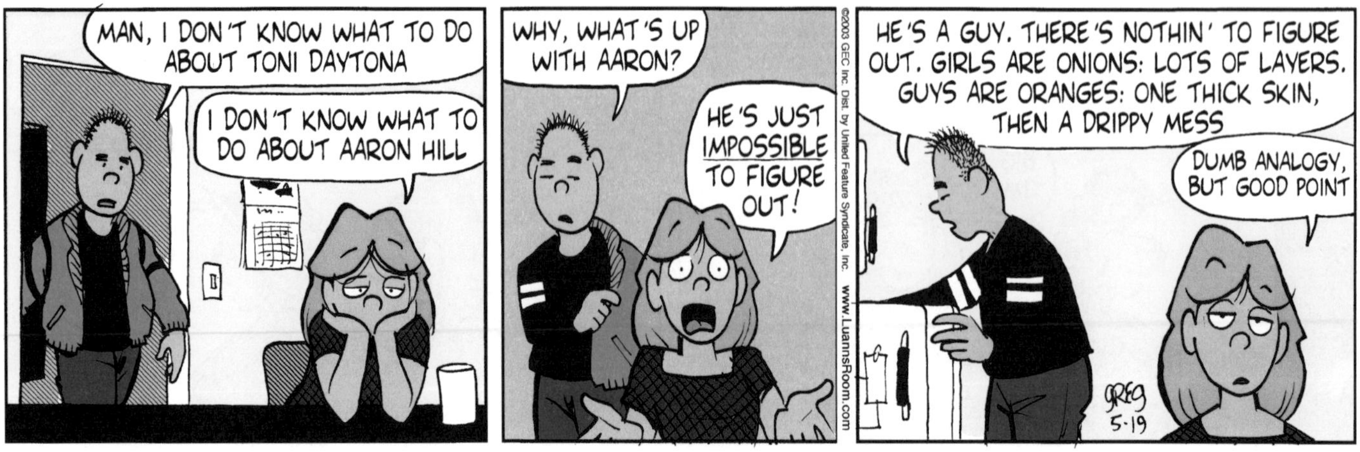
MAN, I DON'T KNOW WHAT TO DO ABOUT TONI DAYTONA
I DON'T KNOW WHAT TO DO ABOUT AARON HILL
WHY, WHAT'S UP WITH AARON?
HE'S JUST IMPOSSIBLE TO FIGURE OUT!
©2003 GEC Inc. Dist. by United Feature Syndicate, Inc. www.LuannsRoom.com
HE'S A GUY. THERE'S NOTHIN' TO FIGURE OUT. GIRLS ARE ONIONS: LOTS OF LAYERS. GUYS ARE ORANGES: ONE THICK SKIN, THEN A DRIPPY MESS
DUMB ANALOGY, BUT GOOD POINT
GREG 5-19

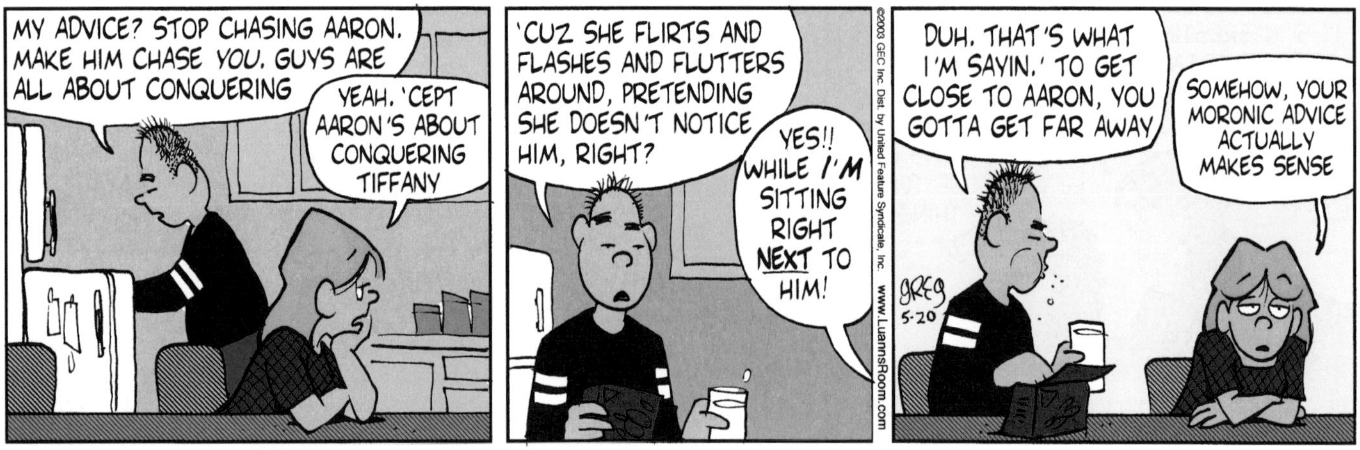
MY ADVICE? STOP CHASING AARON. MAKE HIM CHASE YOU. GUYS ARE ALL ABOUT CONQUERING
YEAH. 'CEPT AARON'S ABOUT CONQUERING TIFFANY
'CUZ SHE FLIRTS AND FLASHES AND FLUTTERS AROUND, PRETENDING SHE DOESN'T NOTICE HIM, RIGHT?
YES!! WHILE I'M SITTING RIGHT NEXT TO HIM!
©2003 GEC Inc. Dist. by United Feature Syndicate, Inc. www.LuannsRoom.com
DUH. THAT'S WHAT I'M SAYIN.' TO GET CLOSE TO AARON, YOU GOTTA GET FAR AWAY
SOMEHOW, YOUR MORONIC ADVICE ACTUALLY MAKES SENSE
GREG 5-20

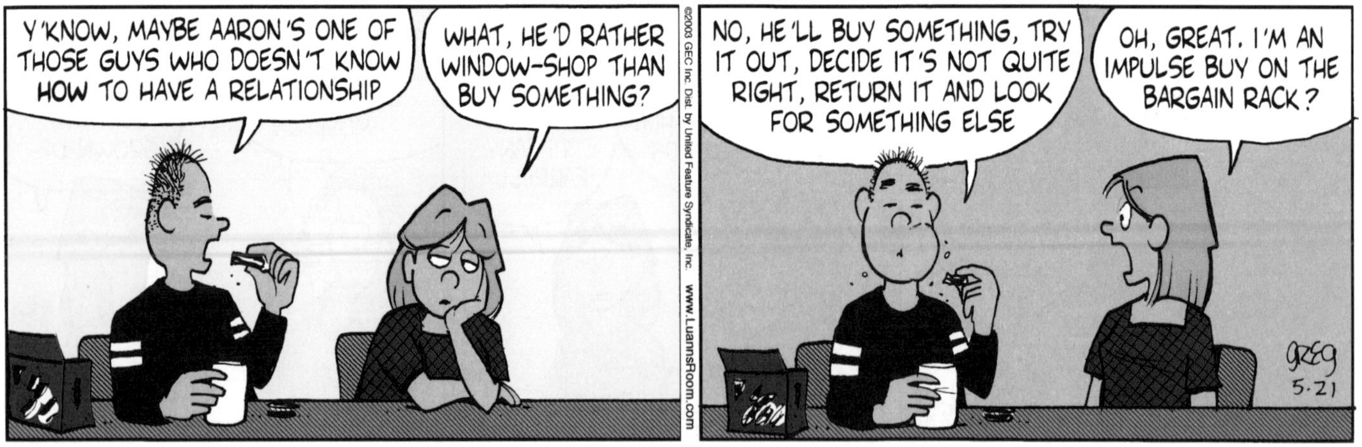
Y'KNOW, MAYBE AARON'S ONE OF THOSE GUYS WHO DOESN'T KNOW HOW TO HAVE A RELATIONSHIP
WHAT, HE'D RATHER WINDOW-SHOP THAN BUY SOMETHING?
©2003 GEC Inc. Dist. by United Feature Syndicate, Inc. www.LuannsRoom.com
NO, HE'LL BUY SOMETHING, TRY IT OUT, DECIDE IT'S NOT QUITE RIGHT, RETURN IT AND LOOK FOR SOMETHING ELSE
OH, GREAT. I'M AN IMPULSE BUY ON THE BARGAIN RACK?
GREG 5-21

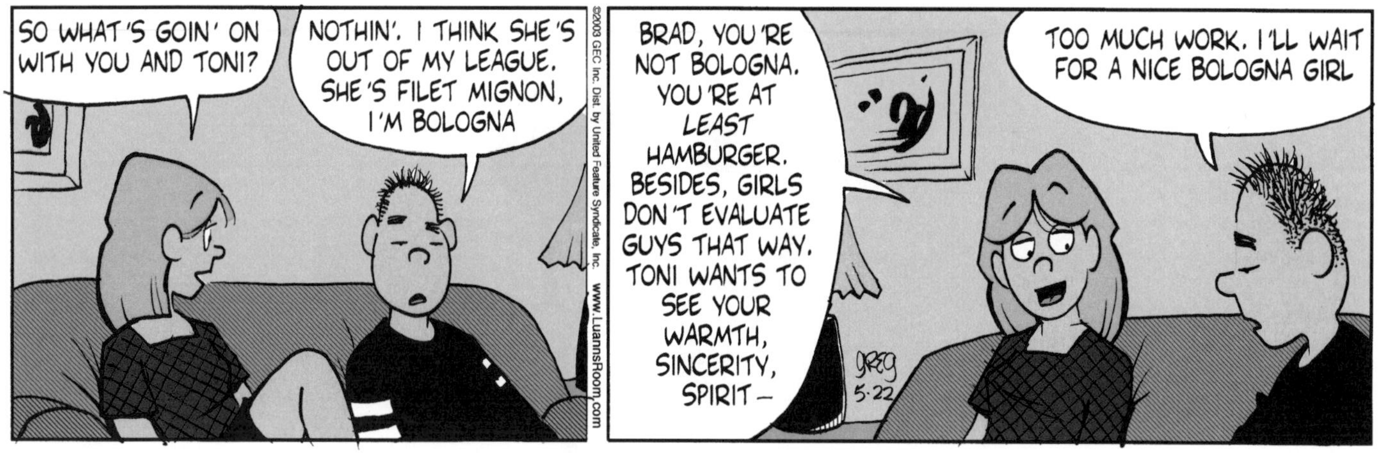
SO WHAT'S GOIN' ON WITH YOU AND TONI?
NOTHIN'. I THINK SHE'S OUT OF MY LEAGUE. SHE'S FILET MIGNON, I'M BOLOGNA
BRAD, YOU'RE NOT BOLOGNA. YOU'RE AT LEAST HAMBURGER. BESIDES, GIRLS DON'T EVALUATE GUYS THAT WAY. TONI WANTS TO SEE YOUR WARMTH, SINCERITY, SPIRIT –
TOO MUCH WORK. I'LL WAIT FOR A NICE BOLOGNA GIRL
©2003 GEC Inc. Dist. by United Feature Syndicate, Inc. www.LuannsRoom.com
GREG 5·22

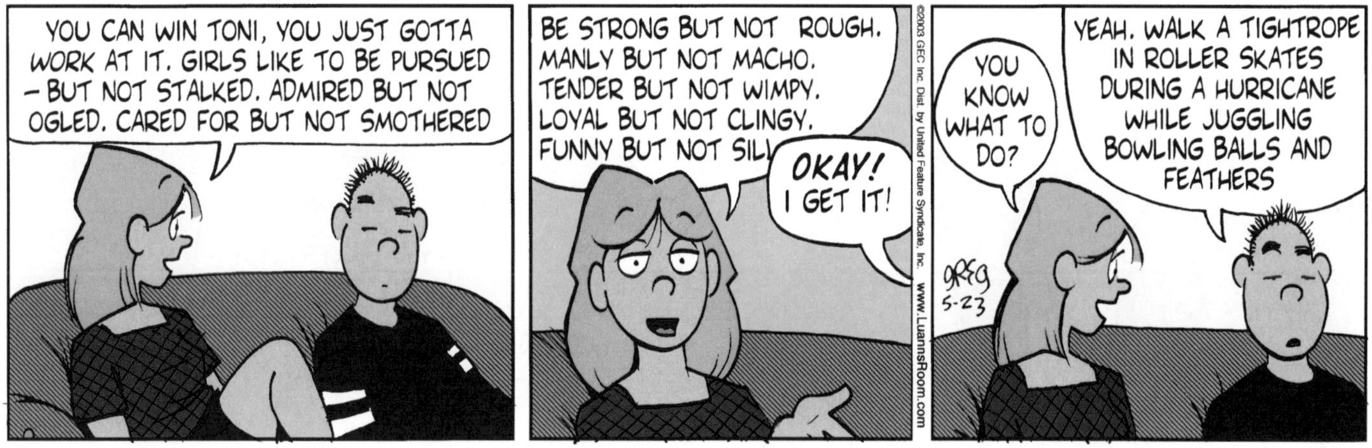
YOU CAN WIN TONI, YOU JUST GOTTA WORK AT IT. GIRLS LIKE TO BE PURSUED – BUT NOT STALKED. ADMIRED BUT NOT OGLED. CARED FOR BUT NOT SMOTHERED
BE STRONG BUT NOT ROUGH. MANLY BUT NOT MACHO. TENDER BUT NOT WIMPY. LOYAL BUT NOT CLINGY. FUNNY BUT NOT SIL
OKAY! I GET IT!
YOU KNOW WHAT TO DO?
YEAH. WALK A TIGHTROPE IN ROLLER SKATES DURING A HURRICANE WHILE JUGGLING BOWLING BALLS AND FEATHERS
©2003 GEC Inc. Dist. by United Feature Syndicate, Inc. www.LuannsRoom.com
GREG 5-23

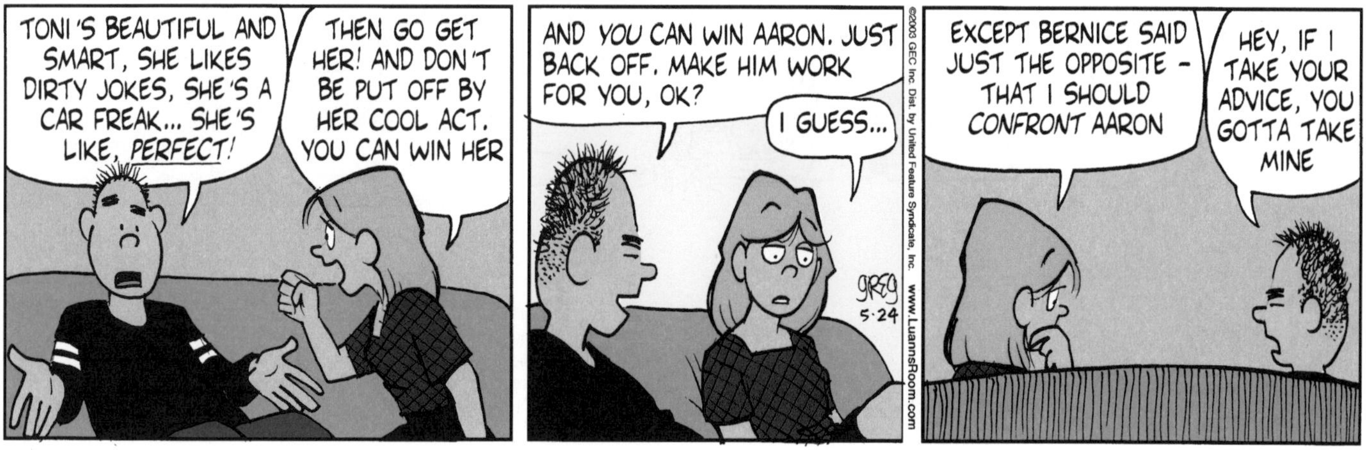
TONI'S BEAUTIFUL AND SMART, SHE LIKES DIRTY JOKES, SHE'S A CAR FREAK... SHE'S LIKE, PERFECT!
THEN GO GET HER! AND DON'T BE PUT OFF BY HER COOL ACT. YOU CAN WIN HER
AND YOU CAN WIN AARON. JUST BACK OFF. MAKE HIM WORK FOR YOU, OK?
I GUESS...
EXCEPT BERNICE SAID JUST THE OPPOSITE – THAT I SHOULD CONFRONT AARON
HEY, IF I TAKE YOUR ADVICE, YOU GOTTA TAKE MINE
©2003 GEC Inc. Dist. by United Feature Syndicate, Inc. www.LuannsRoom.com
GREG 5·24

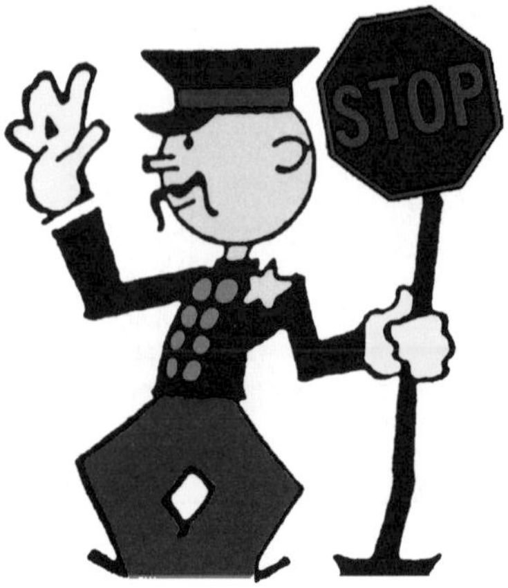
STOP

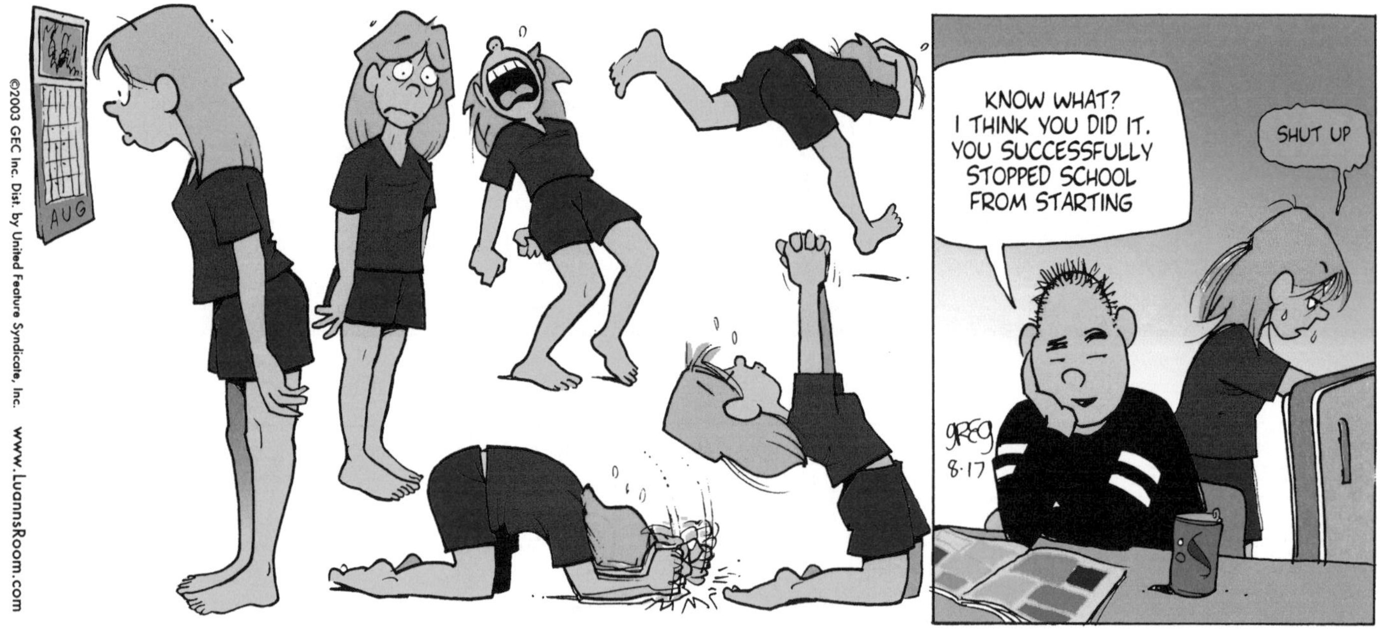
AUG
KNOW WHAT? I THINK YOU DID IT. YOU SUCCESSFULLY STOPPED SCHOOL FROM STARTING
SHUT UP
GREG 8·17
©2003 GEC Inc. Dist. by United Feature Syndicate, Inc.
www.LuannsRoom.com

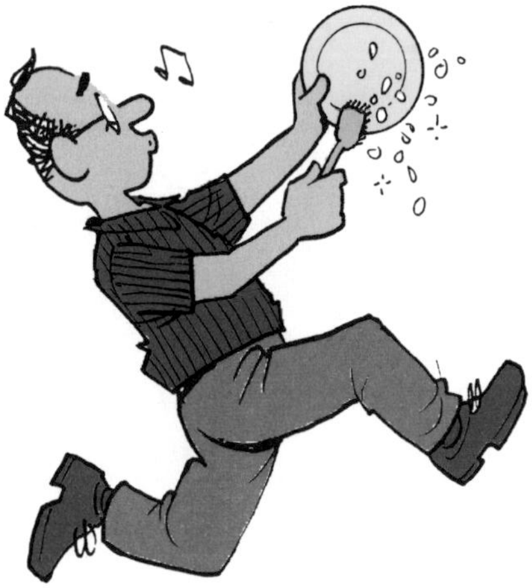

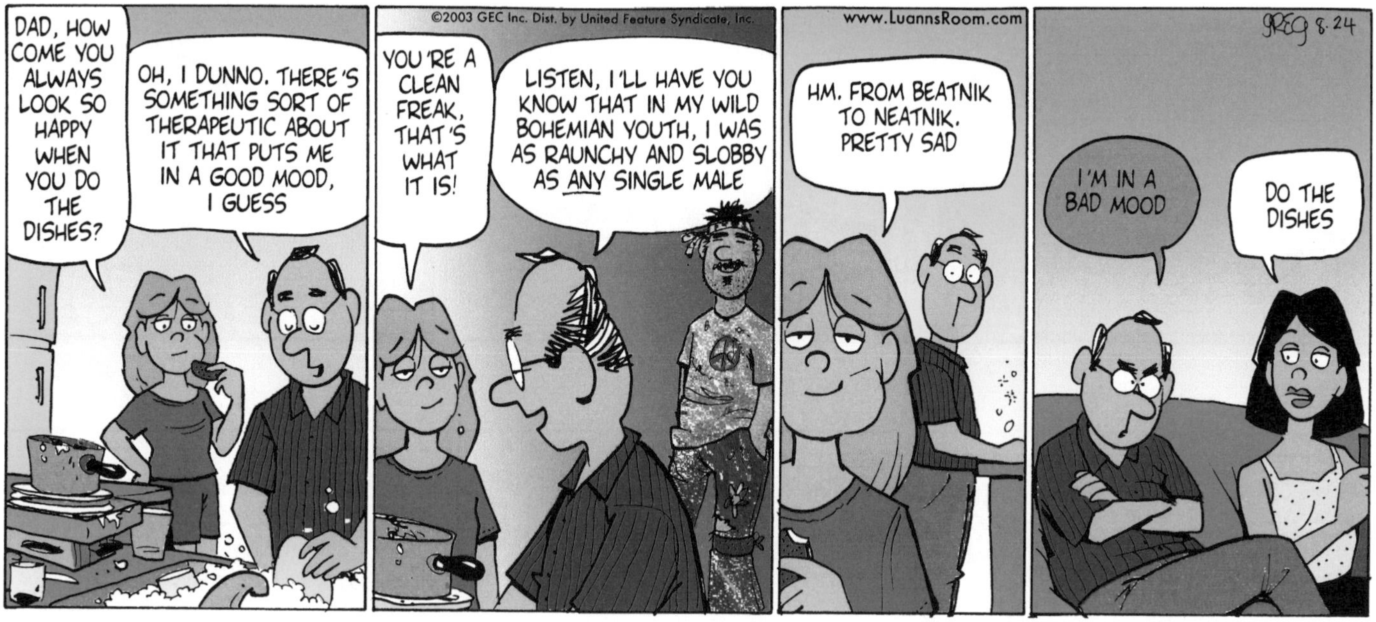

DAD, HOW COME YOU ALWAYS LOOK SO HAPPY WHEN YOU DO THE DISHES?
OH, I DUNNO. THERE'S SOMETHING SORT OF THERAPEUTIC ABOUT IT THAT PUTS ME IN A GOOD MOOD, I GUESS
©2003 GEC Inc. Dist. by United Feature Syndicate, Inc.
YOU'RE A CLEAN FREAK, THAT'S WHAT IT IS!
LISTEN, I'LL HAVE YOU KNOW THAT IN MY WILD BOHEMIAN YOUTH, I WAS AS RAUNCHY AND SLOBBY AS ANY SINGLE MALE
www.LuannsRoom.com
HM. FROM BEATNIK TO NEATNIK. PRETTY SAD
GREG 8.24
I'M IN A BAD MOOD
DO THE DISHES

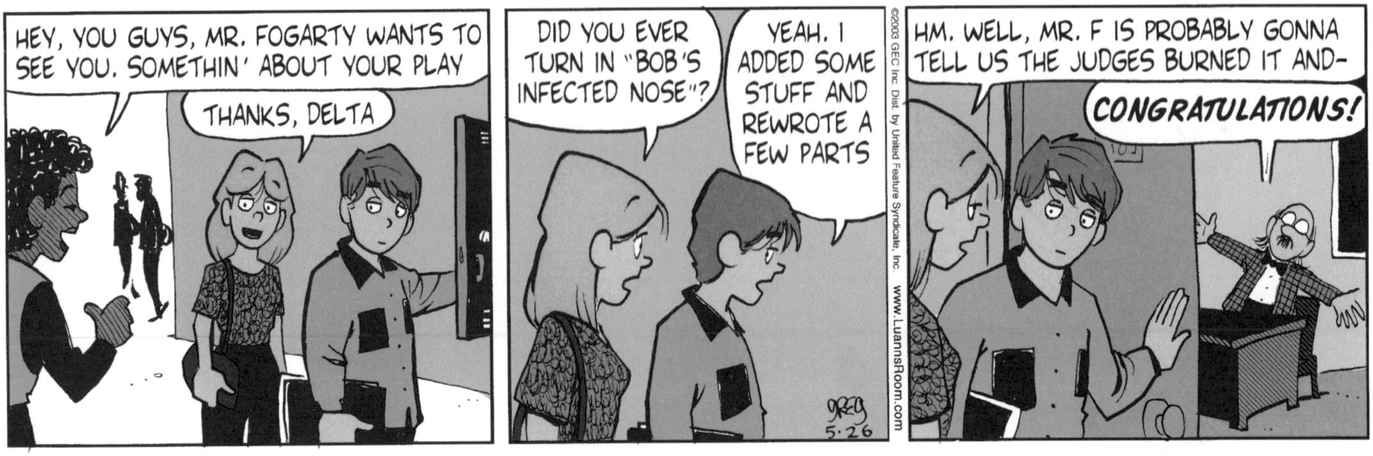
HEY, YOU GUYS, MR. FOGARTY WANTS TO SEE YOU. SOMETHIN' ABOUT YOUR PLAY
THANKS, DELTA
DID YOU EVER TURN IN "BOB'S INFECTED NOSE"?
YEAH. I ADDED SOME STUFF AND REWROTE A FEW PARTS
©2003 GEC Inc. Dist. by United Feature Syndicate, Inc. www.LuannsRoom.com
GREG 5·26
HM. WELL, MR. F IS PROBABLY GONNA TELL US THE JUDGES BURNED IT AND-
CONGRATULATIONS!

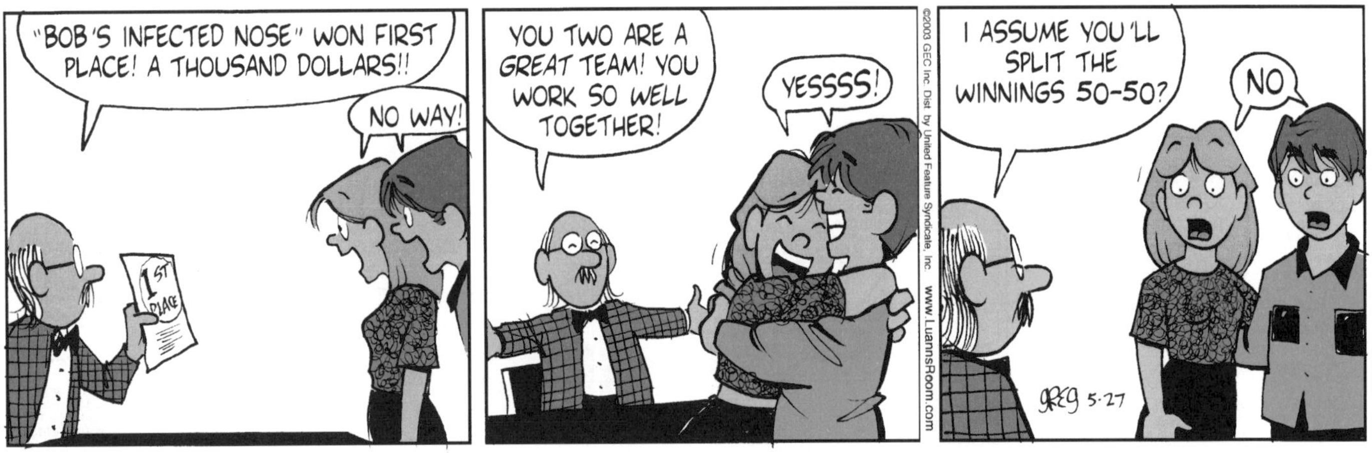
"BOB'S INFECTED NOSE" WON FIRST PLACE! A THOUSAND DOLLARS!!
1ST PLACE
NO WAY!
YOU TWO ARE A GREAT TEAM! YOU WORK SO WELL TOGETHER!
YESSSS!
©2003 GEC Inc. Dist. by United Feature Syndicate, Inc. www.LuannsRoom.com
I ASSUME YOU'LL SPLIT THE WINNINGS 50-50?
NO
GREG 5·27

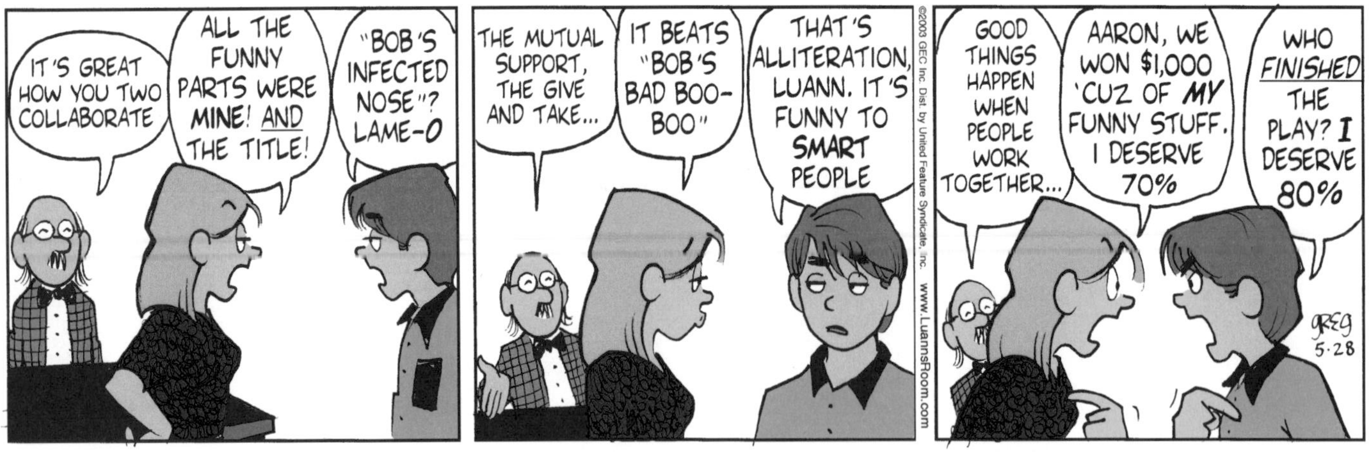
IT'S GREAT HOW YOU TWO COLLABORATE
ALL THE FUNNY PARTS WERE MINE! AND THE TITLE!
"BOB'S INFECTED NOSE"? LAME-O
THE MUTUAL SUPPORT, THE GIVE AND TAKE...
IT BEATS "BOB'S BAD BOO-BOO"
THAT'S ALLITERATION, LUANN. IT'S FUNNY TO SMART PEOPLE
©2003 GEC Inc. Dist. by United Feature Syndicate, Inc. www.LuannsRoom.com
GOOD THINGS HAPPEN WHEN PEOPLE WORK TOGETHER...
AARON, WE WON $1,000 'CUZ OF MY FUNNY STUFF. I DESERVE 70%
WHO FINISHED THE PLAY? I DESERVE 80%
GREG 5·28

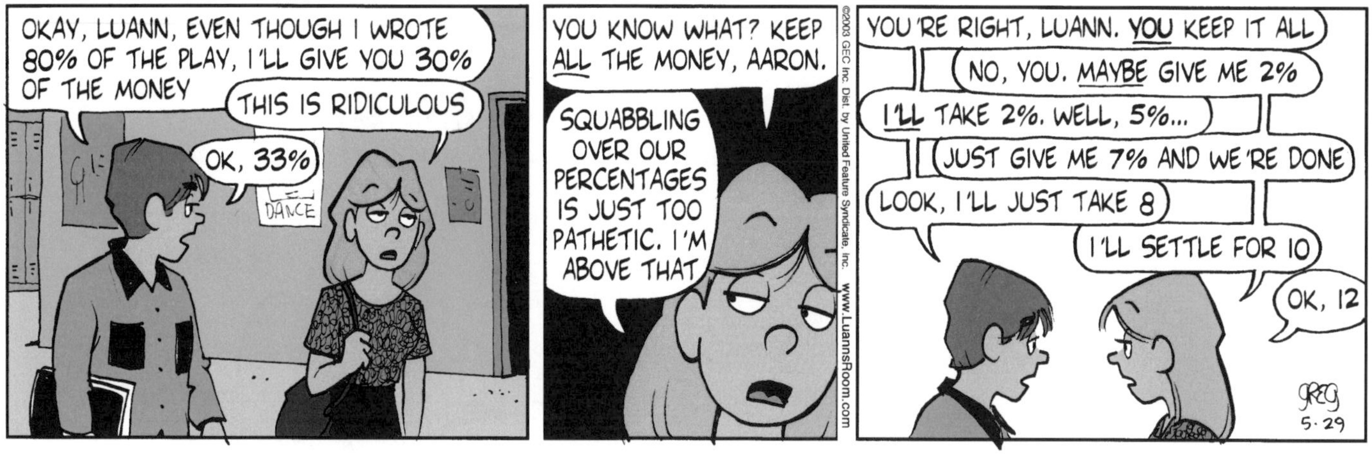
OKAY, LUANN, EVEN THOUGH I WROTE 80% OF THE PLAY, I'LL GIVE YOU 30% OF THE MONEY
THIS IS RIDICULOUS
OK, 33%
DANCE
YOU KNOW WHAT? KEEP ALL THE MONEY, AARON.
SQUABBLING OVER OUR PERCENTAGES IS JUST TOO PATHETIC. I'M ABOVE THAT
©2003 GEC Inc. Dist. by United Feature Syndicate, Inc. www.LuannsRoom.com
YOU'RE RIGHT, LUANN. YOU KEEP IT ALL
NO, YOU. MAYBE GIVE ME 2%
I'LL TAKE 2%. WELL, 5%...
JUST GIVE ME 7% AND WE'RE DONE
LOOK, I'LL JUST TAKE 8
I'LL SETTLE FOR 10
OK, 12
GREG 5·29

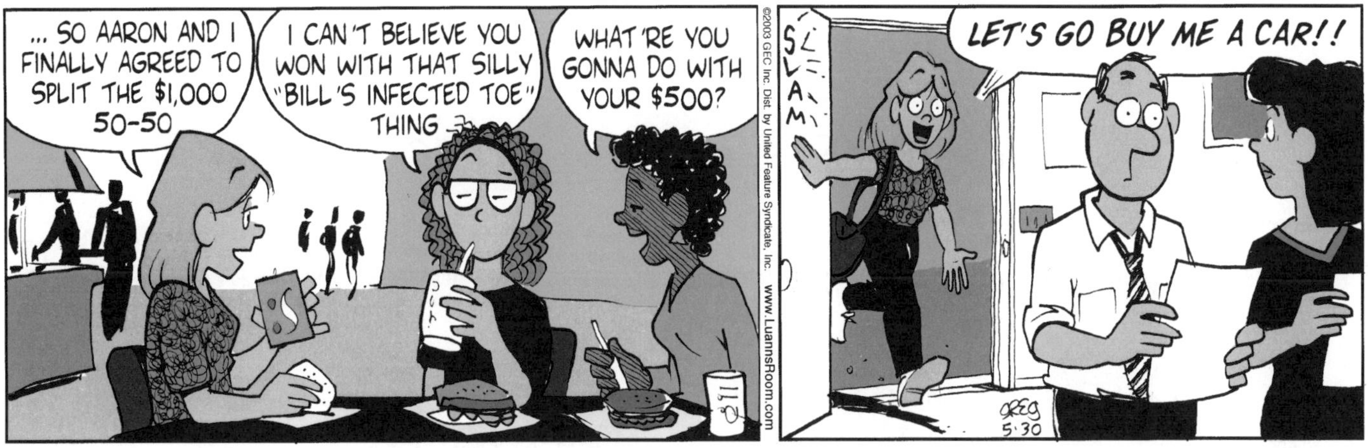
... SO AARON AND I FINALLY AGREED TO SPLIT THE $1,000 50-50
I CAN'T BELIEVE YOU WON WITH THAT SILLY "BILL'S INFECTED TOE" THING
WHAT'RE YOU GONNA DO WITH YOUR $500?
©2003 GEC Inc. Dist. by United Feature Syndicate, Inc. www.LuannsRoom.com
SLAM
LET'S GO BUY ME A CAR!!
GREG 5·30

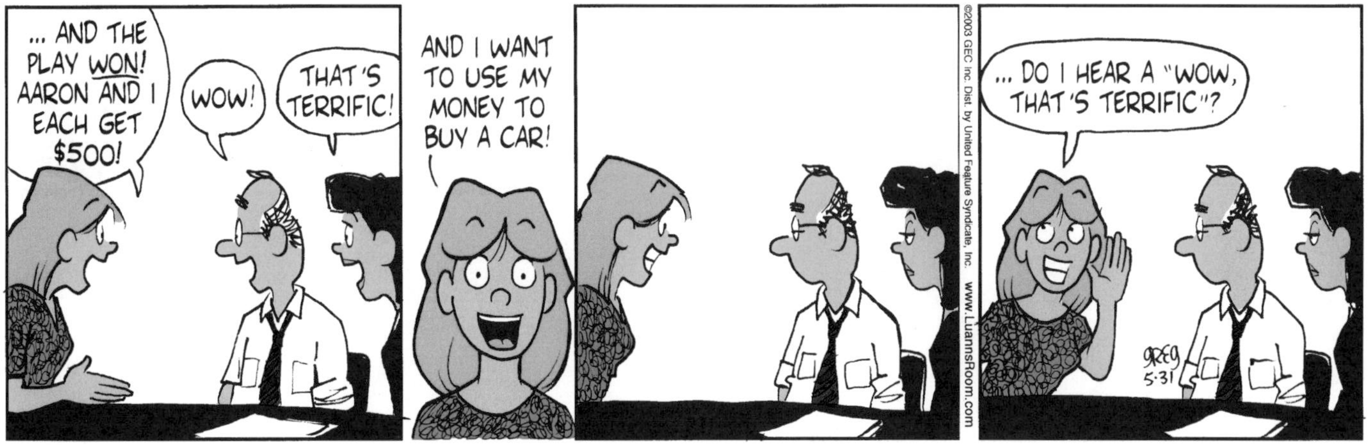
... AND THE PLAY WON! AARON AND I EACH GET $500!
WOW!
THAT'S TERRIFIC!
AND I WANT TO USE MY MONEY TO BUY A CAR!
©2003 GEC Inc. Dist. by United Feature Syndicate, Inc. www.LuannsRoom.com
... DO I HEAR A "WOW, THAT'S TERRIFIC"?
GREG 5·31

edge
you
kay
Ted

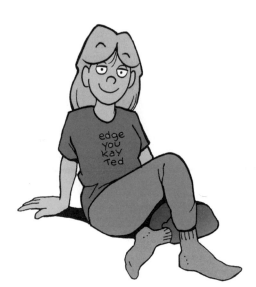

A • POEM • BY • LUANN
I learned a lot this summer
Like how to wax the car
How to jump the battery
And how to change a tire.
I learned to fix a faucet
And how to write a check.
I learned to be more confident
I gained some self-respect.
But now my summer's over
And school's about to start
It's time to study calculus,
Geography and art.
So what will serve me better
When life is hard and cruel...
The things I learned this summer
Or the stuff I learn in school?
HOME DEPOT
A+
ATLAS
GREG 8-31
©2003 GEC Inc. Dist. by United Feature Syndicate, Inc.
www.LuannsRoom.com

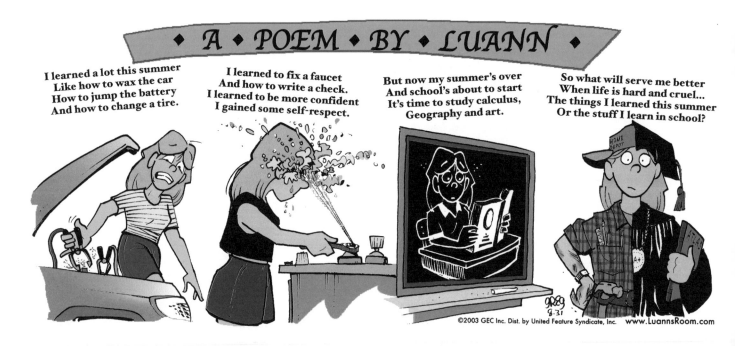

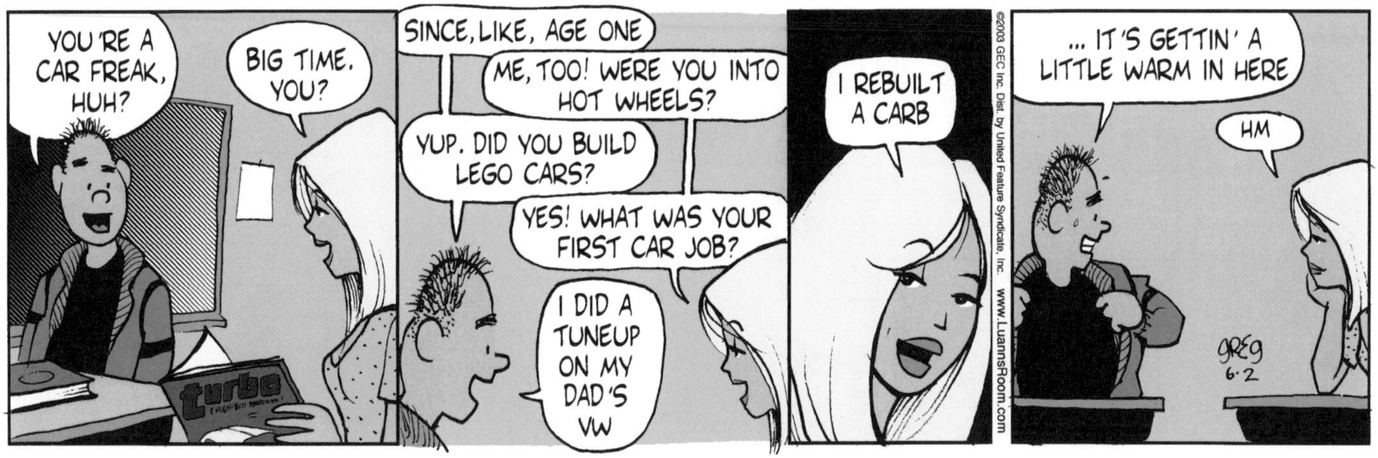
YOU'RE A CAR FREAK, HUH?
BIG TIME. YOU?
SINCE, LIKE, AGE ONE
ME, TOO! WERE YOU INTO HOT WHEELS?
YUP. DID YOU BUILD LEGO CARS?
YES! WHAT WAS YOUR FIRST CAR JOB?
I DID A TUNEUP ON MY DAD'S VW
I REBUILT A CARB
... IT'S GETTIN' A LITTLE WARM IN HERE
HM
©2003 GEC Inc. Dist. by United Feature Syndicate, Inc.
www.LuannsRoom.com
GREG 6·2

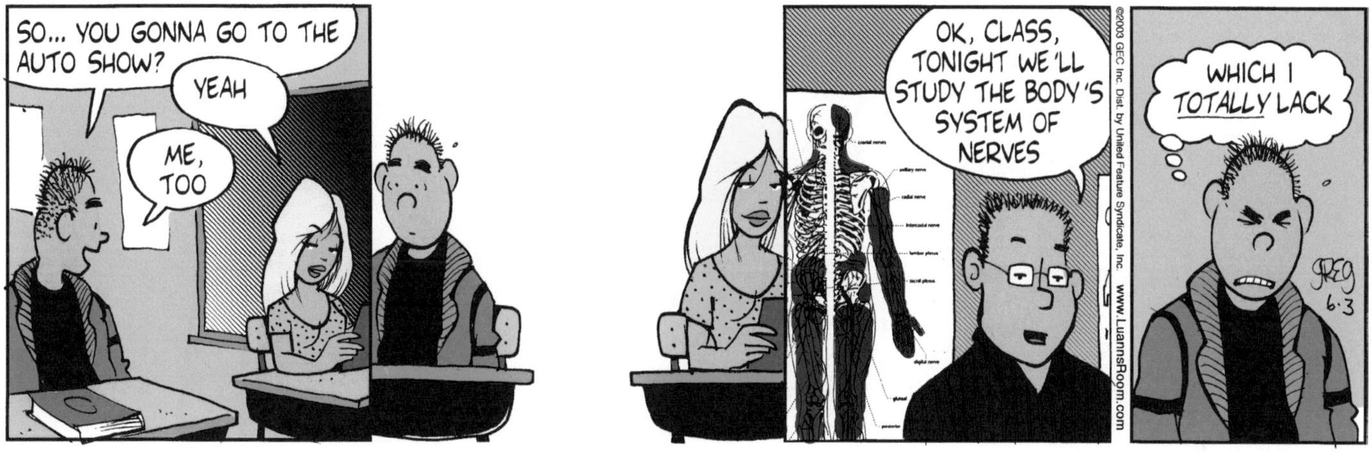
SO... YOU GONNA GO TO THE AUTO SHOW?
YEAH
ME, TOO
OK, CLASS, TONIGHT WE'LL STUDY THE BODY'S SYSTEM OF NERVES
WHICH I TOTALLY LACK
©2003 GEC Inc. Dist. by United Feature Syndicate, Inc.
www.LuannsRoom.com
GREG 6·3

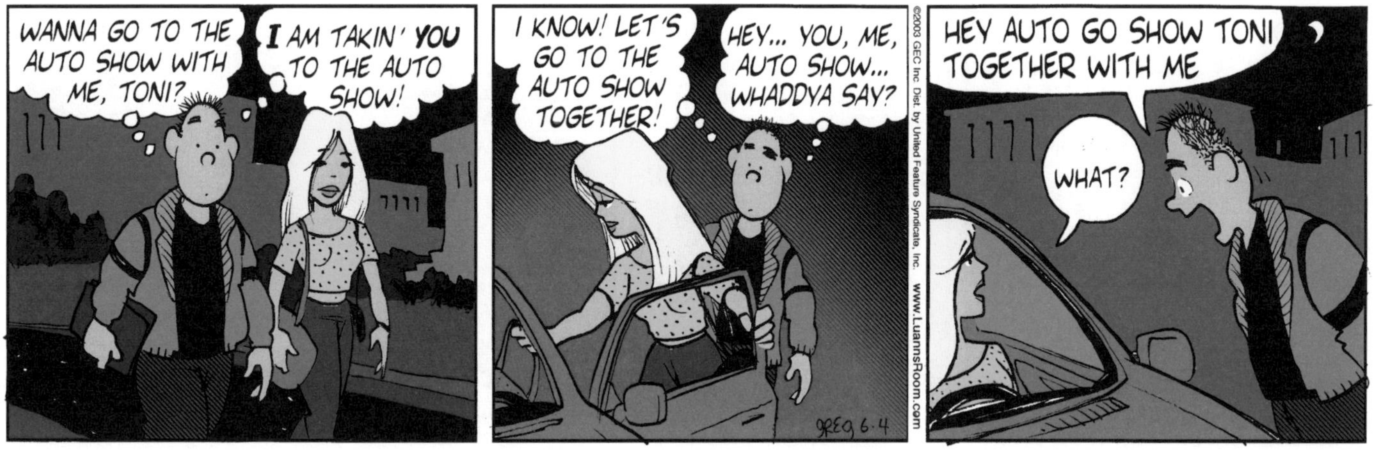
WANNA GO TO THE AUTO SHOW WITH ME, TONI?
I AM TAKIN' YOU TO THE AUTO SHOW!
I KNOW! LET'S GO TO THE AUTO SHOW TOGETHER!
HEY... YOU, ME, AUTO SHOW... WHADDYA SAY?
HEY AUTO GO SHOW TONI TOGETHER WITH ME
WHAT?
©2003 GEC Inc. Dist. by United Feature Syndicate, Inc.
www.LuannsRoom.com
GREG 6·4

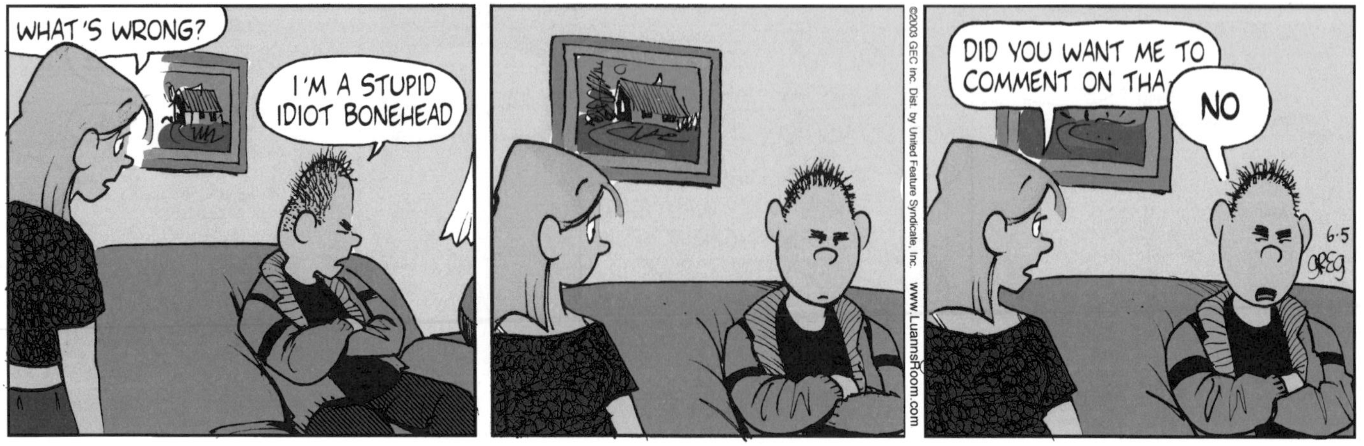
WHAT'S WRONG?
I'M A STUPID IDIOT BONEHEAD
©2003 GEC Inc. Dist. by United Feature Syndicate, Inc. www.LuannsRoom.com
DID YOU WANT ME TO COMMENT ON THA-
NO
6·5 GREG

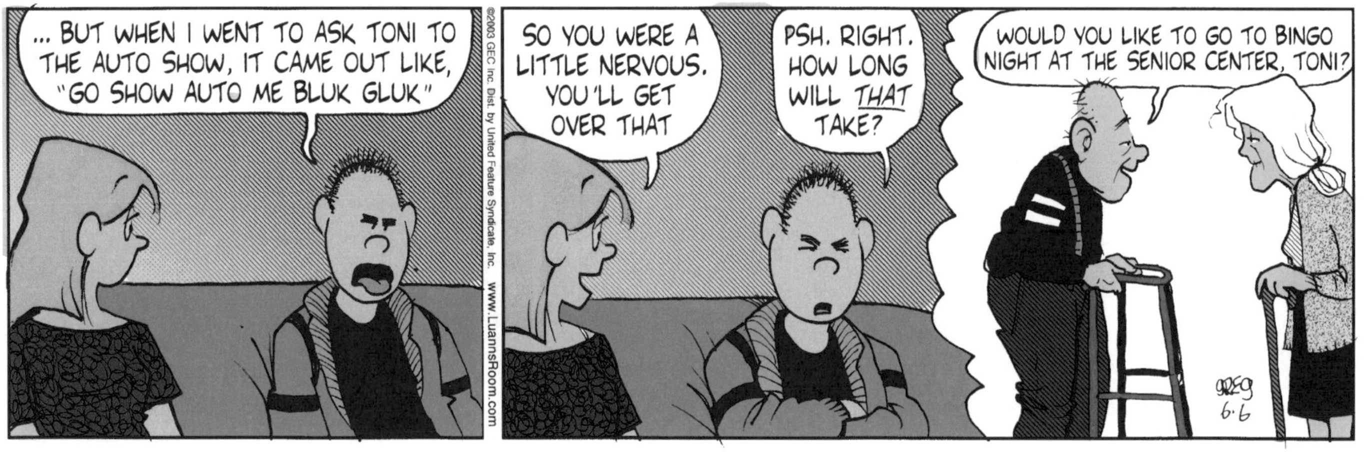
... BUT WHEN I WENT TO ASK TONI TO THE AUTO SHOW, IT CAME OUT LIKE, "GO SHOW AUTO ME BLUK GLUK"
©2003 GEC Inc. Dist. by United Feature Syndicate, Inc. www.LuannsRoom.com
SO YOU WERE A LITTLE NERVOUS. YOU'LL GET OVER THAT
PSH. RIGHT. HOW LONG WILL THAT TAKE?
WOULD YOU LIKE TO GO TO BINGO NIGHT AT THE SENIOR CENTER, TONI?
GREG 6·6

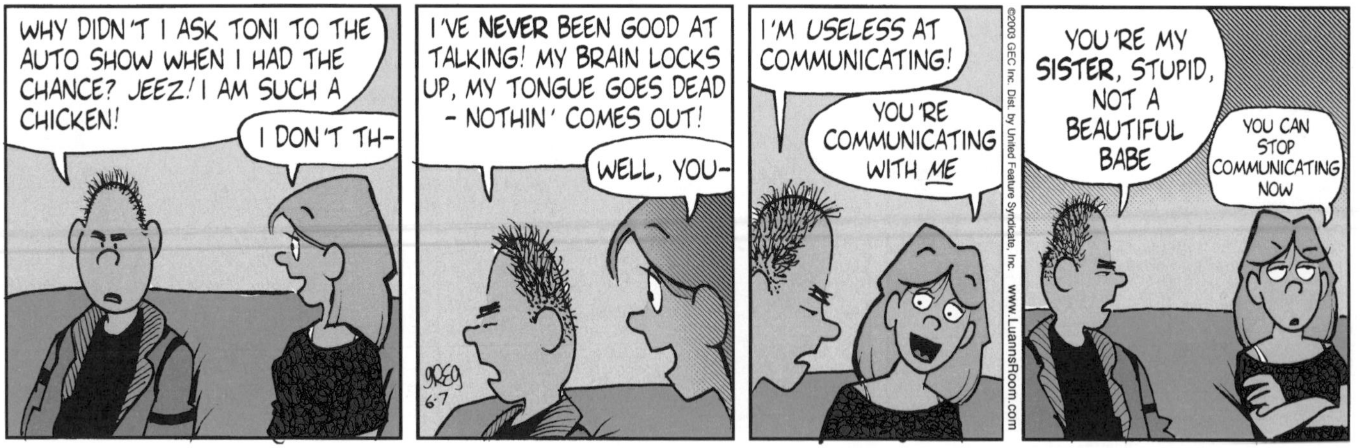
WHY DIDN'T I ASK TONI TO THE AUTO SHOW WHEN I HAD THE CHANCE? JEEZ! I AM SUCH A CHICKEN!
I DON'T TH-
I'VE NEVER BEEN GOOD AT TALKING! MY BRAIN LOCKS UP, MY TONGUE GOES DEAD - NOTHIN' COMES OUT!
WELL, YOU-
GREG 6·7
I'M USELESS AT COMMUNICATING!
YOU'RE COMMUNICATING WITH ME
©2003 GEC Inc. Dist. by United Feature Syndicate, Inc. www.LuannsRoom.com
YOU'RE MY SISTER, STUPID, NOT A BEAUTIFUL BABE
YOU CAN STOP COMMUNICATING NOW

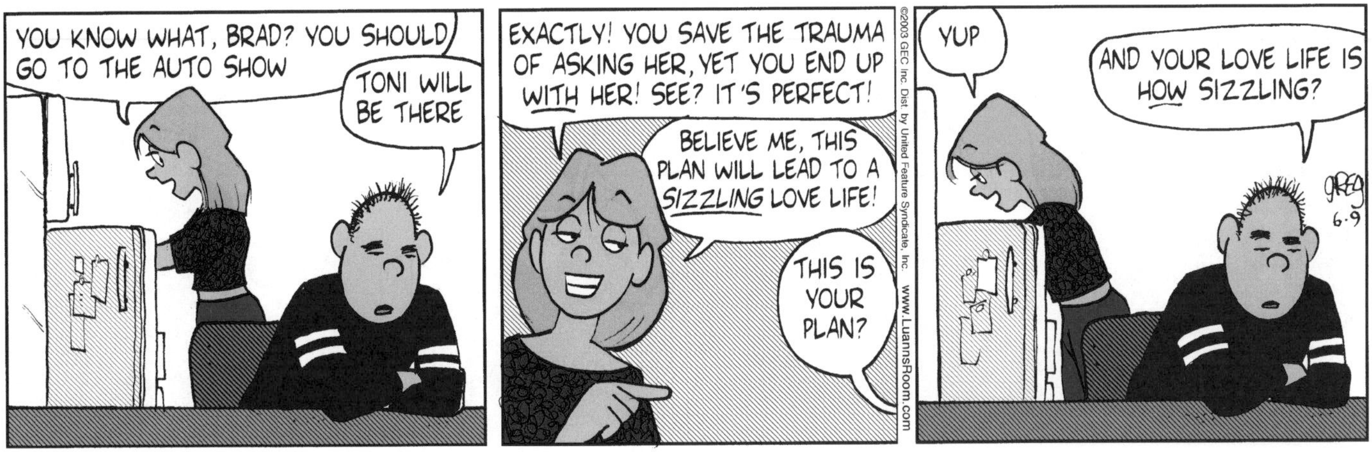
YOU KNOW WHAT, BRAD? YOU SHOULD GO TO THE AUTO SHOW
TONI WILL BE THERE
EXACTLY! YOU SAVE THE TRAUMA OF ASKING HER, YET YOU END UP WITH HER! SEE? IT'S PERFECT!
BELIEVE ME, THIS PLAN WILL LEAD TO A SIZZLING LOVE LIFE!
THIS IS YOUR PLAN?
YUP
AND YOUR LOVE LIFE IS HOW SIZZLING?
GREG 6·9
©2003 GEC Inc. Dist. by United Feature Syndicate, Inc. www.LuannsRoom.com

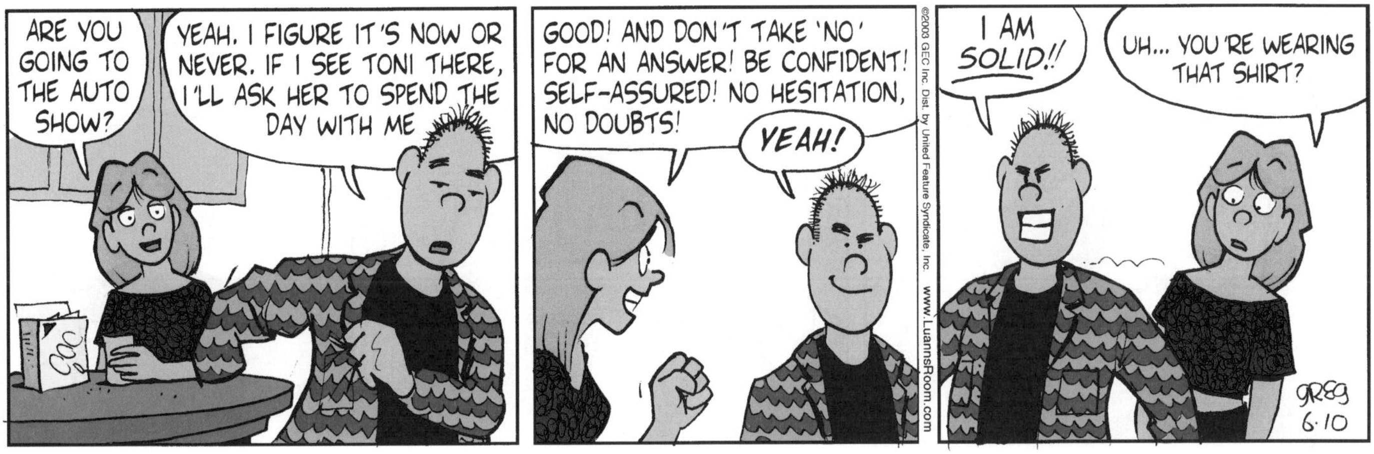
ARE YOU GOING TO THE AUTO SHOW?
YEAH. I FIGURE IT'S NOW OR NEVER. IF I SEE TONI THERE, I'LL ASK HER TO SPEND THE DAY WITH ME
GOOD! AND DON'T TAKE 'NO' FOR AN ANSWER! BE CONFIDENT! SELF-ASSURED! NO HESITATION, NO DOUBTS!
YEAH!
I AM SOLID!!
UH... YOU'RE WEARING THAT SHIRT?
GREG 6·10
©2003 GEC Inc. Dist. by United Feature Syndicate, Inc. www.LuannsRoom.com

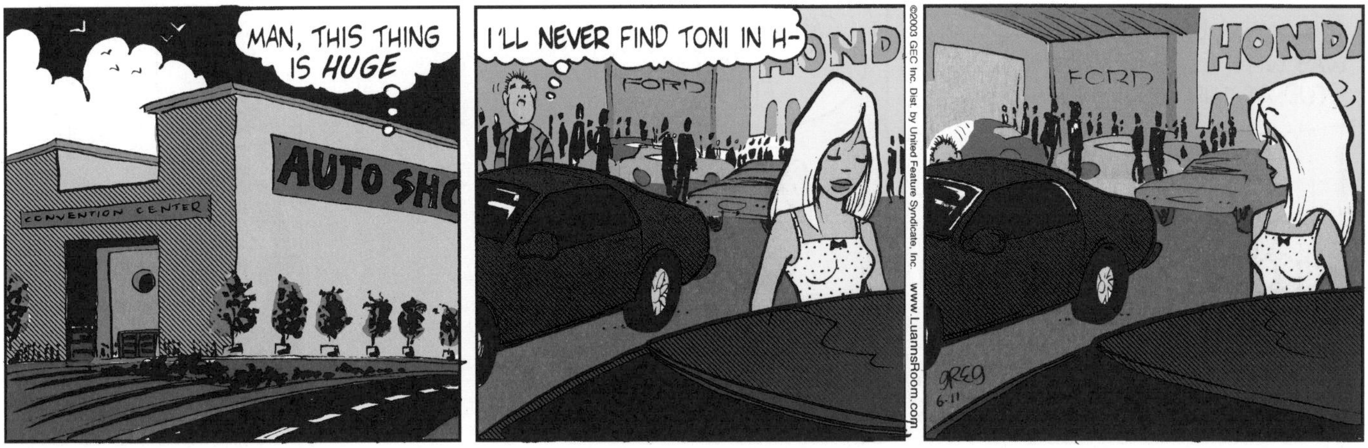
MAN, THIS THING IS HUGE
AUTO SHO
CONVENTION CENTER
I'LL NEVER FIND TONI IN H–
FORD
HOND
HONDA
GREG 6·11
©2003 GEC Inc. Dist. by United Feature Syndicate, Inc. www.LuannsRoom.com

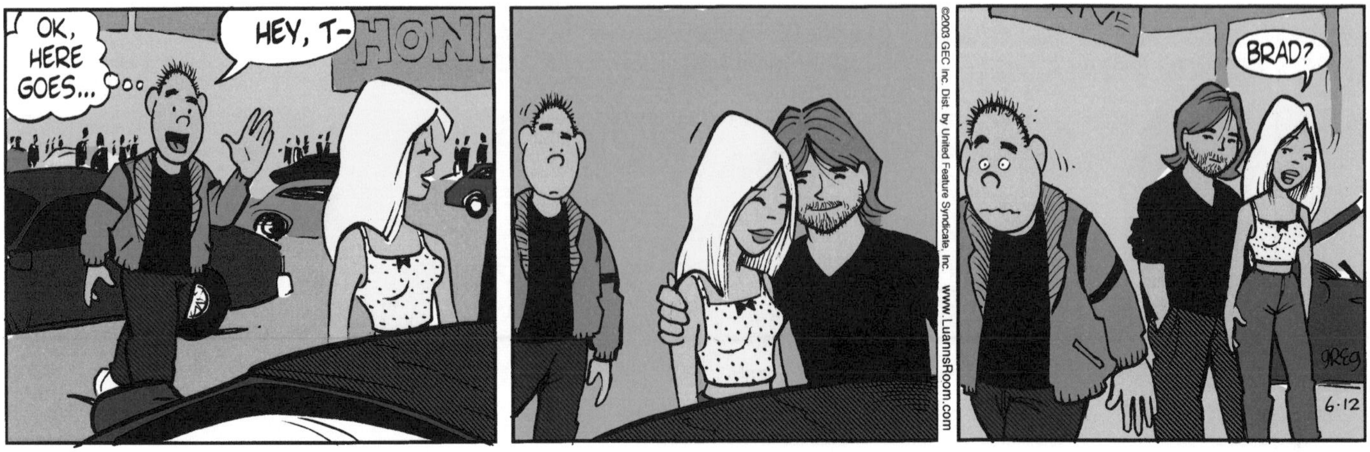
OK, HERE GOES...
HEY, T-
HONI
©2003 GEC Inc. Dist. by United Feature Syndicate, Inc. www.LuannsRoom.com
BRAD?
GREG 6·12

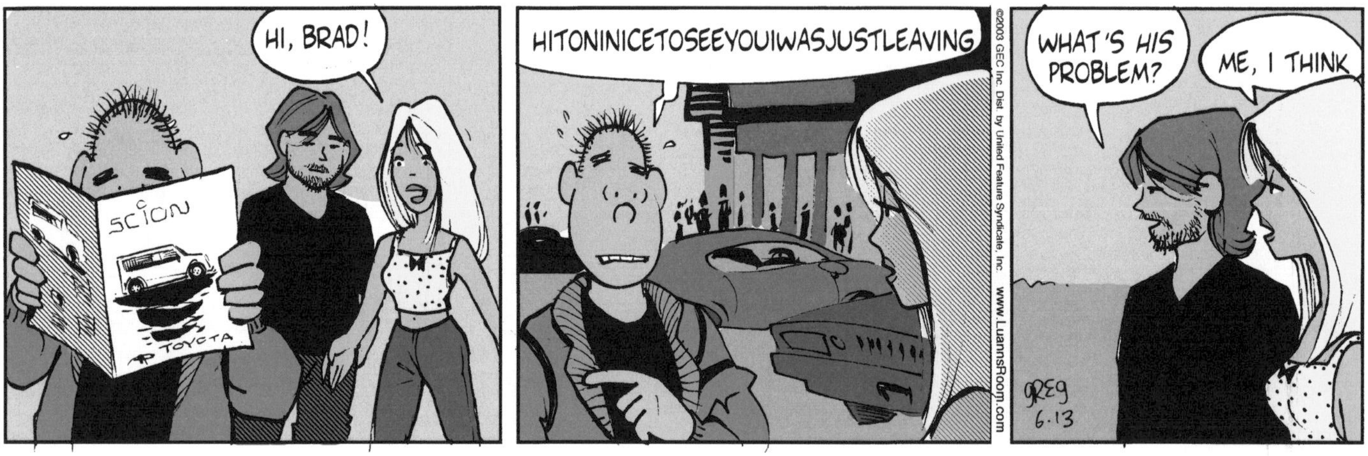
HI, BRAD!
SCION
TOYOTA
HITONINICETOSEEYOUIWASJUSTLEAVING
©2003 GEC Inc. Dist. by United Feature Syndicate, Inc. www.LuannsRoom.com
WHAT'S *HIS* PROBLEM?
ME, I THINK
GREG 6·13

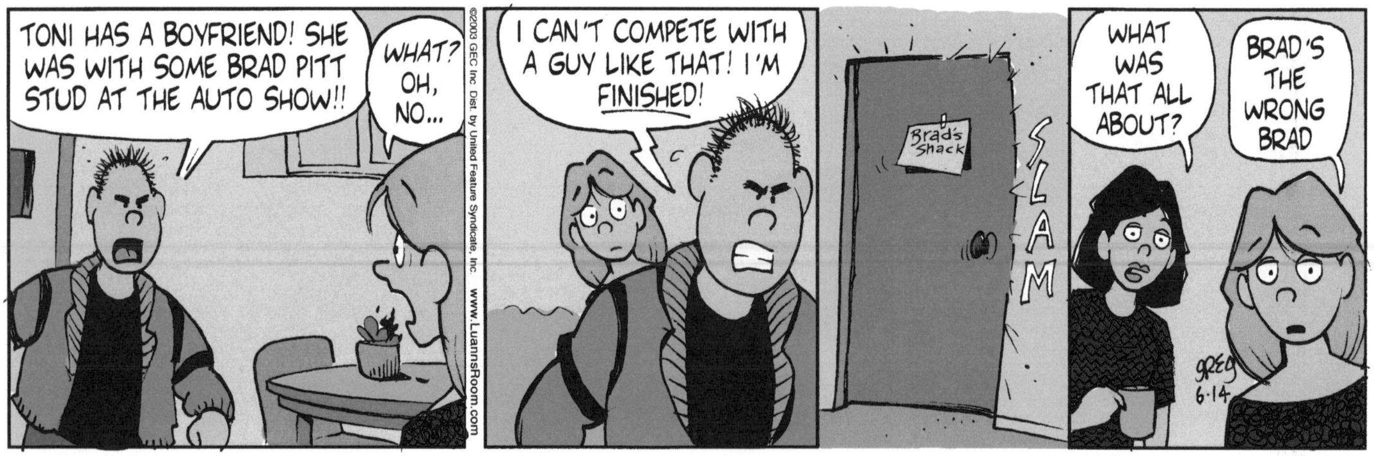
TONI HAS A BOYFRIEND! SHE WAS WITH SOME BRAD PITT STUD AT THE AUTO SHOW!!
WHAT? OH, NO...
©2003 GEC Inc. Dist. by United Feature Syndicate, Inc. www.LuannsRoom.com
I CAN'T COMPETE WITH A GUY LIKE THAT! I'M FINISHED!
Brad's Shack
SLAM
WHAT WAS THAT ALL ABOUT?
BRAD'S THE WRONG BRAD
GREG 6·14

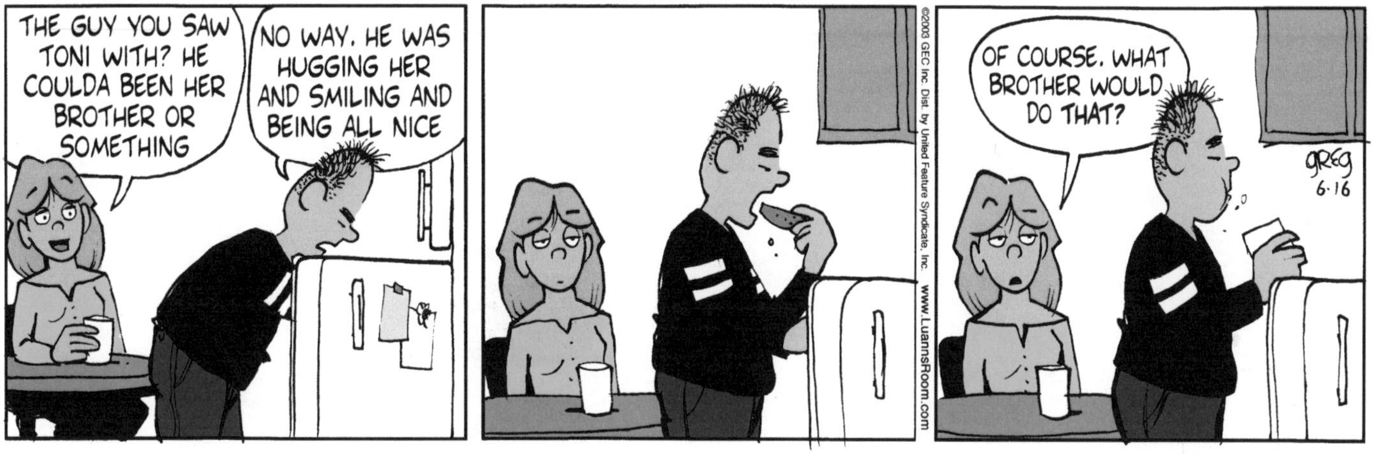
THE GUY YOU SAW TONI WITH? HE COULDA BEEN HER BROTHER OR SOMETHING
NO WAY. HE WAS HUGGING HER AND SMILING AND BEING ALL NICE
OF COURSE. WHAT BROTHER WOULD DO THAT?
GREG 6·16
©2003 GEC Inc. Dist. by United Feature Syndicate, Inc. www.LuannsRoom.com

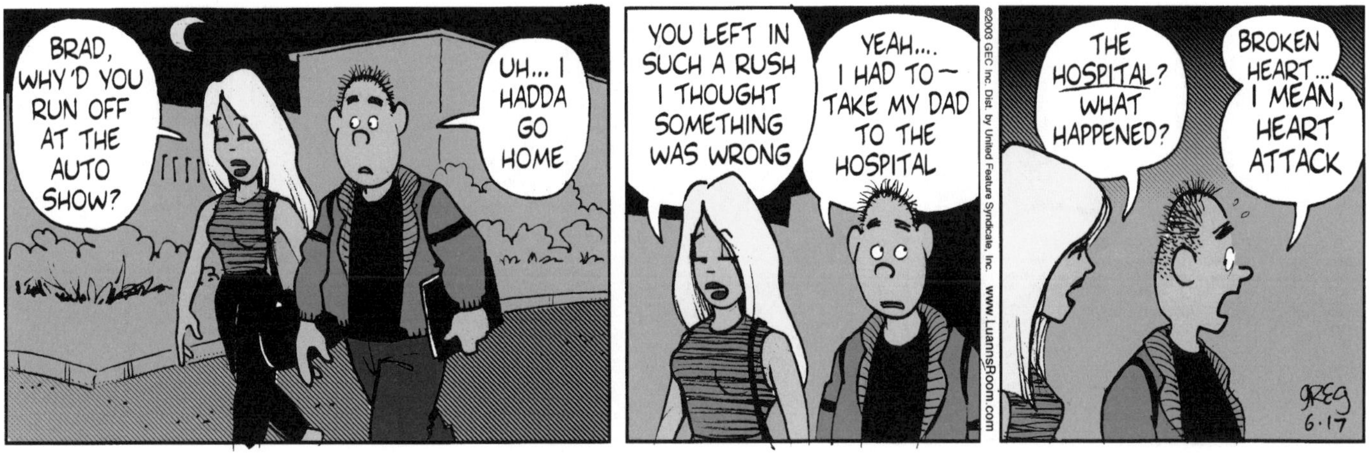
BRAD, WHY'D YOU RUN OFF AT THE AUTO SHOW?
UH... I HADDA GO HOME
YOU LEFT IN SUCH A RUSH I THOUGHT SOMETHING WAS WRONG
YEAH.... I HAD TO— TAKE MY DAD TO THE HOSPITAL
THE HOSPITAL? WHAT HAPPENED?
BROKEN HEART... I MEAN, HEART ATTACK
GREG 6·17
©2003 GEC Inc. Dist. by United Feature Syndicate, Inc. www.LuannsRoom.com

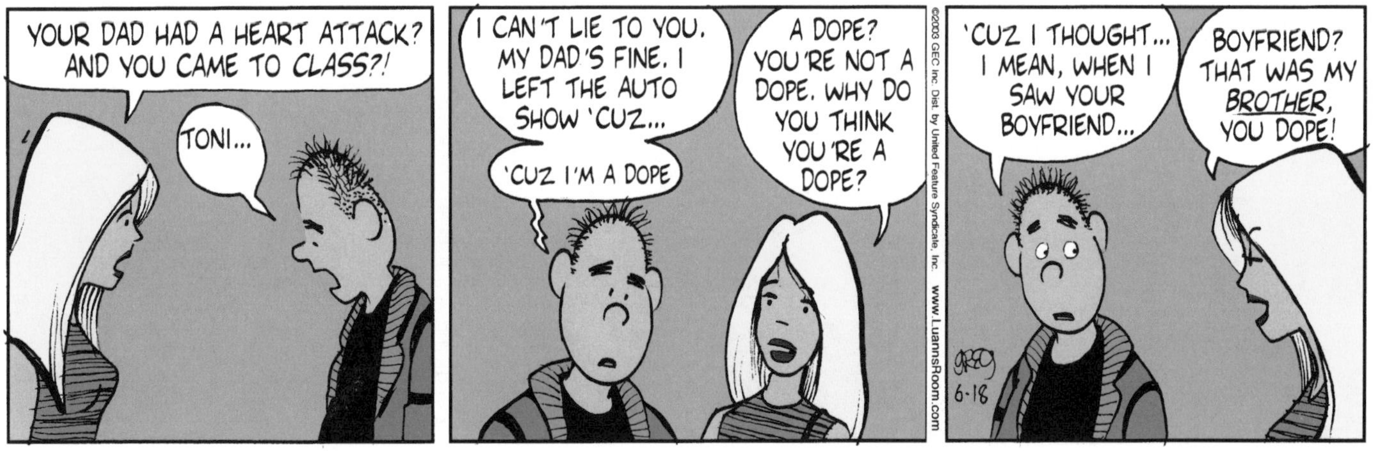
YOUR DAD HAD A HEART ATTACK? AND YOU CAME TO CLASS?!
TONI...
I CAN'T LIE TO YOU. MY DAD'S FINE. I LEFT THE AUTO SHOW 'CUZ...
'CUZ I'M A DOPE
A DOPE? YOU'RE NOT A DOPE. WHY DO YOU THINK YOU'RE A DOPE?
'CUZ I THOUGHT... I MEAN, WHEN I SAW YOUR BOYFRIEND...
BOYFRIEND? THAT WAS MY BROTHER, YOU DOPE!
GREG 6·18
©2003 GEC Inc. Dist. by United Feature Syndicate, Inc. www.LuannsRoom.com

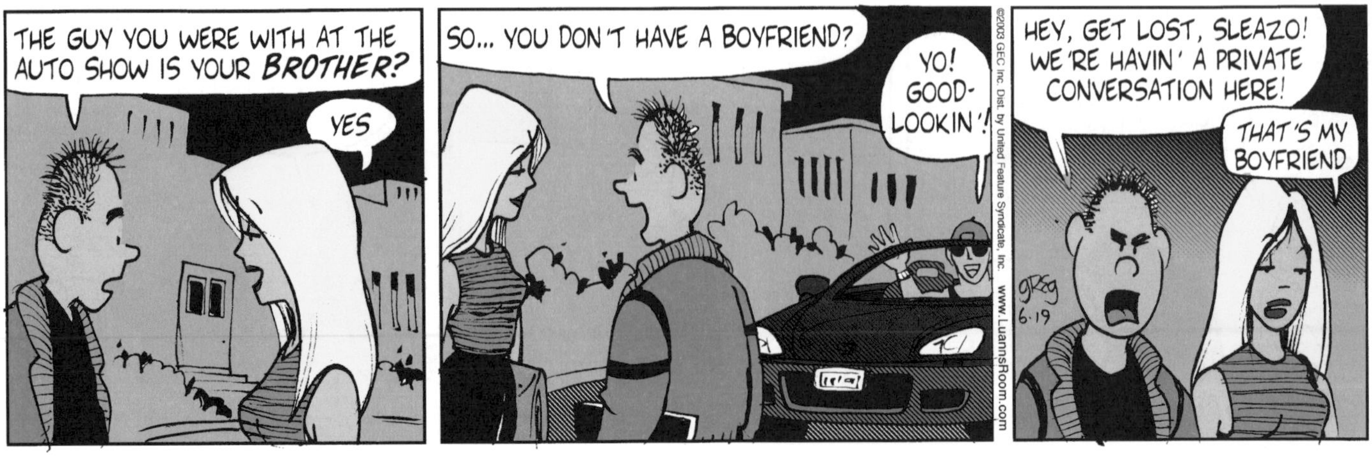
THE GUY YOU WERE WITH AT THE AUTO SHOW IS YOUR BROTHER?
YES
SO... YOU DON'T HAVE A BOYFRIEND?
YO! GOOD-LOOKIN'!
©2003 GEC Inc. Dist. by United Feature Syndicate, Inc.
www.LuannsRoom.com
GREG 6·19
HEY, GET LOST, SLEAZO! WE'RE HAVIN' A PRIVATE CONVERSATION HERE!
THAT'S MY BOYFRIEND

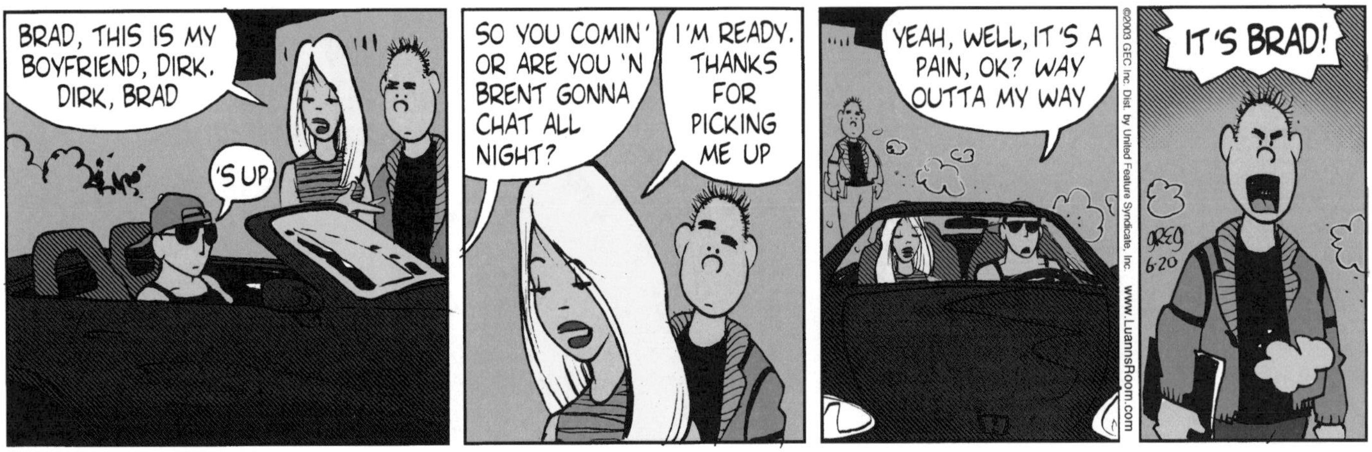
BRAD, THIS IS MY BOYFRIEND, DIRK. DIRK, BRAD
'S UP
SO YOU COMIN' OR ARE YOU 'N BRENT GONNA CHAT ALL NIGHT?
I'M READY. THANKS FOR PICKING ME UP
YEAH, WELL, IT'S A PAIN, OK? WAY OUTTA MY WAY
©2003 GEC Inc. Dist. by United Feature Syndicate, Inc.
www.LuannsRoom.com
IT'S BRAD!
GREG 6·20

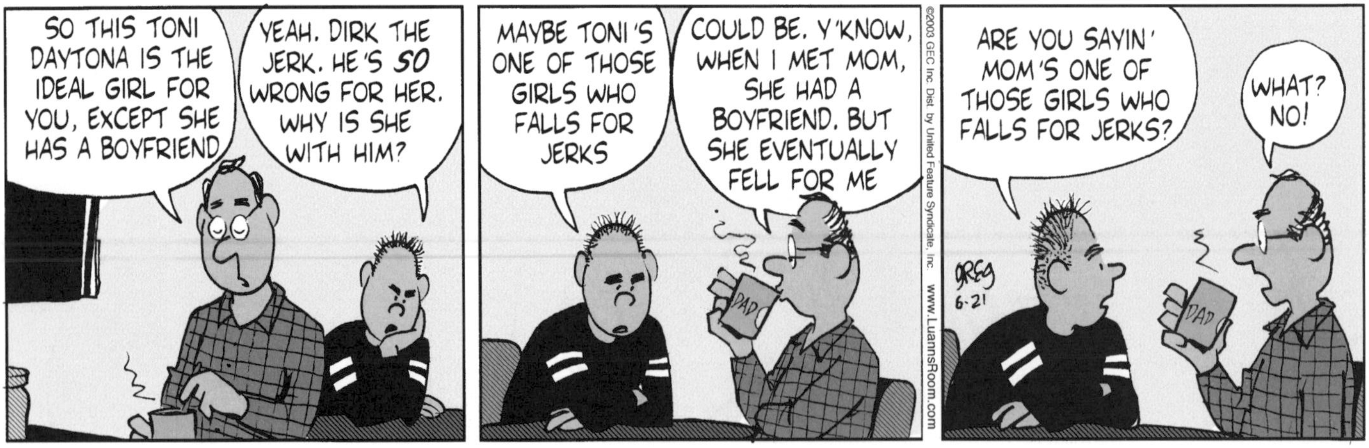
SO THIS TONI DAYTONA IS THE IDEAL GIRL FOR YOU, EXCEPT SHE HAS A BOYFRIEND
YEAH. DIRK THE JERK. HE'S SO WRONG FOR HER. WHY IS SHE WITH HIM?
MAYBE TONI'S ONE OF THOSE GIRLS WHO FALLS FOR JERKS
COULD BE. Y'KNOW, WHEN I MET MOM, SHE HAD A BOYFRIEND. BUT SHE EVENTUALLY FELL FOR ME
DAD
©2003 GEC Inc. Dist. by United Feature Syndicate, Inc.
www.LuannsRoom.com
GREG 6·21
ARE YOU SAYIN' MOM'S ONE OF THOSE GIRLS WHO FALLS FOR JERKS?
WHAT? NO!
DAD

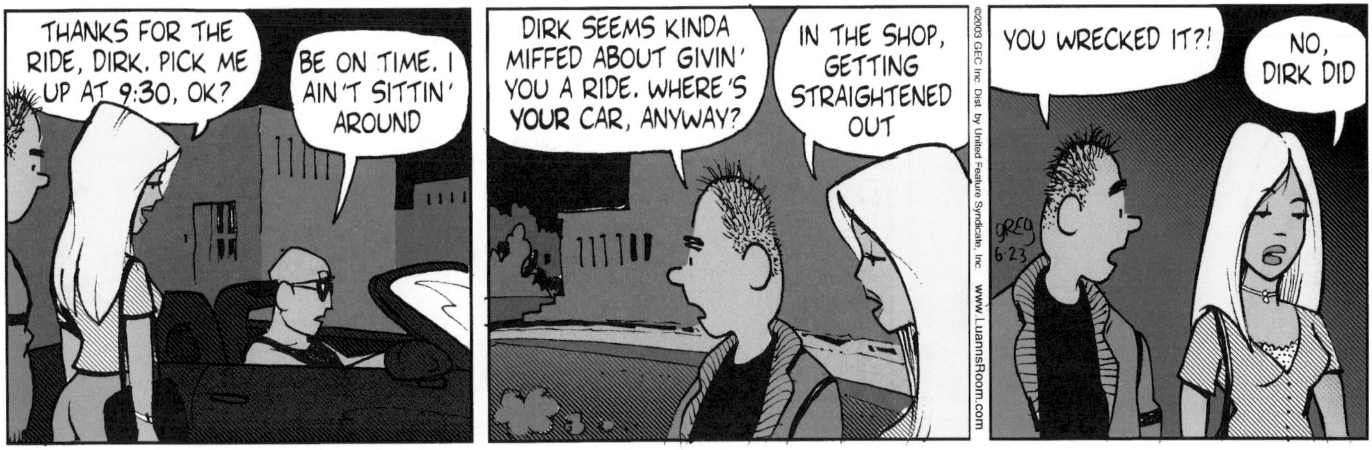
THANKS FOR THE RIDE, DIRK. PICK ME UP AT 9:30, OK?
BE ON TIME. I AIN'T SITTIN' AROUND
DIRK SEEMS KINDA MIFFED ABOUT GIVIN' YOU A RIDE. WHERE'S YOUR CAR, ANYWAY?
IN THE SHOP, GETTING STRAIGHTENED OUT
©2003 GEC Inc. Dist. by United Feature Syndicate, Inc. www.LuannsRoom.com
YOU WRECKED IT?!
NO, DIRK DID
GREG 6·23

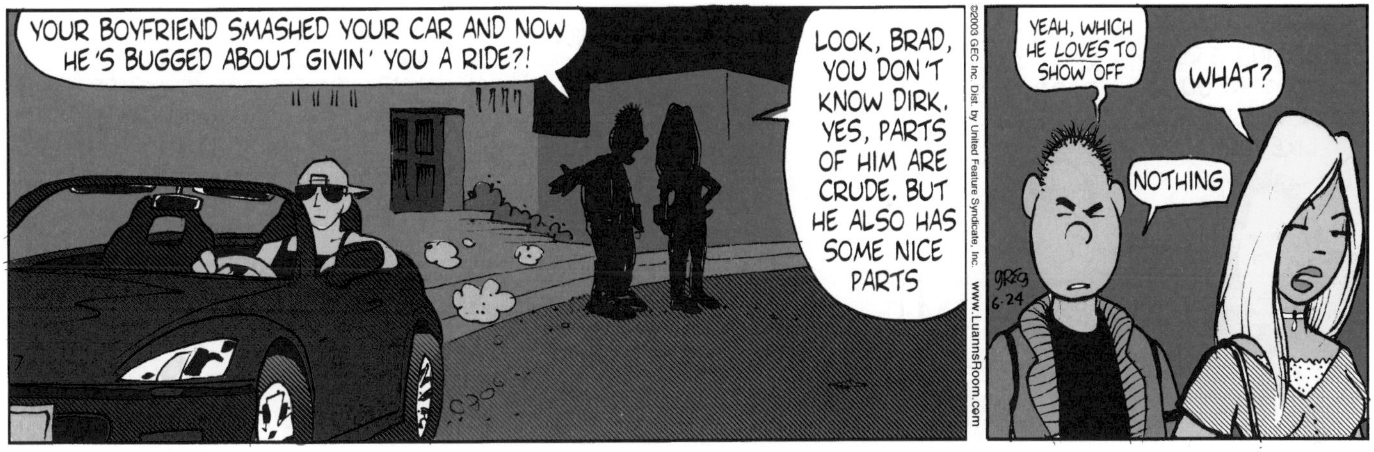
YOUR BOYFRIEND SMASHED YOUR CAR AND NOW HE'S BUGGED ABOUT GIVIN' YOU A RIDE?!
LOOK, BRAD, YOU DON'T KNOW DIRK. YES, PARTS OF HIM ARE CRUDE. BUT HE ALSO HAS SOME NICE PARTS
©2003 GEC Inc. Dist. by United Feature Syndicate, Inc. www.LuannsRoom.com
YEAH, WHICH HE LOVES TO SHOW OFF
WHAT?
NOTHING
GREG 6·24

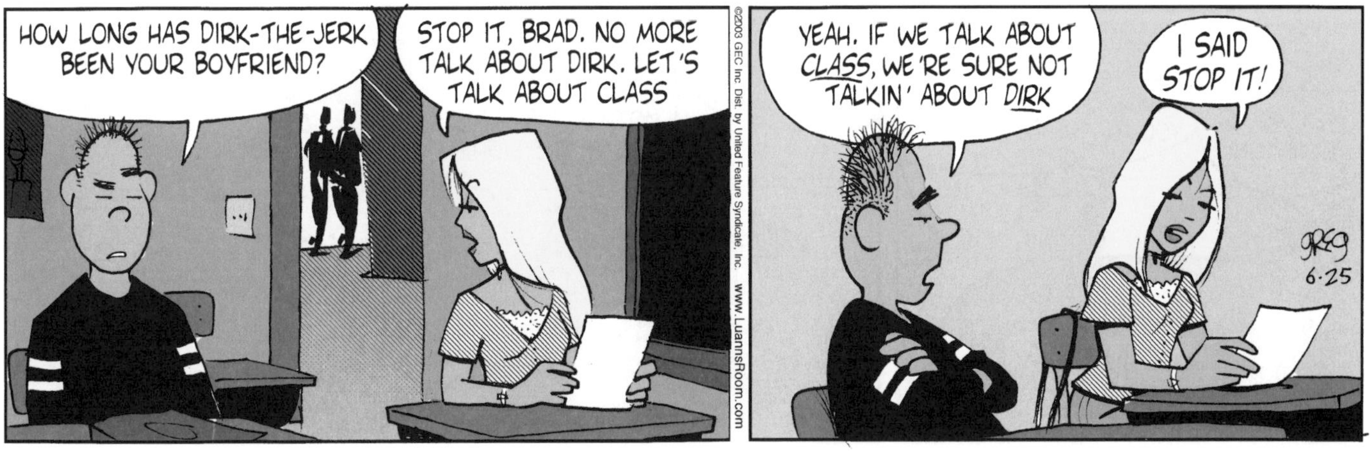
HOW LONG HAS DIRK-THE-JERK BEEN YOUR BOYFRIEND?
STOP IT, BRAD. NO MORE TALK ABOUT DIRK. LET'S TALK ABOUT CLASS
©2003 GEC Inc. Dist. by United Feature Syndicate, Inc. www.LuannsRoom.com
YEAH. IF WE TALK ABOUT CLASS, WE'RE SURE NOT TALKIN' ABOUT DIRK
I SAID STOP IT!
GREG 6·25

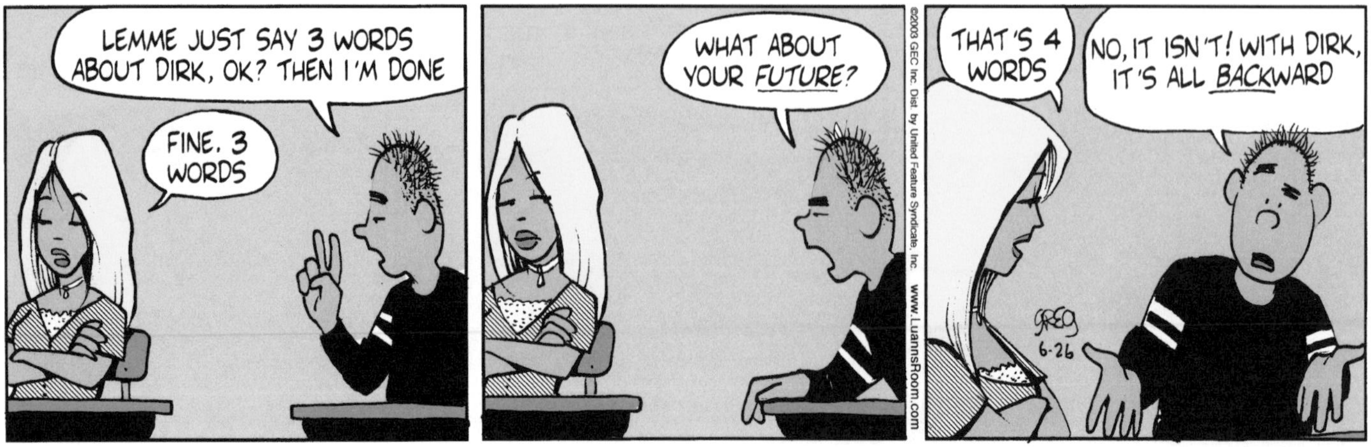
LEMME JUST SAY 3 WORDS ABOUT DIRK, OK? THEN I'M DONE
FINE. 3 WORDS
WHAT ABOUT YOUR FUTURE?
THAT'S 4 WORDS
NO, IT ISN'T! WITH DIRK, IT'S ALL BACKWARD
GREG 6·26
©2003 GEC Inc. Dist. by United Feature Syndicate, Inc. www.LuannsRoom.com

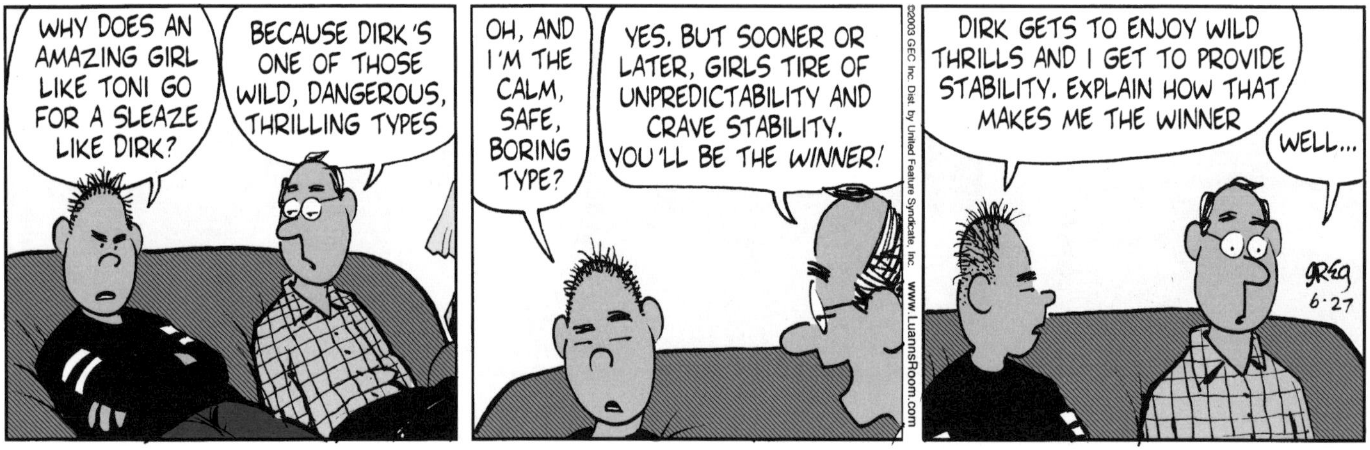
WHY DOES AN AMAZING GIRL LIKE TONI GO FOR A SLEAZE LIKE DIRK?
BECAUSE DIRK'S ONE OF THOSE WILD, DANGEROUS, THRILLING TYPES
OH, AND I'M THE CALM, SAFE, BORING TYPE?
YES. BUT SOONER OR LATER, GIRLS TIRE OF UNPREDICTABILITY AND CRAVE STABILITY. YOU'LL BE THE WINNER!
DIRK GETS TO ENJOY WILD THRILLS AND I GET TO PROVIDE STABILITY. EXPLAIN HOW THAT MAKES ME THE WINNER
WELL...
GREG 6·27
©2003 GEC Inc. Dist. by United Feature Syndicate, Inc. www.LuannsRoom.com

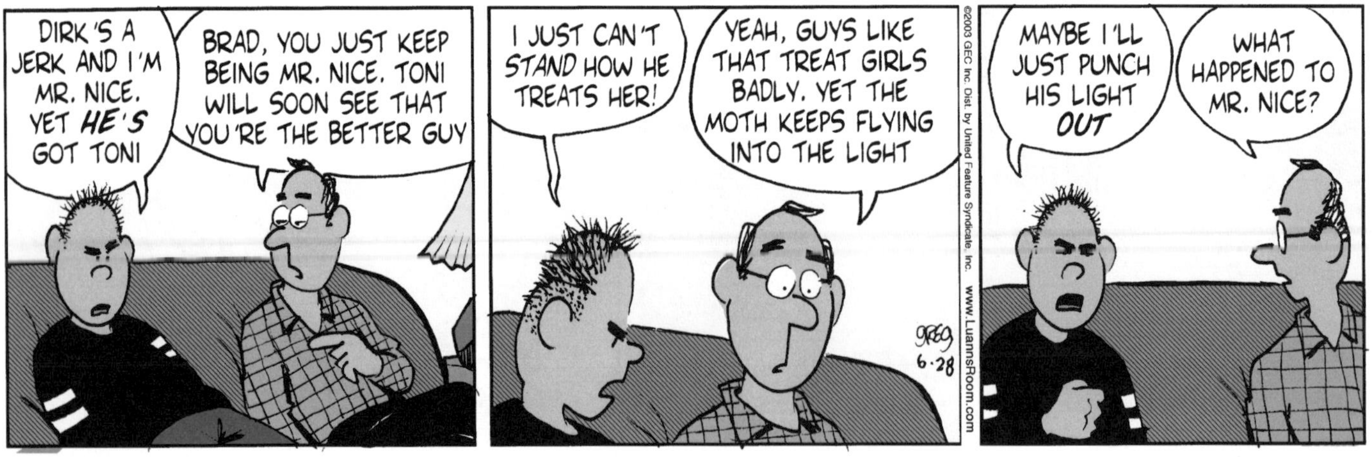
DIRK'S A JERK AND I'M MR. NICE. YET HE'S GOT TONI
BRAD, YOU JUST KEEP BEING MR. NICE. TONI WILL SOON SEE THAT YOU'RE THE BETTER GUY
I JUST CAN'T STAND HOW HE TREATS HER!
YEAH, GUYS LIKE THAT TREAT GIRLS BADLY. YET THE MOTH KEEPS FLYING INTO THE LIGHT
MAYBE I'LL JUST PUNCH HIS LIGHT OUT
WHAT HAPPENED TO MR. NICE?
GREG 6·28
©2003 GEC Inc. Dist. by United Feature Syndicate, Inc. www.LuannsRoom.com

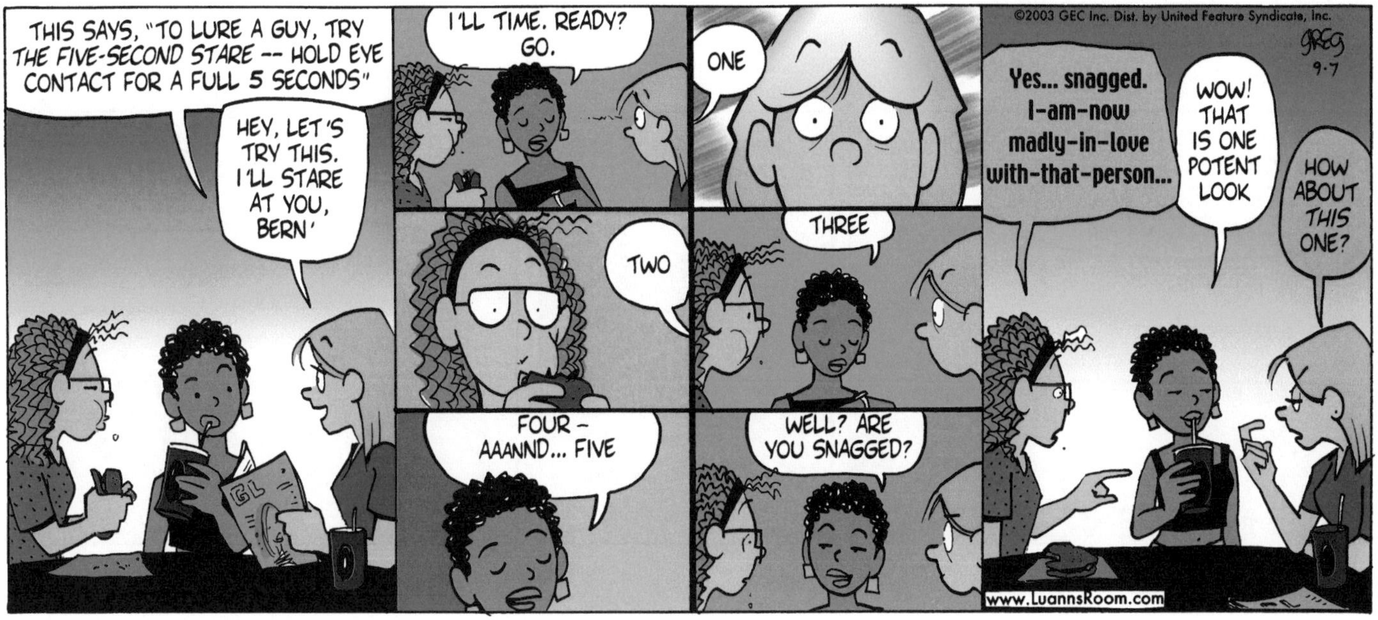
THIS SAYS, "TO LURE A GUY, TRY THE FIVE-SECOND STARE -- HOLD EYE CONTACT FOR A FULL 5 SECONDS"
HEY, LET'S TRY THIS. I'LL STARE AT YOU, BERN'
I'LL TIME. READY? GO.
ONE
TWO
THREE
FOUR - AAANND... FIVE
WELL? ARE YOU SNAGGED?
©2003 GEC Inc. Dist. by United Feature Syndicate, Inc.
GREG 9-7
Yes... snagged. I-am-now madly-in-love with-that-person...
WOW! THAT IS ONE POTENT LOOK
HOW ABOUT THIS ONE?
www.LuannsRoom.com

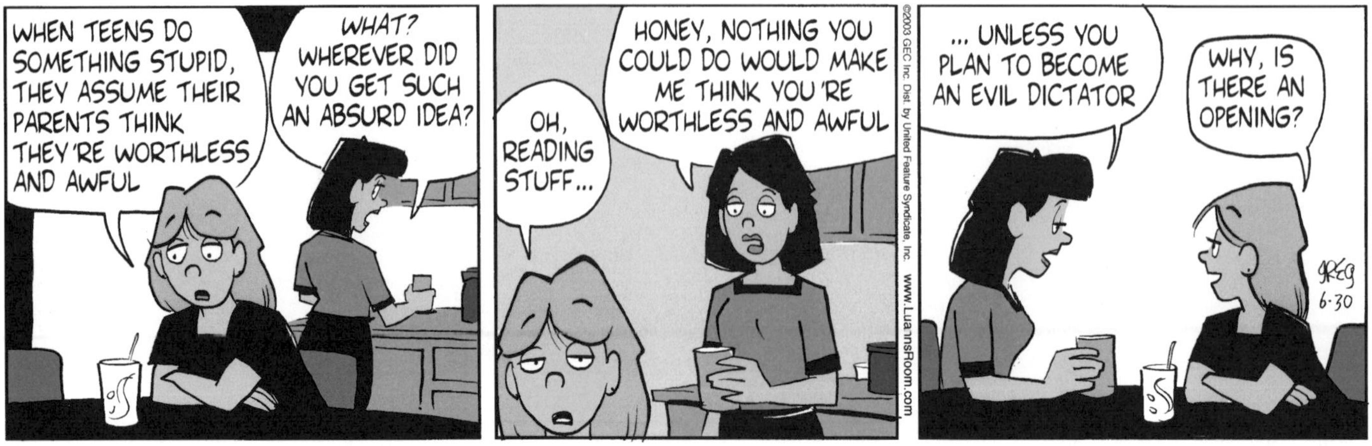
WHEN TEENS DO SOMETHING STUPID, THEY ASSUME THEIR PARENTS THINK THEY'RE WORTHLESS AND AWFUL
WHAT? WHEREVER DID YOU GET SUCH AN ABSURD IDEA?
OH, READING STUFF...
HONEY, NOTHING YOU COULD DO WOULD MAKE ME THINK YOU'RE WORTHLESS AND AWFUL
©2003 GEC Inc. Dist. by United Feature Syndicate, Inc.
www.LuannsRoom.com
... UNLESS YOU PLAN TO BECOME AN EVIL DICTATOR
WHY, IS THERE AN OPENING?
GREG 6-30

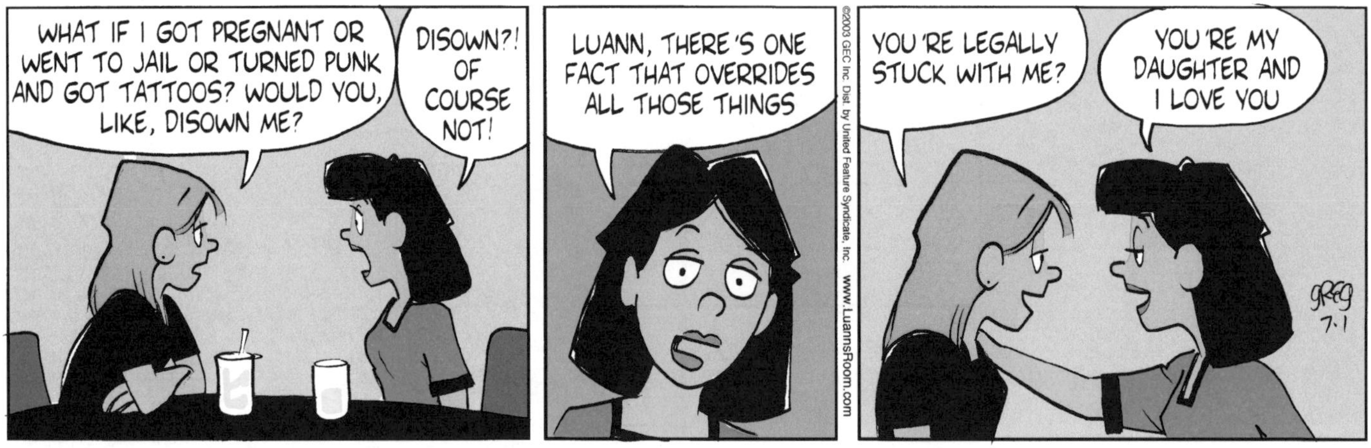
WHAT IF I GOT PREGNANT OR WENT TO JAIL OR TURNED PUNK AND GOT TATTOOS? WOULD YOU, LIKE, DISOWN ME?
DISOWN?! OF COURSE NOT!
©2003 GEC Inc. Dist. by United Feature Syndicate, Inc.
www.LuannsRoom.com
LUANN, THERE'S ONE FACT THAT OVERRIDES ALL THOSE THINGS
YOU'RE LEGALLY STUCK WITH ME?
YOU'RE MY DAUGHTER AND I LOVE YOU
GREG 7-1

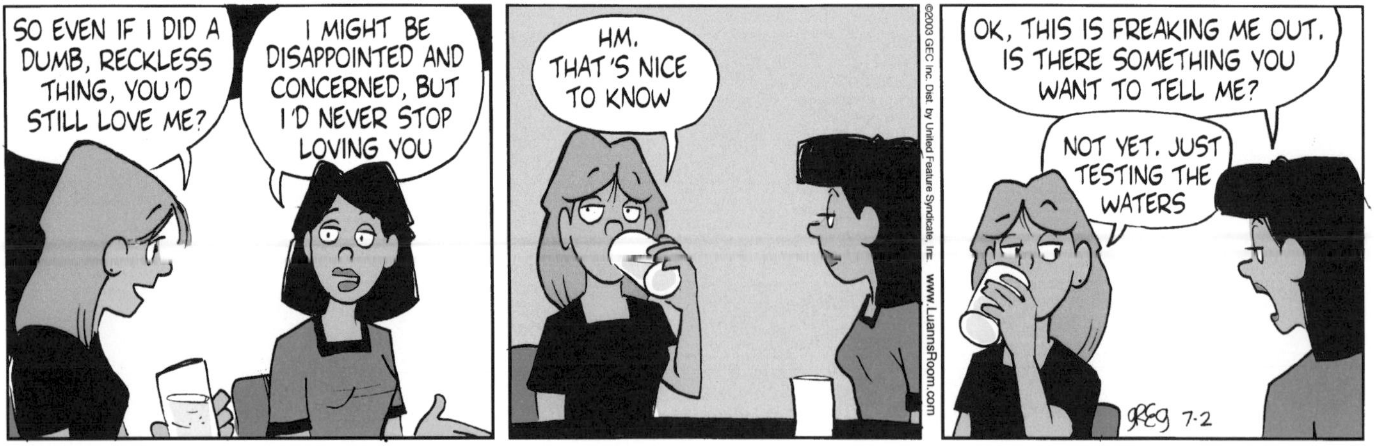
SO EVEN IF I DID A DUMB, RECKLESS THING, YOU'D STILL LOVE ME?
I MIGHT BE DISAPPOINTED AND CONCERNED, BUT I'D NEVER STOP LOVING YOU
HM. THAT'S NICE TO KNOW
©2003 GEC Inc. Dist. by United Feature Syndicate, Inc.
www.LuannsRoom.com
OK, THIS IS FREAKING ME OUT. IS THERE SOMETHING YOU WANT TO TELL ME?
NOT YET. JUST TESTING THE WATERS
GREG 7-2

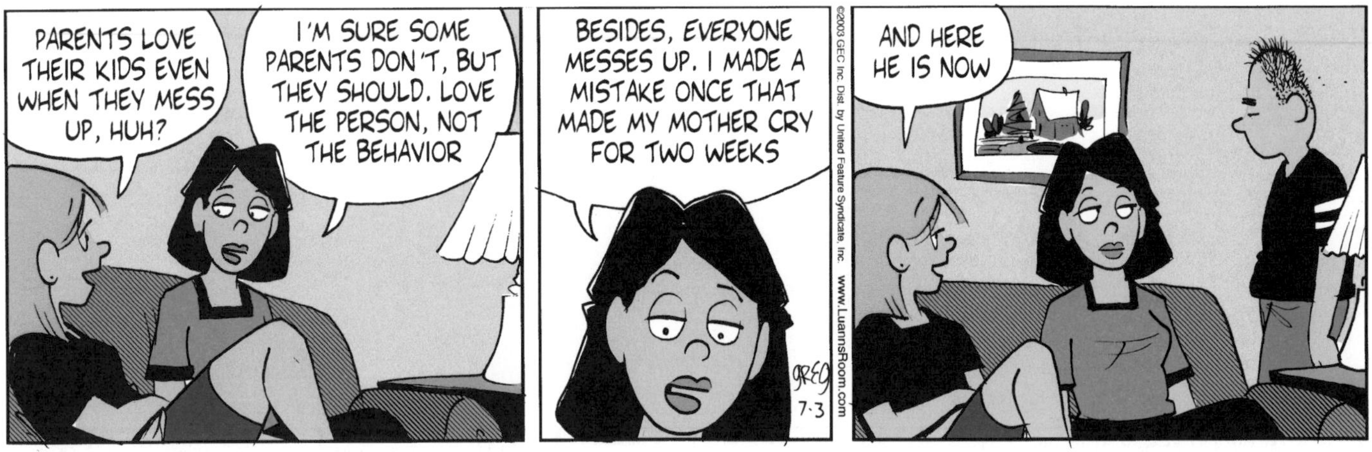
PARENTS LOVE THEIR KIDS EVEN WHEN THEY MESS UP, HUH?
I'M SURE SOME PARENTS DON'T, BUT THEY SHOULD. LOVE THE PERSON, NOT THE BEHAVIOR
BESIDES, EVERYONE MESSES UP. I MADE A MISTAKE ONCE THAT MADE MY MOTHER CRY FOR TWO WEEKS
AND HERE HE IS NOW
GREG 7·3
©2003 GEC Inc. Dist. by United Feature Syndicate, Inc. www.LuannsRoom.com

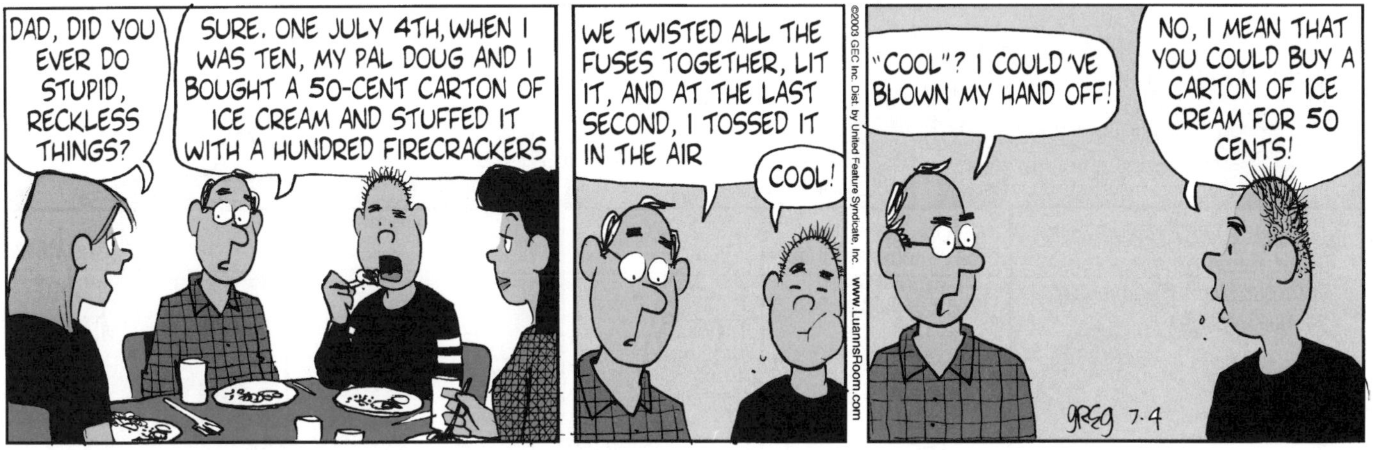
DAD, DID YOU EVER DO STUPID, RECKLESS THINGS?
SURE. ONE JULY 4TH, WHEN I WAS TEN, MY PAL DOUG AND I BOUGHT A 50-CENT CARTON OF ICE CREAM AND STUFFED IT WITH A HUNDRED FIRECRACKERS
WE TWISTED ALL THE FUSES TOGETHER, LIT IT, AND AT THE LAST SECOND, I TOSSED IT IN THE AIR
COOL!
"COOL"? I COULD'VE BLOWN MY HAND OFF!
NO, I MEAN THAT YOU COULD BUY A CARTON OF ICE CREAM FOR 50 CENTS!
GREG 7·4
©2003 GEC Inc. Dist. by United Feature Syndicate, Inc. www.LuannsRoom.com

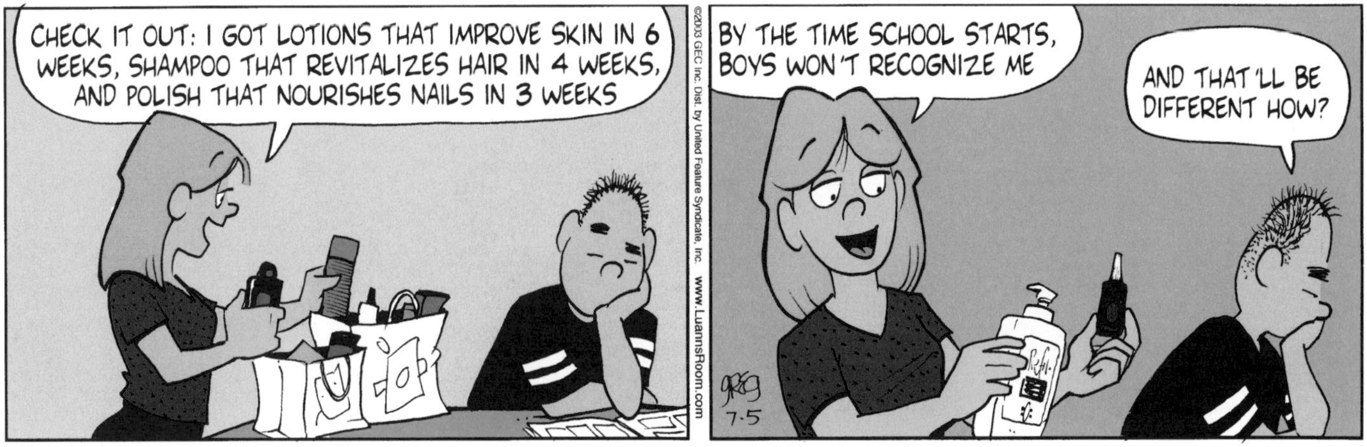
CHECK IT OUT: I GOT LOTIONS THAT IMPROVE SKIN IN 6 WEEKS, SHAMPOO THAT REVITALIZES HAIR IN 4 WEEKS, AND POLISH THAT NOURISHES NAILS IN 3 WEEKS
BY THE TIME SCHOOL STARTS, BOYS WON'T RECOGNIZE ME
AND THAT'LL BE DIFFERENT HOW?
GREG 7·5
©2003 GEC Inc. Dist. by United Feature Syndicate, Inc. www.LuannsRoom.com

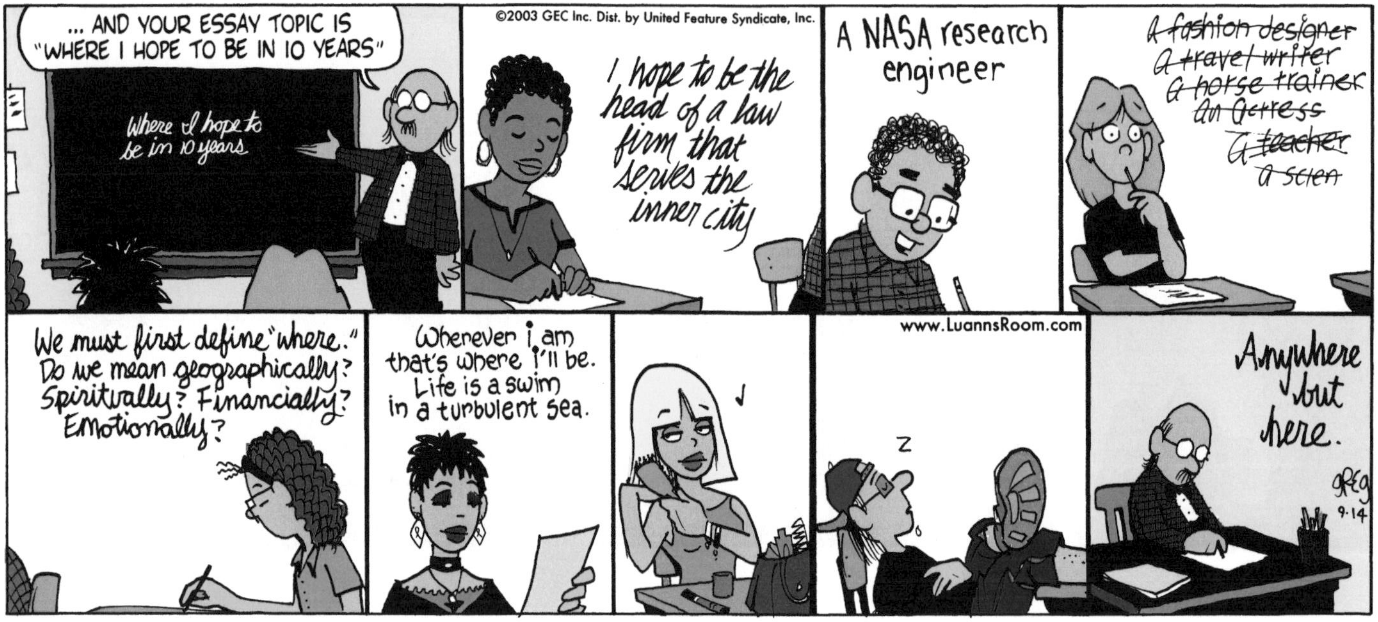
... AND YOUR ESSAY TOPIC IS "WHERE I HOPE TO BE IN 10 YEARS"
Where I hope to be in 10 years
©2003 GEC Inc. Dist. by United Feature Syndicate, Inc.
I hope to be the head of a law firm that serves the inner city
A NASA research engineer
A fashion designer
A travel writer
A horse trainer
An actress
A teacher
A scien
We must first define "where." Do we mean geographically? Spiritually? Financially? Emotionally?
Whenever I am that's where I'll be. Life is a swim in a turbulent sea.
Z
www.LuannsRoom.com
Anywhere but here.
GREG 9·14

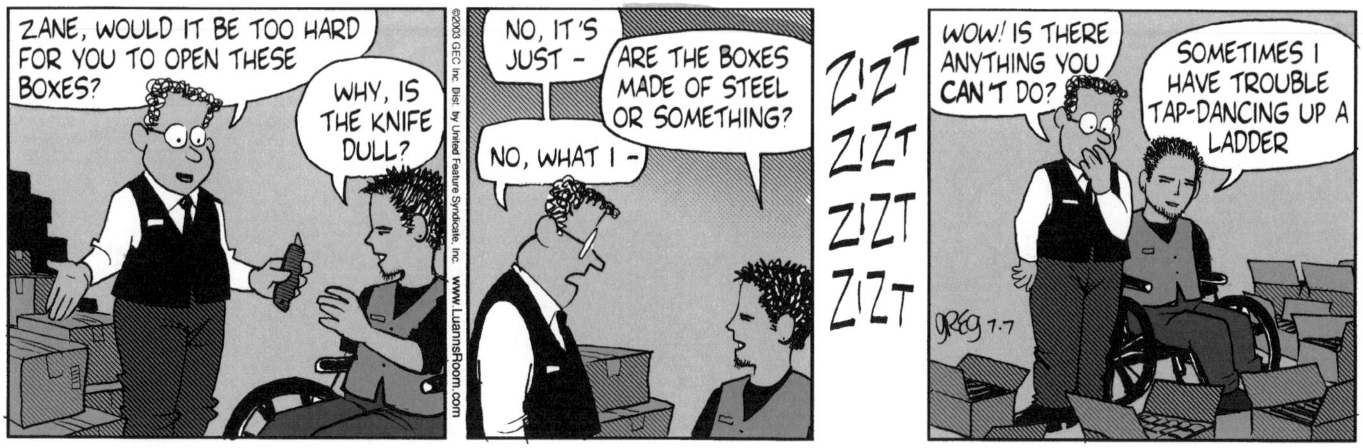
ZANE, WOULD IT BE TOO HARD FOR YOU TO OPEN THESE BOXES?
WHY, IS THE KNIFE DULL?
©2003 GEC Inc. Dist. by United Feature Syndicate, Inc. www.LuannsRoom.com
NO, IT'S JUST –
ARE THE BOXES MADE OF STEEL OR SOMETHING?
NO, WHAT I –
ZIZT ZIZT ZIZT ZIZT
WOW! IS THERE ANYTHING YOU CAN'T DO?
SOMETIMES I HAVE TROUBLE TAP-DANCING UP A LADDER
GREG 7-7

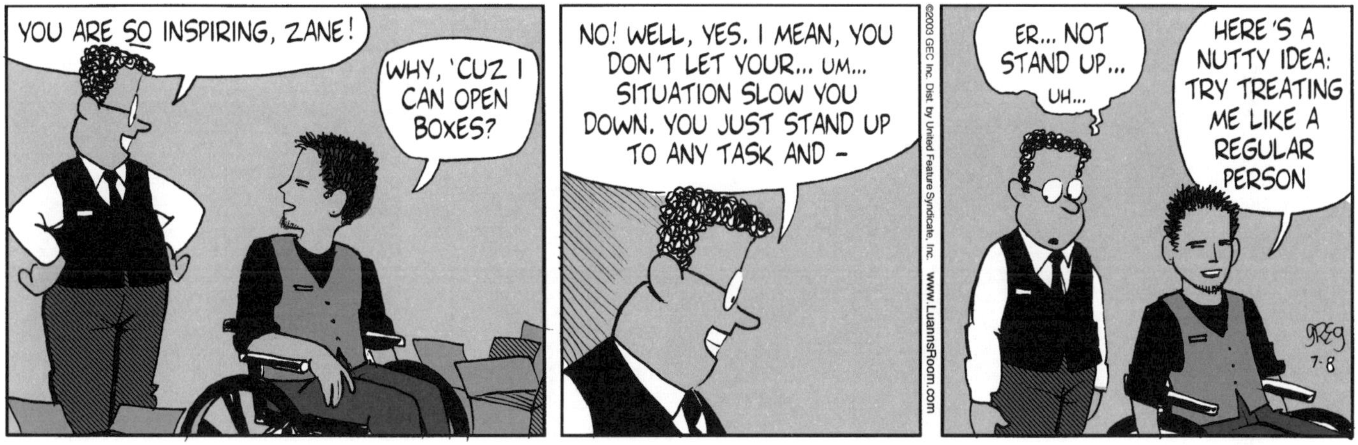
YOU ARE SO INSPIRING, ZANE!
WHY, 'CUZ I CAN OPEN BOXES?
NO! WELL, YES. I MEAN, YOU DON'T LET YOUR... UM... SITUATION SLOW YOU DOWN. YOU JUST STAND UP TO ANY TASK AND –
©2003 GEC Inc. Dist. by United Feature Syndicate, Inc. www.LuannsRoom.com
ER... NOT STAND UP... UH...
HERE'S A NUTTY IDEA: TRY TREATING ME LIKE A REGULAR PERSON
GREG 7-8

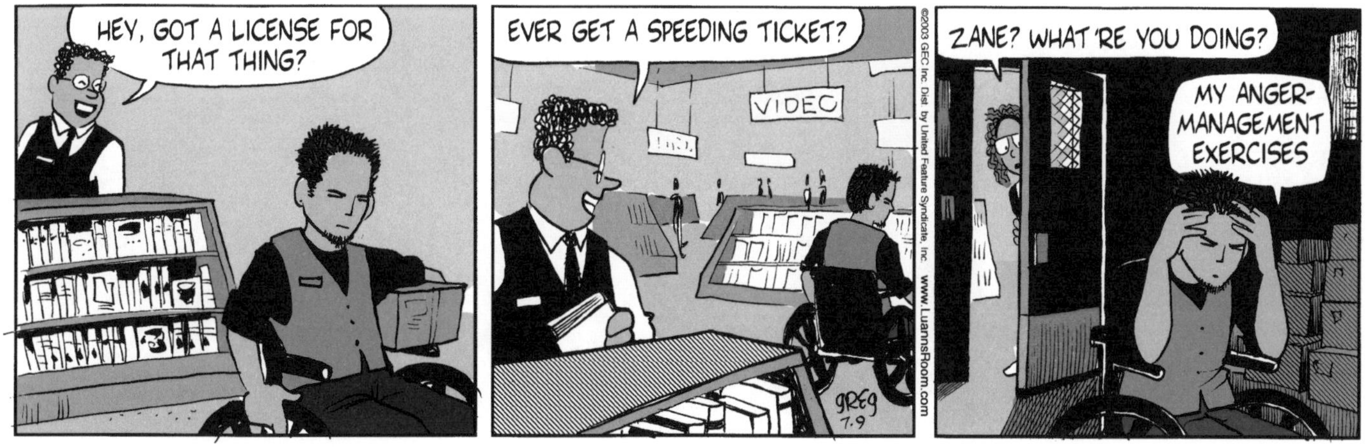
HEY, GOT A LICENSE FOR THAT THING?
EVER GET A SPEEDING TICKET?
VIDEO
GREG 7-9
©2003 GEC Inc. Dist. by United Feature Syndicate, Inc. www.LuannsRoom.com
ZANE? WHAT'RE YOU DOING?
MY ANGER-MANAGEMENT EXERCISES

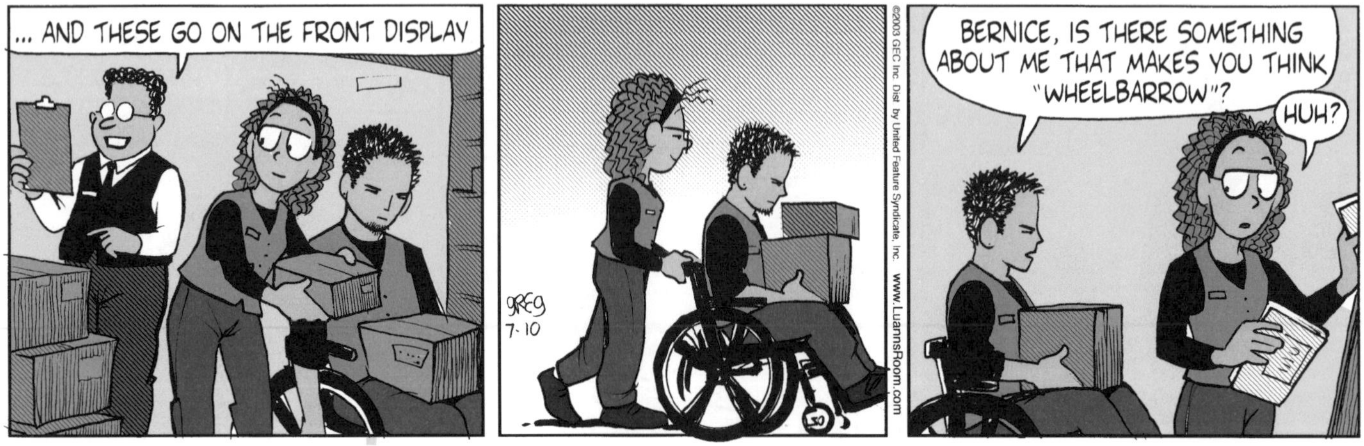
... AND THESE GO ON THE FRONT DISPLAY
©2003 GEC Inc. Dist. by United Feature Syndicate, Inc.
www.LuannsRoom.com
GREG 7-10
BERNICE, IS THERE SOMETHING ABOUT ME THAT MAKES YOU THINK "WHEELBARROW"?
HUH?

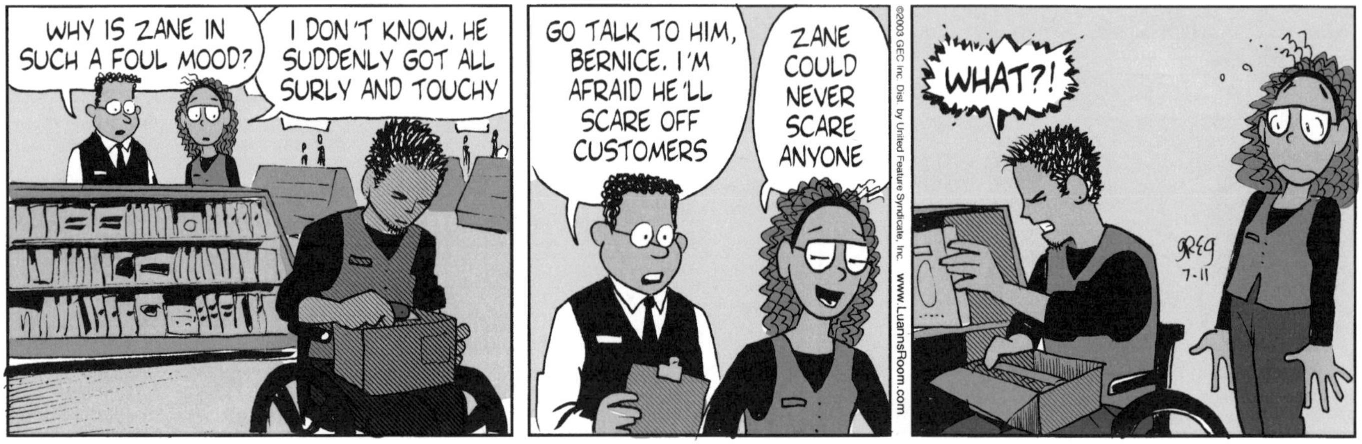
WHY IS ZANE IN SUCH A FOUL MOOD?
I DON'T KNOW. HE SUDDENLY GOT ALL SURLY AND TOUCHY
GO TALK TO HIM, BERNICE. I'M AFRAID HE'LL SCARE OFF CUSTOMERS
ZANE COULD NEVER SCARE ANYONE
©2003 GEC Inc. Dist. by United Feature Syndicate, Inc.
www.LuannsRoom.com
WHAT?!
GREG 7-11

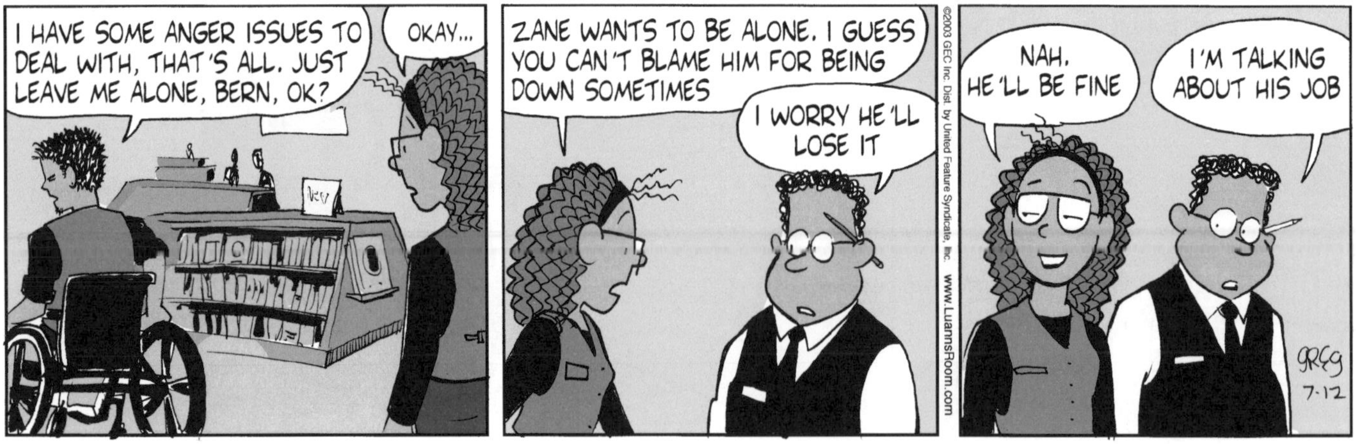
I HAVE SOME ANGER ISSUES TO DEAL WITH, THAT'S ALL. JUST LEAVE ME ALONE, BERN, OK?
OKAY...
ZANE WANTS TO BE ALONE. I GUESS YOU CAN'T BLAME HIM FOR BEING DOWN SOMETIMES
I WORRY HE'LL LOSE IT
©2003 GEC Inc. Dist. by United Feature Syndicate, Inc.
www.LuannsRoom.com
NAH. HE'LL BE FINE
I'M TALKING ABOUT HIS JOB
GREG 7-12

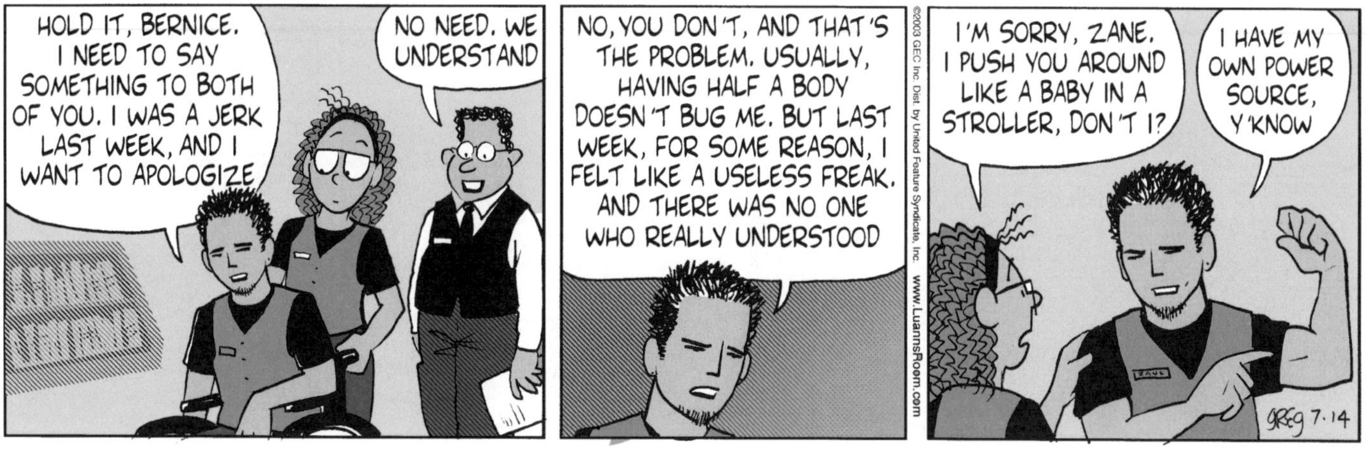
HOLD IT, BERNICE. I NEED TO SAY SOMETHING TO BOTH OF YOU. I WAS A JERK LAST WEEK, AND I WANT TO APOLOGIZE
NO NEED. WE UNDERSTAND
NO, YOU DON'T, AND THAT'S THE PROBLEM. USUALLY, HAVING HALF A BODY DOESN'T BUG ME. BUT LAST WEEK, FOR SOME REASON, I FELT LIKE A USELESS FREAK. AND THERE WAS NO ONE WHO REALLY UNDERSTOOD
I'M SORRY, ZANE. I PUSH YOU AROUND LIKE A BABY IN A STROLLER, DON'T I?
I HAVE MY OWN POWER SOURCE, Y'KNOW
GREG 7·14

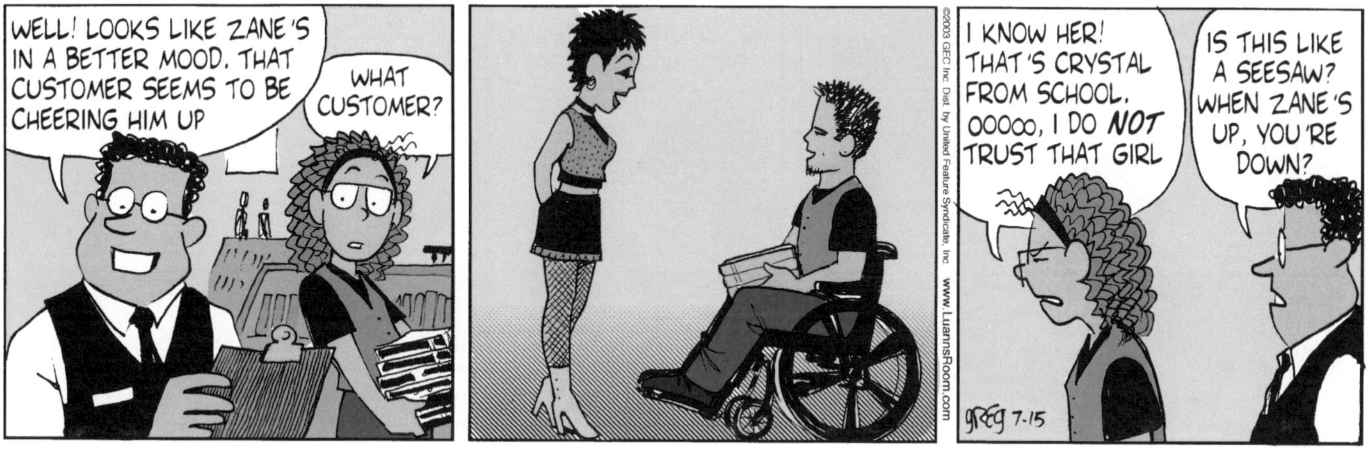
WELL! LOOKS LIKE ZANE'S IN A BETTER MOOD. THAT CUSTOMER SEEMS TO BE CHEERING HIM UP
WHAT CUSTOMER?
I KNOW HER! THAT'S CRYSTAL FROM SCHOOL. OOOOO, I DO **NOT** TRUST THAT GIRL
IS THIS LIKE A SEESAW? WHEN ZANE'S UP, YOU'RE DOWN?
GREG 7·15

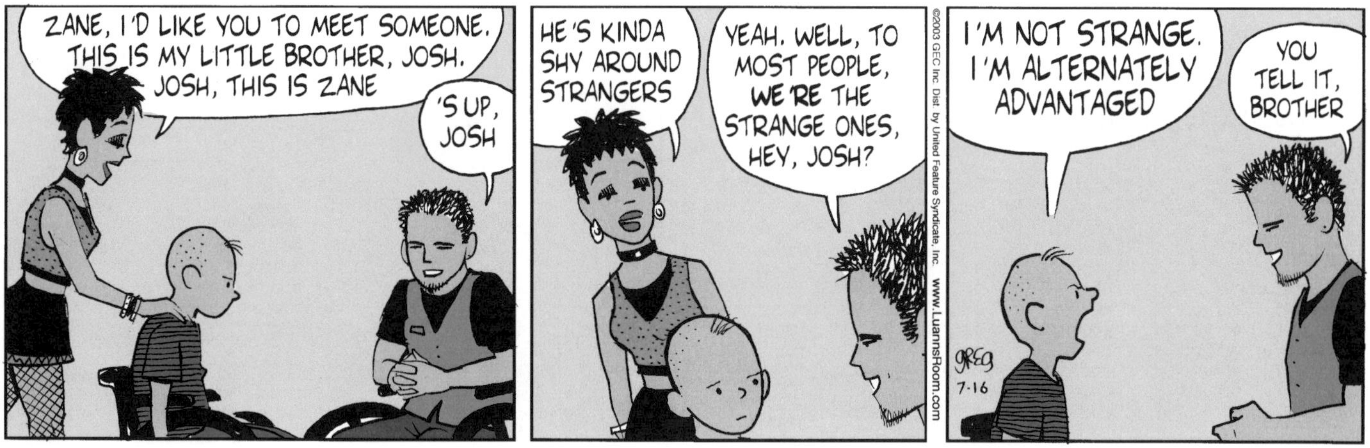
ZANE, I'D LIKE YOU TO MEET SOMEONE. THIS IS MY LITTLE BROTHER, JOSH. JOSH, THIS IS ZANE
'S UP, JOSH
HE'S KINDA SHY AROUND STRANGERS
YEAH. WELL, TO MOST PEOPLE, **WE'RE** THE STRANGE ONES, HEY, JOSH?
I'M NOT STRANGE. I'M ALTERNATELY ADVANTAGED
YOU TELL IT, BROTHER
GREG 7·16

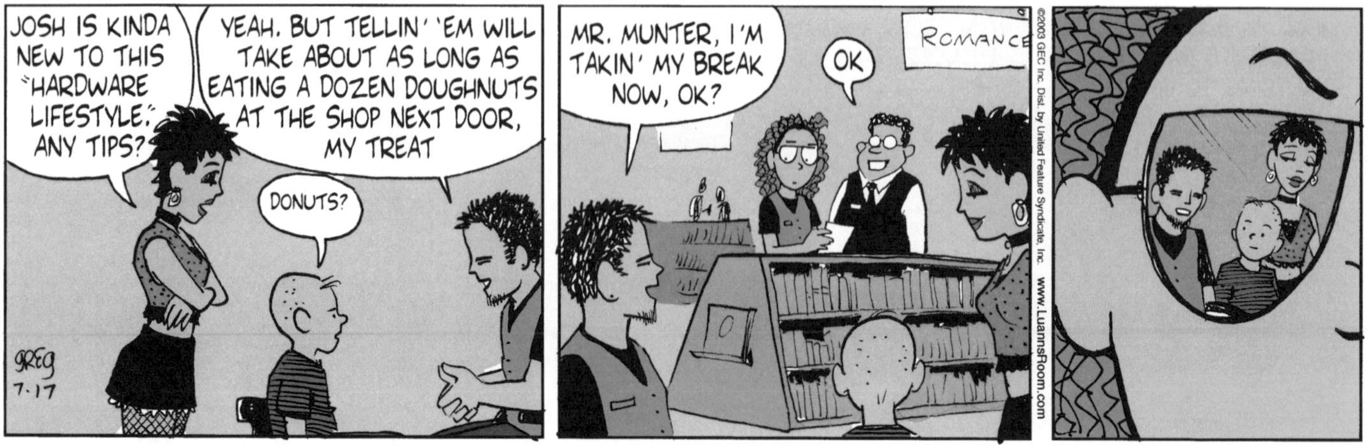
JOSH IS KINDA NEW TO THIS "HARDWARE LIFESTYLE." ANY TIPS?
YEAH. BUT TELLIN' 'EM WILL TAKE ABOUT AS LONG AS EATING A DOZEN DOUGHNUTS AT THE SHOP NEXT DOOR, MY TREAT
DONUTS?
GREG 7·17
MR. MUNTER, I'M TAKIN' MY BREAK NOW, OK?
OK
ROMANCE
©2003 GEC Inc. Dist. by United Feature Syndicate, Inc. www.LuannsRoom.com

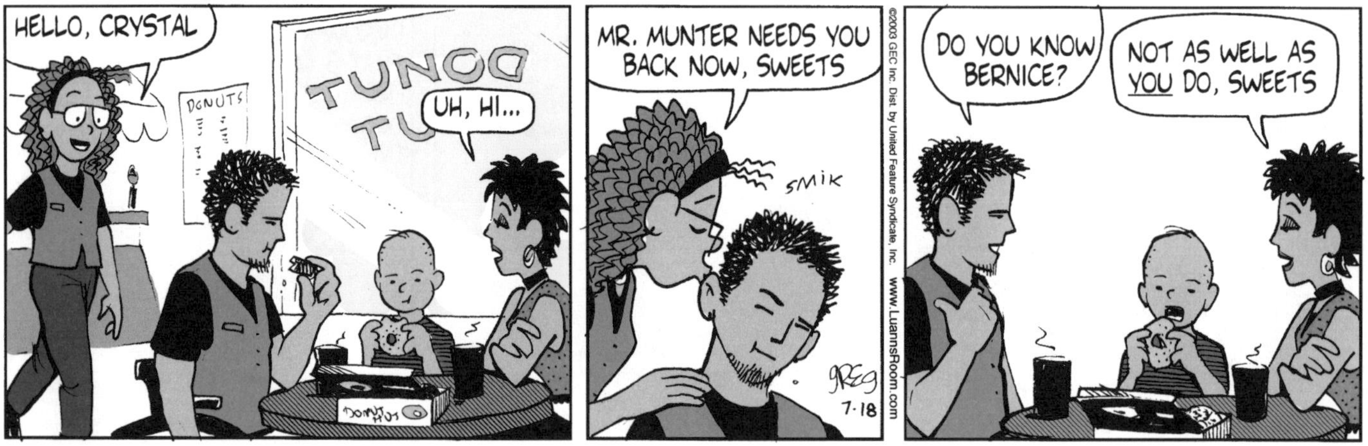
HELLO, CRYSTAL
DONUTS
DONUT
UH, HI...
MR. MUNTER NEEDS YOU BACK NOW, SWEETS
SMIK
GREG 7·18
©2003 GEC Inc. Dist. by United Feature Syndicate, Inc. www.LuannsRoom.com
DO YOU KNOW BERNICE?
NOT AS WELL AS YOU DO, SWEETS

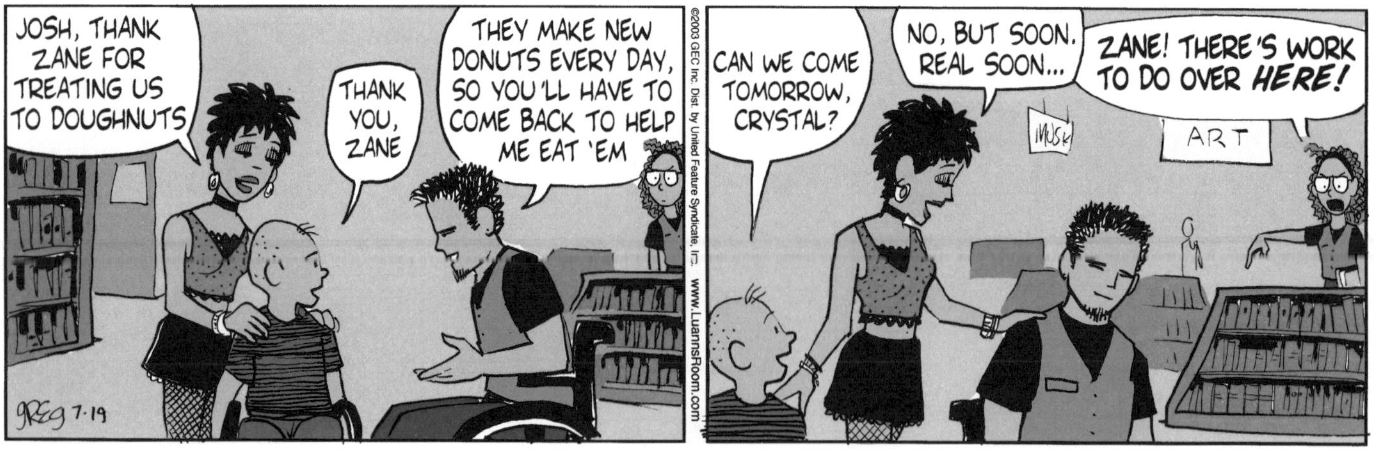
JOSH, THANK ZANE FOR TREATING US TO DOUGHNUTS
THANK YOU, ZANE
THEY MAKE NEW DONUTS EVERY DAY, SO YOU'LL HAVE TO COME BACK TO HELP ME EAT 'EM
GREG 7·19
©2003 GEC Inc. Dist. by United Feature Syndicate, Inc. www.LuannsRoom.com
CAN WE COME TOMORROW, CRYSTAL?
NO, BUT SOON. REAL SOON...
ZANE! THERE'S WORK TO DO OVER HERE!
MUSIC
ART

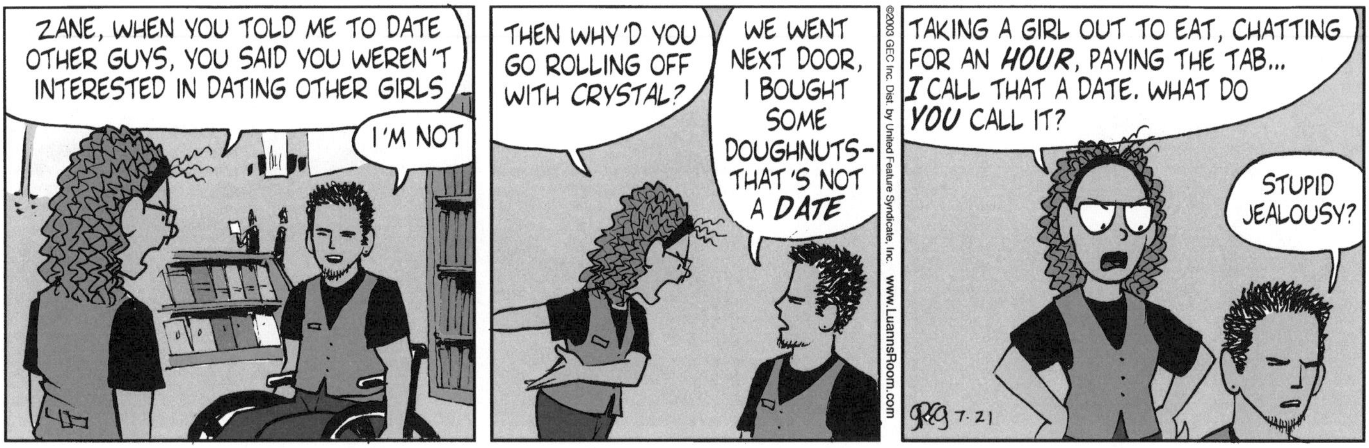
ZANE, WHEN YOU TOLD ME TO DATE OTHER GUYS, YOU SAID YOU WEREN'T INTERESTED IN DATING OTHER GIRLS
I'M NOT
THEN WHY'D YOU GO ROLLING OFF WITH CRYSTAL?
WE WENT NEXT DOOR, I BOUGHT SOME DOUGHNUTS- THAT'S NOT A DATE
©2003 GEC Inc. Dist. by United Feature Syndicate, Inc.
www.LuannsRoom.com
TAKING A GIRL OUT TO EAT, CHATTING FOR AN HOUR, PAYING THE TAB... I CALL THAT A DATE. WHAT DO YOU CALL IT?
STUPID JEALOUSY?
GREG 7.21

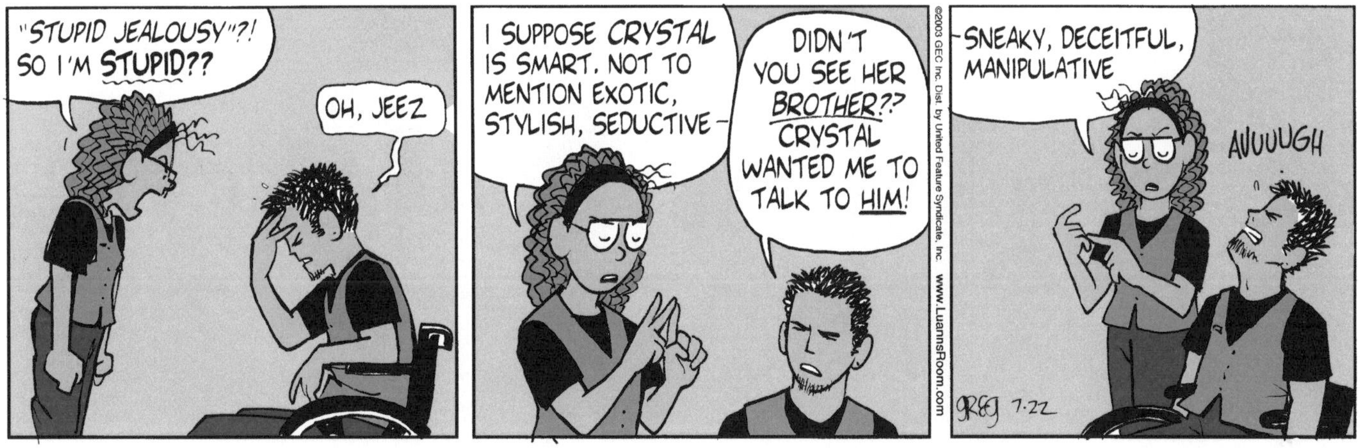
"STUPID JEALOUSY"?! SO I'M STUPID??
OH, JEEZ
I SUPPOSE CRYSTAL IS SMART. NOT TO MENTION EXOTIC, STYLISH, SEDUCTIVE-
DIDN'T YOU SEE HER BROTHER?? CRYSTAL WANTED ME TO TALK TO HIM!
©2003 GEC Inc. Dist. by United Feature Syndicate, Inc.
www.LuannsRoom.com
-SNEAKY, DECEITFUL, MANIPULATIVE
AUUUUGH
GREG 7.22

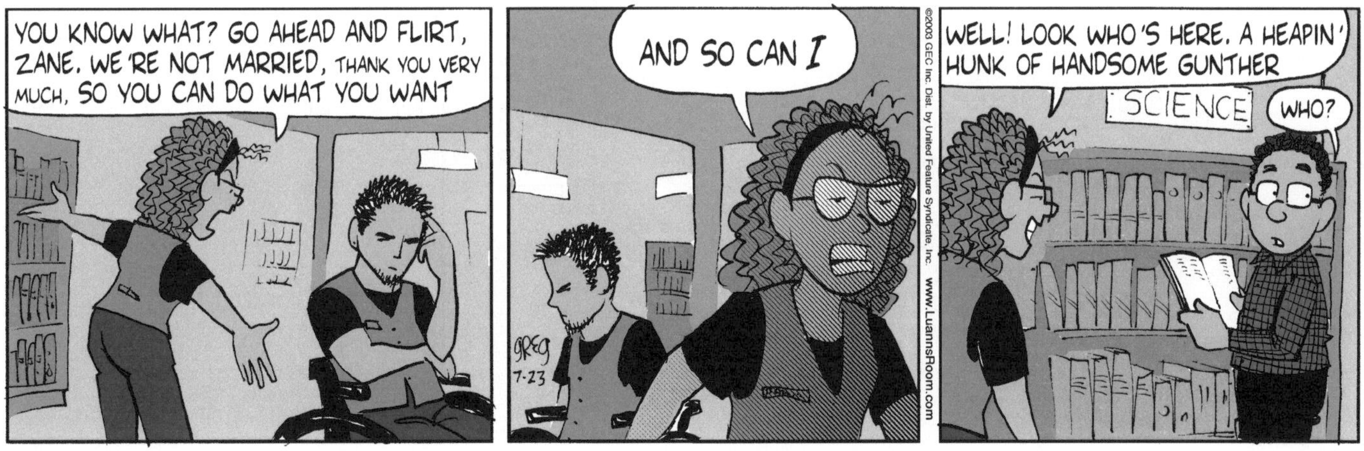
YOU KNOW WHAT? GO AHEAD AND FLIRT, ZANE. WE'RE NOT MARRIED, THANK YOU VERY MUCH, SO YOU CAN DO WHAT YOU WANT
AND SO CAN I
GREG 7-23
©2003 GEC Inc. Dist. by United Feature Syndicate, Inc.
www.LuannsRoom.com
WELL! LOOK WHO'S HERE. A HEAPIN' HUNK OF HANDSOME GUNTHER
SCIENCE
WHO?

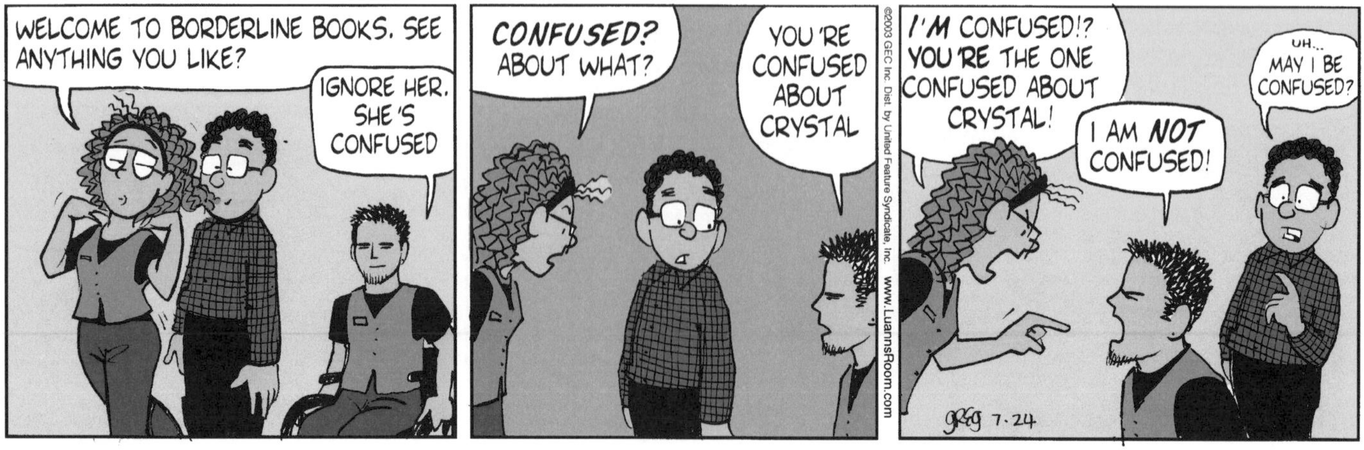
WELCOME TO BORDERLINE BOOKS. SEE ANYTHING YOU LIKE?
IGNORE HER. SHE'S CONFUSED
CONFUSED? ABOUT WHAT?
YOU'RE CONFUSED ABOUT CRYSTAL
©2003 GEC Inc. Dist. by United Feature Syndicate, Inc.
www.LuannsRoom.com
I'M CONFUSED!? YOU'RE THE ONE CONFUSED ABOUT CRYSTAL!
I AM NOT CONFUSED!
UH... MAY I BE CONFUSED?
GREG 7·24

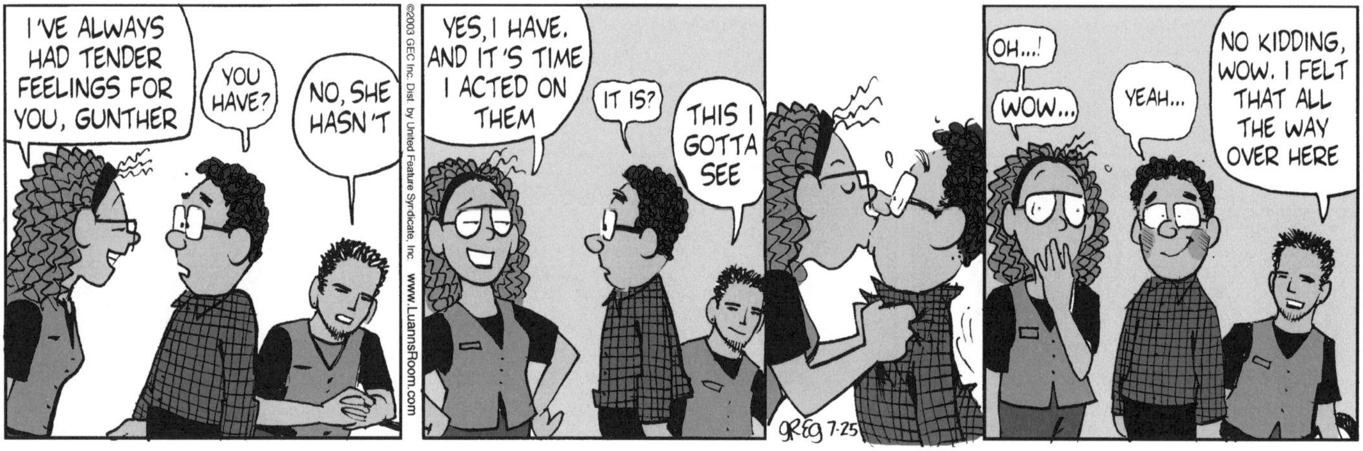
I'VE ALWAYS HAD TENDER FEELINGS FOR YOU, GUNTHER
YOU HAVE?
NO, SHE HASN'T
©2003 GEC Inc. Dist. by United Feature Syndicate, Inc.
www.LuannsRoom.com
YES, I HAVE. AND IT'S TIME I ACTED ON THEM
IT IS?
THIS I GOTTA SEE
GREG 7·25
OH...!
WOW...
YEAH...
NO KIDDING, WOW. I FELT THAT ALL THE WAY OVER HERE

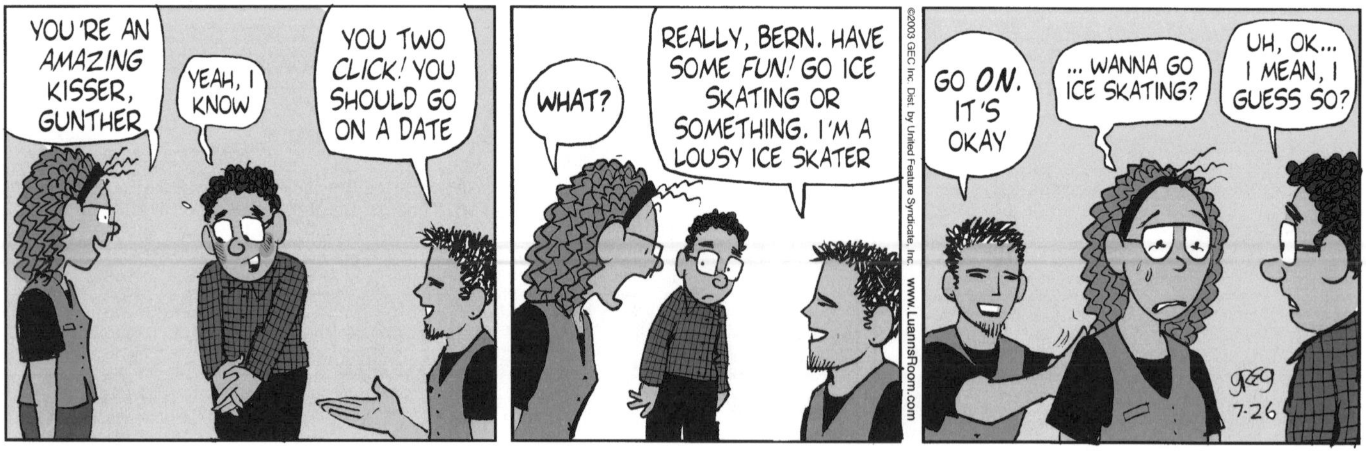
YOU'RE AN AMAZING KISSER, GUNTHER
YEAH, I KNOW
YOU TWO CLICK! YOU SHOULD GO ON A DATE
WHAT?
REALLY, BERN. HAVE SOME FUN! GO ICE SKATING OR SOMETHING. I'M A LOUSY ICE SKATER
©2003 GEC Inc. Dist. by United Feature Syndicate, Inc.
www.LuannsRoom.com
GO ON. IT'S OKAY
... WANNA GO ICE SKATING?
UH, OK... I MEAN, I GUESS SO?
GREG 7·26

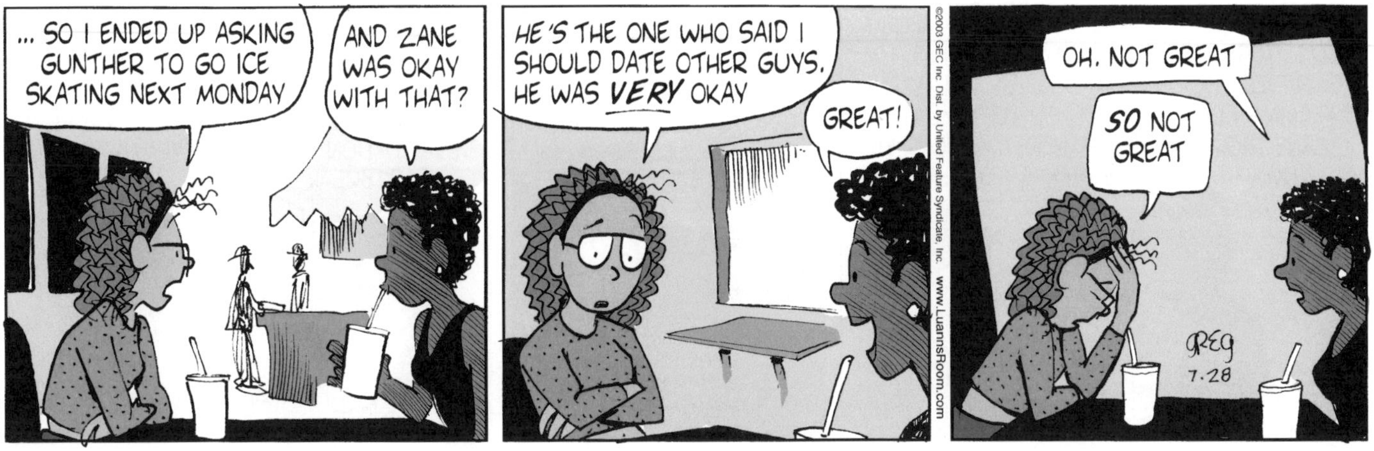
... SO I ENDED UP ASKING GUNTHER TO GO ICE SKATING NEXT MONDAY
AND ZANE WAS OKAY WITH THAT?
HE'S THE ONE WHO SAID I SHOULD DATE OTHER GUYS. HE WAS VERY OKAY
GREAT!
©2003 GEC Inc. Dist. by United Feature Syndicate, Inc. www.LuannsRoom.com
OH. NOT GREAT
SO NOT GREAT
GREG 7-28

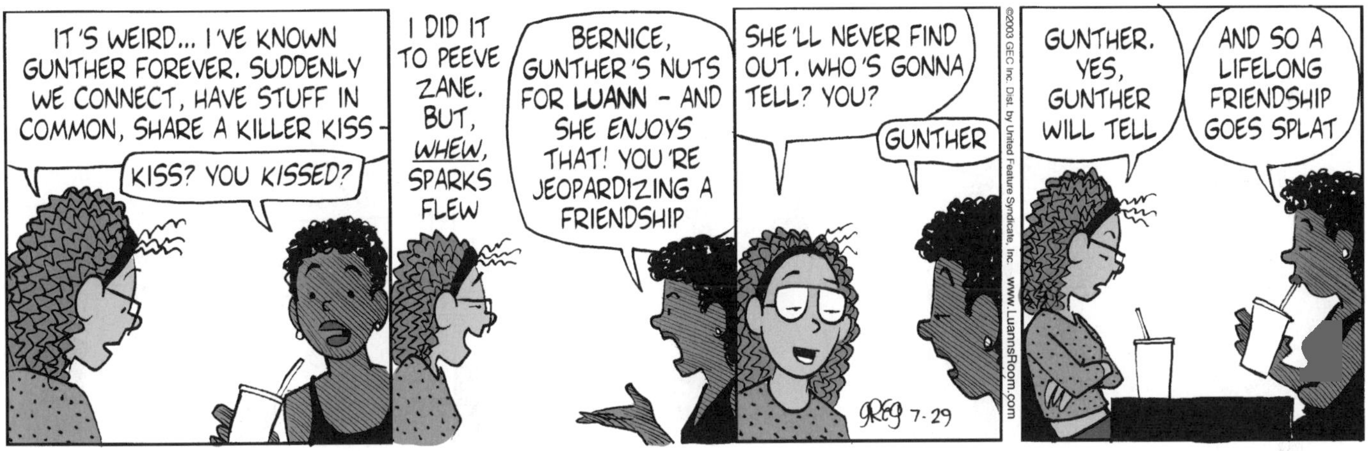
IT'S WEIRD... I'VE KNOWN GUNTHER FOREVER. SUDDENLY WE CONNECT, HAVE STUFF IN COMMON, SHARE A KILLER KISS-
KISS? YOU KISSED?
I DID IT TO PEEVE ZANE. BUT, WHEW, SPARKS FLEW
BERNICE, GUNTHER'S NUTS FOR LUANN - AND SHE ENJOYS THAT! YOU'RE JEOPARDIZING A FRIENDSHIP
SHE'LL NEVER FIND OUT. WHO'S GONNA TELL? YOU?
GUNTHER
GREG 7-29
©2003 GEC Inc. Dist. by United Feature Syndicate, Inc. www.LuannsRoom.com
GUNTHER. YES, GUNTHER WILL TELL
AND SO A LIFELONG FRIENDSHIP GOES SPLAT

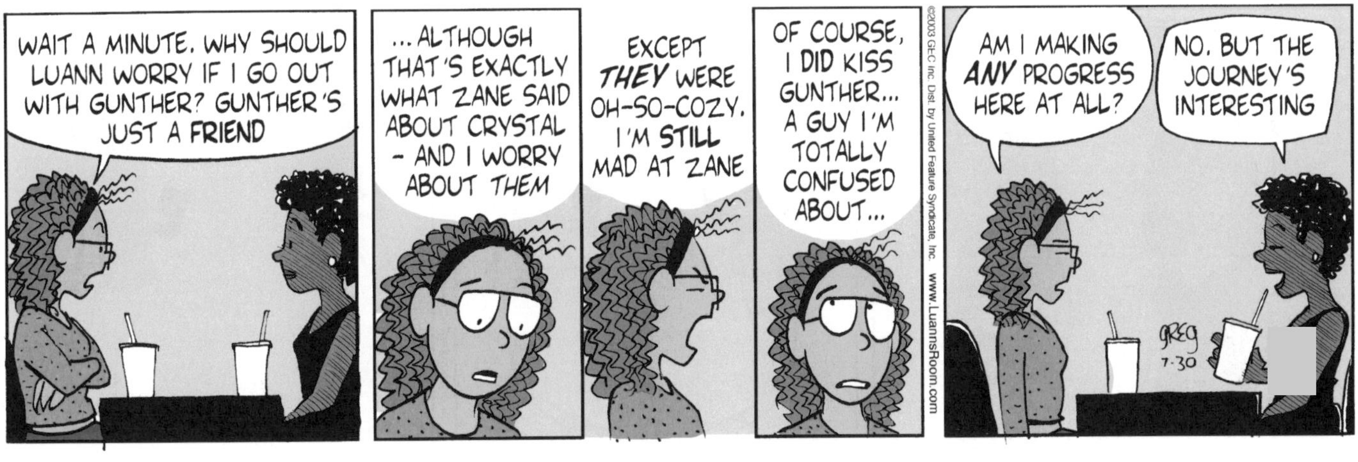
WAIT A MINUTE. WHY SHOULD LUANN WORRY IF I GO OUT WITH GUNTHER? GUNTHER'S JUST A FRIEND
...ALTHOUGH THAT'S EXACTLY WHAT ZANE SAID ABOUT CRYSTAL - AND I WORRY ABOUT THEM
EXCEPT THEY WERE OH-SO-COZY. I'M STILL MAD AT ZANE
OF COURSE, I DID KISS GUNTHER... A GUY I'M TOTALLY CONFUSED ABOUT...
©2003 GEC Inc. Dist. by United Feature Syndicate, Inc. www.LuannsRoom.com
AM I MAKING ANY PROGRESS HERE AT ALL?
NO. BUT THE JOURNEY'S INTERESTING
GREG 7-30

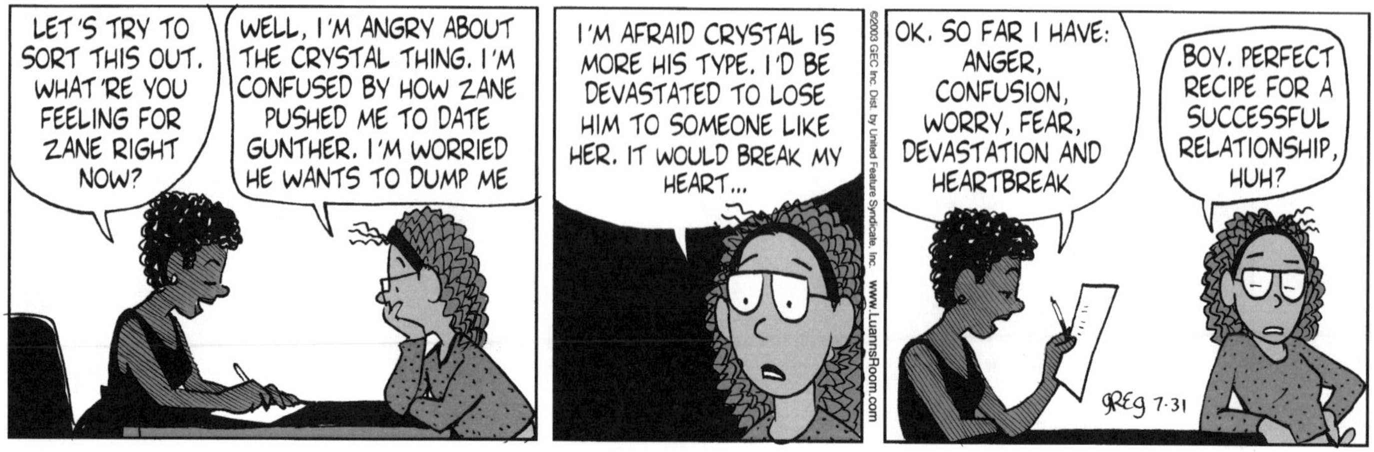
LET'S TRY TO SORT THIS OUT. WHAT'RE YOU FEELING FOR ZANE RIGHT NOW?
WELL, I'M ANGRY ABOUT THE CRYSTAL THING. I'M CONFUSED BY HOW ZANE PUSHED ME TO DATE GUNTHER. I'M WORRIED HE WANTS TO DUMP ME
I'M AFRAID CRYSTAL IS MORE HIS TYPE. I'D BE DEVASTATED TO LOSE HIM TO SOMEONE LIKE HER. IT WOULD BREAK MY HEART...
©2003 GEC Inc. Dist. by United Feature Syndicate, Inc. www.LuannsRoom.com
OK. SO FAR I HAVE: ANGER, CONFUSION, WORRY, FEAR, DEVASTATION AND HEARTBREAK
BOY. PERFECT RECIPE FOR A SUCCESSFUL RELATIONSHIP, HUH?
GREG 7·31

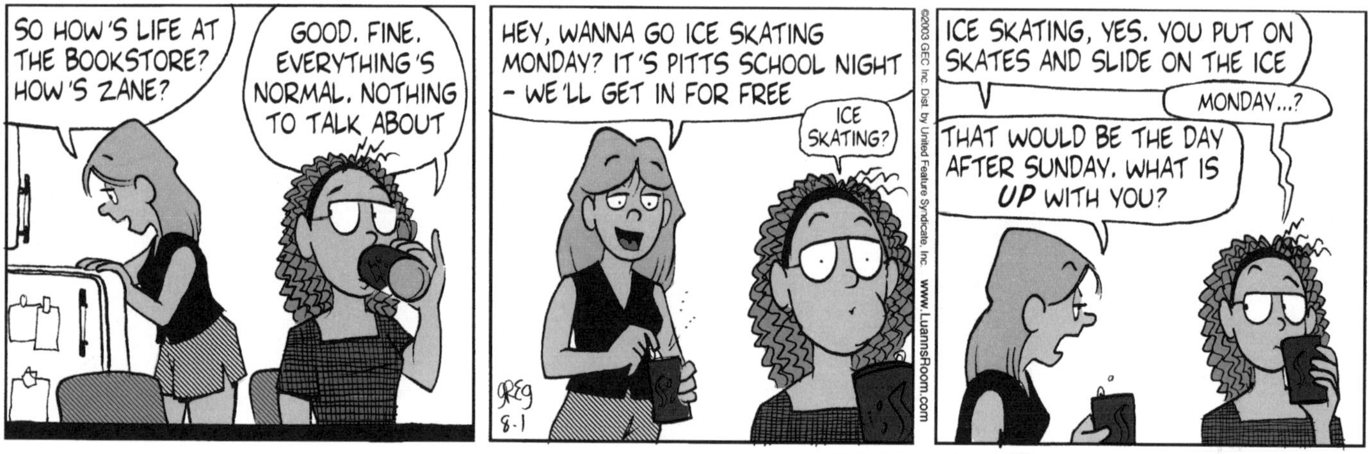
SO HOW'S LIFE AT THE BOOKSTORE? HOW'S ZANE?
GOOD. FINE. EVERYTHING'S NORMAL. NOTHING TO TALK ABOUT
GREG 8·1
HEY, WANNA GO ICE SKATING MONDAY? IT'S PITTS SCHOOL NIGHT - WE'LL GET IN FOR FREE
ICE SKATING?
©2003 GEC Inc. Dist. by United Feature Syndicate, Inc. www.LuannsRoom.com
ICE SKATING, YES. YOU PUT ON SKATES AND SLIDE ON THE ICE
MONDAY...?
THAT WOULD BE THE DAY AFTER SUNDAY. WHAT IS *UP* WITH YOU?

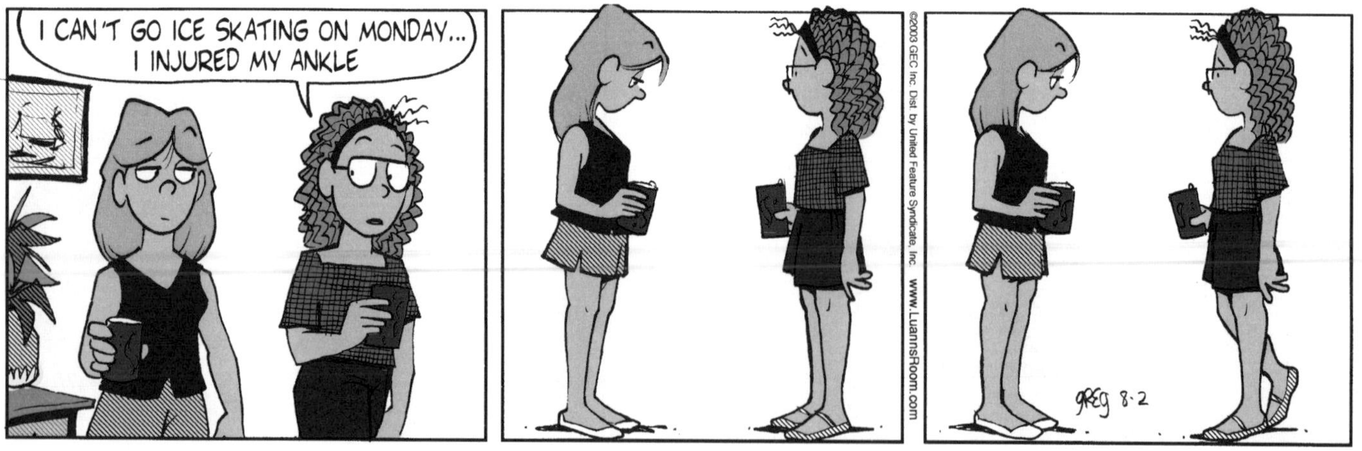
I CAN'T GO ICE SKATING ON MONDAY... I INJURED MY ANKLE
©2003 GEC Inc. Dist. by United Feature Syndicate, Inc. www.LuannsRoom.com
GREG 8·2

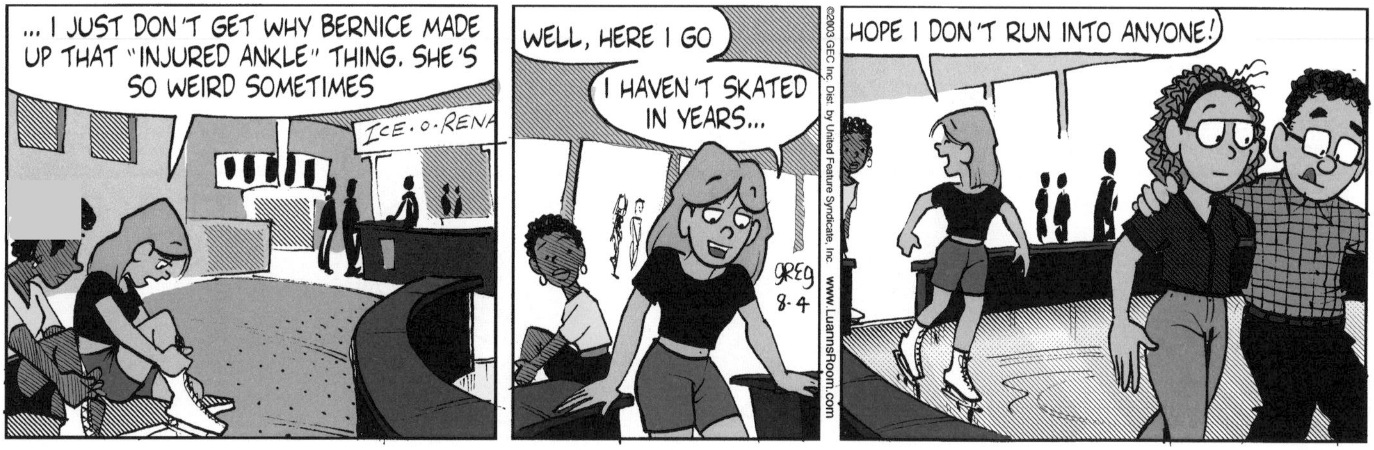
... I JUST DON'T GET WHY BERNICE MADE UP THAT "INJURED ANKLE" THING. SHE'S SO WEIRD SOMETIMES
ICE-O-RENA
WELL, HERE I GO
I HAVEN'T SKATED IN YEARS...
GREG 8·4
©2003 GEC Inc. Dist. by United Feature Syndicate, Inc. www.LuannsRoom.com
HOPE I DON'T RUN INTO ANYONE!

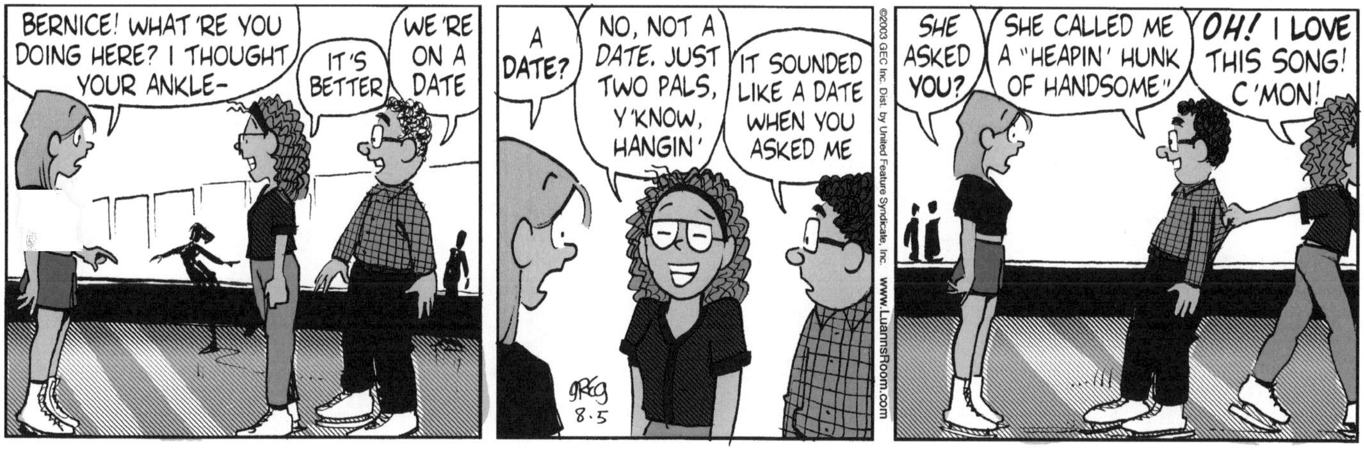
BERNICE! WHAT'RE YOU DOING HERE? I THOUGHT YOUR ANKLE-
IT'S BETTER
WE'RE ON A DATE
A DATE?
NO, NOT A DATE. JUST TWO PALS, Y'KNOW, HANGIN'
IT SOUNDED LIKE A DATE WHEN YOU ASKED ME
GREG 8·5
©2003 GEC Inc. Dist. by United Feature Syndicate, Inc. www.LuannsRoom.com
SHE ASKED YOU?
SHE CALLED ME A "HEAPIN' HUNK OF HANDSOME"
OH! I LOVE THIS SONG! C'MON!

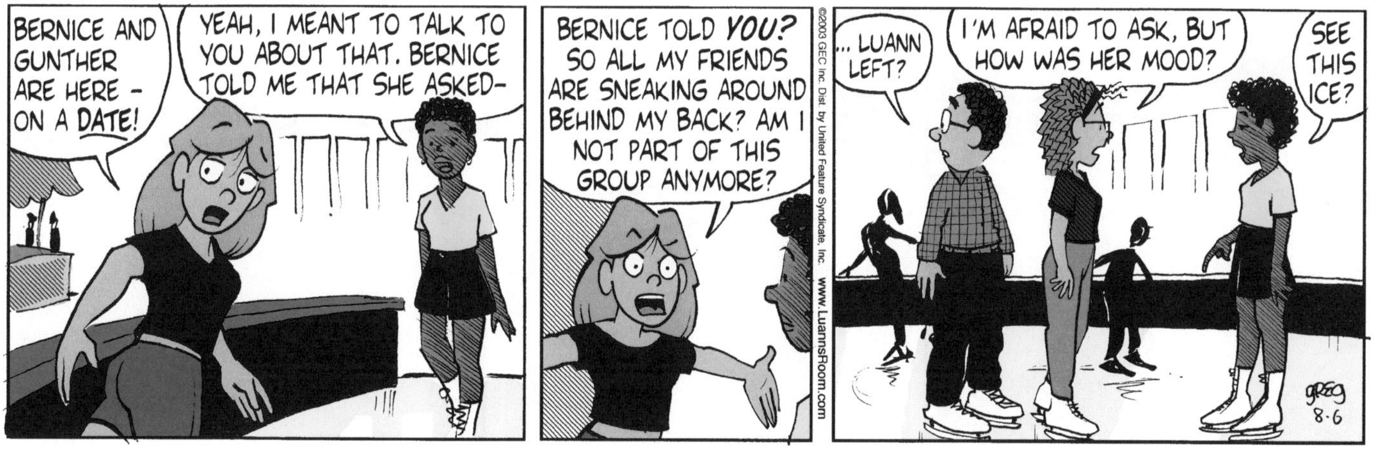
BERNICE AND GUNTHER ARE HERE - ON A DATE!
YEAH, I MEANT TO TALK TO YOU ABOUT THAT. BERNICE TOLD ME THAT SHE ASKED-
BERNICE TOLD YOU? SO ALL MY FRIENDS ARE SNEAKING AROUND BEHIND MY BACK? AM I NOT PART OF THIS GROUP ANYMORE?
©2003 GEC Inc. Dist. by United Feature Syndicate, Inc. www.LuannsRoom.com
... LUANN LEFT?
I'M AFRAID TO ASK, BUT HOW WAS HER MOOD?
SEE THIS ICE?
GREG 8·6

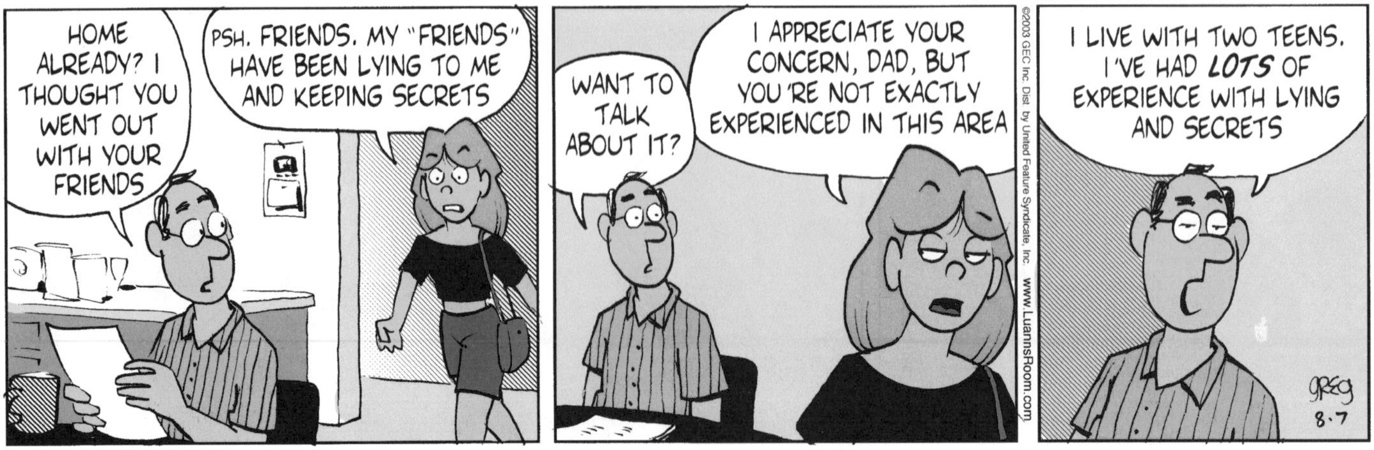
HOME ALREADY? I THOUGHT YOU WENT OUT WITH YOUR FRIENDS
PSH. FRIENDS. MY "FRIENDS" HAVE BEEN LYING TO ME AND KEEPING SECRETS
WANT TO TALK ABOUT IT?
I APPRECIATE YOUR CONCERN, DAD, BUT YOU'RE NOT EXACTLY EXPERIENCED IN THIS AREA
©2003 GEC Inc. Dist. by United Feature Syndicate, Inc. www.LuannsRoom.com
I LIVE WITH TWO TEENS. I'VE HAD ***LOTS*** OF EXPERIENCE WITH LYING AND SECRETS
GREG 8·7

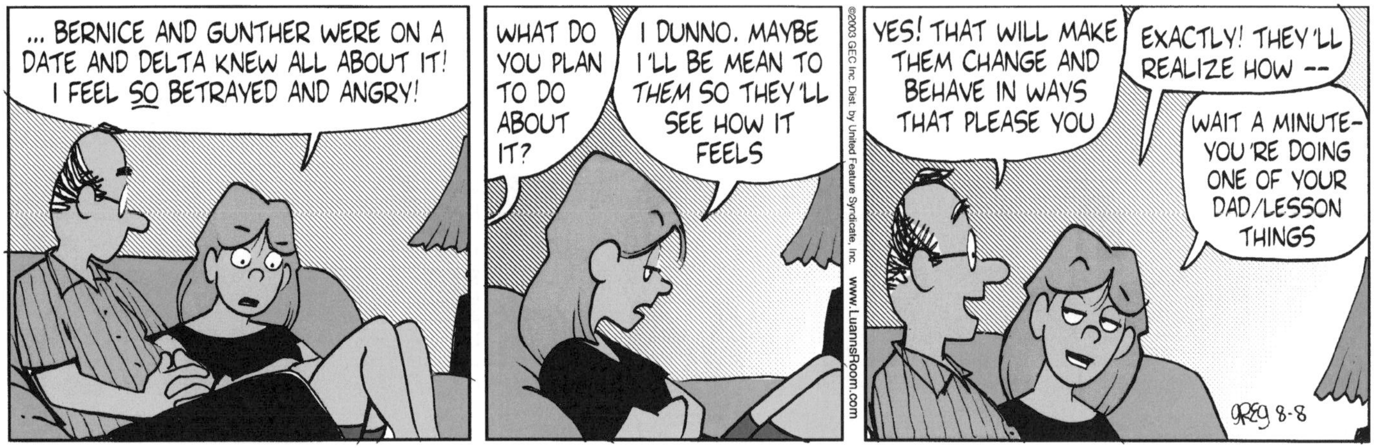
... BERNICE AND GUNTHER WERE ON A DATE AND DELTA KNEW ALL ABOUT IT! I FEEL SO BETRAYED AND ANGRY!
WHAT DO YOU PLAN TO DO ABOUT IT?
I DUNNO. MAYBE I'LL BE MEAN TO *THEM* SO THEY'LL SEE HOW IT FEELS
©2003 GEC Inc. Dist. by United Feature Syndicate, Inc. www.LuannsRoom.com
YES! THAT WILL MAKE THEM CHANGE AND BEHAVE IN WAYS THAT PLEASE YOU
EXACTLY! THEY'LL REALIZE HOW --
WAIT A MINUTE- YOU'RE DOING ONE OF YOUR DAD/LESSON THINGS
GREG 8-8

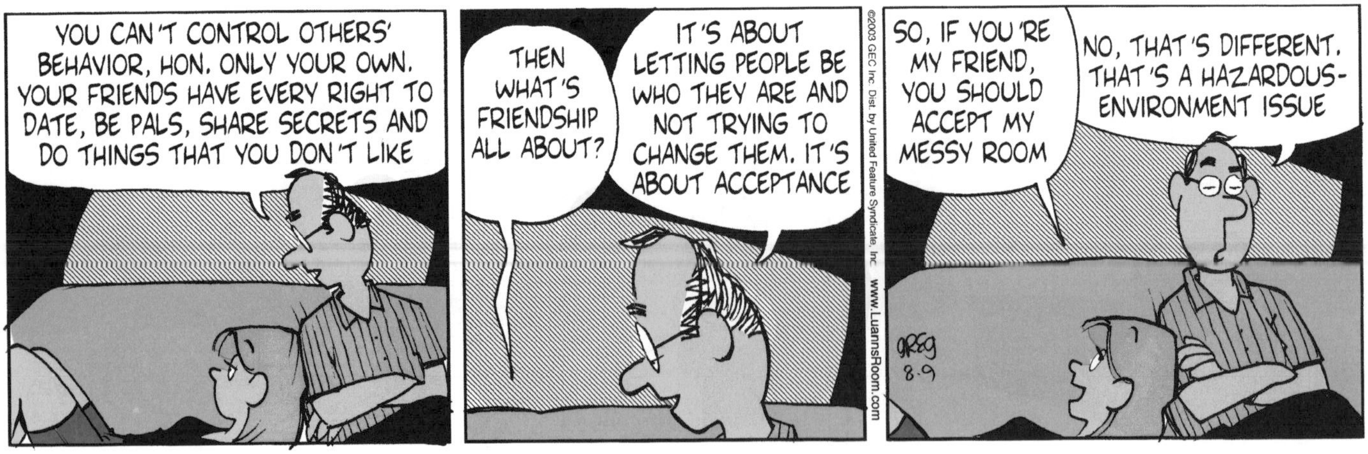
YOU CAN'T CONTROL OTHERS' BEHAVIOR, HON. ONLY YOUR OWN. YOUR FRIENDS HAVE EVERY RIGHT TO DATE, BE PALS, SHARE SECRETS AND DO THINGS THAT YOU DON'T LIKE
THEN WHAT'S FRIENDSHIP ALL ABOUT?
IT'S ABOUT LETTING PEOPLE BE WHO THEY ARE AND NOT TRYING TO CHANGE THEM. IT'S ABOUT ACCEPTANCE
©2003 GEC Inc. Dist. by United Feature Syndicate, Inc. www.LuannsRoom.com
SO, IF YOU'RE MY FRIEND, YOU SHOULD ACCEPT MY MESSY ROOM
NO, THAT'S DIFFERENT. THAT'S A HAZARDOUS-ENVIRONMENT ISSUE
GREG 8·9

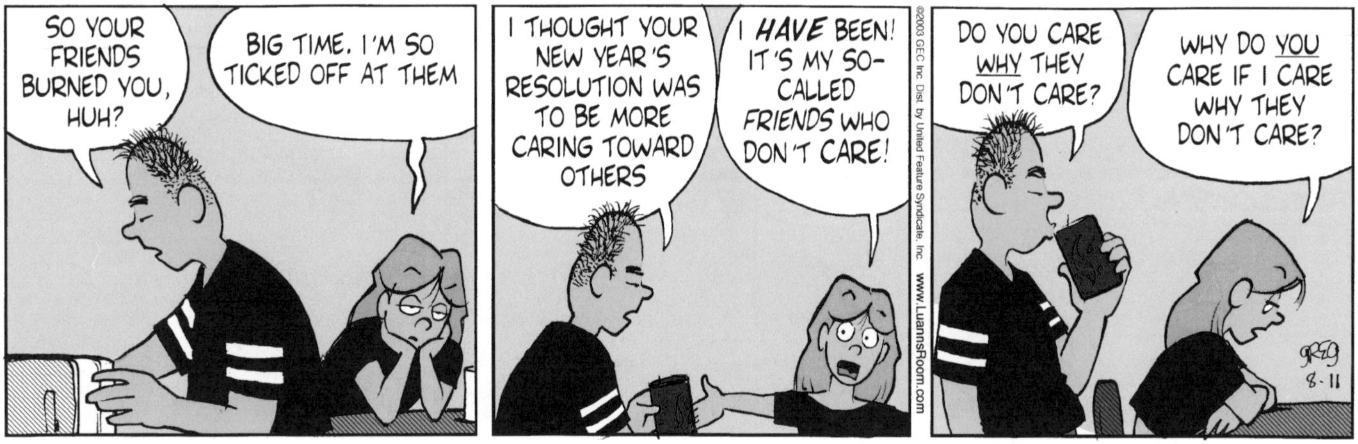
SO YOUR FRIENDS BURNED YOU, HUH?
BIG TIME. I'M SO TICKED OFF AT THEM
I THOUGHT YOUR NEW YEAR'S RESOLUTION WAS TO BE MORE CARING TOWARD OTHERS
I *HAVE* BEEN! IT'S MY SO-CALLED *FRIENDS* WHO DON'T CARE!
DO YOU CARE WHY THEY DON'T CARE?
WHY DO YOU CARE IF I CARE WHY THEY DON'T CARE?
©2003 GEC Inc. Dist. by United Feature Syndicate, Inc.
www.LuannsRoom.com
GREG 8-11

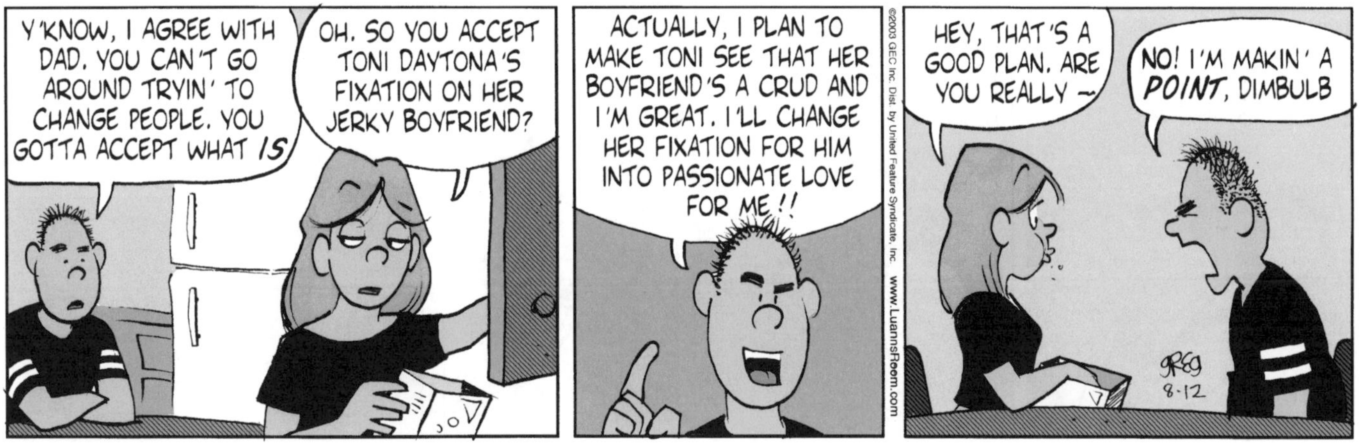
Y'KNOW, I AGREE WITH DAD. YOU CAN'T GO AROUND TRYIN' TO CHANGE PEOPLE. YOU GOTTA ACCEPT WHAT *IS*
OH. SO YOU ACCEPT TONI DAYTONA'S FIXATION ON HER JERKY BOYFRIEND?
ACTUALLY, I PLAN TO MAKE TONI SEE THAT HER BOYFRIEND'S A CRUD AND I'M GREAT. I'LL CHANGE HER FIXATION FOR HIM INTO PASSIONATE LOVE FOR ME!!
HEY, THAT'S A GOOD PLAN. ARE YOU REALLY ~
NO! I'M MAKIN' A ***POINT***, DIMBULB
©2003 GEC Inc. Dist. by United Feature Syndicate, Inc.
www.LuannsRoom.com
GREG 8-12

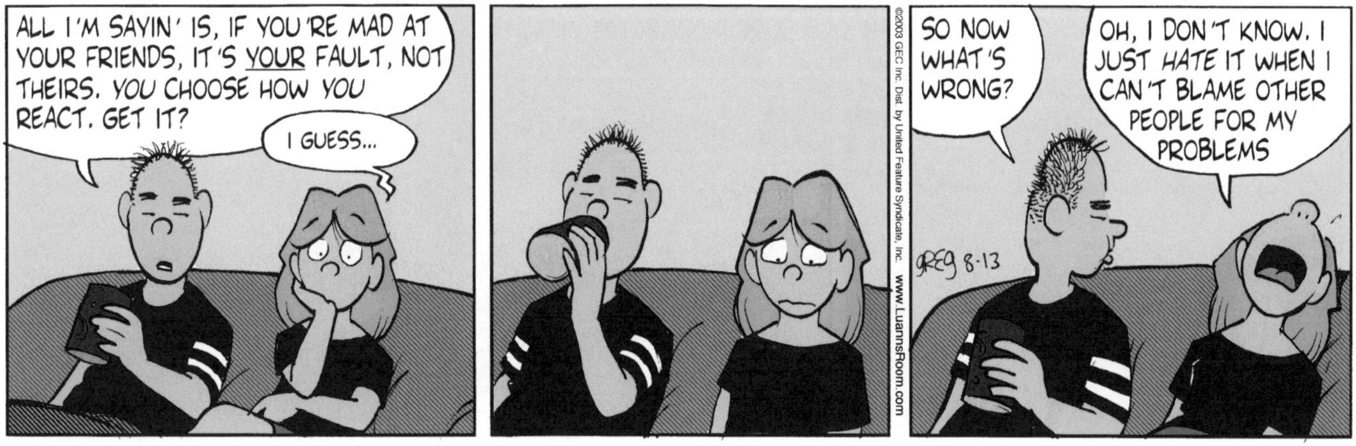
ALL I'M SAYIN' IS, IF YOU'RE MAD AT YOUR FRIENDS, IT'S YOUR FAULT, NOT THEIRS. *YOU* CHOOSE HOW *YOU* REACT. GET IT?
I GUESS...
SO NOW WHAT'S WRONG?
OH, I DON'T KNOW. I JUST *HATE* IT WHEN I CAN'T BLAME OTHER PEOPLE FOR MY PROBLEMS
©2003 GEC Inc. Dist. by United Feature Syndicate, Inc.
www.LuannsRoom.com
GREG 8-13

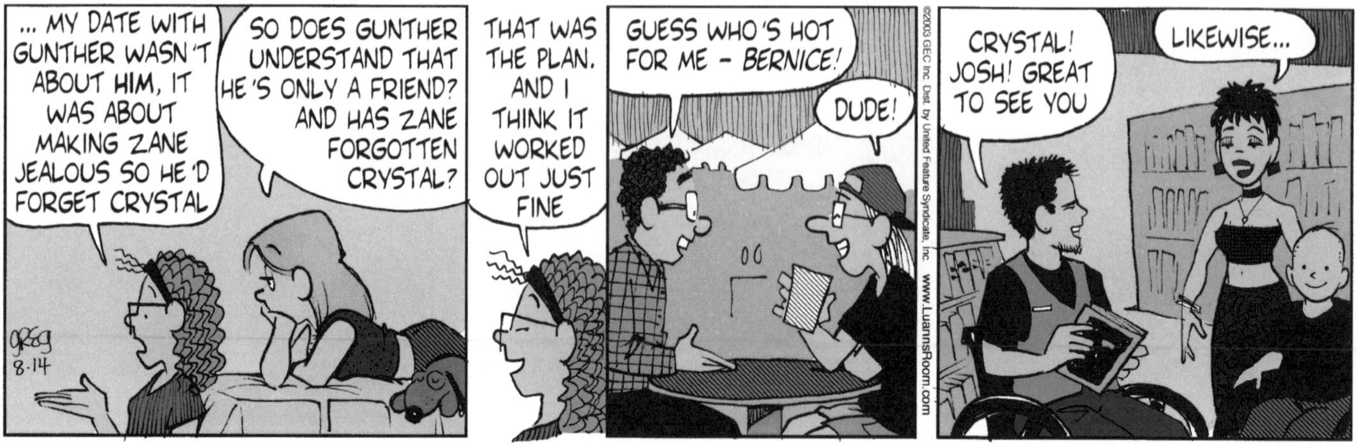
... MY DATE WITH GUNTHER WASN'T ABOUT **HIM**, IT WAS ABOUT MAKING ZANE JEALOUS SO HE'D FORGET CRYSTAL
SO DOES GUNTHER UNDERSTAND THAT HE'S ONLY A FRIEND? AND HAS ZANE FORGOTTEN CRYSTAL?
GREG 8·14
THAT WAS THE PLAN. AND I THINK IT WORKED OUT JUST FINE
GUESS WHO'S HOT FOR ME – *BERNICE!*
DUDE!
©2003 GEC Inc. Dist. by United Feature Syndicate, Inc. www.LuannsRoom.com
CRYSTAL! JOSH! GREAT TO SEE YOU
LIKEWISE...

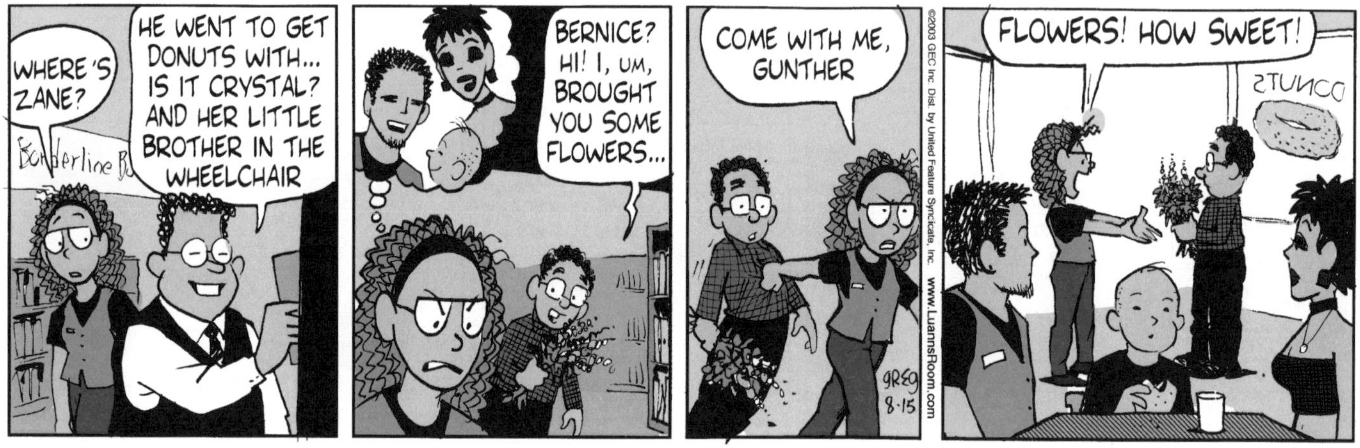
WHERE'S ZANE?
HE WENT TO GET DONUTS WITH... IS IT CRYSTAL? AND HER LITTLE BROTHER IN THE WHEELCHAIR
BERNICE? HI! I, UM, BROUGHT YOU SOME FLOWERS...
©2003 GEC Inc. Dist. by United Feature Syndicate, Inc. www.LuannsRoom.com
COME WITH ME, GUNTHER
GREG 8·15
FLOWERS! HOW SWEET!

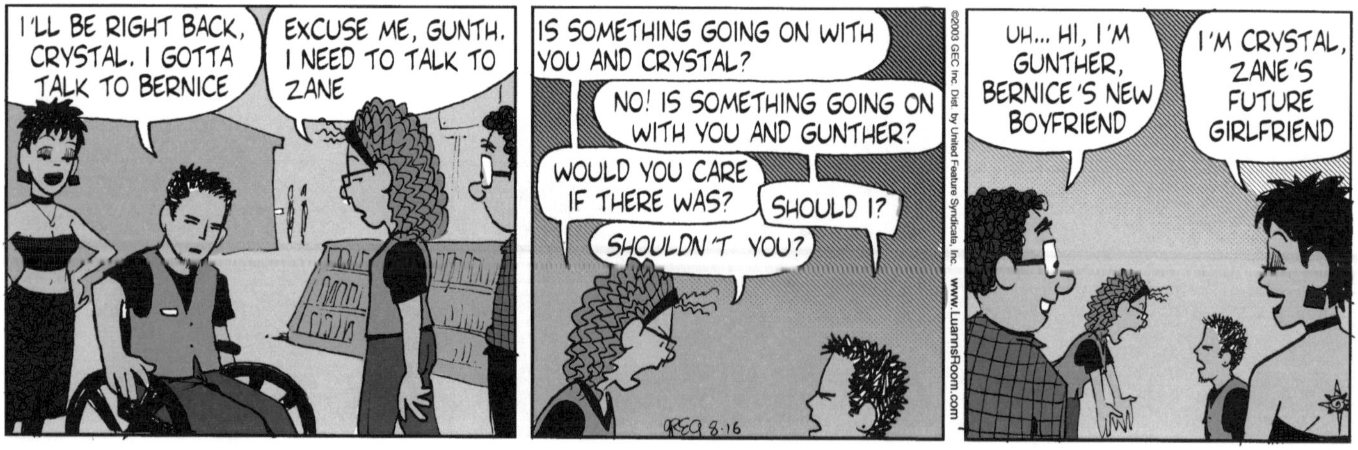
I'LL BE RIGHT BACK, CRYSTAL. I GOTTA TALK TO BERNICE
EXCUSE ME, GUNTH. I NEED TO TALK TO ZANE
IS SOMETHING GOING ON WITH YOU AND CRYSTAL?
NO! IS SOMETHING GOING ON WITH YOU AND GUNTHER?
WOULD YOU CARE IF THERE WAS?
SHOULD I?
SHOULDN'T YOU?
GREG 8·16
©2003 GEC Inc. Dist. by United Feature Syndicate, Inc. www.LuannsRoom.com
UH... HI, I'M GUNTHER, BERNICE'S NEW BOYFRIEND
I'M CRYSTAL, ZANE'S FUTURE GIRLFRIEND

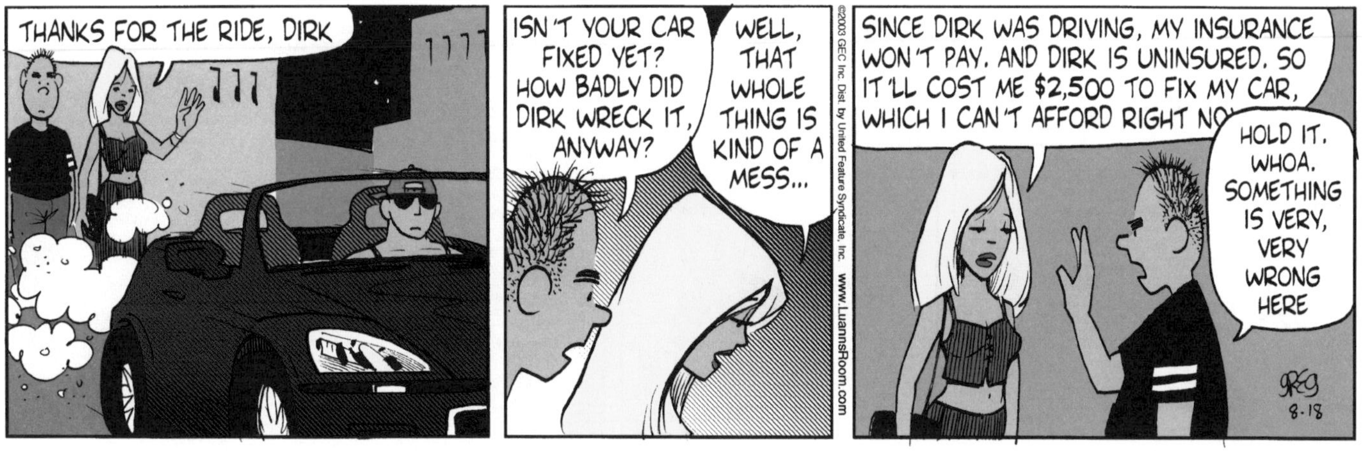
THANKS FOR THE RIDE, DIRK
ISN'T YOUR CAR FIXED YET? HOW BADLY DID DIRK WRECK IT, ANYWAY?
WELL, THAT WHOLE THING IS KIND OF A MESS...
SINCE DIRK WAS DRIVING, MY INSURANCE WON'T PAY. AND DIRK IS UNINSURED. SO IT'LL COST ME $2,500 TO FIX MY CAR, WHICH I CAN'T AFFORD RIGHT NO
HOLD IT. WHOA. SOMETHING IS VERY, VERY WRONG HERE
GREG 8·18

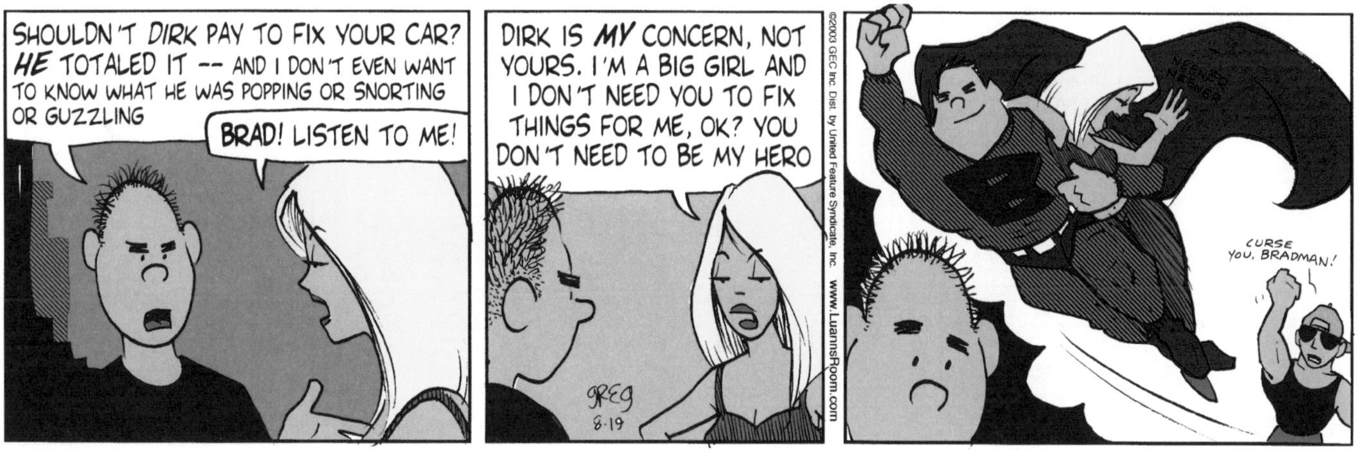
SHOULDN'T DIRK PAY TO FIX YOUR CAR? HE TOTALED IT -- AND I DON'T EVEN WANT TO KNOW WHAT HE WAS POPPING OR SNORTING OR GUZZLING
BRAD! LISTEN TO ME!
DIRK IS MY CONCERN, NOT YOURS. I'M A BIG GIRL AND I DON'T NEED YOU TO FIX THINGS FOR ME, OK? YOU DON'T NEED TO BE MY HERO
GREG 8·19
CURSE YOU, BRADMAN!

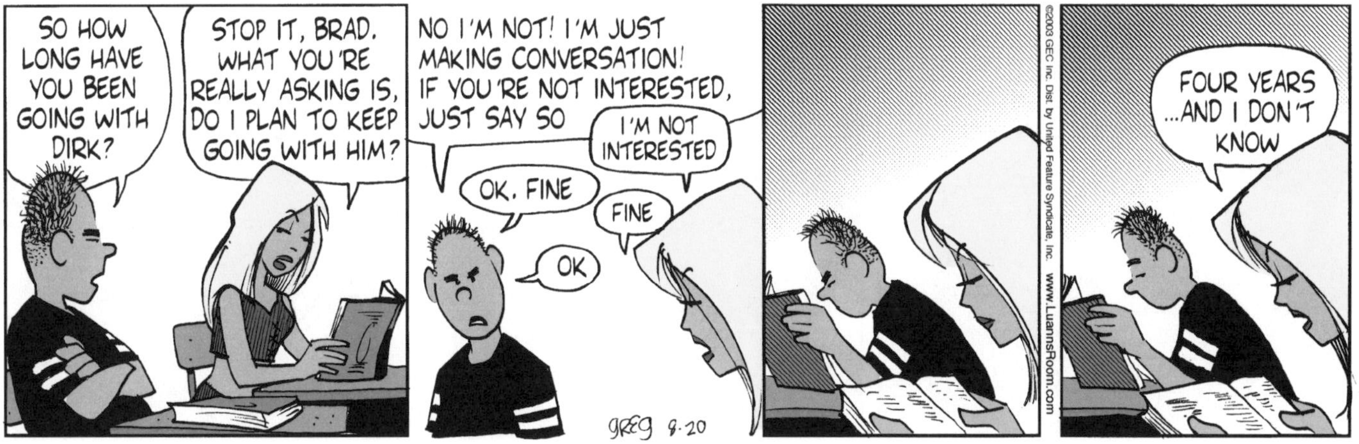
SO HOW LONG HAVE YOU BEEN GOING WITH DIRK?
STOP IT, BRAD. WHAT YOU'RE REALLY ASKING IS, DO I PLAN TO KEEP GOING WITH HIM?
NO I'M NOT! I'M JUST MAKING CONVERSATION! IF YOU'RE NOT INTERESTED, JUST SAY SO
I'M NOT INTERESTED
OK. FINE
FINE
OK
FOUR YEARS ...AND I DON'T KNOW
GREG 8·20

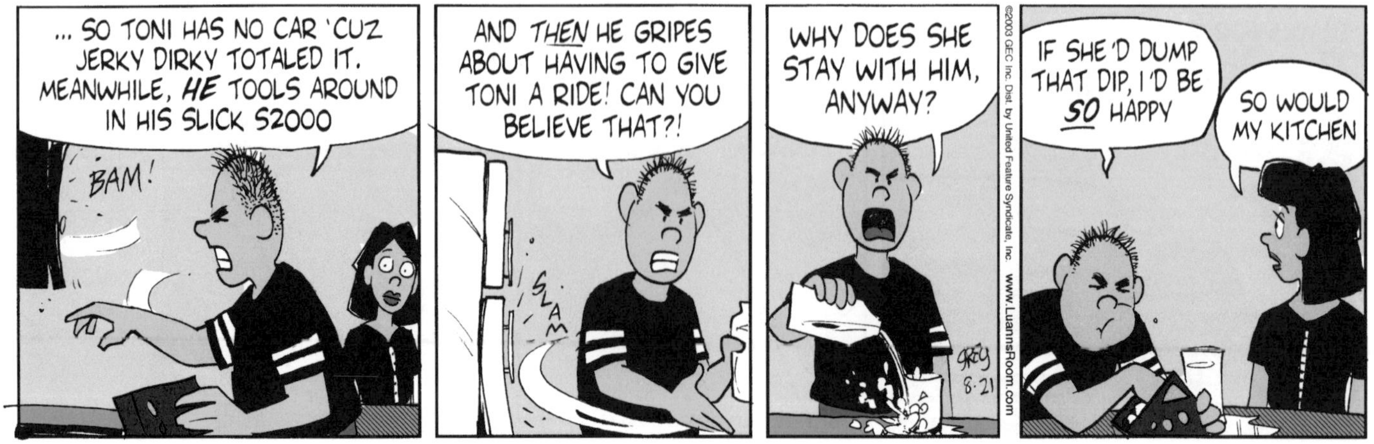
... SO TONI HAS NO CAR 'CUZ JERKY DIRKY TOTALED IT. MEANWHILE, HE TOOLS AROUND IN HIS SLICK S2000
BAM!
AND THEN HE GRIPES ABOUT HAVING TO GIVE TONI A RIDE! CAN YOU BELIEVE THAT?!
SLAM
WHY DOES SHE STAY WITH HIM, ANYWAY?
©2003 GEC Inc. Dist. by United Feature Syndicate, Inc. www.LuannsRoom.com
GREG 8·21
IF SHE'D DUMP THAT DIP, I'D BE SO HAPPY
SO WOULD MY KITCHEN

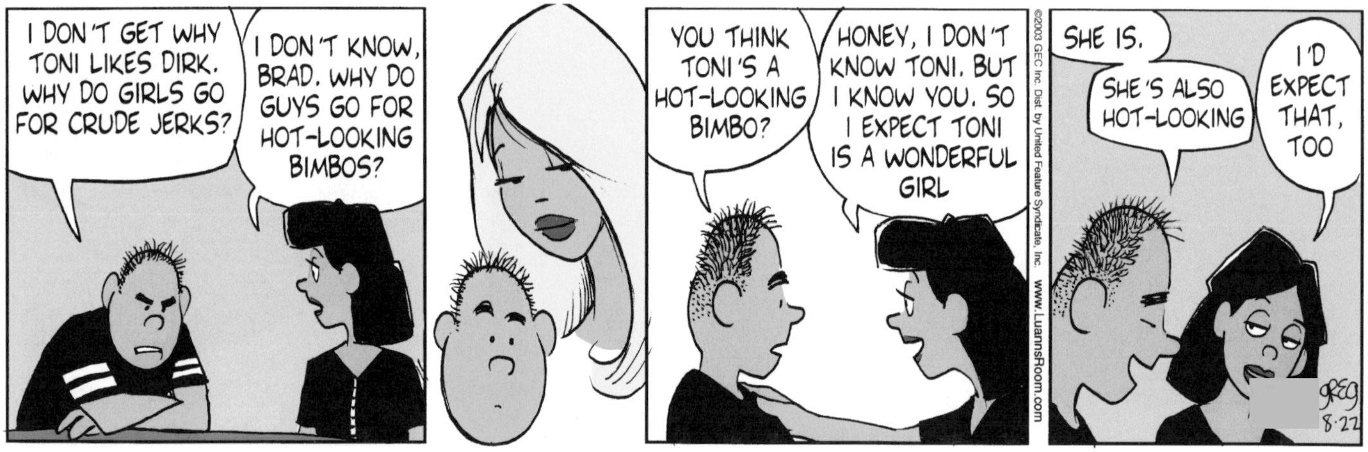
I DON'T GET WHY TONI LIKES DIRK. WHY DO GIRLS GO FOR CRUDE JERKS?
I DON'T KNOW, BRAD. WHY DO GUYS GO FOR HOT-LOOKING BIMBOS?
YOU THINK TONI'S A HOT-LOOKING BIMBO?
HONEY, I DON'T KNOW TONI. BUT I KNOW YOU. SO I EXPECT TONI IS A WONDERFUL GIRL
©2003 GEC Inc. Dist. by United Feature Syndicate, Inc. www.LuannsRoom.com
SHE IS.
SHE'S ALSO HOT-LOOKING
I'D EXPECT THAT, TOO
GREG 8·22

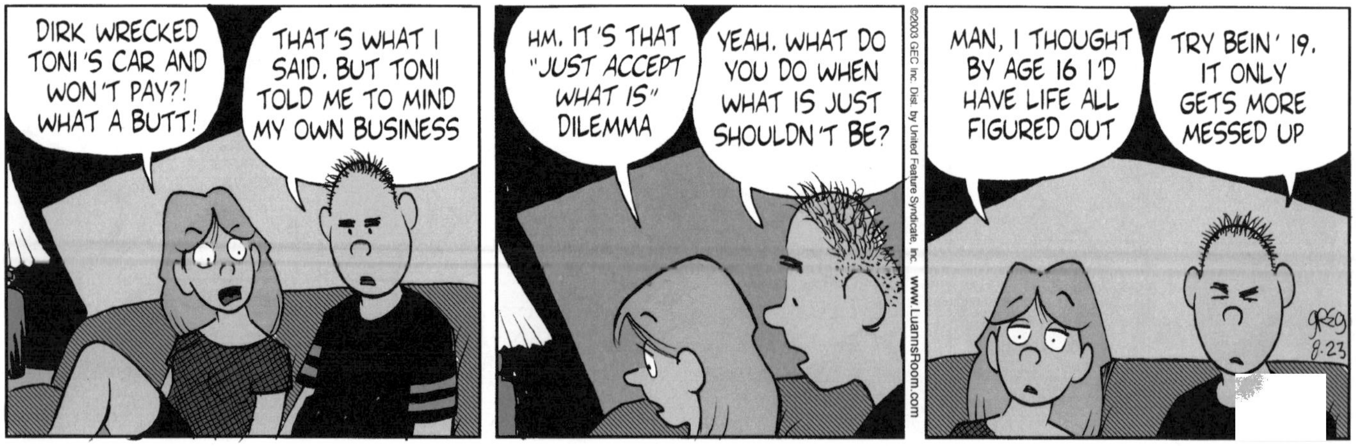
DIRK WRECKED TONI'S CAR AND WON'T PAY?! WHAT A BUTT!
THAT'S WHAT I SAID. BUT TONI TOLD ME TO MIND MY OWN BUSINESS
HM. IT'S THAT "JUST ACCEPT WHAT IS" DILEMMA
YEAH. WHAT DO YOU DO WHEN WHAT IS JUST SHOULDN'T BE?
©2003 GEC Inc. Dist. by United Feature Syndicate, Inc. www.LuannsRoom.com
MAN, I THOUGHT BY AGE 16 I'D HAVE LIFE ALL FIGURED OUT
TRY BEIN' 19. IT ONLY GETS MORE MESSED UP
GREG 8·23

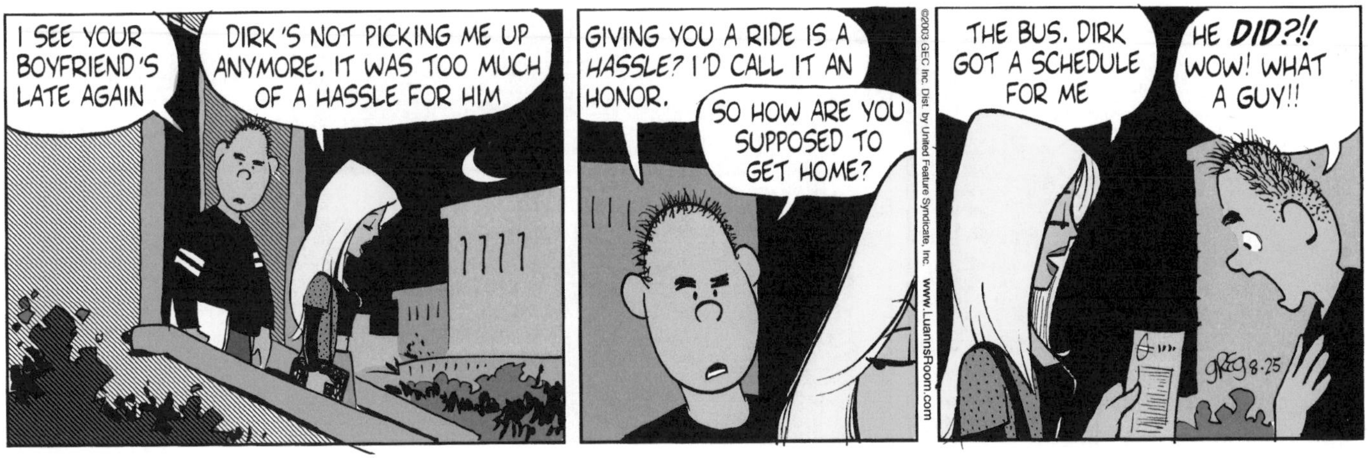
I SEE YOUR BOYFRIEND'S LATE AGAIN
DIRK'S NOT PICKING ME UP ANYMORE. IT WAS TOO MUCH OF A HASSLE FOR HIM
GIVING YOU A RIDE IS A *HASSLE?* I'D CALL IT AN HONOR.
SO HOW ARE YOU SUPPOSED TO GET HOME?
THE BUS. DIRK GOT A SCHEDULE FOR ME
HE ***DID?!!*** WOW! WHAT A GUY!!
GREG 8-25
©2003 GEC Inc. Dist. by United Feature Syndicate, Inc. www.LuannsRoom.com

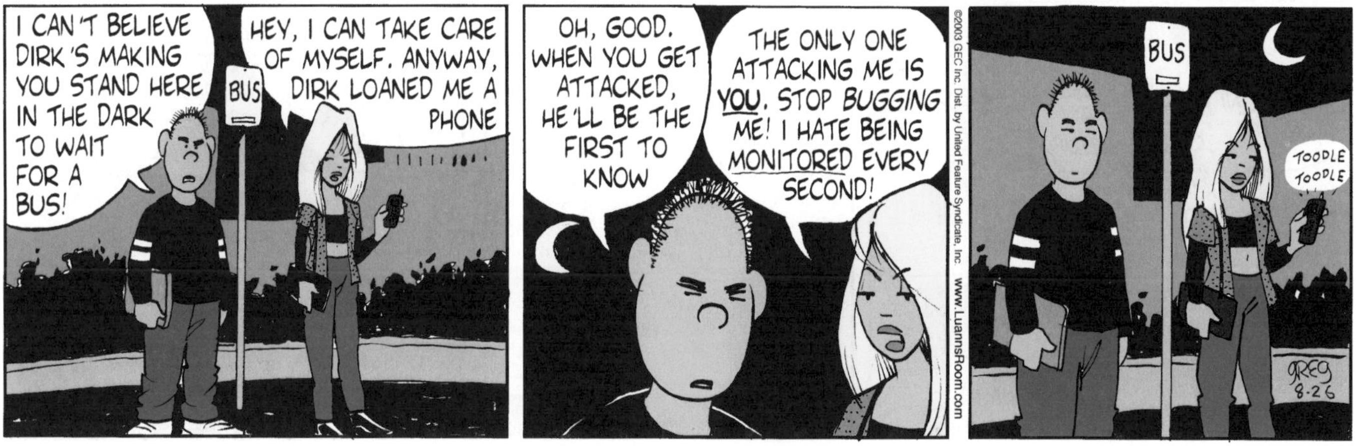
I CAN'T BELIEVE DIRK'S MAKING YOU STAND HERE IN THE DARK TO WAIT FOR A BUS!
BUS
HEY, I CAN TAKE CARE OF MYSELF. ANYWAY, DIRK LOANED ME A PHONE
OH, GOOD. WHEN YOU GET ATTACKED, HE'LL BE THE FIRST TO KNOW
THE ONLY ONE ATTACKING ME IS YOU. STOP *BUGGING* ME! I HATE BEING MONITORED EVERY SECOND!
BUS
TOODLE TOODLE
GREG 8-26
©2003 GEC Inc. Dist. by United Feature Syndicate, Inc. www.LuannsRoom.com

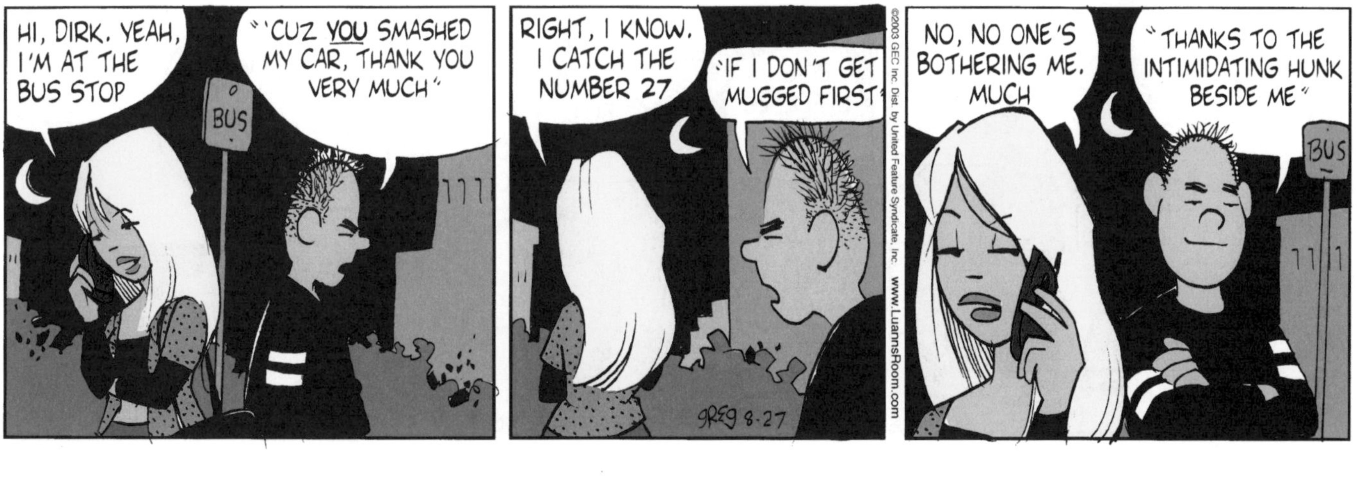
HI, DIRK. YEAH, I'M AT THE BUS STOP
"'CUZ YOU SMASHED MY CAR, THANK YOU VERY MUCH"
BUS
RIGHT, I KNOW. I CATCH THE NUMBER 27
"IF I DON'T GET MUGGED FIRST"
GREG 8-27
NO, NO ONE'S BOTHERING ME. MUCH
"THANKS TO THE INTIMIDATING HUNK BESIDE ME"
BUS
©2003 GEC Inc. Dist. by United Feature Syndicate, Inc. www.LuannsRoom.com

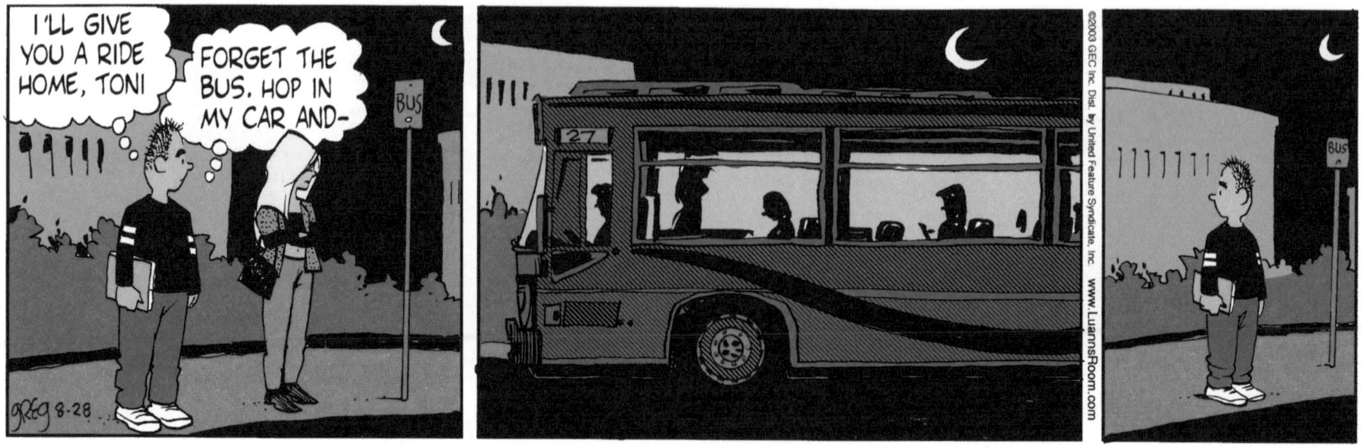
I'LL GIVE YOU A RIDE HOME, TONI
FORGET THE BUS. HOP IN MY CAR AND-
BUS
27
GREG 8-28
©2003 GEC Inc. Dist. by United Feature Syndicate, Inc. www.LuannsRoom.com

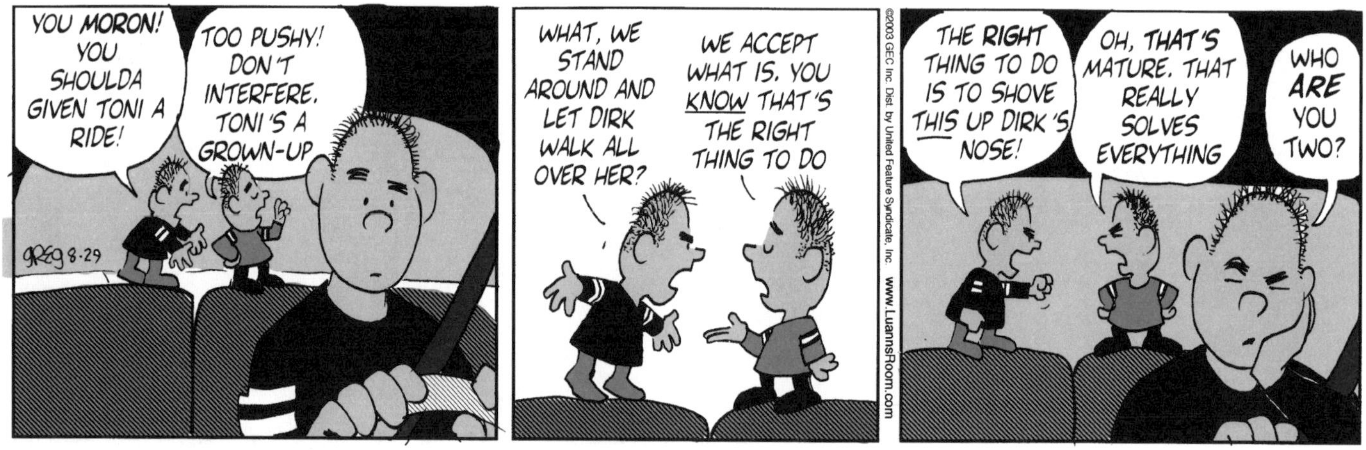
YOU MORON! YOU SHOULDA GIVEN TONI A RIDE!
TOO PUSHY! DON'T INTERFERE. TONI'S A GROWN-UP
GREG 8-29
WHAT, WE STAND AROUND AND LET DIRK WALK ALL OVER HER?
WE ACCEPT WHAT IS. YOU KNOW THAT'S THE RIGHT THING TO DO
©2003 GEC Inc. Dist. by United Feature Syndicate, Inc. www.LuannsRoom.com
THE RIGHT THING TO DO IS TO SHOVE THIS UP DIRK'S NOSE!
OH, THAT'S MATURE. THAT REALLY SOLVES EVERYTHING
WHO ARE YOU TWO?

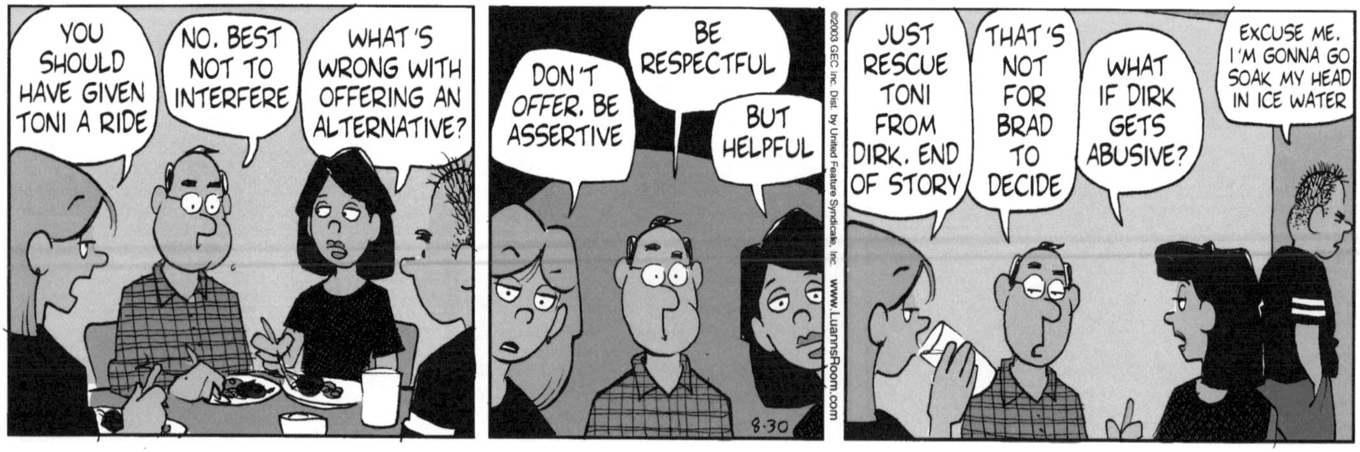
YOU SHOULD HAVE GIVEN TONI A RIDE
NO. BEST NOT TO INTERFERE
WHAT'S WRONG WITH OFFERING AN ALTERNATIVE?
DON'T OFFER. BE ASSERTIVE
BE RESPECTFUL
BUT HELPFUL
8-30
©2003 GEC Inc. Dist. by United Feature Syndicate, Inc. www.LuannsRoom.com
JUST RESCUE TONI FROM DIRK. END OF STORY
THAT'S NOT FOR BRAD TO DECIDE
WHAT IF DIRK GETS ABUSIVE?
EXCUSE ME. I'M GONNA GO SOAK MY HEAD IN ICE WATER

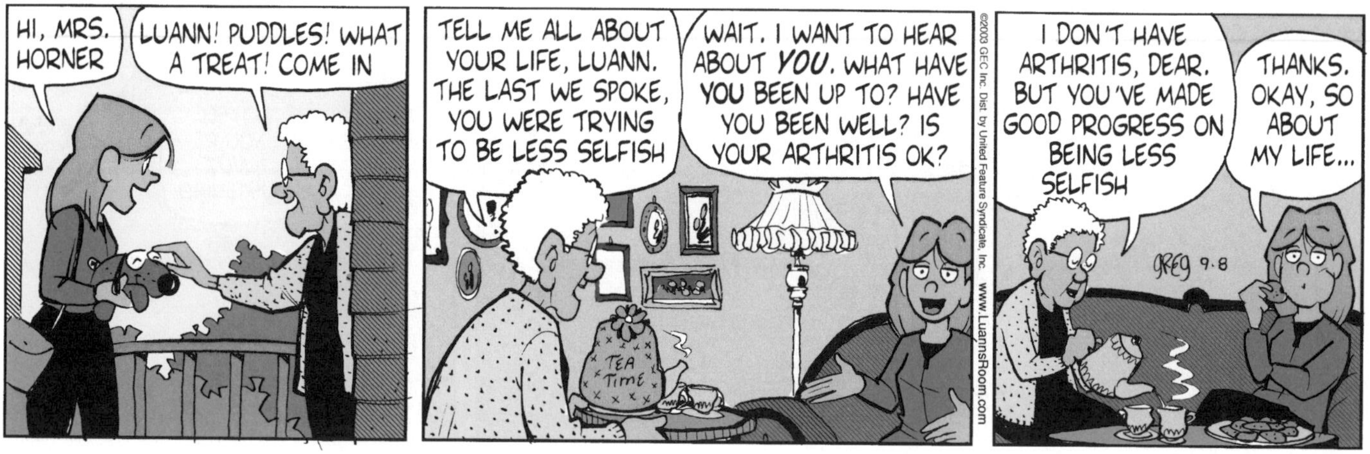
HI, MRS. HORNER
LUANN! PUDDLES! WHAT A TREAT! COME IN
TELL ME ALL ABOUT YOUR LIFE, LUANN. THE LAST WE SPOKE, YOU WERE TRYING TO BE LESS SELFISH
WAIT. I WANT TO HEAR ABOUT ***YOU***. WHAT HAVE YOU BEEN UP TO? HAVE YOU BEEN WELL? IS YOUR ARTHRITIS OK?
TEA TIME
©2003 GEC Inc. Dist. by United Feature Syndicate, Inc. www.LuannsRoom.com
I DON'T HAVE ARTHRITIS, DEAR. BUT YOU'VE MADE GOOD PROGRESS ON BEING LESS SELFISH
THANKS. OKAY, SO ABOUT MY LIFE...
GREG 9.8

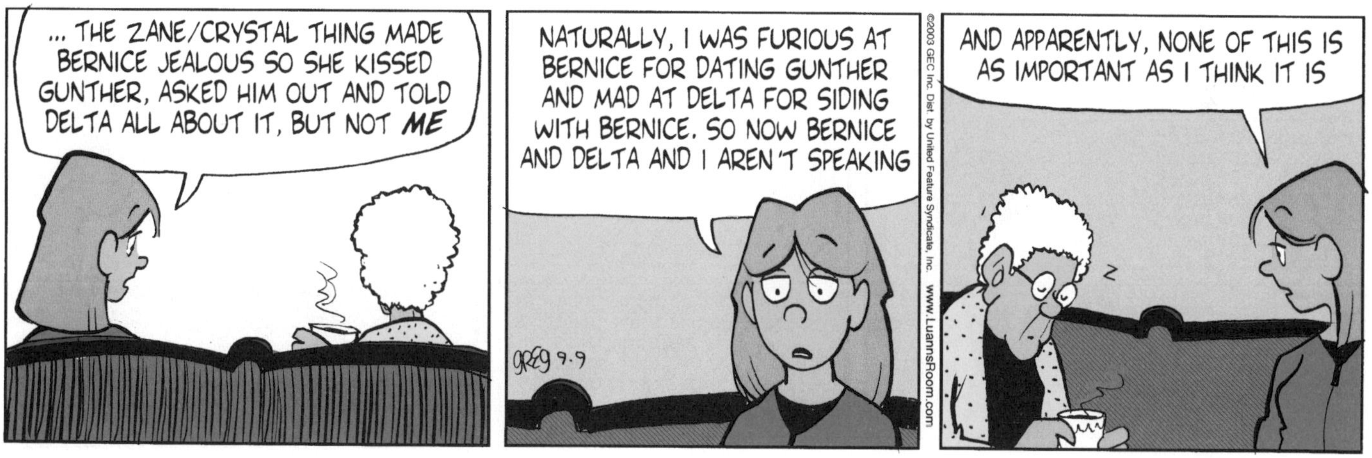
... THE ZANE/CRYSTAL THING MADE BERNICE JEALOUS SO SHE KISSED GUNTHER, ASKED HIM OUT AND TOLD DELTA ALL ABOUT IT, BUT NOT ***ME***
GREG 9.9
NATURALLY, I WAS FURIOUS AT BERNICE FOR DATING GUNTHER AND MAD AT DELTA FOR SIDING WITH BERNICE. SO NOW BERNICE AND DELTA AND I AREN'T SPEAKING
©2003 GEC Inc. Dist. by United Feature Syndicate, Inc. www.LuannsRoom.com
AND APPARENTLY, NONE OF THIS IS AS IMPORTANT AS I THINK IT IS
Z

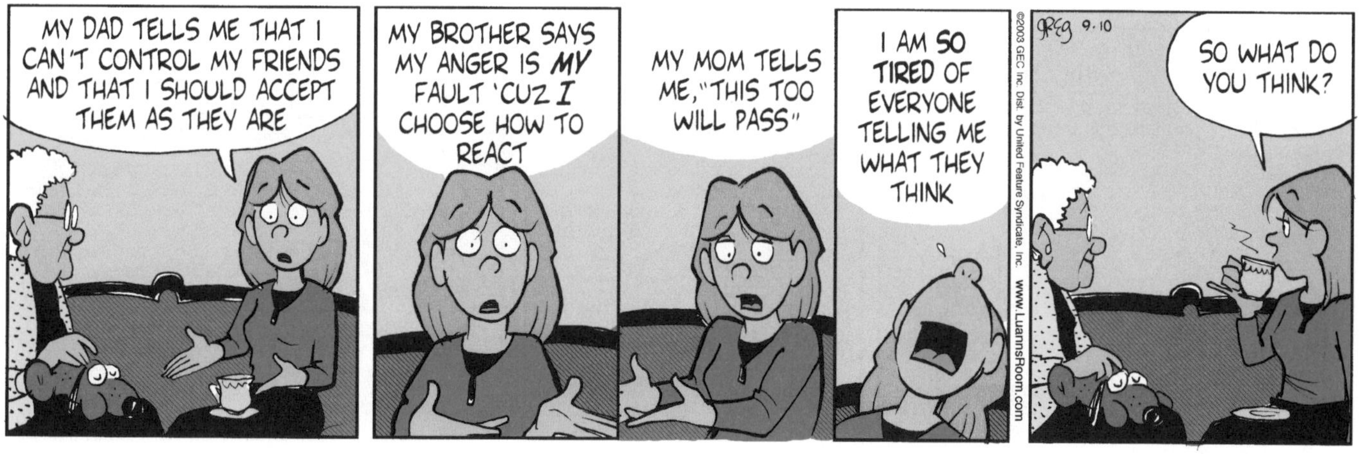
MY DAD TELLS ME THAT I CAN'T CONTROL MY FRIENDS AND THAT I SHOULD ACCEPT THEM AS THEY ARE
MY BROTHER SAYS MY ANGER IS ***MY*** FAULT 'CUZ ***I*** CHOOSE HOW TO REACT
MY MOM TELLS ME, "THIS TOO WILL PASS"
I AM **SO TIRED** OF EVERYONE TELLING ME WHAT THEY THINK
©2003 GEC Inc. Dist. by United Feature Syndicate, Inc. www.LuannsRoom.com
GREG 9.10
SO WHAT DO YOU THINK?

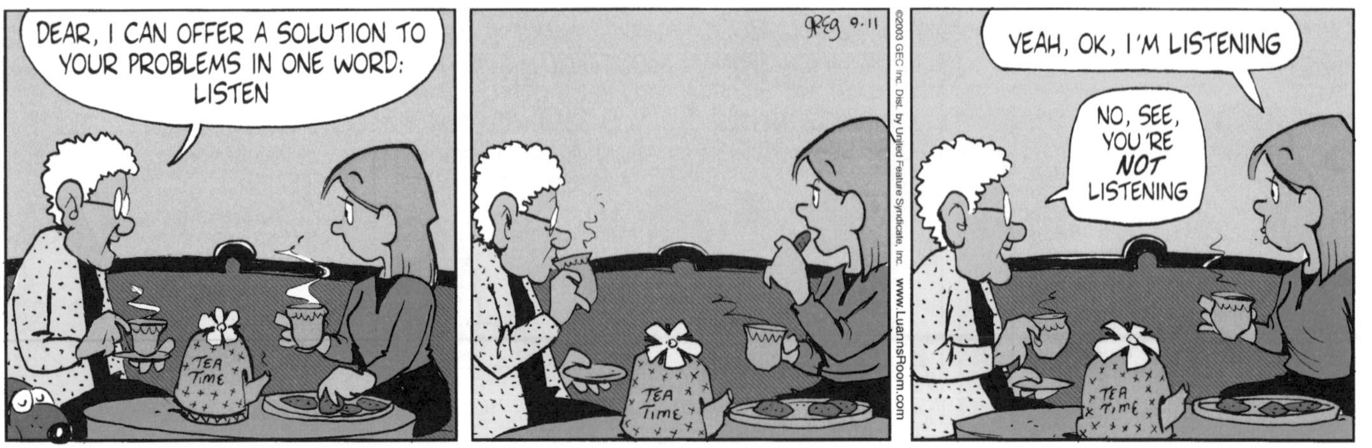
DEAR, I CAN OFFER A SOLUTION TO YOUR PROBLEMS IN ONE WORD: LISTEN
TEA TIME
GREG 9·11
©2003 GEC Inc. Dist. by United Feature Syndicate, Inc. www.LuannsRoom.com
YEAH, OK, I'M LISTENING
NO, SEE, YOU'RE *NOT* LISTENING

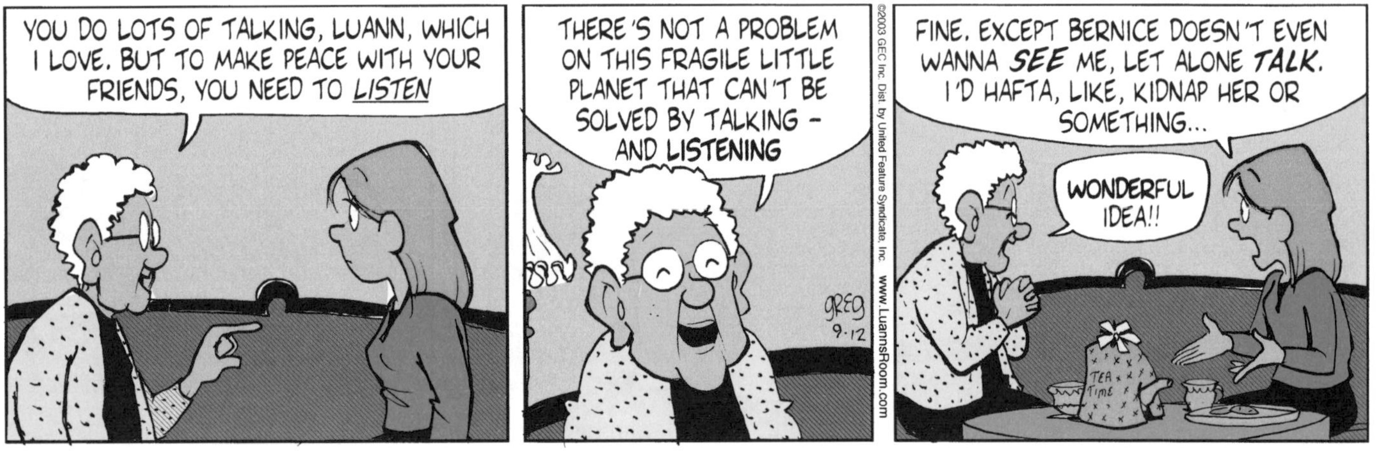
YOU DO LOTS OF TALKING, LUANN, WHICH I LOVE. BUT TO MAKE PEACE WITH YOUR FRIENDS, YOU NEED TO LISTEN
THERE'S NOT A PROBLEM ON THIS FRAGILE LITTLE PLANET THAT CAN'T BE SOLVED BY TALKING – AND **LISTENING**
GREG 9·12
©2003 GEC Inc. Dist. by United Feature Syndicate, Inc. www.LuannsRoom.com
FINE. EXCEPT BERNICE DOESN'T EVEN WANNA ***SEE*** ME, LET ALONE ***TALK***. I'D HAFTA, LIKE, KIDNAP HER OR SOMETHING...
WONDERFUL IDEA!!

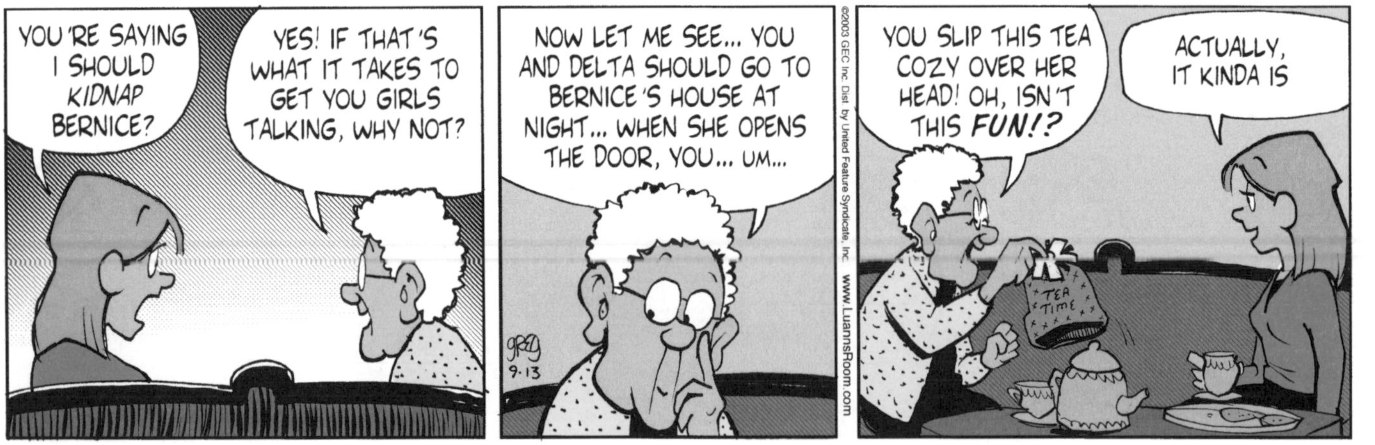
YOU'RE SAYING I SHOULD *KIDNAP* BERNICE?
YES! IF THAT'S WHAT IT TAKES TO GET YOU GIRLS TALKING, WHY NOT?
GREG 9·13
NOW LET ME SEE... YOU AND DELTA SHOULD GO TO BERNICE'S HOUSE AT NIGHT... WHEN SHE OPENS THE DOOR, YOU... UM...
©2003 GEC Inc. Dist. by United Feature Syndicate, Inc. www.LuannsRoom.com
YOU SLIP THIS TEA COZY OVER HER HEAD! OH, ISN'T THIS ***FUN!?***
ACTUALLY, IT KINDA IS
TEA TIME

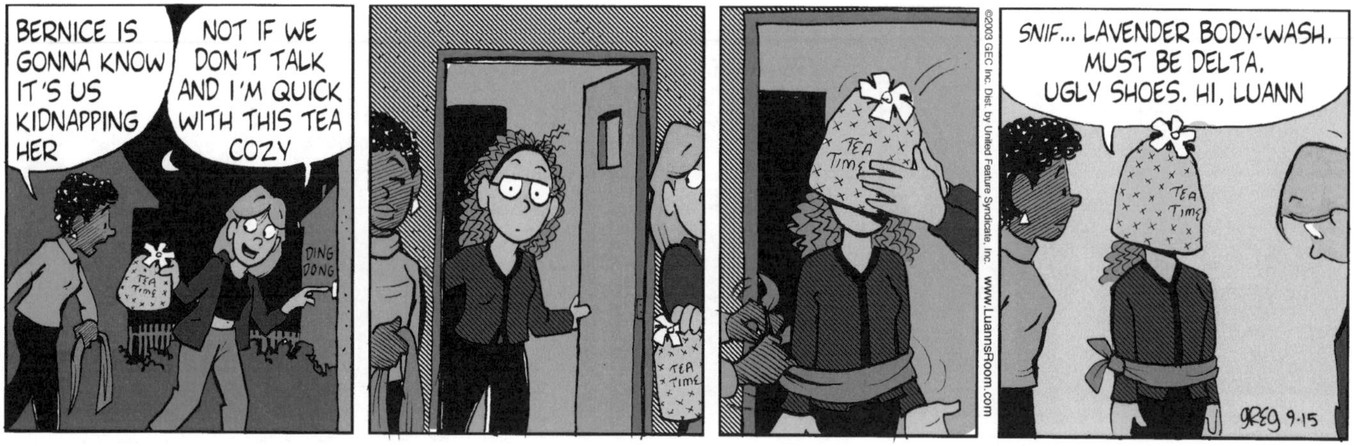
BERNICE IS GONNA KNOW IT'S US KIDNAPPING HER
NOT IF WE DON'T TALK AND I'M QUICK WITH THIS TEA COZY
DING DONG
TEA TIME
©2003 GEC Inc. Dist. by United Feature Syndicate, Inc.
www.LuannsRoom.com
SNIF... LAVENDER BODY-WASH. MUST BE DELTA. UGLY SHOES. HI, LUANN
GREG 9.15

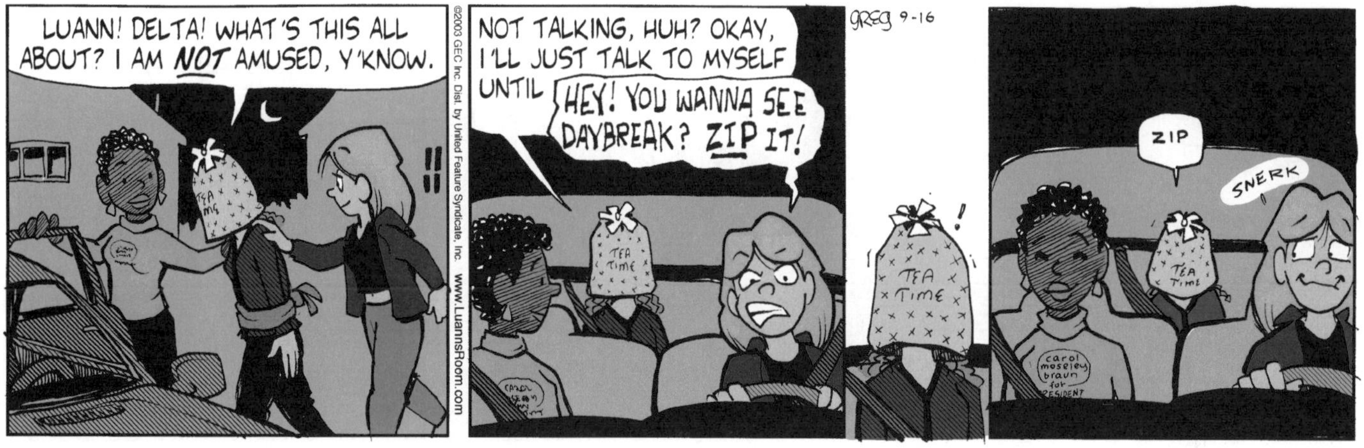
LUANN! DELTA! WHAT'S THIS ALL ABOUT? I AM NOT AMUSED, Y'KNOW.
!!
©2003 GEC Inc. Dist. by United Feature Syndicate, Inc.
www.LuannsRoom.com
NOT TALKING, HUH? OKAY, I'LL JUST TALK TO MYSELF UNTIL
HEY! YOU WANNA SEE DAYBREAK? ZIP IT!
GREG 9-16
TEA TIME
!
ZIP
SNERK
carol moseley braun for PRESIDENT

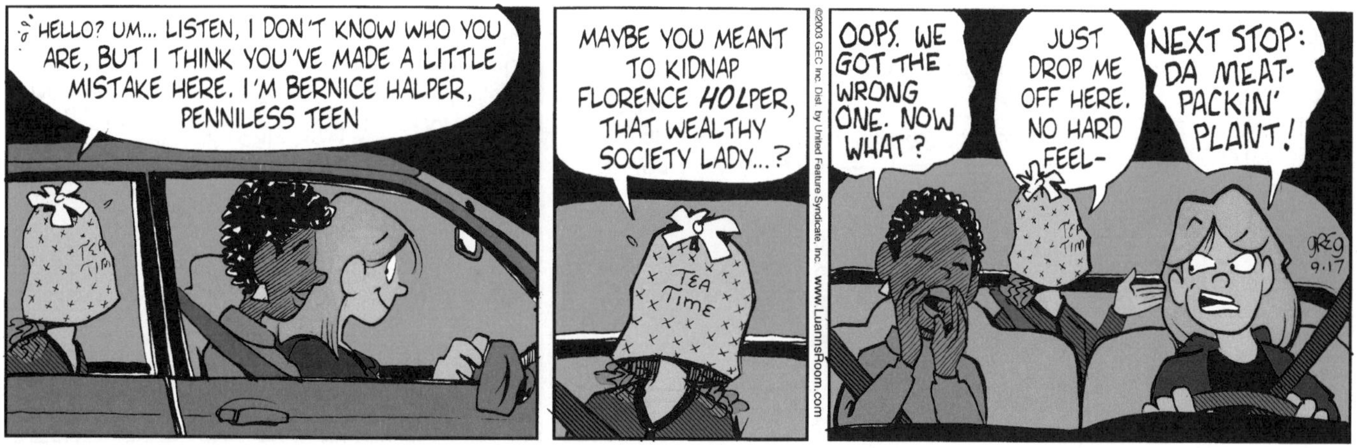
HELLO? UM... LISTEN, I DON'T KNOW WHO YOU ARE, BUT I THINK YOU'VE MADE A LITTLE MISTAKE HERE. I'M BERNICE HALPER, PENNILESS TEEN
MAYBE YOU MEANT TO KIDNAP FLORENCE HOLPER, THAT WEALTHY SOCIETY LADY...?
TEA TIME
©2003 GEC Inc. Dist. by United Feature Syndicate, Inc.
www.LuannsRoom.com
OOPS. WE GOT THE WRONG ONE. NOW WHAT?
JUST DROP ME OFF HERE. NO HARD FEEL-
NEXT STOP: DA MEAT-PACKIN' PLANT!
GREG 9.17

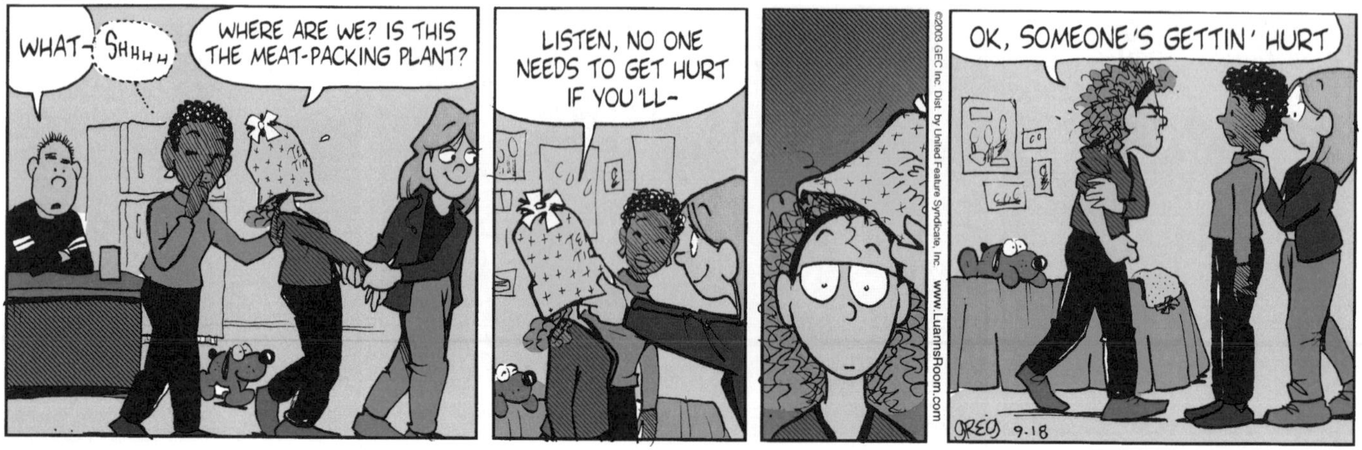
WHAT-
SHHHH
WHERE ARE WE? IS THIS THE MEAT-PACKING PLANT?
LISTEN, NO ONE NEEDS TO GET HURT IF YOU'LL-
©2003 GEC Inc. Dist. by United Feature Syndicate, Inc. www.LuannsRoom.com
OK, SOMEONE'S GETTIN' HURT
GREG 9.18

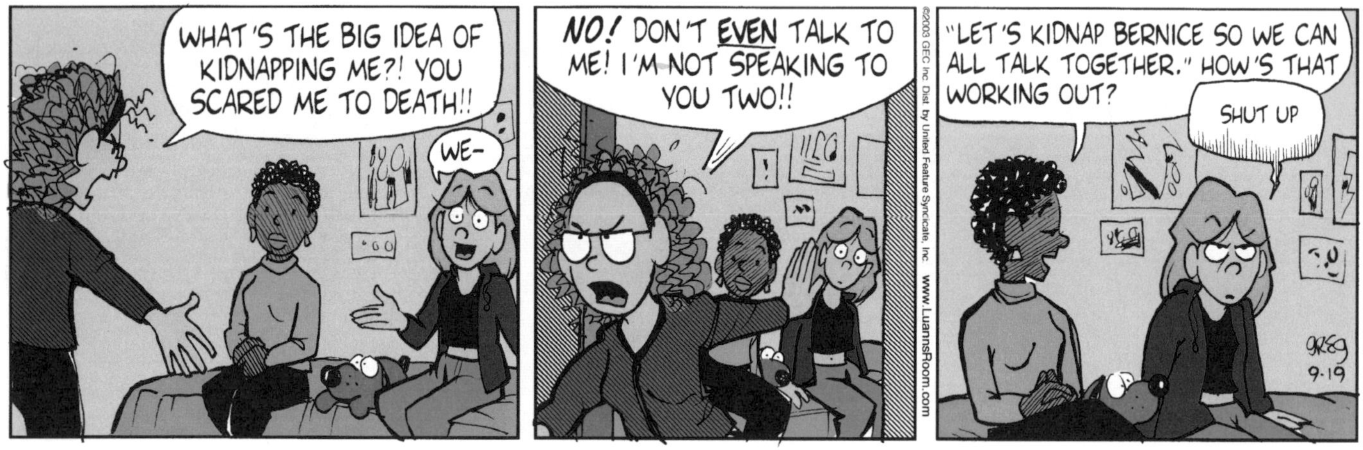
WHAT'S THE BIG IDEA OF KIDNAPPING ME?! YOU SCARED ME TO DEATH!!
WE-
NO! DON'T EVEN TALK TO ME! I'M NOT SPEAKING TO YOU TWO!!
©2003 GEC Inc. Dist. by United Feature Syndicate, Inc. www.LuannsRoom.com
"LET'S KIDNAP BERNICE SO WE CAN ALL TALK TOGETHER." HOW'S THAT WORKING OUT?
SHUT UP
GREG 9.19

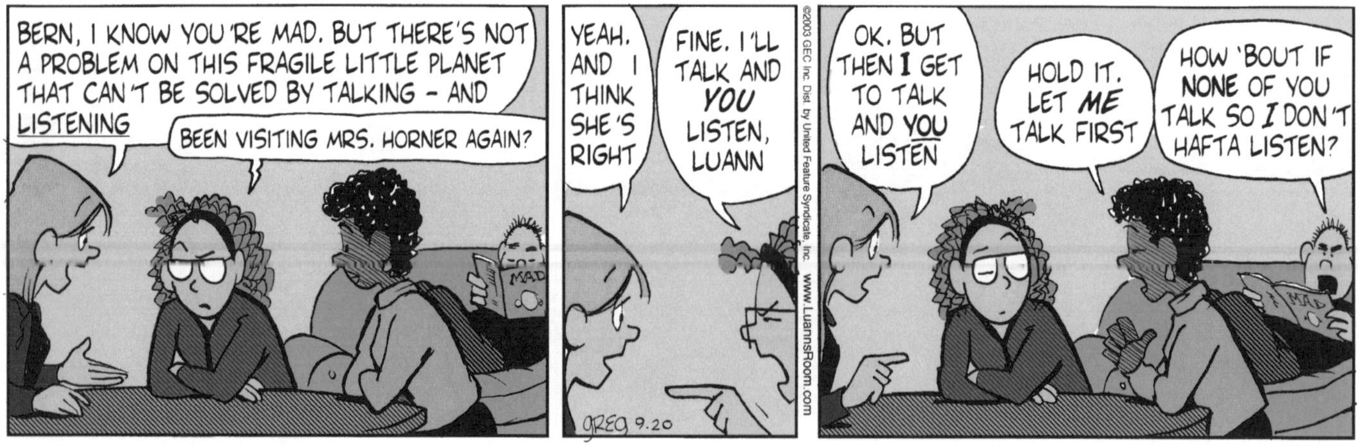
BERN, I KNOW YOU'RE MAD. BUT THERE'S NOT A PROBLEM ON THIS FRAGILE LITTLE PLANET THAT CAN'T BE SOLVED BY TALKING - AND LISTENING
BEEN VISITING MRS. HORNER AGAIN?
YEAH. AND I THINK SHE'S RIGHT
FINE. I'LL TALK AND YOU LISTEN, LUANN
GREG 9.20
©2003 GEC Inc. Dist. by United Feature Syndicate, Inc. www.LuannsRoom.com
OK. BUT THEN I GET TO TALK AND YOU LISTEN
HOLD IT. LET ME TALK FIRST
HOW 'BOUT IF NONE OF YOU TALK SO I DON'T HAFTA LISTEN?

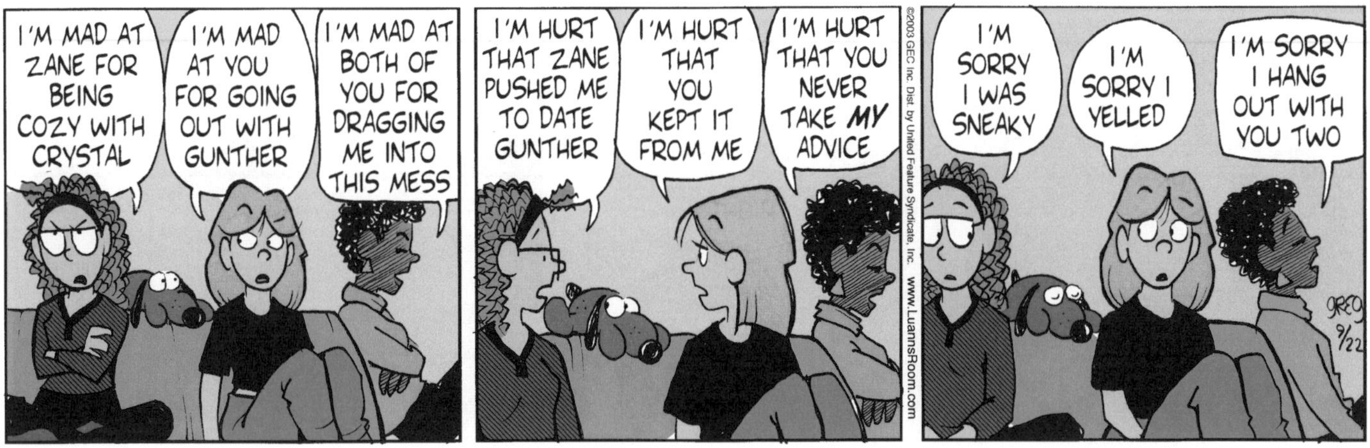
I'M MAD AT ZANE FOR BEING COZY WITH CRYSTAL
I'M MAD AT YOU FOR GOING OUT WITH GUNTHER
I'M MAD AT BOTH OF YOU FOR DRAGGING ME INTO THIS MESS
I'M HURT THAT ZANE PUSHED ME TO DATE GUNTHER
I'M HURT THAT YOU KEPT IT FROM ME
I'M HURT THAT YOU NEVER TAKE *MY* ADVICE
©2003 GEC Inc. Dist. by United Feature Syndicate, Inc.
www.LuannsRoom.com
I'M SORRY I WAS SNEAKY
I'M SORRY I YELLED
I'M SORRY I HANG OUT WITH YOU TWO
GREG 9/22

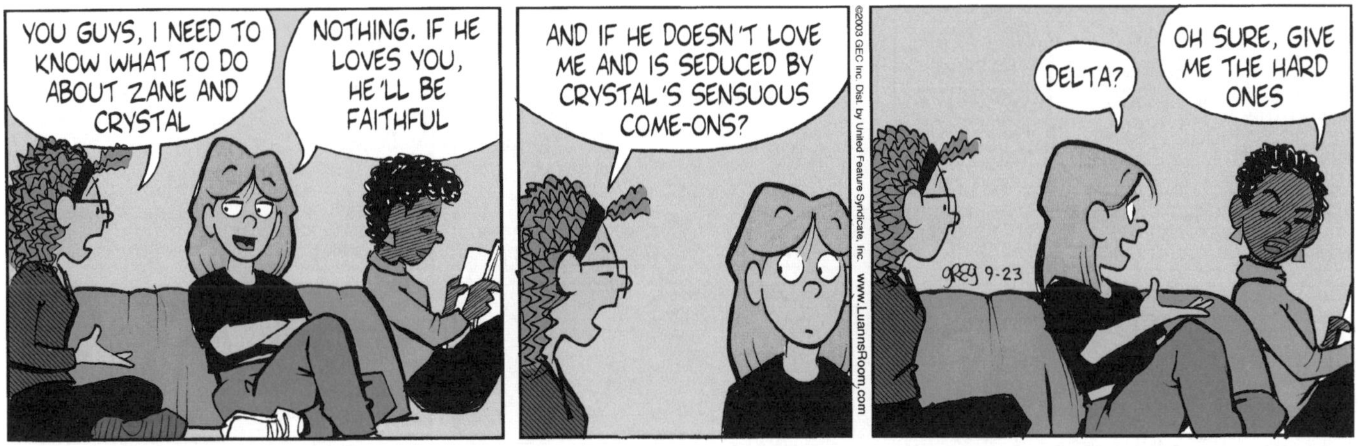
YOU GUYS, I NEED TO KNOW WHAT TO DO ABOUT ZANE AND CRYSTAL
NOTHING. IF HE LOVES YOU, HE'LL BE FAITHFUL
AND IF HE DOESN'T LOVE ME AND IS SEDUCED BY CRYSTAL'S SENSUOUS COME-ONS?
©2003 GEC Inc. Dist. by United Feature Syndicate, Inc.
www.LuannsRoom.com
DELTA?
OH SURE, GIVE ME THE HARD ONES
GREG 9-23

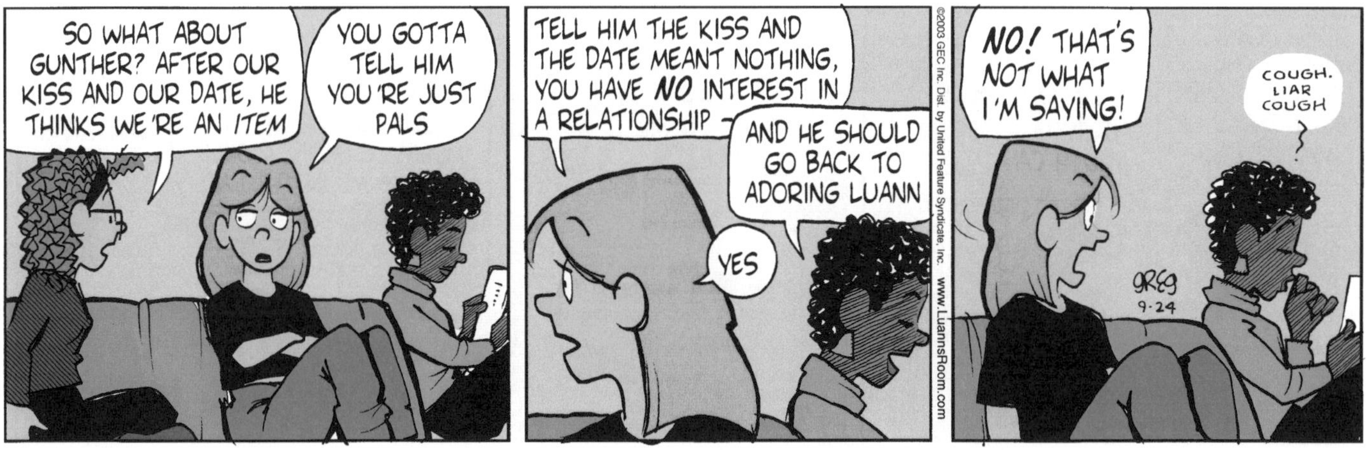
SO WHAT ABOUT GUNTHER? AFTER OUR KISS AND OUR DATE, HE THINKS WE'RE AN *ITEM*
YOU GOTTA TELL HIM YOU'RE JUST PALS
TELL HIM THE KISS AND THE DATE MEANT NOTHING, YOU HAVE *NO* INTEREST IN A RELATIONSHIP –
AND HE SHOULD GO BACK TO ADORING LUANN
YES
©2003 GEC Inc. Dist. by United Feature Syndicate, Inc.
www.LuannsRoom.com
NO! THAT'S NOT WHAT I'M SAYING!
COUGH. LIAR COUGH
GREG 9-24

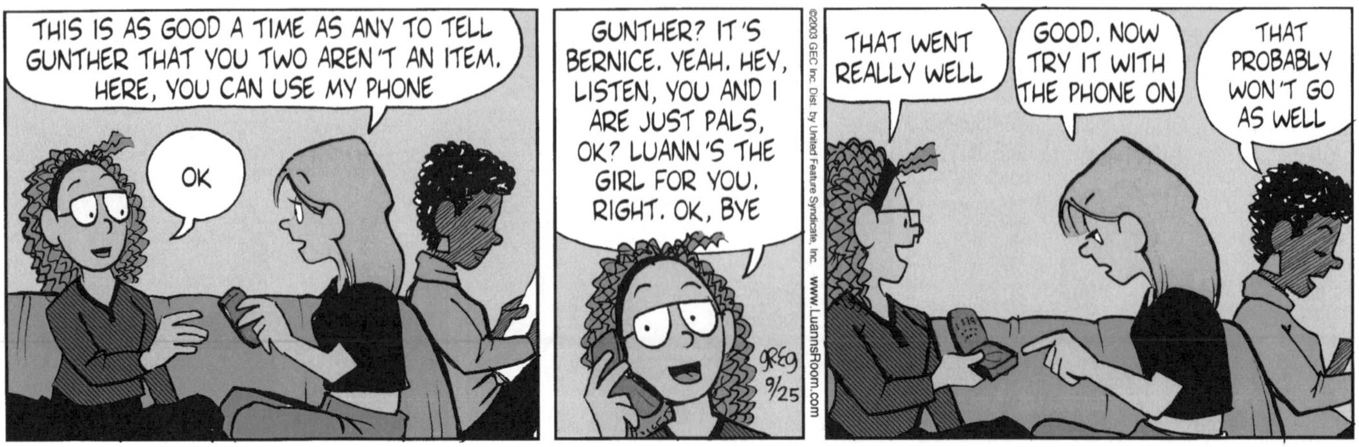
THIS IS AS GOOD A TIME AS ANY TO TELL GUNTHER THAT YOU TWO AREN'T AN ITEM. HERE, YOU CAN USE MY PHONE
OK
GUNTHER? IT'S BERNICE. YEAH. HEY, LISTEN, YOU AND I ARE JUST PALS, OK? LUANN'S THE GIRL FOR YOU. RIGHT. OK, BYE
GREG 9/25
THAT WENT REALLY WELL
GOOD. NOW TRY IT WITH THE PHONE ON
THAT PROBABLY WON'T GO AS WELL

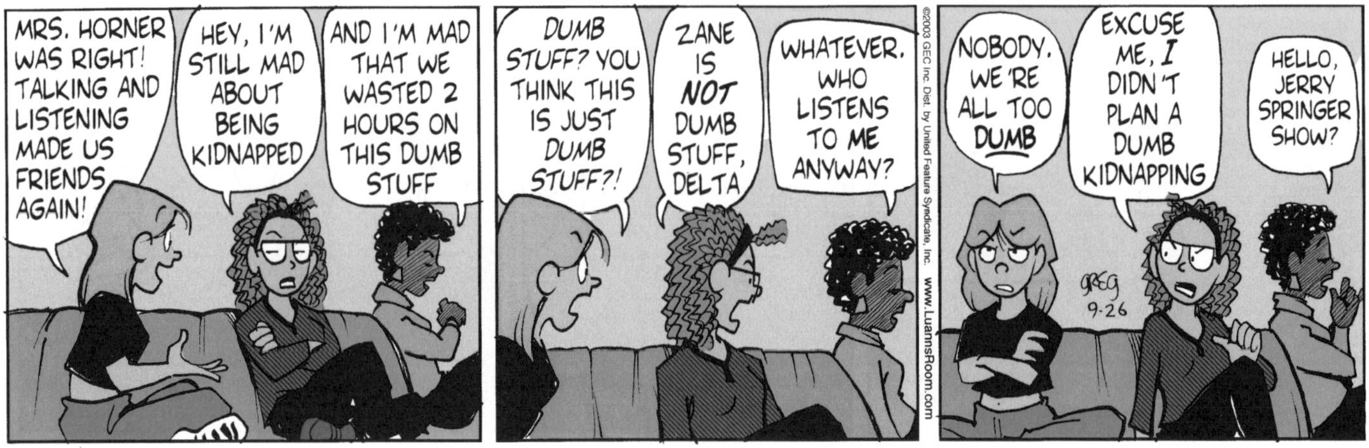
MRS. HORNER WAS RIGHT! TALKING AND LISTENING MADE US FRIENDS AGAIN!
HEY, I'M STILL MAD ABOUT BEING KIDNAPPED
AND I'M MAD THAT WE WASTED 2 HOURS ON THIS DUMB STUFF
DUMB STUFF? YOU THINK THIS IS JUST DUMB STUFF?!
ZANE IS NOT DUMB STUFF, DELTA
WHATEVER. WHO LISTENS TO ME ANYWAY?
NOBODY. WE'RE ALL TOO DUMB
EXCUSE ME, I DIDN'T PLAN A DUMB KIDNAPPING
HELLO, JERRY SPRINGER SHOW?
GREG 9-26

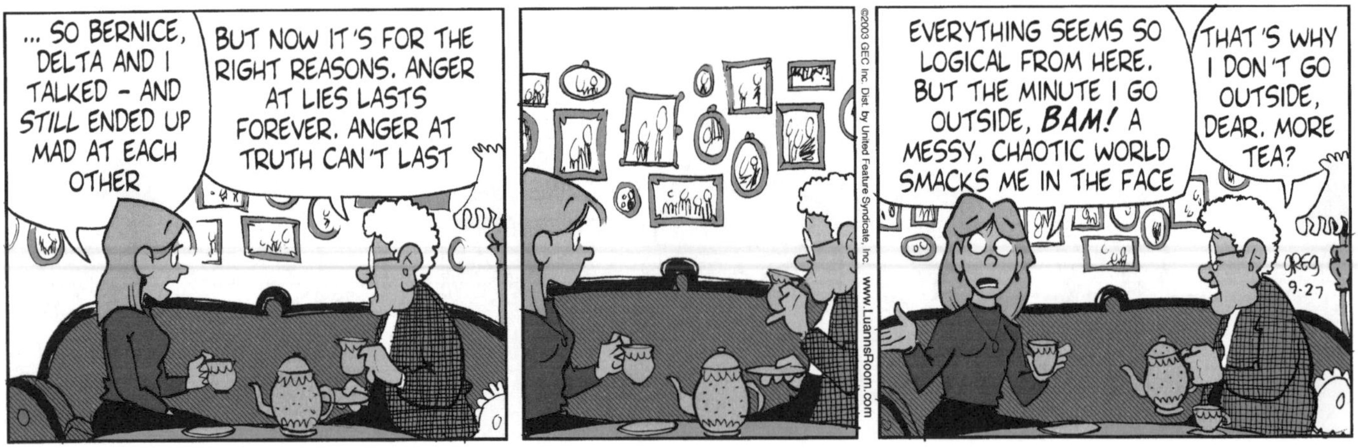
... SO BERNICE, DELTA AND I TALKED – AND STILL ENDED UP MAD AT EACH OTHER
BUT NOW IT'S FOR THE RIGHT REASONS. ANGER AT LIES LASTS FOREVER. ANGER AT TRUTH CAN'T LAST
EVERYTHING SEEMS SO LOGICAL FROM HERE. BUT THE MINUTE I GO OUTSIDE, BAM! A MESSY, CHAOTIC WORLD SMACKS ME IN THE FACE
THAT'S WHY I DON'T GO OUTSIDE, DEAR. MORE TEA?
GREG 9-27

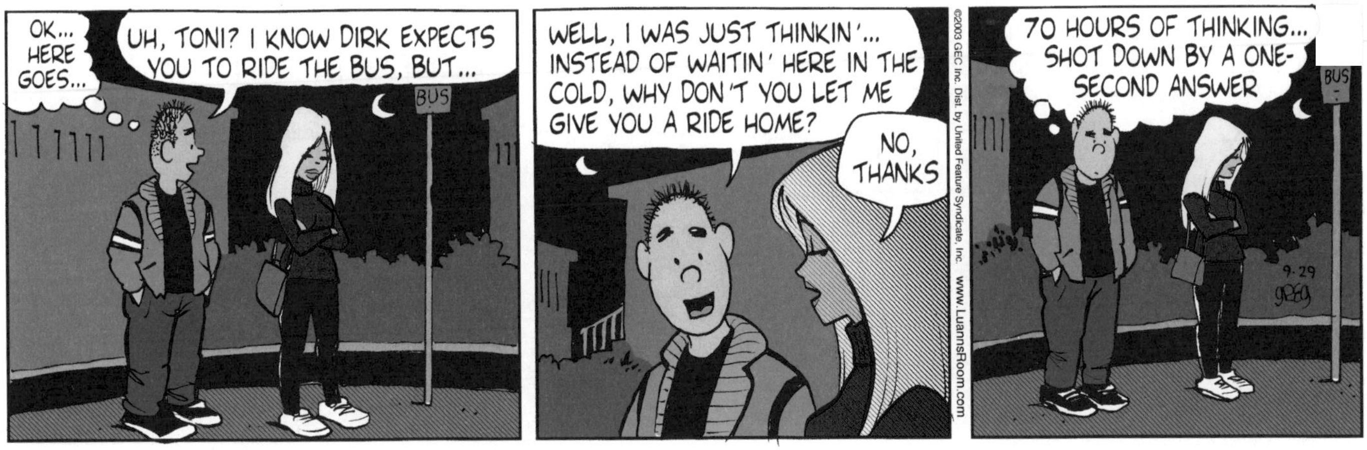

OK... HERE GOES...
UH, TONI? I KNOW DIRK EXPECTS YOU TO RIDE THE BUS, BUT...
BUS
WELL, I WAS JUST THINKIN'... INSTEAD OF WAITIN' HERE IN THE COLD, WHY DON'T YOU LET ME GIVE YOU A RIDE HOME?
NO, THANKS
©2003 GEC Inc. Dist. by United Feature Syndicate, Inc. www.LuannsRoom.com
70 HOURS OF THINKING... SHOT DOWN BY A ONE-SECOND ANSWER
BUS
9-29 GREG

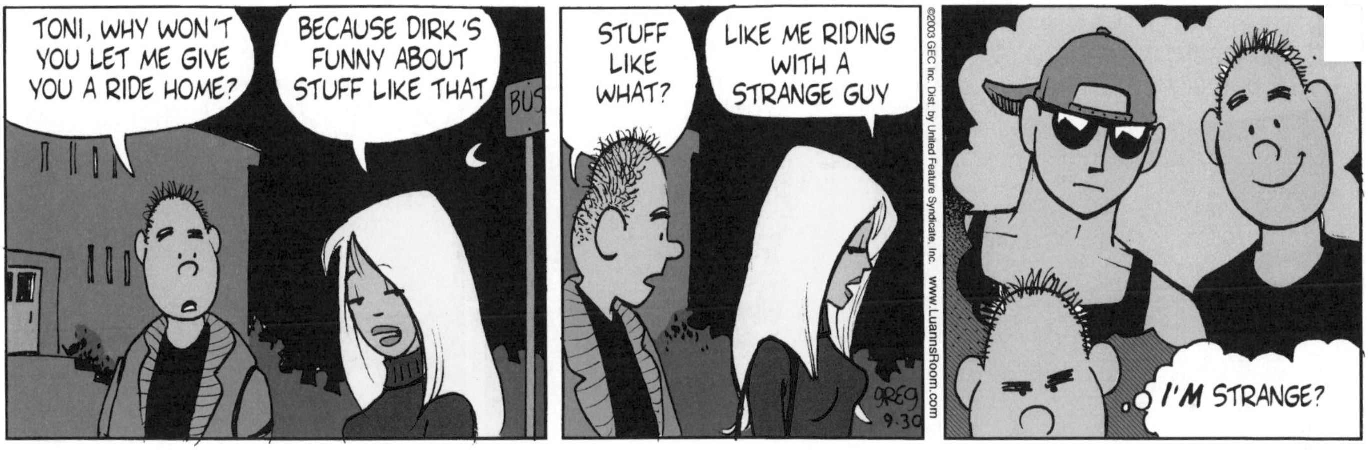

TONI, WHY WON'T YOU LET ME GIVE YOU A RIDE HOME?
BECAUSE DIRK'S FUNNY ABOUT STUFF LIKE THAT
BUS
GREG 9-30
STUFF LIKE WHAT?
LIKE ME RIDING WITH A STRANGE GUY
©2003 GEC Inc. Dist. by United Feature Syndicate, Inc. www.LuannsRoom.com
I'M STRANGE?

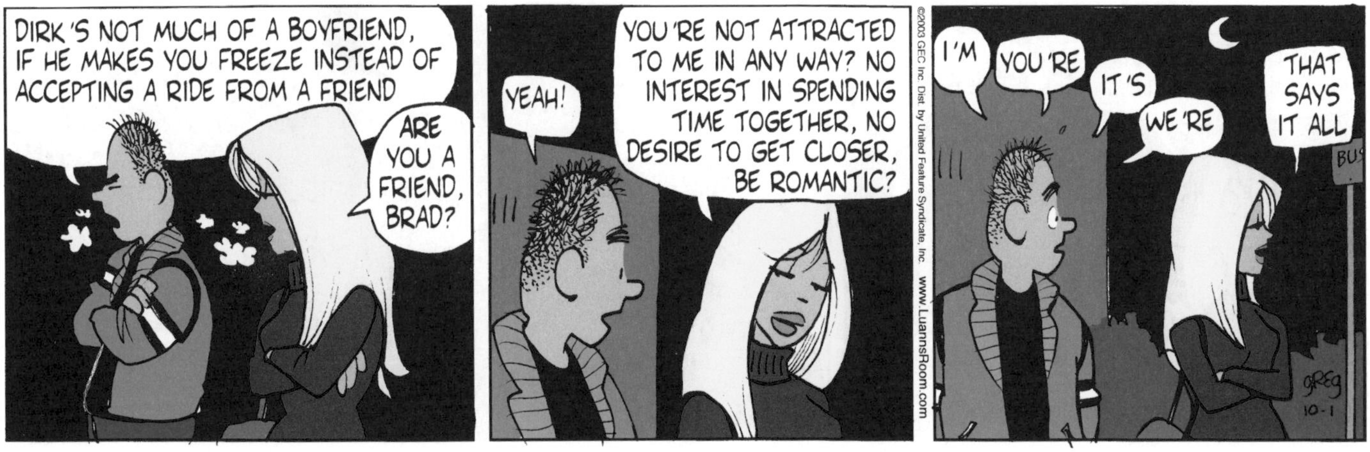

DIRK'S NOT MUCH OF A BOYFRIEND, IF HE MAKES YOU FREEZE INSTEAD OF ACCEPTING A RIDE FROM A FRIEND
ARE YOU A FRIEND, BRAD?
YEAH!
YOU'RE NOT ATTRACTED TO ME IN ANY WAY? NO INTEREST IN SPENDING TIME TOGETHER, NO DESIRE TO GET CLOSER, BE ROMANTIC?
©2003 GEC Inc. Dist. by United Feature Syndicate, Inc. www.LuannsRoom.com
I'M
YOU'RE
IT'S
WE'RE
THAT SAYS IT ALL
BUS
GREG 10-1

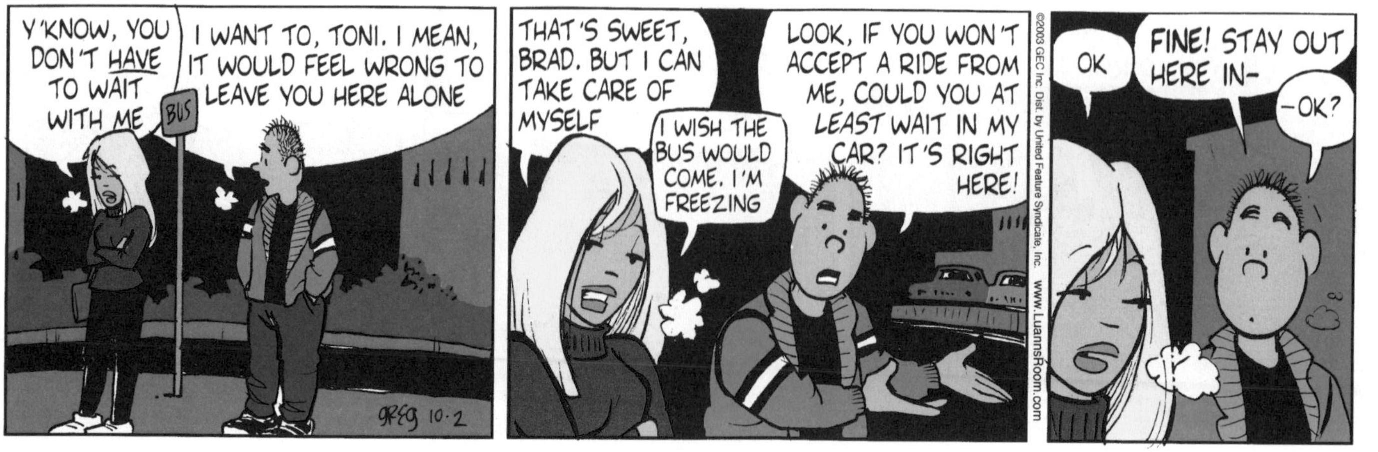
Y'KNOW, YOU DON'T HAVE TO WAIT WITH ME
BUS
I WANT TO, TONI. I MEAN, IT WOULD FEEL WRONG TO LEAVE YOU HERE ALONE
GREG 10·2
THAT'S SWEET, BRAD. BUT I CAN TAKE CARE OF MYSELF
I WISH THE BUS WOULD COME. I'M FREEZING
LOOK, IF YOU WON'T ACCEPT A RIDE FROM ME, COULD YOU AT LEAST WAIT IN MY CAR? IT'S RIGHT HERE!
©2003 GEC Inc. Dist. by United Feature Syndicate, Inc. www.LuannsRoom.com
OK
FINE! STAY OUT HERE IN-
-OK?

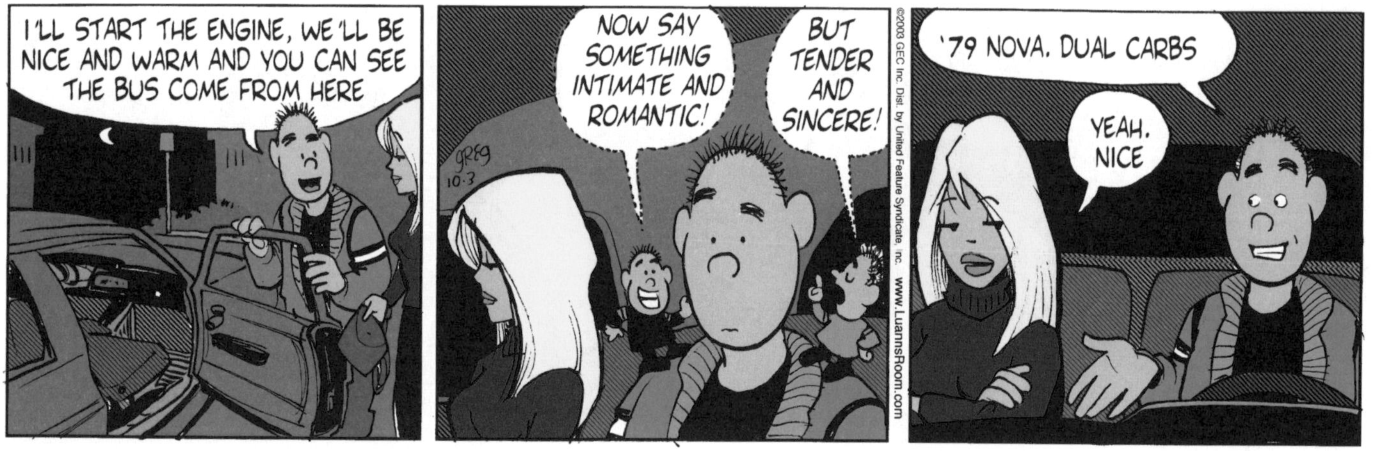
I'LL START THE ENGINE, WE'LL BE NICE AND WARM AND YOU CAN SEE THE BUS COME FROM HERE
GREG 10·3
NOW SAY SOMETHING INTIMATE AND ROMANTIC!
BUT TENDER AND SINCERE!
©2003 GEC Inc. Dist. by United Feature Syndicate, Inc. www.LuannsRoom.com
'79 NOVA. DUAL CARBS
YEAH. NICE

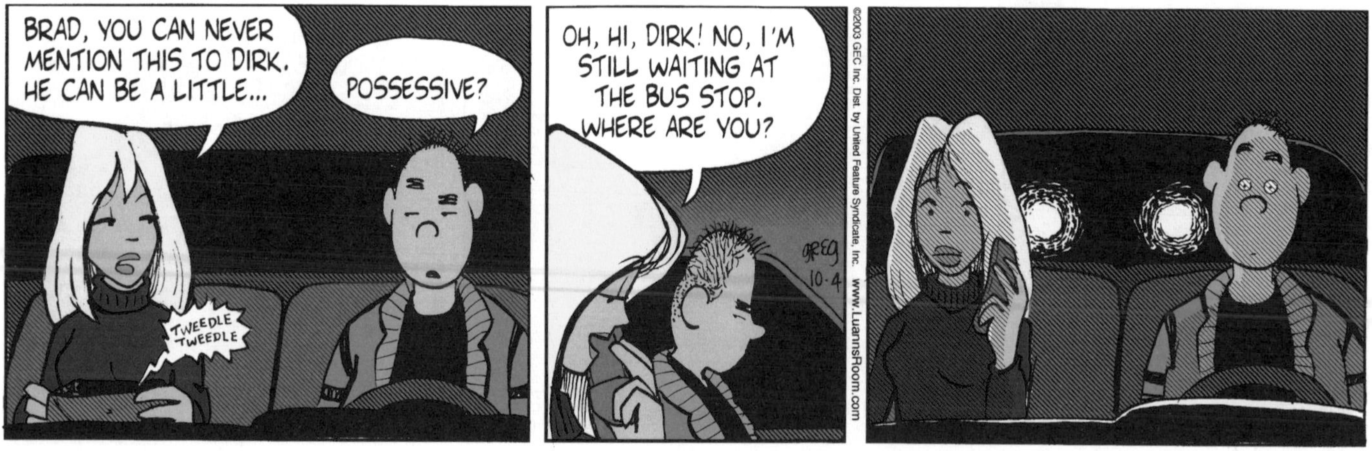
BRAD, YOU CAN NEVER MENTION THIS TO DIRK. HE CAN BE A LITTLE...
POSSESSIVE?
TWEEDLE TWEEDLE
©2003 GEC Inc. Dist. by United Feature Syndicate, Inc. www.LuannsRoom.com
OH, HI, DIRK! NO, I'M STILL WAITING AT THE BUS STOP. WHERE ARE YOU?
GREG 10·4

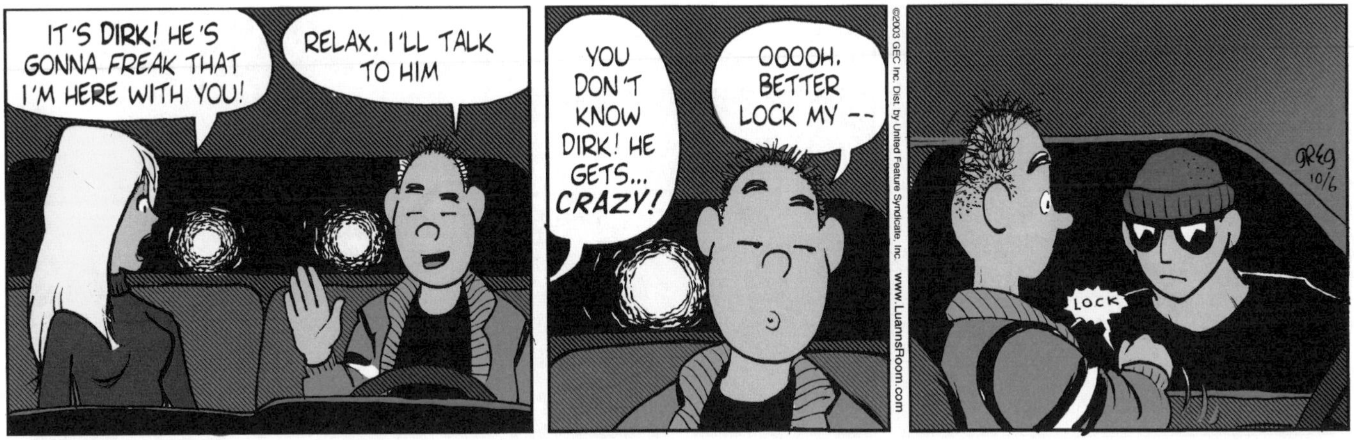
IT'S DIRK! HE'S GONNA FREAK THAT I'M HERE WITH YOU!
RELAX. I'LL TALK TO HIM
YOU DON'T KNOW DIRK! HE GETS... CRAZY!
OOOOH. BETTER LOCK MY --
LOCK
GREG 10/6
©2003 GEC Inc. Dist. by United Feature Syndicate, Inc. www.LuannsRoom.com

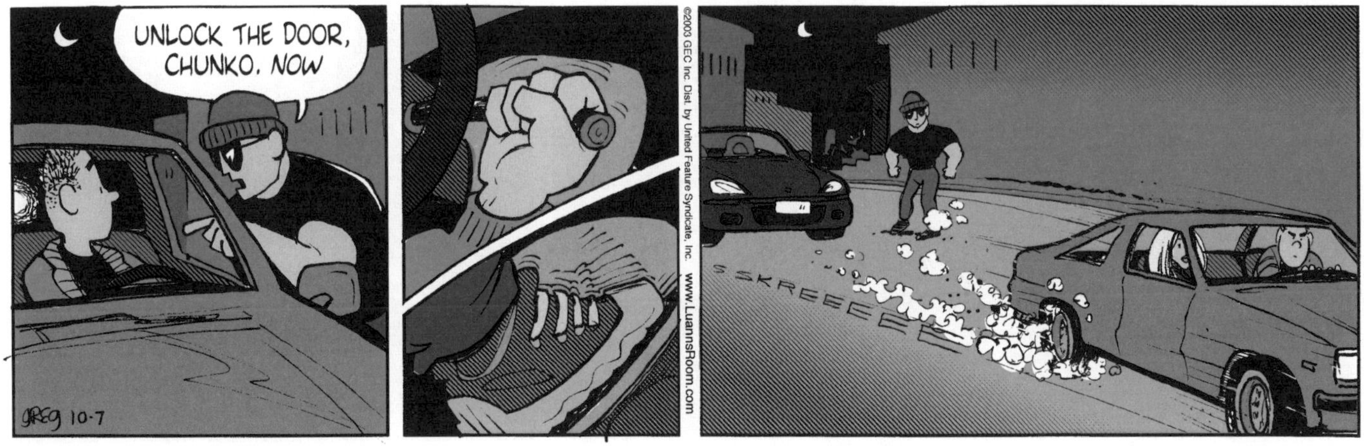
UNLOCK THE DOOR, CHUNKO. NOW
GREG 10-7
SSKREEEEEE
©2003 GEC Inc. Dist. by United Feature Syndicate, Inc. www.LuannsRoom.com

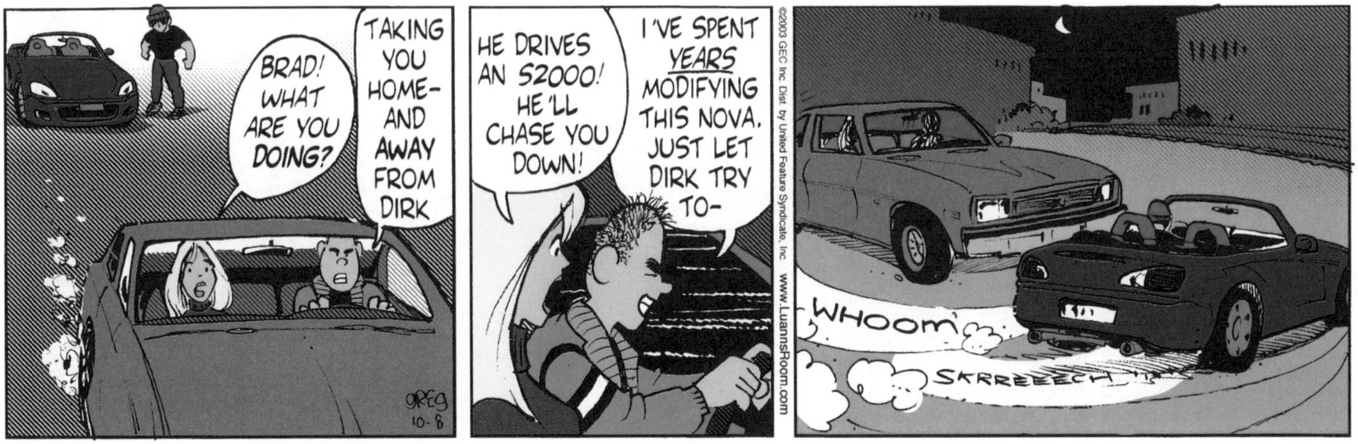
BRAD! WHAT ARE YOU DOING?
TAKING YOU HOME- AND AWAY FROM DIRK
GREG 10-8
HE DRIVES AN S2000! HE'LL CHASE YOU DOWN!
I'VE SPENT YEARS MODIFYING THIS NOVA. JUST LET DIRK TRY TO-
WHOOM
SKRREEEECH
©2003 GEC Inc. Dist. by United Feature Syndicate, Inc. www.LuannsRoom.com

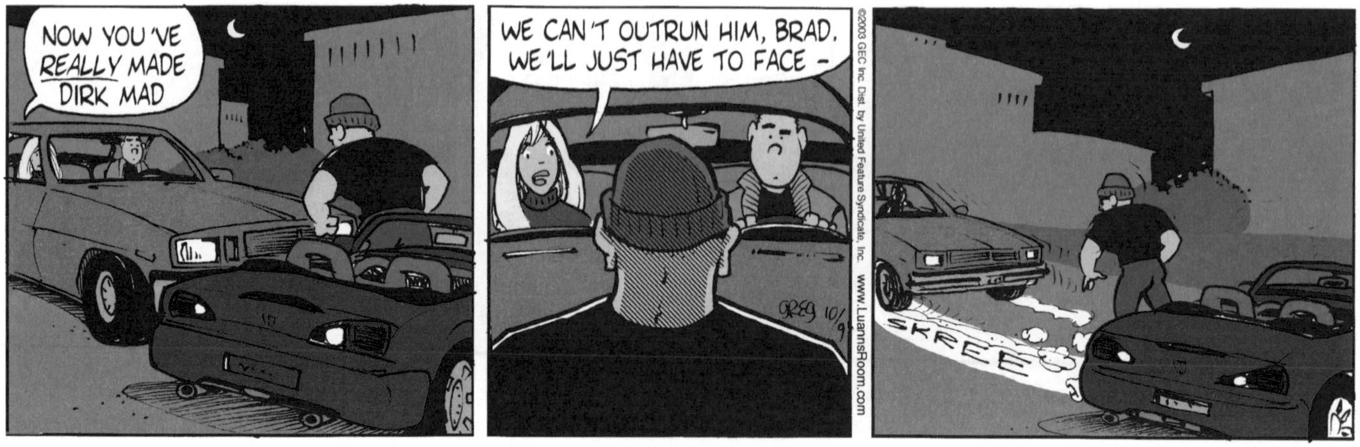
NOW YOU'VE REALLY MADE DIRK MAD
WE CAN'T OUTRUN HIM, BRAD. WE'LL JUST HAVE TO FACE –
GREG 10/9
©2003 GEC Inc. Dist. by United Feature Syndicate, Inc. www.LuannsRoom.com
SKREE

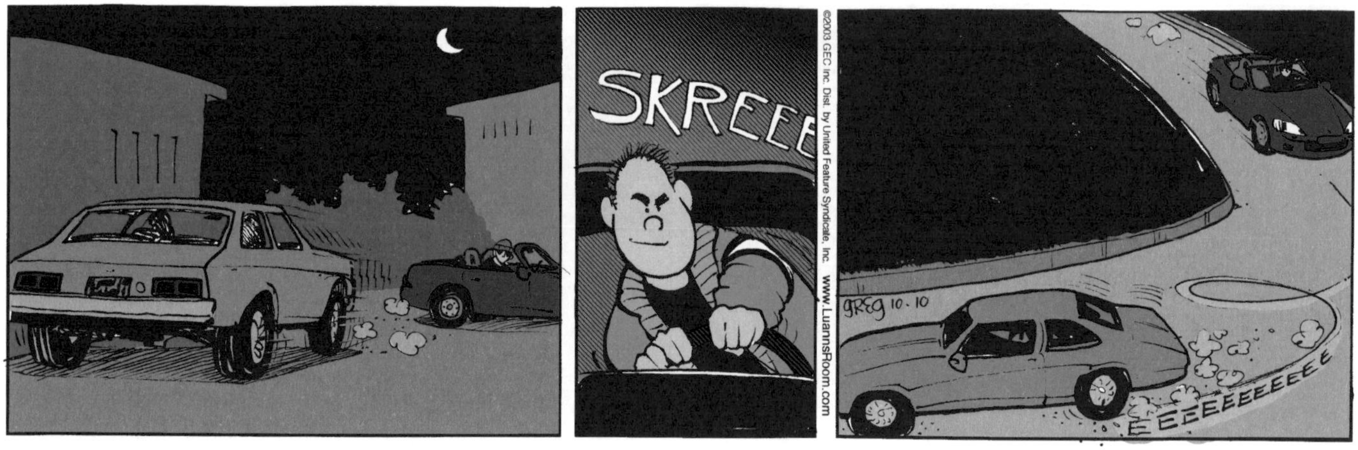
©2003 GEC Inc. Dist. by United Feature Syndicate, Inc. www.LuannsRoom.com
SKREEE
GREG 10.10

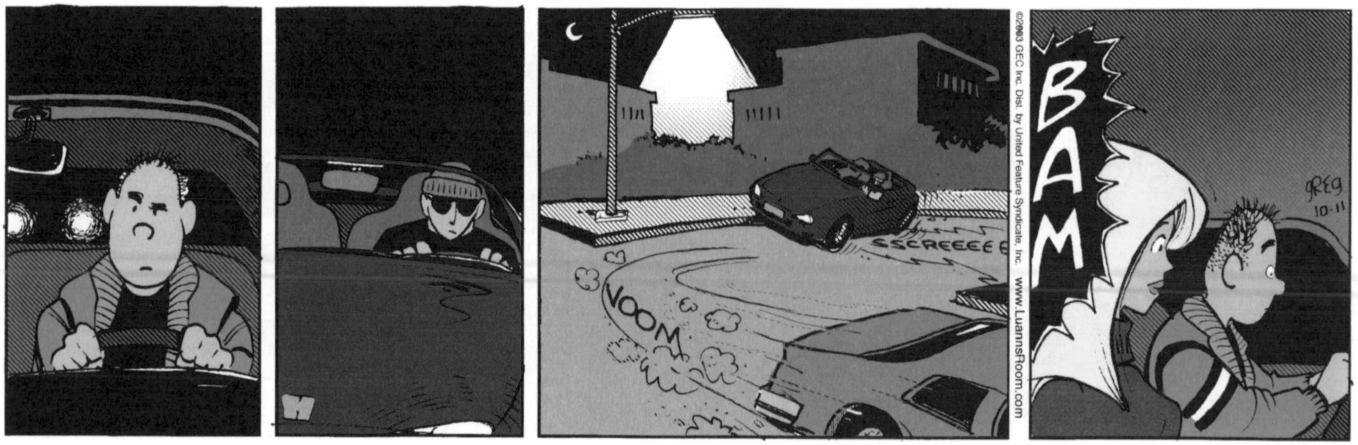
VOOM
©2003 GEC Inc. Dist. by United Feature Syndicate, Inc. www.LuannsRoom.com
BAM
GREG 10-11

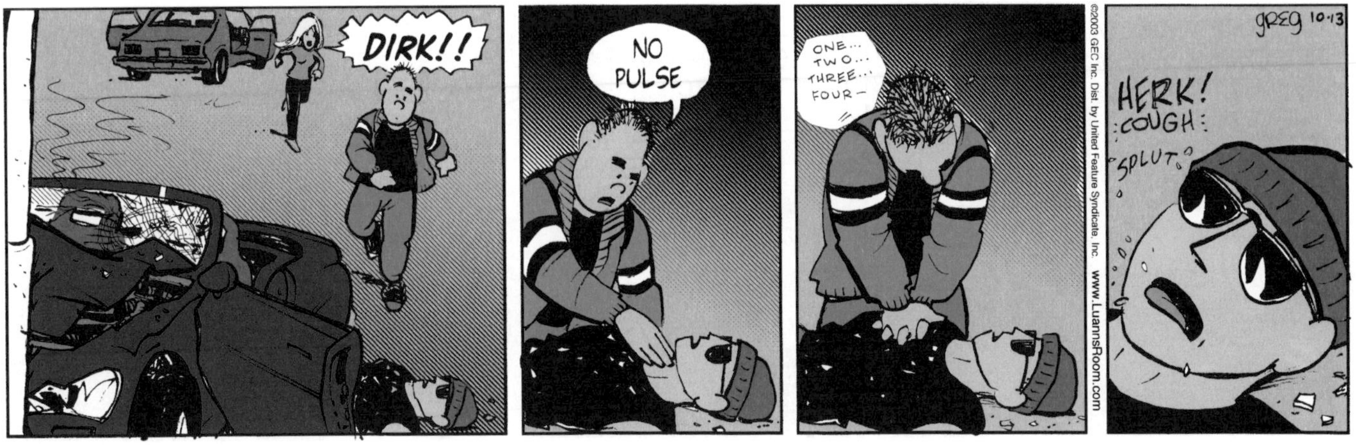
DIRK!!
NO PULSE
ONE... TWO... THREE... FOUR—
©2003 GEC Inc. Dist. by United Feature Syndicate, Inc. www.LuannsRoom.com
GREG 10-13
HERK!
COUGH
SPLUT

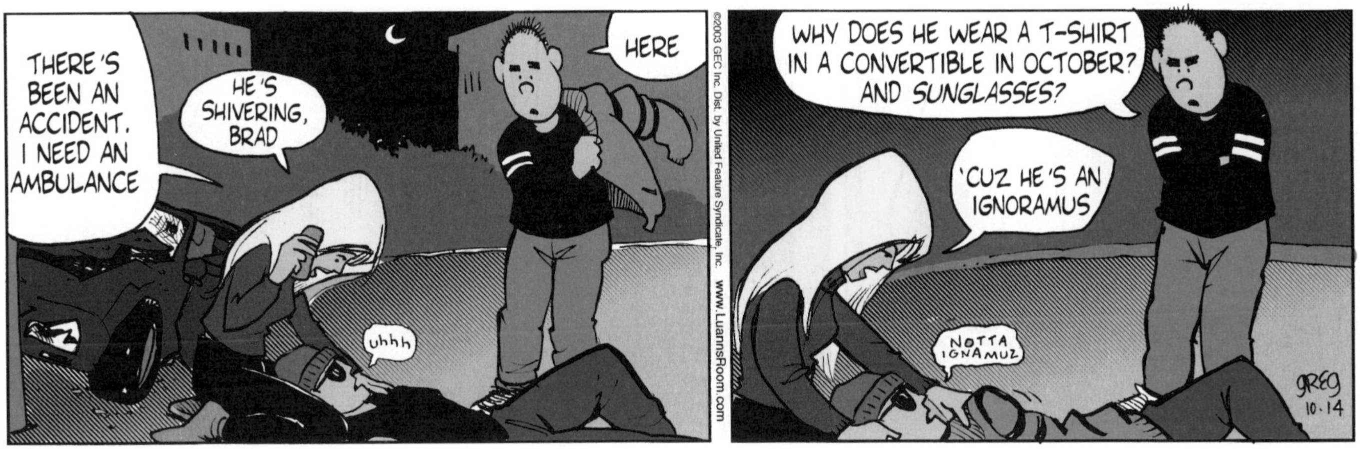
THERE'S BEEN AN ACCIDENT. I NEED AN AMBULANCE
HE'S SHIVERING, BRAD
HERE
uhhh
©2003 GEC Inc. Dist. by United Feature Syndicate, Inc. www.LuannsRoom.com
WHY DOES HE WEAR A T-SHIRT IN A CONVERTIBLE IN OCTOBER? AND SUNGLASSES?
'CUZ HE'S AN IGNORAMUS
NOTTA IGNAMUZ
GREG 10-14

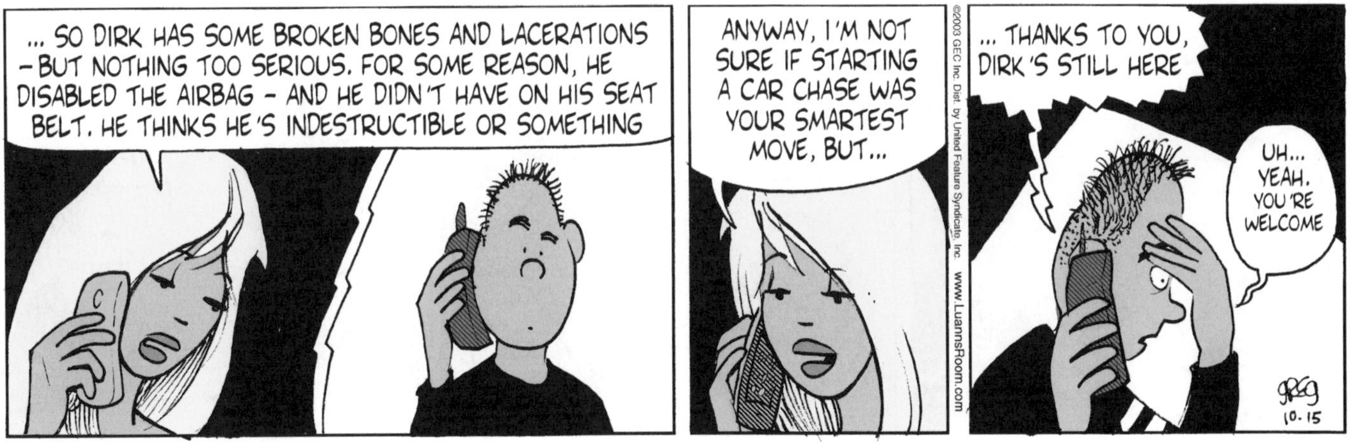
... SO DIRK HAS SOME BROKEN BONES AND LACERATIONS – BUT NOTHING TOO SERIOUS. FOR SOME REASON, HE DISABLED THE AIRBAG – AND HE DIDN'T HAVE ON HIS SEAT BELT. HE THINKS HE'S INDESTRUCTIBLE OR SOMETHING
ANYWAY, I'M NOT SURE IF STARTING A CAR CHASE WAS YOUR SMARTEST MOVE, BUT...
©2003 GEC Inc. Dist. by United Feature Syndicate, Inc. www.LuannsRoom.com
... THANKS TO YOU, DIRK'S STILL HERE
UH... YEAH. YOU'RE WELCOME
GREG 10-15

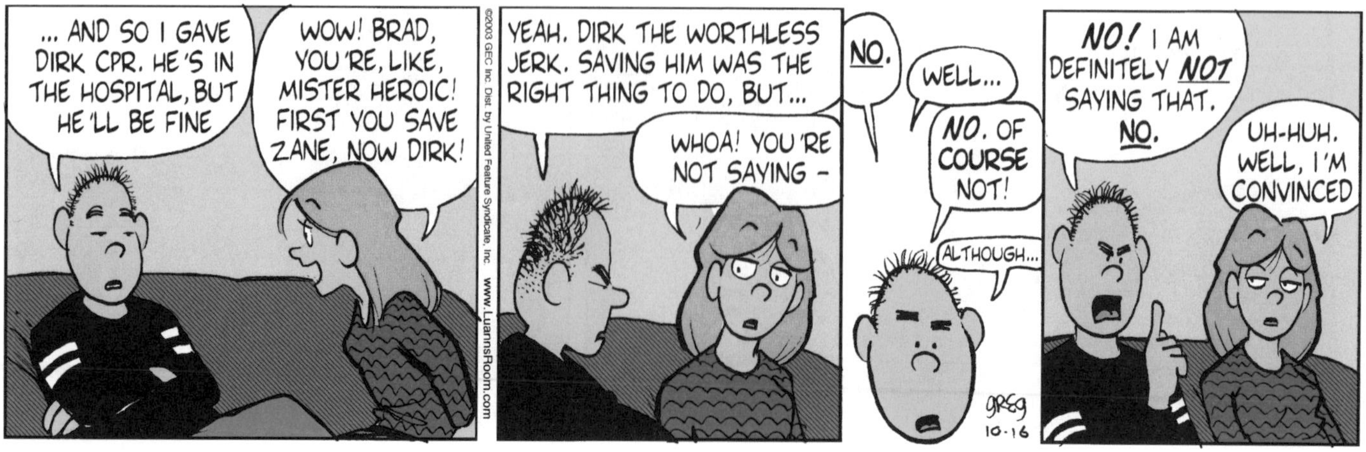
... AND SO I GAVE DIRK CPR. HE'S IN THE HOSPITAL, BUT HE'LL BE FINE
WOW! BRAD, YOU'RE, LIKE, MISTER HEROIC! FIRST YOU SAVE ZANE, NOW DIRK!
©2003 GEC Inc. Dist. by United Feature Syndicate, Inc. www.LuannsRoom.com
YEAH. DIRK THE WORTHLESS JERK. SAVING HIM WAS THE RIGHT THING TO DO, BUT...
WHOA! YOU'RE NOT SAYING –
NO.
WELL...
NO. OF COURSE NOT!
ALTHOUGH...
GREG 10-16
NO! I AM DEFINITELY NOT SAYING THAT. NO.
UH-HUH. WELL, I'M CONVINCED

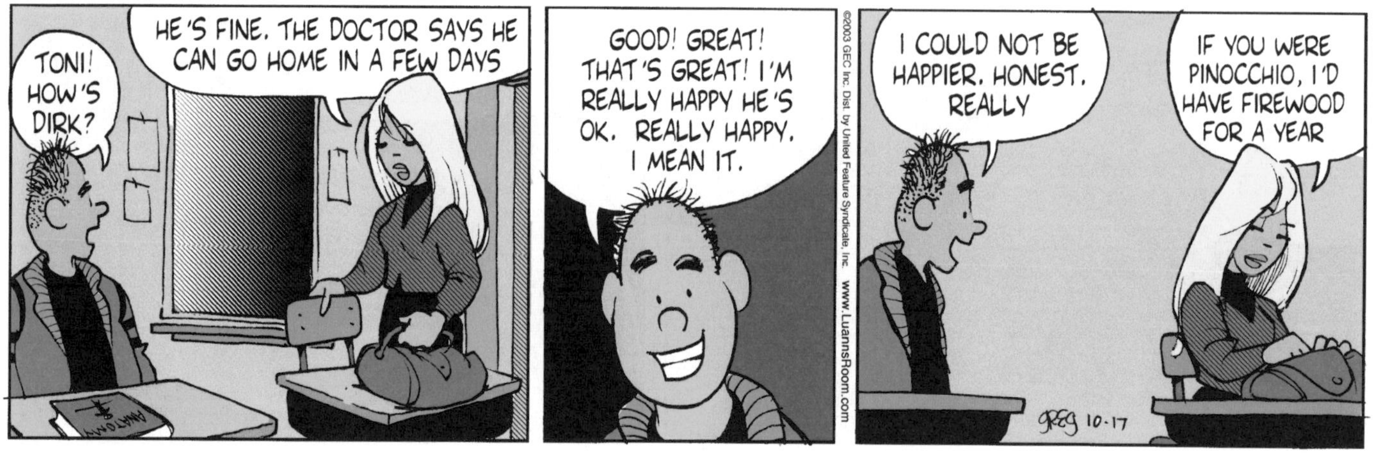
TONI! HOW'S DIRK?
HE'S FINE. THE DOCTOR SAYS HE CAN GO HOME IN A FEW DAYS
GOOD! GREAT! THAT'S GREAT! I'M REALLY HAPPY HE'S OK. REALLY HAPPY. I MEAN IT.
©2003 GEC Inc. Dist. by United Feature Syndicate, Inc. www.LuannsRoom.com
I COULD NOT BE HAPPIER. HONEST. REALLY
IF YOU WERE PINOCCHIO, I'D HAVE FIREWOOD FOR A YEAR
GREG 10-17

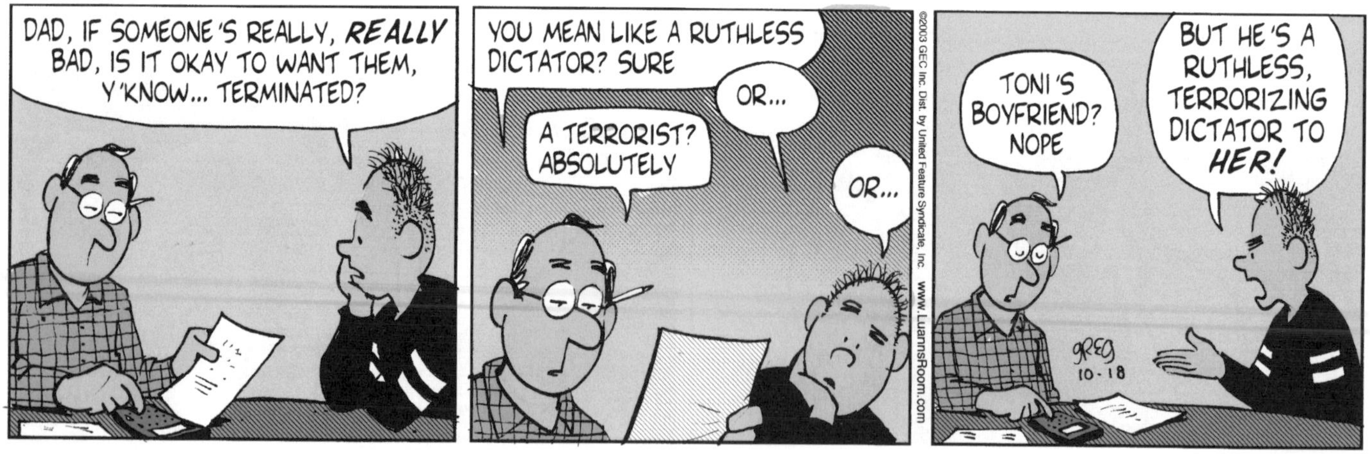
DAD, IF SOMEONE'S REALLY, REALLY BAD, IS IT OKAY TO WANT THEM, Y'KNOW... TERMINATED?
YOU MEAN LIKE A RUTHLESS DICTATOR? SURE
OR...
A TERRORIST? ABSOLUTELY
OR...
©2003 GEC Inc. Dist. by United Feature Syndicate, Inc. www.LuannsRoom.com
TONI'S BOYFRIEND? NOPE
BUT HE'S A RUTHLESS, TERRORIZING DICTATOR TO HER!
GREG 10-18

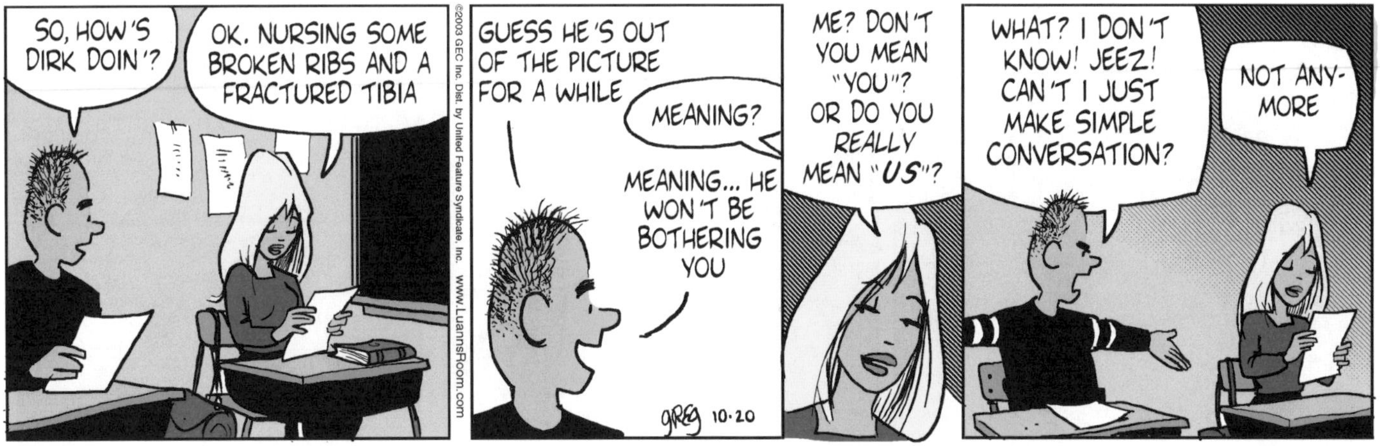
SO, HOW'S DIRK DOIN'?
OK. NURSING SOME BROKEN RIBS AND A FRACTURED TIBIA
©2003 GEC Inc. Dist. by United Feature Syndicate, Inc. www.LuannsRoom.com
GUESS HE'S OUT OF THE PICTURE FOR A WHILE
MEANING?
MEANING... HE WON'T BE BOTHERING YOU
GREG 10·20
ME? DON'T YOU MEAN "YOU"? OR DO YOU REALLY MEAN "US"?
WHAT? I DON'T KNOW! JEEZ! CAN'T I JUST MAKE SIMPLE CONVERSATION?
NOT ANY-MORE

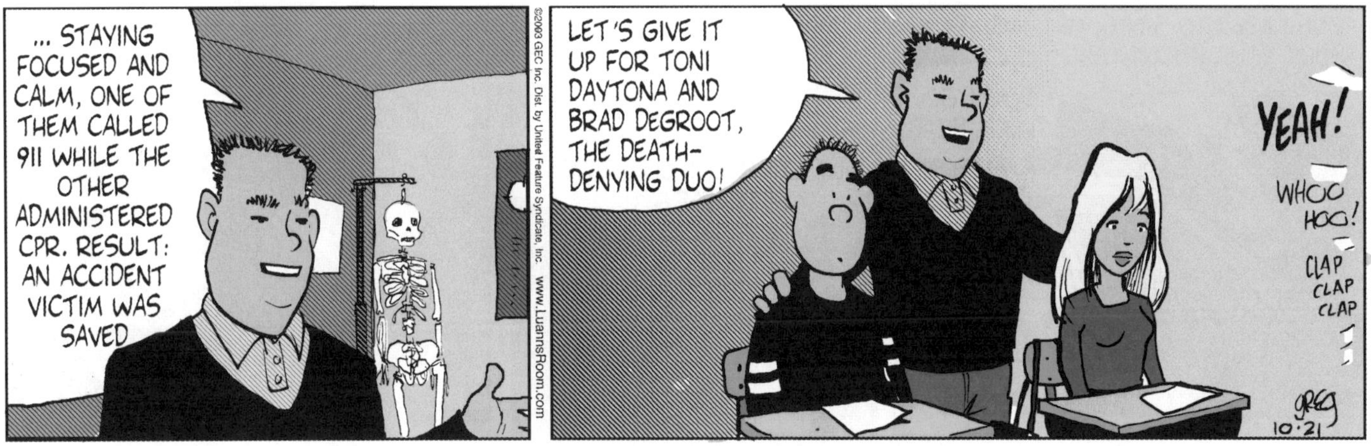
... STAYING FOCUSED AND CALM, ONE OF THEM CALLED 911 WHILE THE OTHER ADMINISTERED CPR. RESULT: AN ACCIDENT VICTIM WAS SAVED
©2003 GEC Inc. Dist. by United Feature Syndicate, Inc. www.LuannsRoom.com
LET'S GIVE IT UP FOR TONI DAYTONA AND BRAD DEGROOT, THE DEATH-DENYING DUO!
YEAH!
WHOO HOO!
CLAP CLAP CLAP
GREG 10·21

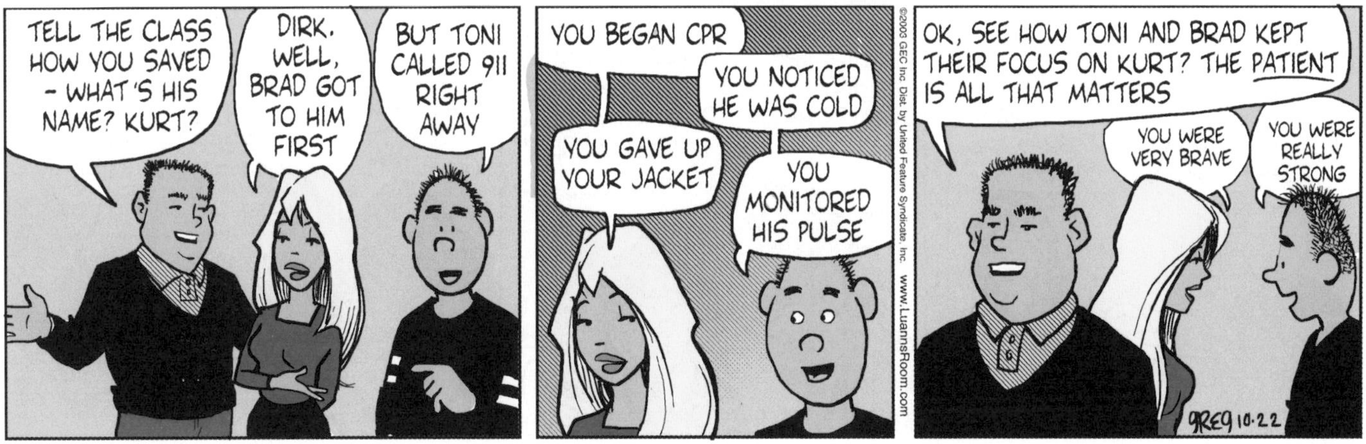
TELL THE CLASS HOW YOU SAVED - WHAT'S HIS NAME? KURT?
DIRK. WELL, BRAD GOT TO HIM FIRST
BUT TONI CALLED 911 RIGHT AWAY
YOU BEGAN CPR
YOU NOTICED HE WAS COLD
YOU GAVE UP YOUR JACKET
YOU MONITORED HIS PULSE
©2003 GEC Inc. Dist. by United Feature Syndicate, Inc. www.LuannsRoom.com
OK, SEE HOW TONI AND BRAD KEPT THEIR FOCUS ON KURT? THE PATIENT IS ALL THAT MATTERS
YOU WERE VERY BRAVE
YOU WERE REALLY STRONG
GREG 10·22

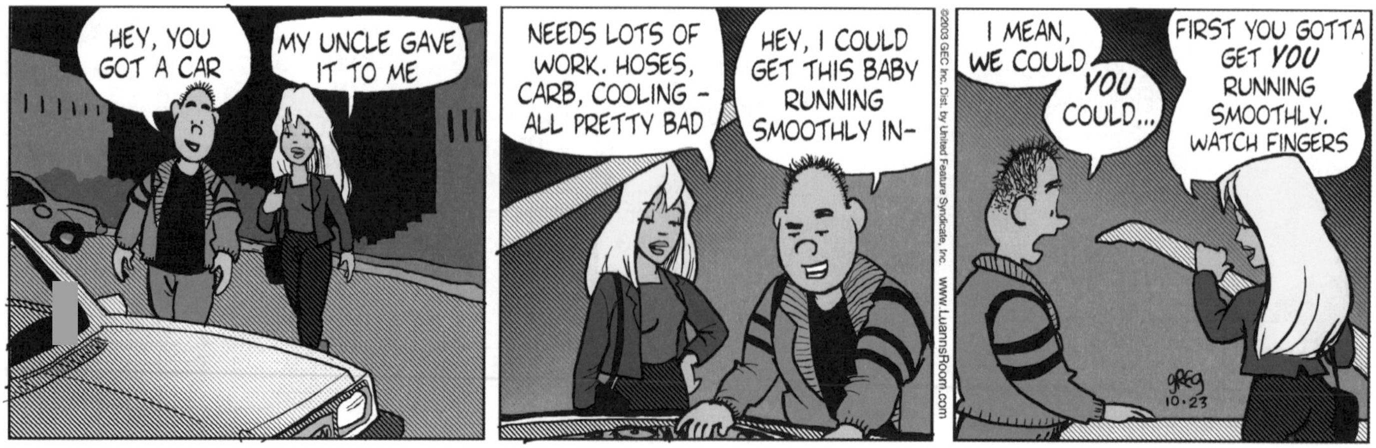
HEY, YOU GOT A CAR
MY UNCLE GAVE IT TO ME
NEEDS LOTS OF WORK. HOSES, CARB, COOLING - ALL PRETTY BAD
HEY, I COULD GET THIS BABY RUNNING SMOOTHLY IN-
©2003 GEC Inc. Dist. by United Feature Syndicate, Inc. www.LuannsRoom.com
I MEAN, WE COULD
YOU COULD...
FIRST YOU GOTTA GET YOU RUNNING SMOOTHLY. WATCH FINGERS
GREG 10·23

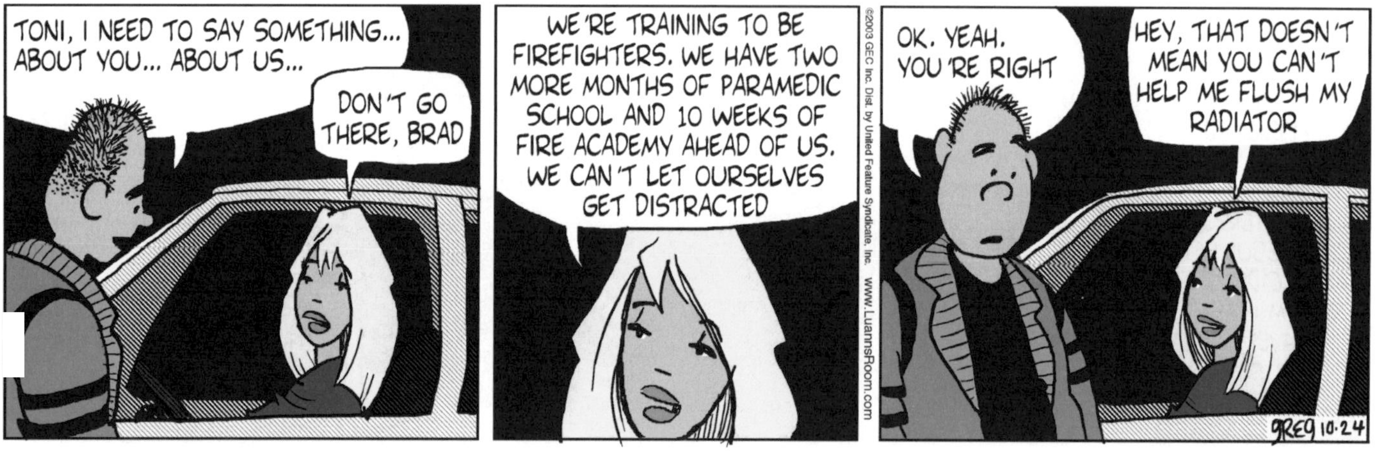
TONI, I NEED TO SAY SOMETHING... ABOUT YOU... ABOUT US...
DON'T GO THERE, BRAD
WE'RE TRAINING TO BE FIREFIGHTERS. WE HAVE TWO MORE MONTHS OF PARAMEDIC SCHOOL AND 10 WEEKS OF FIRE ACADEMY AHEAD OF US. WE CAN'T LET OURSELVES GET DISTRACTED
©2003 GEC Inc. Dist. by United Feature Syndicate, Inc. www.LuannsRoom.com
OK. YEAH. YOU'RE RIGHT
HEY, THAT DOESN'T MEAN YOU CAN'T HELP ME FLUSH MY RADIATOR
GREG 10·24

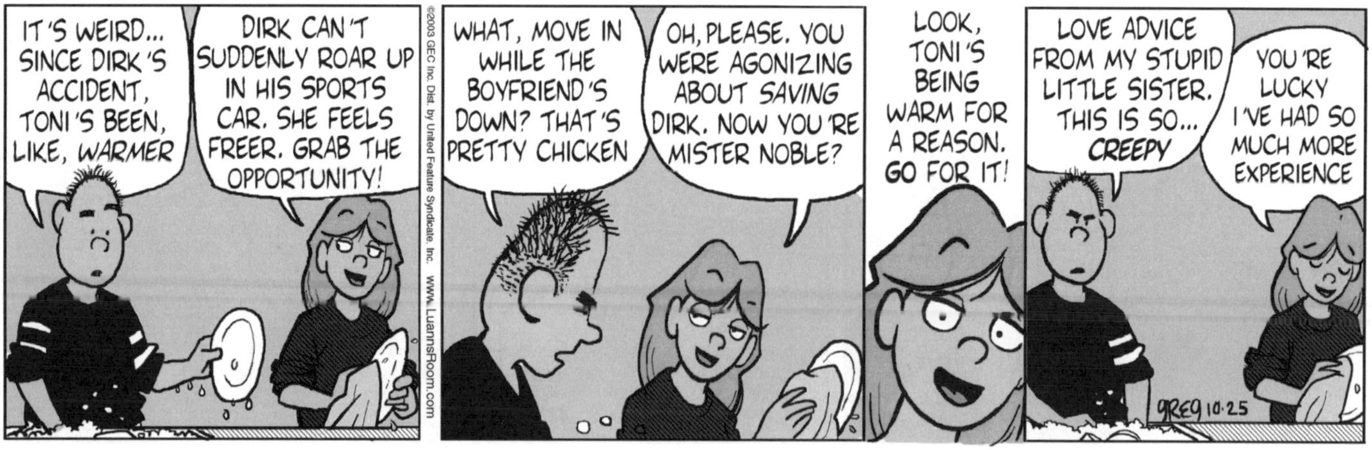
IT'S WEIRD... SINCE DIRK'S ACCIDENT, TONI'S BEEN, LIKE, WARMER
DIRK CAN'T SUDDENLY ROAR UP IN HIS SPORTS CAR. SHE FEELS FREER. GRAB THE OPPORTUNITY!
©2003 GEC Inc. Dist. by United Feature Syndicate, Inc. www.LuannsRoom.com
WHAT, MOVE IN WHILE THE BOYFRIEND'S DOWN? THAT'S PRETTY CHICKEN
OH, PLEASE. YOU WERE AGONIZING ABOUT SAVING DIRK. NOW YOU'RE MISTER NOBLE?
LOOK, TONI'S BEING WARM FOR A REASON. GO FOR IT!
LOVE ADVICE FROM MY STUPID LITTLE SISTER. THIS IS SO... CREEPY
YOU'RE LUCKY I'VE HAD SO MUCH MORE EXPERIENCE
GREG 10·25

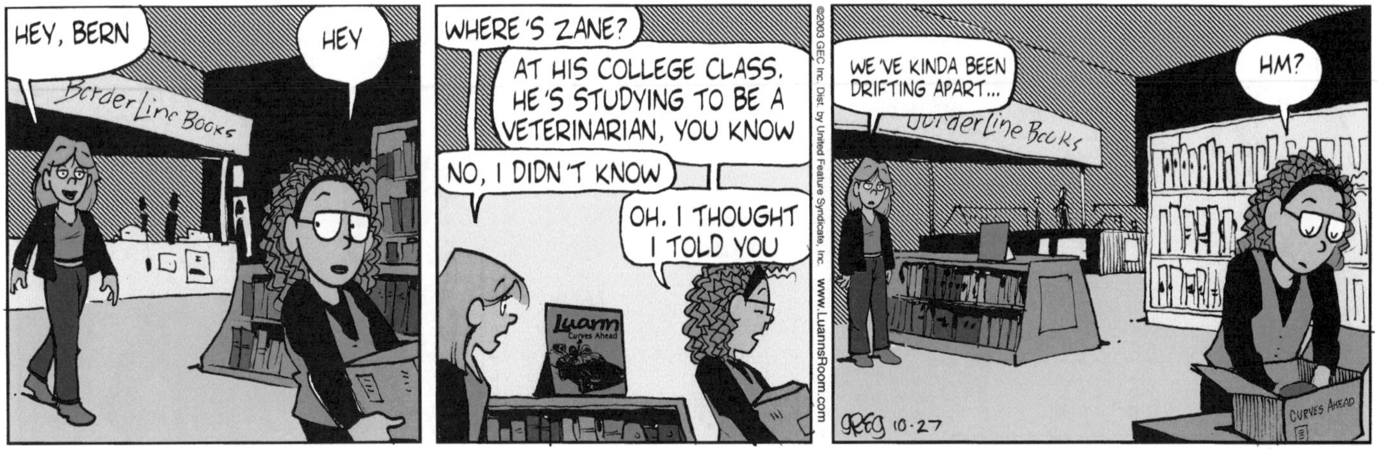
HEY, BERN
HEY
BorderLine Books
WHERE'S ZANE?
AT HIS COLLEGE CLASS. HE'S STUDYING TO BE A VETERINARIAN, YOU KNOW
NO, I DIDN'T KNOW
OH. I THOUGHT I TOLD YOU
Luann Curves Ahead
©2003 GEC Inc. Dist. by United Feature Syndicate, Inc. www.LuannsRoom.com
WE'VE KINDA BEEN DRIFTING APART...
HM?
BorderLine Books
CURVES AHEAD
GREG 10-27

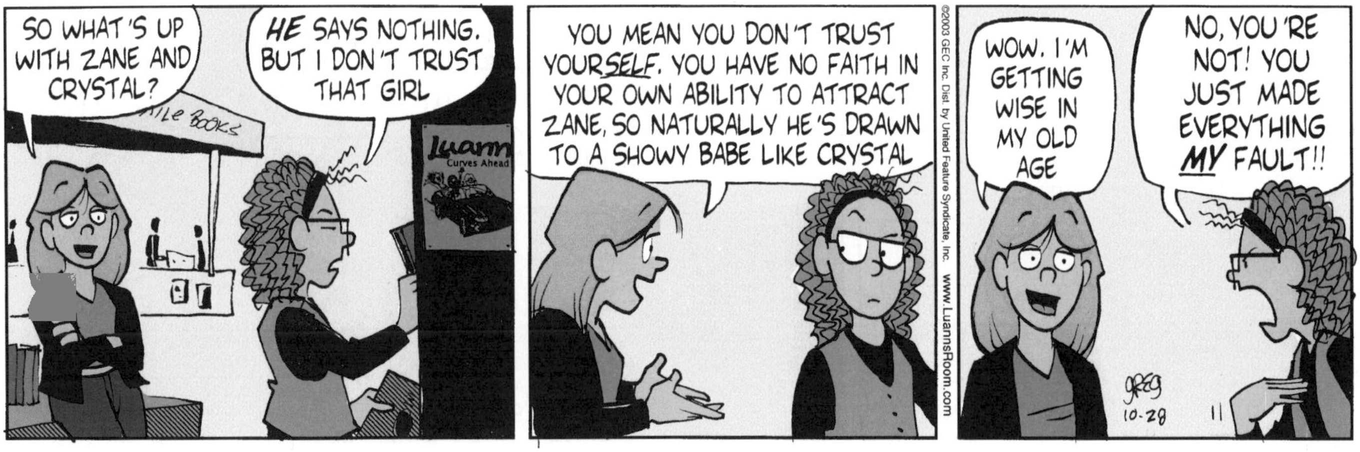
SO WHAT'S UP WITH ZANE AND CRYSTAL?
HE SAYS NOTHING. BUT I DON'T TRUST THAT GIRL
Luann Curves Ahead
YOU MEAN YOU DON'T TRUST YOURSELF. YOU HAVE NO FAITH IN YOUR OWN ABILITY TO ATTRACT ZANE, SO NATURALLY HE'S DRAWN TO A SHOWY BABE LIKE CRYSTAL
©2003 GEC Inc. Dist. by United Feature Syndicate, Inc. www.LuannsRoom.com
WOW. I'M GETTING WISE IN MY OLD AGE
NO, YOU'RE NOT! YOU JUST MADE EVERYTHING MY FAULT!!
GREG 10-28

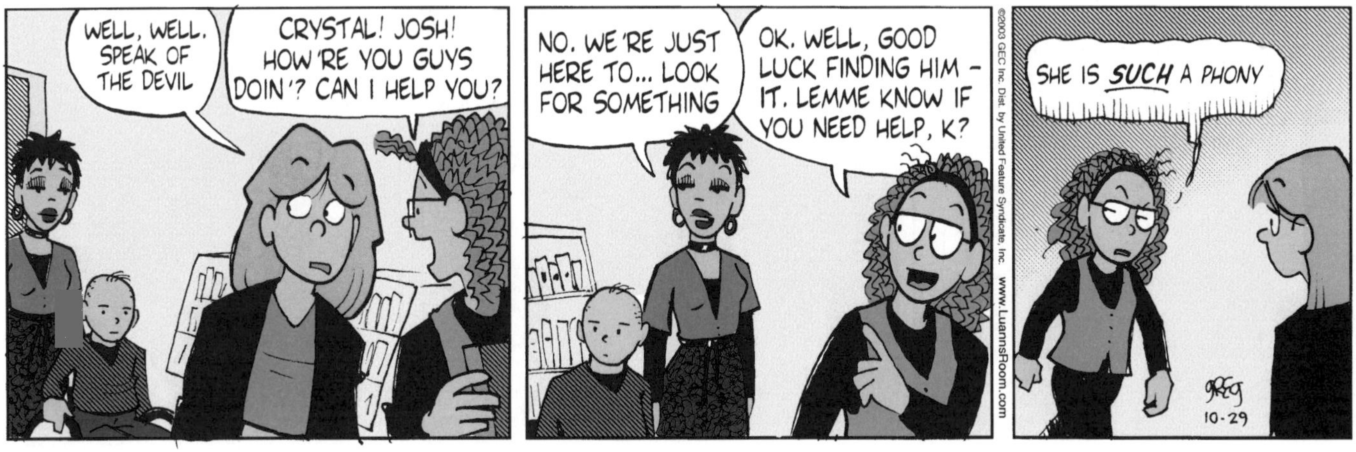
WELL, WELL. SPEAK OF THE DEVIL
CRYSTAL! JOSH! HOW'RE YOU GUYS DOIN'? CAN I HELP YOU?
NO. WE'RE JUST HERE TO... LOOK FOR SOMETHING
OK. WELL, GOOD LUCK FINDING HIM – IT. LEMME KNOW IF YOU NEED HELP, K?
©2003 GEC Inc. Dist. by United Feature Syndicate, Inc. www.LuannsRoom.com
SHE IS SUCH A PHONY
GREG 10-29

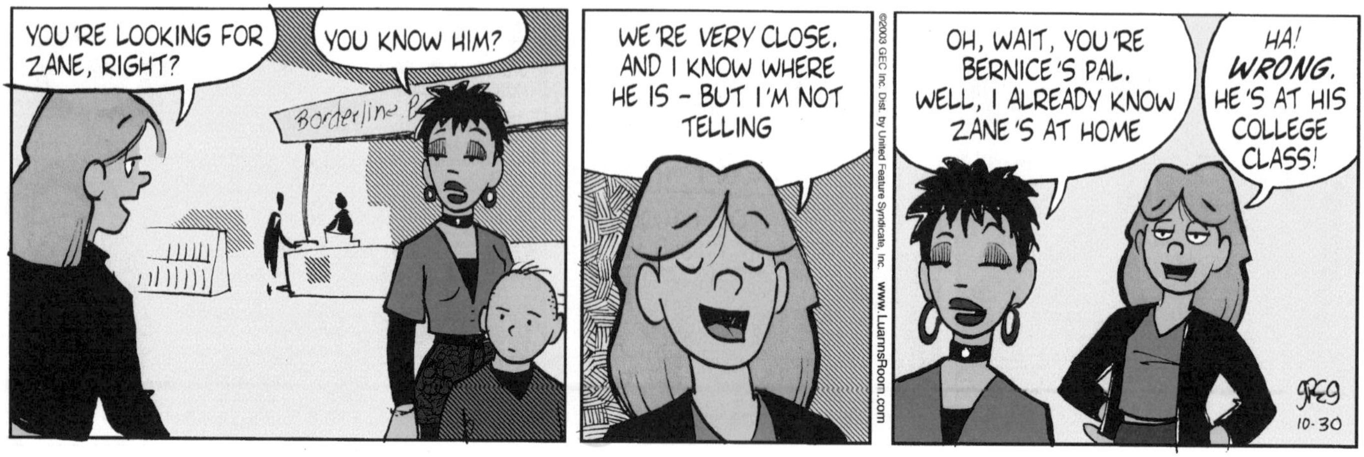
YOU'RE LOOKING FOR ZANE, RIGHT?
YOU KNOW HIM?
Borderline
WE'RE VERY CLOSE. AND I KNOW WHERE HE IS – BUT I'M NOT TELLING
©2003 GEC Inc. Dist. by United Feature Syndicate, Inc. www.LuannsRoom.com
OH, WAIT, YOU'RE BERNICE'S PAL. WELL, I ALREADY KNOW ZANE'S AT HOME
HA! WRONG. HE'S AT HIS COLLEGE CLASS!
GREG
10-30

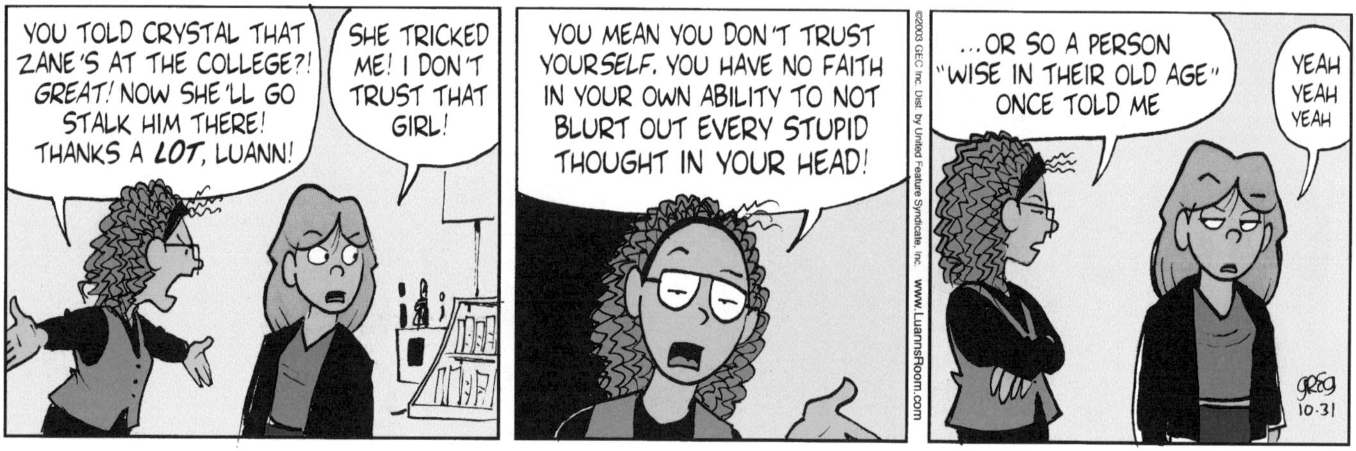
YOU TOLD CRYSTAL THAT ZANE'S AT THE COLLEGE?! GREAT! NOW SHE'LL GO STALK HIM THERE! THANKS A LOT, LUANN!
SHE TRICKED ME! I DON'T TRUST THAT GIRL!
YOU MEAN YOU DON'T TRUST YOURSELF. YOU HAVE NO FAITH IN YOUR OWN ABILITY TO NOT BLURT OUT EVERY STUPID THOUGHT IN YOUR HEAD!
©2003 GEC Inc. Dist. by United Feature Syndicate, Inc. www.LuannsRoom.com
...OR SO A PERSON "WISE IN THEIR OLD AGE" ONCE TOLD ME
YEAH YEAH YEAH
GREG
10-31

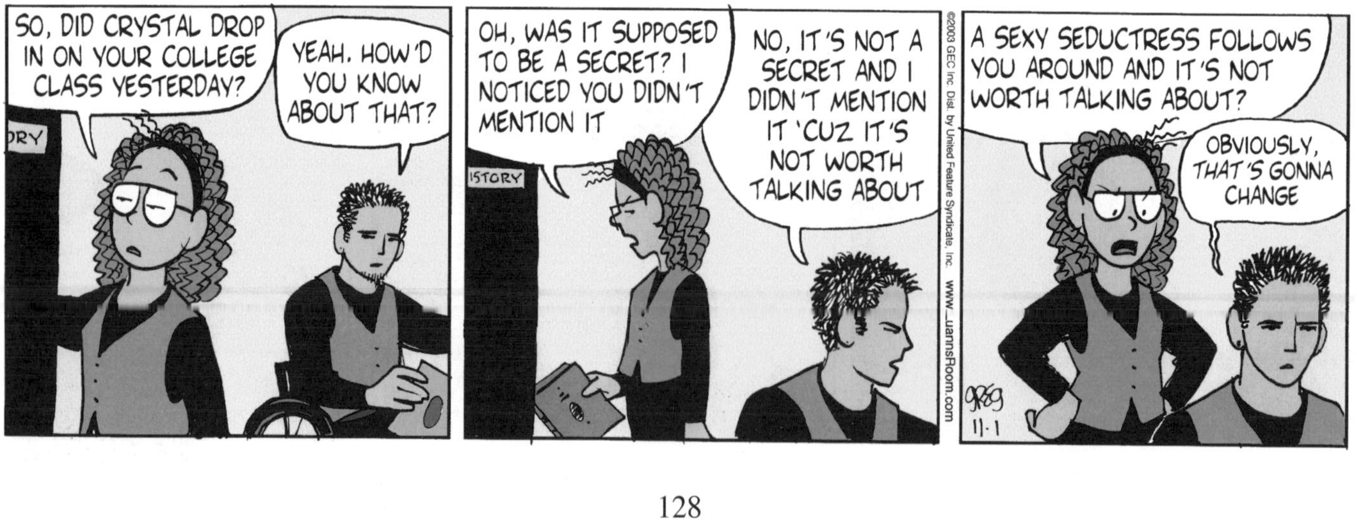
SO, DID CRYSTAL DROP IN ON YOUR COLLEGE CLASS YESTERDAY?
YEAH. HOW'D YOU KNOW ABOUT THAT?
OH, WAS IT SUPPOSED TO BE A SECRET? I NOTICED YOU DIDN'T MENTION IT
NO, IT'S NOT A SECRET AND I DIDN'T MENTION IT 'CUZ IT'S NOT WORTH TALKING ABOUT
©2003 GEC Inc. Dist. by United Feature Syndicate, Inc. www.LuannsRoom.com
A SEXY SEDUCTRESS FOLLOWS YOU AROUND AND IT'S NOT WORTH TALKING ABOUT?
OBVIOUSLY, THAT'S GONNA CHANGE
GREG
11-1